WATCH-FIRES
ON THE MOUNTAINS:
THE LIFE AND WRITINGS OF
ETHEL JOHNS

ETHEL JOHNS, *circa* 1919
Courtesy of the Vancouver General Hospital

Watch-fires on the mountains: the life and writings of Ethel Johns

Margaret M. Street

UNIVERSITY OF TORONTO PRESS

© University of Toronto Press 1973
Toronto and Buffalo
Printed in Canada
Reprinted in 2018
ISBN 0-8020-1987-0
ISBN 978-1-4875-7359-1 (paper)
LC 72-98026

TO THE MEMORY OF
ETHEL JOHNS

Contents

Acknowledgments / ix
Prologue / xiii

PART ONE: 1879–1902

1 Childhood / 3
2 Life on the Reserve / 10
3 Ethel Johns – Pupil Nurse / 20

PART TWO: 1902–1914

4 Early Practice of Nursing / 33
5 The *Nurses' Alumnae Journal* of the
   Winnipeg General Hospital / 41
6 High Adventure / 53
7 A Champion for Nurse Registration / 58
8 The McKellar General Hospital / 65

PART THREE: 1914–1919

9 Teachers College, Columbia University / 75
10 The Children's Hospital of Winnipeg / 83
11 The Manitoba Public Welfare Commission / 93
12 An End and a Beginning / 102

PART FOUR: 1919–1925

13 The Hospital and the University / 115
14 The Department of Nursing of The University of
   British Columbia / 126
15 A Time of Testing / 138
16 Ethel Johns Reports / 149

PART FIVE: 1925-1932

17 Service under the Rockefeller Foundation /165
18 New York Hospital–Cornell Medical College Association Project / 174

PART SIX: 1933-1944

19 Ethel Johns, Editor, *The Canadian Nurse* / 187
20 The Canadian Nurses' Association and the Journal / 196
21 A Time for Expansion / 207
22 Ethel Johns Off Duty / 216
23 Full Flower / 223

PART SEVEN: 1944-1968

24 New Horizons / 237
25 The Johns Hopkins Project / 248
26 Full Circle / 258
27 Another Task for Ethel Johns / 267
28 The Setting Sun / 277
Epilogue / 284
Chapter Notes / 286
Bibliography / 307
Addendum /318
Index / 321

Acknowledgments

The project to write a biography of the late Ethel Johns was undertaken as a personal commitment, to mark the Golden Jubilee, in 1969, of the University of British Columbia School of Nursing, of which she was the first director. A major objective was to identify and record Miss Johns' influence as a leader in helping to shape the history of nursing in Canada. A further aim was to investigate her contribution to nursing internationally. Ethel Johns' writings, over more than fifty years of this century, both reflected and commented upon the passing scene in nursing and its relation with other groups and the broad community of which it was a part. Through her writings, she gave vigorous expression to her convictions about areas of nursing education and practice in which reforms were needed. For this reason, and because her personal characteristics were revealed in her writings, the present book includes many excerpts from them. Whatever grace and vitality the narrative may possess are, therefore, due in large measure to Ethel Johns' own literary ability, and I am happy indeed to acknowledge my debt to her.

Valuable assistance in this project was given by Ethel Johns' relatives, former students, friends, and associates. In addition, many organizations generously granted access to their records. To one and all I express my grateful thanks. Their individual contributions are acknowledged in the chapter notes.

The National Trust Company kindly placed Miss Johns' papers at my disposal, with the understanding that royalties accruing from the book's publication would be used to establish an Ethel Johns Memorial Scholarship fund for the assistance of students enrolled in the Master of Science in Nursing programme of the University of British Columbia.

The Canada Council awarded grants in support of the project. The President and the Board of Governors of the University of British Columbia, upon the recommendation of the School of Nursing, approved a sabbatical leave of one year which enabled me to make substantial progress in the work. During that period, the Woodward Biomedical Library of the University placed an enclosed carrell at my disposal, thus facilitating the work of research and writing.

Dorothy Percy, Kathleen Ruane, and Edna Rossiter gave valuable assistance with the preliminary research. Margaret Allemang, Jessie Morrison, and Sheila Rymer contributed in various ways to expedite the search for information. Anthony Blicq, at that time the director of the Publications Centre of the University of British Columbia, gave some helpful initial guidance; so, too, did Teresa Christy in New York. Rae Chittick graciously consented to serve as an informal adviser.

Librarians and archivists gave courteous and efficient assistance. In particular, I want to thank the following: Margaret Parkin and the staff of the Library, Canadian Nurses' Association; Anna Leith and the staff of the Woodward Biomedical Library, especially Margaret Leighton; Mrs H. Rosenfeld, librarian of the Toronto General Hospital School of Nursing; Sheilagh Jameson, archivist of the Glenbow-Alberta Institute, and members of her staff; and Phyllis Mutasio, supervisor of the Central files, National League for Nursing, New York.

Virginia Henderson placed at my disposal the resources of the Nursing Studies Index Unit at the Yale University School of Nursing, while Mary Elizabeth Tennant and Hazel Goff shared with me their recollections of the nursing programme of the Rockefeller Foundation in Europe, in which Ethel Johns participated.

I am grateful to the individuals, organizations, and publishers who allowed me to use excerpts from their publications. The Canadian Nurses' Association authorized quotations from the writings of Ethel Johns and others which appeared in *The Canadian Nurse*. The Nurses' Alumnae Association of the Winnipeg General Hospital permitted the use of passages from the *Nurses' Alumnae Journal*. The J.B. Lippincott Company granted permission to quote from *Just Plain Nursing*. Kennethe Haig and Thomas Allan and Sons allowed the inclusion of an excerpt from *Brave Harvest*. Donald C. Masters kindly gave me a copy of the memorandum which Miss Johns wrote for him on 'The Winnipeg General Strike,' and the University of Toronto Press concurred in authorizing the use of excerpts from this material and from Professor Masters' book of the same title. Mrs C. Bernard Brack and Eileen Flanagan graciously allowed me to quote from letters which Ethel Johns had written to them; and Margaret Leighton contributed the letters which her late aunt, Amy Lee, had received from Miss Johns.

The manuscript was read initially by Rae Chittick, Evelyn Mallory, and Helen Mussallem. Subsequently, it was read by Muriel Uprichard, Dr William C. Gibson, Elizabeth McCann, Margaret Leighton, Lucille Blayney, and Emily Mayhew. A number of other persons reviewed sections of the manuscript. Among these was Jane Fredeman, who evaluated an early section of the work from the point of view of style.

Gertrude Stevenson carried out the final editing of the manuscript. The constructive comments of these critics were very helpful and I am much indebted to them. Any errors or deficiencies which remain in the book are my responsibility alone.

A special word of thanks is due to my sister, Bertha, who lived cheerfully with this book in the making and whose unfaltering confidence in its completion was reassuring.

I am particularly pleased to record my grateful thanks to Jean Houston, executive editor of the University of Toronto Press, whose interest and sound guidance were a source of strength in the final phase of the project.

This book has been published with the help of a grant from the Social Science Research Council, using funds provided by the Canada Council; a grant towards purchase from the Canadian Nurses' Association; and grants towards publication from the University of British Columbia, the Faculty of Applied Science of the University of British Columbia, the Alberta Association of Registered Nurses, the Manitoba Association of Registered Nurses, the Winnipeg General Hospital, the Winnipeg General Hospital Nurses' Alumnae, the Association of Nurses of the Province of Quebec, the Registered Nurses' Association of British Columbia, and the Alumnae Association of the Calgary General Hospital School of Nursing. To all these bodies I acknowledge my indebtedness and express my heartfelt thanks.

Vancouver   MARGARET M. STREET

Prologue

Ethel Johns had passed her eighty-ninth birthday when she faced a hard decision. Frail and sick, she recognized at last that she could no longer remain in the small house with the mountain view, purchased nineteen years earlier with the help of a legacy from her friend, Cora Hind.

On a Monday morning late in May 1968 she walked resolutely out of her home, supported on one side by a faithful woman who had been her part-time helper for several years, and on the other by the friend who was to drive her to the hospital. With her, she took a few carefully chosen articles: a small framed snapshot of a young man, a dictionary, her radio, a copy of *The Johns Hopkins Hospital School of Nursing, 1869–1949,* and – hidden from view – three chapters of the autobiography started some ten years earlier but destined never to be completed.

Left behind on a table near the door were the portable typewriter on which, for so many years, she had done all her writing, and a neat little pile of green cloth-bound volumes of *Just Plain Nursing*. Abandoned without a backward glance were row upon row of well-loved books, ancestral plates ranged above the fireplace, antique silver and china in the cabinet, doctoral gown and hood in the closet. She knew she would not see her home or cherished possessions again. She had not long to endure the sorrow of separation from her familiar environment or the awareness of approaching dissolution. She died quietly on 2 September 1968, and few at the time marked the passing of this pioneer of the Canadian West and twentieth-century nursing. Yet the story of her life and work is worthy of record.

Graduating in 1902 from the Training School for Nurses of the Winnipeg General Hospital, Ethel Johns began her work shortly after the close of the Victorian era. Launched with other 'new career women' on the flood tide of the young twentieth century, she was to be part of its turbulence for over forty years of professional practice. Wars and depression, labour unrest, unprecedented advances in medical science and technology, rising demands for high standards of health services, widespread social change: all were to place extraordinary pressures upon the evolving profession of nursing.

Reference is often made to the 'giants' of nursing, the women who assumed leadership in the formative years of the profession. They would have been the first to disclaim heroic stature; be that as it may, they were women of superior ability, intelligence, vision, courage, and dedication. In Ethel Johns' view, they were responsible for blazing the trail and lighting watch-fires on the mountains, for the guidance of those who would follow. She was one of their number.

PART ONE: 1879–1902

1

Childhood

Ethel Johns was proud of the Celtic blood that ran in her veins. She took a quiet satisfaction in the achievements of her ancestors and rejoiced in the exploits of some of the more colourful members of the family. 'For several generations,' she wrote, 'my father's family flourished in the town of Helston, in Cornwall, and one of its members seems to have been a rugged individualist. Early in the eighteenth century, he got himself elected as mayor and, when his term expired, refused to surrender the seals of office until he had settled a controversy in which he had become involved. The archives show that he hung on quite unlawfully for a whole year and then, having vanquished his opponent, marched out, flags flying and drums beating ...'[1]

She was equally delighted with the family member who was reputed to have performed a daring feat of climbing the Lizard Cliffs, dressed in top hat and pantaloons with strap over the instep and carrying his walking stick. Writing in 1948 to her cousin, Archbishop Philip Carrington, she enquired about the identity of this gentleman and added: 'I am proud of him, whoever he was, and I hope that I inherited a little of his audacity. I know that I got a good share of his love of wild flowers and birds and all *free* things on this green earth ...' The gentleman was her father's uncle, the Reverend Charles Alexander Johns, in his day a noted botanist, writer, and teacher. Ethel Johns, it seems, was unaware that her father, as a boy, had often visited his uncle Charles and so had come under the influence of this scholarly clergyman. Another lad in whom Charles Johns took a special interest was one of his pupils, Charles Kingsley – later to become a celebrated writer – who was to acknowledge his debt to his old teacher in one of his books.[2]

Bennett George Johns (Charles' brother and the grandfather of Ethel) was born at Plympton, Devon, in the year 1820. He attended Dublin University, from which he obtained a Master of Arts degree. From 1842 to 1847 he was on the staff of St Mark's College, Chelsea, where the principal was Derwent Coleridge, son of the poet, Samuel T. Coleridge. Prior to his ordination in 1847, Bennett had been influenced by the High Church movement at Oxford, and had dreamed of being a celibate. Archbishop Carrington states that Bennett at that time went to stay with his brother Charles at Helston, in order to meditate and retreat from the world, and he adds:

...But he had forgotten the Helston Furry, the prehistoric folkdance on May 8 (still going on) when the people took partners and danced through the streets, in and out of every house, in at the front door and out at the back, for they all had to be open. He found himself linked with a 'wild Scotch girl,' Delphinea Hepburn (a 'mad Hebburn' – for so it was pronounced) and within a week they were married. Delphinea Sophia Hepburn thus became Mrs Bennett Johns, and the grandmother of Ethel. *Her* grandfather was Lord Belmerino, leader of the Jacobites in 1745, who was executed in the Tower of London in 1746, the last man to be beheaded in England with an axe. Ethel was very proud of this Scotch Jacobite descent. She united Highland Scots with Cornish and Welsh ...[3]

By 1851, Bennett Johns was lecturing at King's College, London, where George Eliot was among his pupils. In 1852, he was appointed chaplain, secretary, and treasurer to the London School for the Blind, a post which he held for thirty-two years. True to the literary tradition of the Johns Family, he wrote and published several books including: *History of Spain, Sermons to the Blind,* and *Blind People, Their Works and Ways.* He was a frequent contributor to periodicals and for forty years he reviewed books for *The Morning Post.* About the latter activity, his granddaughter Ethel (in her autobiography) made a single delighted comment: 'His reviews of the works of a Victorian lady novelist had a pungency all their own. A romance by the redoubtable Rhoda Broughton, entitled "Cometh up as a flower," was dismissed in seven words: "And is cut down like the grass."' From the London School for the Blind, Bennett retired to parish work and died in 1900.

Bennett's daughter, Dellie Sophia Adcock, wrote on 4 February 1948 to her niece Ethel, in response to the latter's request for information about her father's family. Concerning her mother (Ethel's grandmother) – the original Delphinea – Mrs Adcock reported only that she had died in 1870, at the time of her own birth. Her father remarried two years later, and there was a second family. She had vivid memories of her father: he had many friends in London among whom were the bishops, canons, and dean of St Paul's Cathedral. He belonged to the Savage Club and the Authors' Club. He was on the Royal Commission for the Blind, and was often invited to civic dinners. A fine preacher, he put church work first in his life. In appearance he was very like Lord Tennyson, for whom he was mistaken on two occasions, 'in his wide-awake hat in winter and a broad Scotch plaid wrap over his coat.' A very handsome man, he was a distinctive figure in a crowd, with his blue eyes and black hair which was later, at eighty, only streaked with silver. He was quiet and absent-minded, but a great worker, and very dear to his daughter Dellie: 'I used to escape from our governess when lessons were over,' she wrote, 'and sit on a little tin box in his study and often he would forget I was there. Friends dropped in, various authors and artists, Charles Dickens among them. There was reading aloud every evening and music quartettes. He had a lovely tenor voice ...'

This, then was the father of Henry Incledon Johns and the home environment at the London School for the Blind in which he passed his boyhood. Of this period of her father's life, Ethel Johns made only one comment in her memoirs: 'He once told us that his most vivid memory was that of seeing and hearing Charles Dickens give a reading from his novel, Oliver Twist. Those blind people followed his every word with such rapt attention that Dickens himself was deeply moved.'

The combination of family tradition, heredity, and environment made it almost inevitable that Henry Johns would receive a classical education and be prepared for service in the Church. In due course, he enrolled as a student in Oriel College, Oxford University, and later graduated in Arts from Trinity College, Dublin. In 1878, he married a Welsh girl, Amy Robinson. Their first child, Ethel Mary, was born on 13 May 1879, in the village of Meonstoke, Southampton, where her father was curate of the local church. As soon as she was old enough to be critical of her parents' choice of a second name, she seems to have discarded it except for legal purposes. For many years she adopted the time-honoured family name of Incledon, borne by her father. A number of her writings were signed, 'Ethel Incledon Johns,' and a calling card in 1910 was inscribed, 'Ethel I. Johns.' A second child, Owen, was born to the young couple on 2 November 1881.

When Ethel Johns was seven years old, Amy Johns went with the two children to stay with her father, John Robinson, who lived in Denbigh, North Wales. The reason for this move is not known. For Ethel and

Owen, the parting from their father must have been traumatic, but this was probably alleviated to some extent by their interest in new surroundings. They were enrolled in an 'infant school' in Denbigh which was conducted by two maiden ladies, the Misses Elizabeth and Maria Hubbard. Of this experience, Miss Johns was later to recall that, although she could read and write at the time she started school, she had 'no luck with even the simplest arithmetic. Whenever the class recited the multiplication tables, loudly and in unison, I stumbled along without much idea of what they meant. Miss Maria did her best to help, but I have never been quite sure of seven times eight ...'

John Robinson was administrator of the North Wales County Lunatic Asylum. Reference to him is made in a brief history of the institution written on the occasion of its centenary. The writers of this paper give a vivid picture of the conditions that led to the founding of the hospital:

... Very few 'asylums' existed at the beginning of the nineteenth century, and little was done for the mentally afflicted. Their plight was, in fact, at that time, so deplorable that public enquiries were caused to be made and much suffering and deprivation was brought to light. In England conditions were bad, but in Wales the lack of accommodation was felt to a far greater extent as the worst cases for whom it was absolutely essential to provide accommodation had to be sent to English 'Asylums' where their sufferings were often aggravated for want of care and treatment by doctors and nurses who understood their language ...[4]

Through public subscription by concerned individuals which was augmented by financial aid from the counties of North Wales, a hospital to accommodate two hundred mentally ill patients was erected at Denbigh and opened in 1848. Soon it was necessary to add wings to the building, and by 1865 the bed capacity had increased to four hundred. John Robinson, formerly on the staff of the Gloucester Mental Hospital, was appointed as the first Steward and Clerk of the Board of the North Wales County Lunatic Asylum. He held this post for forty years, until his death. Mute evidence of the regard in which he was held by the staff of the institution is offered by a family heirloom, treasured through the years by Ethel Johns, an antique silver ink-well engraved: 'Presented to Mr. J.C. Robinson by the artizans, attendants, and servants of the N.W.C.L. Asylum upon the occasion of attaining his majority, April 18th, 1866.'

Almost a century later, his granddaughter Ethel recorded in her autobiography that John Robinson had once been connected with a local police force and had seen 'lunatics' bound hand and foot, filthy and neglected, committed to jail because there was nowhere else to put them. Although John Robinson had no responsibility for the medical care of the patients, she said, 'he must have had an intuitive realization of the value of occupation in the treatment of mental illness. The Asylum farm was his pride and joy and he never tired of persuading patients to work on it ...' She added: 'His political views were decidedly radical and he fought hard for the abolition of church tithes ...'

Young Ethel was captivated by her genial Welsh grandfather and the stories he told her: 'The Welsh side of the family originally hailed from the Isle of Anglesey and owned a small farm, conveniently close to the sea, where they were darkly suspected of lending aid and comfort to smugglers and of storing contraband in the barn; an accusation that grandfather stoutly denied though with a twinkle in his eye ...' She was entranced when she was allowed to accompany her grandfather to hear the Welsh choirs singing in the open air at a national festival.

Meanwhile in 1888, Ethel's father left England for Canada to work among the Indians.[5] Missionaries and teachers were in demand for the young Dominion, and in response to the call many clergymen of various denominations were leaving England to settle in the new land. He must have had serious doubts about the wisdom of this step. Gently reared in a sheltered home by his scholarly father, educated in the classics, securely engaged in the work of a quiet rural parish, he must have wondered whether he was fitted for the rugged life of a pioneer settler, what amenities his wife and children might expect on an Indian reserve, and of what social and educational advantages his children would be deprived. These were weighty questions, to which the young curate could have found, at best, uncertain answers. Henry Johns' initial destination in Canada is unknown. Some evidence exists that his intention was to carry on missionary work, but no information has been found as to whether he actually did so prior to his appointment (in 1889) as teacher on the Wabigoon Reserve in northwestern Ontario.[6] The Indians of this band were Ojibways, all of whom were reported to be pagan even as late as 1895.[7]

Life in her grandfather's home seems to have been placid and congenial for Ethel, but one day in 1888 all this changed. When the two children came home from school, they were told that they must be very quiet because their grandfather was ill. Three days later he died. Shortly thereafter, Amy Johns told her daughter that she was going to Canada to join her husband, but that Ethel was to stay behind and go to boarding-school for awhile. The decision must have been made in advance of John Robinson's death, and it could not have been an easy one.

Had her grandfather lived, temporary separation from mother and father might have been easier to bear; but Ethel was still suffering from her loss when her mother, too, left her. Seventy years later, Ethel Johns could still recall vividly her feelings upon being told that her mother was to go to Canada alone: '... The desolation that swept over me could only have been experienced by a child. Children are not consoled by being assured that the pain of parting will soon be over. They do not believe that it will ever end. After a few miserable weeks, mother left us and I went to boarding school ...'[8] At the age of nine, Ethel Johns was already no stranger to loneliness and she had to learn to rely upon her own inner resources.

The arrangements made by his mother for the care and schooling of Owen are not recorded, but Ethel was placed in a boarding-school in Denbigh where the only familiar feature was the lovely Welsh landscape, the valley of the Clwyd. The new pupil was assigned to a narrow bed in a long dormitory and shown a chest of drawers in which she was instructed to arrange her possessions neatly. She was given a uniform and a set of rules. Her formal education began the next day. Contrary to her expectations, she later recalled, it proved to be 'a happy as well as a profitable experience. It was only the holidays that were lonely and wretched, but of this no more need be said ...' The mistresses were good teachers and the instruction, although narrow in scope, was thorough. Discipline was severe but 'there was a sort of rough justice about it. Examinations were fairly stiff and if you failed you were not promoted. If you broke a rule, you had to eat your meals alone and in silence at a table facing a blank wall adorned only by a plaster cast of the Apollo Belvedere. I got to know him pretty well ...'[9]

Ethel Johns' recollections of extracurricular activities give a charming glimpse into this late Victorian boarding-school for young ladies:

... There was a large playground, surrounded by individual flower beds which the pupils were expected to tend. Nothing ever grew in mine except some depressing greyish green plants called Stars of Bethlehem. By common consent my plot was used as a burial ground for any dead bird or mouse that we happened to find and I was allowed to conduct the obsequies. This was my first experience in public speaking and I enjoyed it immensely.

No matter what the weather might be, we went for a daily walk, two by two, in the traditional crocodile. Sometimes in the Spring, we were taken to a nearby wood and permitted to break ranks. There were violets and primroses, hyacinths and daffodils everywhere, but we had to promise not to touch them. On Sundays we went to St Hilary's Church where, from our seats in the gallery, we could look down into the nave. In the centre of it there was the tomb of a Crusader with his arms crossed over the hilt of his great sword ...

Some uncertainty exists as to the length of time Ethel Johns remained in this boarding-school, and the year of her departure for Canada, but weighing the available evidence, it appears that she and her brother Owen sailed from England in the late summer or early fall of 1892. A log house had now been built for the Johns family on the Wabigoon reserve, and their parents and small brother Alexander awaited their arrival there.

2

Life on the Reserve

Ethel Johns would never forget the voyage or the arrival in Canada; she gave a graphic account of these events in her autobiography:

... In September, my brother and I sailed from Liverpool on the S.S. Sardinian, a dreadful old tub that rolled and pitched unmercifully. It was not until we reached the Gulf of St Lawrence that I managed to crawl out on deck when my brother called out that here was Canada, and to come and look at it. Cold and seasick, I clung to the rail and gazed at the dim outline of the coast in the fading twilight. Incidentally, my brother had been in rude health throughout the voyage and, with the assistance of a kindred spirit from the United States of America, had managed to make a public nuisance of himself as only a small boy can.

In Montreal we were taken in charge by a fatherly railway official who told me what to do when we arrived at our destination. The train would reach Wabigoon Lake at two in the morning, and, although there was no station, would stop long enough to set us down at the side of the track. There we were to stay until someone from the Hudson's Bay Company's fur-trading post came to pick us up. Mother had warned me about this already. We were not to be frightened. When the time came, the kindly porter helped us to jump off and put down our luggage beside us. Then the train pulled out and the tail lights disappeared round a curve. The stars were very bright and all around us were the pointed fir trees. Nothing else, not even a sound. At last, three lanterns came bobbing down the track toward us. It was the Hudson's Bay officer and two Indian boys to carry the bags. Mother was waiting for us at the Post. Had we been frightened? Yes, a little but it was alright now ...

The following morning, Amy Johns with her son and daughter travelled across the lake in a birchbark canoe paddled by two Indians. The morning air was crisp and invigorating, the view of absorbing interest to the young travellers:

... The rocky shores were covered with trees almost to the water's edge, most of them evergreen, with here and there a cluster of birch or poplar glowing with autumn colour against the dusky background of the pines. On the western shore we could see the school house and beyond it a circle of wigwams and, as we reached the landing, there was Father waiting for us, and beside him the new little Canadian brother who didn't seem at all pleased to see us, but greeted our arrival with a dismal wail. Indian men, women and children, accompanied by innumerable yelping dogs, gathered round to gaze with frank curiosity at this family reunion ...[1]

It is easy to imagine the excitement of the newcomers and their parents as they entered their Canadian home for the first time together. Ethel Johns was later to write a vivid description of her initial impressions:

... The log house in which we were to live stood high on a rocky point above the lake with a winding footpath leading down to the beach. The living room was covered with Indian reed mats and in one corner stood a little upright piano. In the centre, was a large boxstove and, carefully ranged on wall brackets, were the Chinese plates that I had last seen in Grandfather's house in Denbigh. Out in the kitchen, a fire crackled in the cook-stove and beside it was a big woodbox and a stand for water pails. On a shelf at the foot of the stairs, there was a row of brightly polished coal-oil lamps. The three small bedrooms were separated by canvas partitions, and, much to our delight, each bed had a white fur coverlet woven by the Indians out of strips of rabbit skin ...

Shortly after her arrival, Ethel started going each day to the school on the reserve where her father was the teacher. The restless environment of the classroom proved unfavourable to concentration on her studies: it was noisy, the pupils were hard to control, and frequently they had to be allowed to go outside to play. Yet Mr Johns found time to help his daughter, who was struggling to master the unfamiliar Canadian textbooks, and in the evenings he encouraged her to read as her fancy dictated. 'Fortunately,' she recalled, 'there were lots of books, some of them strange reading for a girl of fourteen, but everything was grist that came to my mill and none of it did me any harm. Indeed, I owe to my father that priceless gift – a love of books and reading – that Logan Pearson Smith once called "this joy not dimmed by age, this polite but unpunished vice, this selfish, serene, life-long intoxication" ...'

Some details about the school in which Henry Johns (and later his wife and daughter) taught are found in the reports of the Indian Agent and the Inspector in whose jurisdiction the Wabigoon reserve was located.[2] The Ojibway Indians comprising this band at first resisted the Inspector's request that they build a school. The Chief and his son (a councillor) had put the proposal before the band in 1885, but it was rejected. The reason for this is not recorded; but the Inspector, reporting in the same year to the Superintendent-General of Indian Affairs, voiced concern that, in a number of reserves, the Indians were refusing to build schools because of their understanding that it was the responsibility of the government to provide both buildings and teachers. Another factor that may have contributed to the resistance of the Wabigoon band was the belief, prevalent among Indians who clung to their paganism (as was the case with the Ojibways) that their children would be educated into other creeds which would adversely affect their existence and separate them from their parents in a future life. Whatever the cause of their hesitation, by 1886 the Indian agent, John McIntyre, was able to report that the school house was nearly completed and that a Protestant teacher had been requested. In his report for the year 1887, he noted that the school building, constructed of logs, was sixteen by twenty feet in size and that it was 'nicely ceiled and boarded inside, with floors of dressed lumber.' He also stated that, with lumber left over from the construction of the school, he had had an addition of twelve feet built for the teacher's room.

Further information about the school on the Wabigoon reserve is found in the 'Tabular Statements' concerning the condition of various Indian schools in the Dominion, published in the *Annual Reports* of the Department of Indian Affairs. From this source it is learned that the first teacher in the Wabigoon school was appointed in 1886, that he remained one year, and was followed in succession by two other men, each of whom departed within twelve months. Henry I. Johns was appointed teacher there commencing in July 1889 and his salary was the regular stipend of three hundred dollars per annum paid by the Department of Indian Affairs to teachers in schools which were wholly supported by the government. A supplementary allowance of twelve dollars per annum was granted for each pupil over the number of twenty-five, up to a total of forty-two; but the total salary for the year was not to exceed five hundred and four dollars. The enrolment for the first year of Mr Johns' tenure was twenty-one; for the remaining years of his service, it fluctuated from slightly below twenty-five to a little above thirty. The denomination of this school for the years 1889–92 was reported as 'Episcopal,' although it was not subsidized by the Church of England at that time. In 1893, it was listed as 'Undenominational.'

That the financial arrangement for teachers in government-controlled schools in the reserves was totally inadequate was pointed out in the 1885 report of Inspector E. McColl of the Manitoba Superintendency, in whose district the reserves in northwestern Ontario fell.[3] He stated emphatically that it was very difficult, if not impossible, to attract competent teachers at this salary, which was just half of that paid in provincial schools. To this handicap had to be added the hardships of life on the reserves, the lack of suitable living accommodation and congenial society, and the high cost of obtaining food and other supplies in isolated places. Despite the strong representations made by Inspector McColl, the *Annual Reports* of the Indian Department show that the stipend of three hundred dollars was to remain in effect for the remainder of the nineteenth and into the twentieth century. This had implications for the Johns family: Henry Johns could not make provision for the future economic security of his wife and children, nor, after his premature death, could Amy Johns do so on the same salary. Ethel Johns was later to assume considerable financial responsibility for her mother and (when necessary) for other members of the family as well.

Yet the lot of the Johns family was probably better than that prevailing on many of the other reserves in Canada at that time. The log cabin was comfortable and homelike. As noted by the Indian Agent in his annual report of August 1892, 'The cattle here are in good condition, and the gardens are looking well. Mr Johns, the teacher, has a splendid garden filled with vegetables ...' Official records show that the vegetables grown by the Indians of this band (under the instruction and supervision of the Indian Agent) included potatoes and corn on the reserve, and, on the island outside its boundaries, potatoes, turnips, carrots, peas, beans, onions, and pumpkins. Berries were plentiful, and fishing was excellent.

Another favourable factor on the Wabigoon reserve was the calibre and influence of the chief, Shabaqua. The high regard in which this man was held was attested in an account of his death published in *The*

Wabigoon Star and Dryden, Dinorwic, and Manitou District Advertiser, in the issue of 9 October 1902: '... The late Chief, who is the last of a long line of rulers that, up to comparatively modern times, had led the oft victorious Ojibway against their hereditary foe, the Sioux, was noted for his open mindedness and genial manner. Many of his friends among the white inhabitants of the district, endeared to him by his noble qualities, will deplore his untimely decease.'[4]

In the months following their arrival, Ethel and Owen made friends with the Indian children and soon picked up a working knowledge of their language. From their new friends, too, they learned woodcraft and other useful skills such as paddling a canoe and using an axe to chop down a dead tree for firewood. When winter came, they went out on snowshoes upon the frozen lake and helped the Indian boys to build a wind-break from fir boughs. Then they chopped a hole in the ice, baited their hooks, and waited for the fish to bite. Even small Alexander was able to achieve success in this sport.

As soon as the days grew longer, the Indians departed for their Spring hunting grounds. Ethel was later to record the scene in her autobiography: '... Barking dogs were harnessed to the toboggans, babies were tucked into moss-filled cradles and slung with deerskin thongs to the backs of their patient mothers. Away they all went across the lake and nothing was left of the encampment but bare poles and the blackened circles where the fires had burned all winter long. For us, this was the loneliest time of all ...' With the arrival of summer, the Indians returned and school started again. Ethel was now allowed to help with the teaching and the older children took quite an interest in her 'clumsy efforts' to spell out Ojibway words on the blackboard. But it was difficult to hold their attention since 'they tired easily and would wander away to pick berries or else their parents would take them to a distant shallow bay to help with the rice harvest by beating grains into canoes with the flat blades of their cedar paddles ...'

Nor was this the only distraction to the pupils of the Wabigoon reserve school. In mid-summer came an important break in all normal activities of the band. This was the medawin or medicine dance, held in a large enclosure, the shebandowan, '... open to the sky and surrounded by a screen of birchbark fastened to bent poles, gaily decorated with flowering branches and coloured streamers ...' The medawin followed the traditional rites:

... The earth was beaten flat and the drummers crouched at either end while the medicine men chanted their wild song and the dancers revolved around them, the men in one circle and the women in another, moving in opposite directions. These rites went on for three days and three nights until all concerned were utterly exhausted. The Chief and his councillors had ruled against any religious instruction being given in the school and the governmental authorities had tacitly admitted that they had a right to follow their pagan custom. So, when the excitement died down, the children came back to school as though nothing had happened ...

As the months went by, Ethel found much to occupy her time. By diligent study, she acquired sufficient grasp of the Ojibway language to serve as interpreter for the Chief when a representative of the Indian Department paid a visit. In the school, her father's 'strong but quiet influence' was beginning to have an effect. The Indian Agent, in his annual report of 24 August 1892 noted that, 'The children here are fairly regular in attendance at school and I am much pleased with the progress they have made. Mrs Johns is teaching the girls to sew and knit; samples of the latter shown us would compare favorably with that of any white woman. The teacher and his family are on very friendly terms with the Indians, by whom they are well liked and respected.'

So the months and the seasons passed by, and Ethel found that she was too busy to be lonely. But the pleasant family life was to be cut short. In the early fall of 1895, calamity swiftly fell upon the Johns family. Miss Johns, in a few poignant sentences of her autobiography, later told of the tragedy:

... One afternoon in October, when I had stayed home to study, my mother went alone through the wood to school. Suddenly, I heard the sound of someone running toward the house and a breathless Indian boy told me to come quickly. He would not tell me what had happened and it was not until I reached the school that I knew that my mother had found my father lying beside the path breathing heavily and quite unconscious. An hour later, it was all over and we were left desolate.

There was no one to turn to for help except the Hudson's Bay officer and he read the Burial Service over the grave on an island far out in the lake where we often spent our summer evenings. Now it was cold and bleak and a freezing rain fell on the coffin lid. When it grew dusk, I slipped out of the house and went down to the water's edge. Looking over toward the island, I saw that according to their own burial custom the Indians had lighted a fire beside the grave. There could have been no greater consolation than that living flame in the gathering darkness ...[5]

So Henry Johns, forty-two years of age, died as quietly as he had lived. The loss to his family was shattering. Alexander, six years old, and Owen, a lad of fourteen, were deprived of the guidance and companionship of their father. Ethel, at sixteen, lost a beloved parent and teacher whom she had known too short a time but whose influence on her life she would always remember with gratitude. Upon the shoulders of Amy Johns fell the responsibility of supporting her children.

In this crisis, Mrs Johns conferred with her daughter. They discussed returning to England but agreed that this would be unwise, since they would then become dependent upon relatives who were not themselves well-off. At last a plan evolved: Amy Johns would apply to the Indian Department for her late husband's position, on the understanding that Ethel would help with the teaching. Within a month, word was received that the application had been accepted. The Chief had been consulted and had given his approval: 'The widow is good medicine woman and the girl can speak our language.'[6]

The decision to remain on the reserve, while almost inevitable under the circumstances, cannot have been made easily: its disadvantages were evident. Owen would have to go to boarding-school; no other course of action would be suitable for him. Financially this would be hard to manage, and Amy Johns would lose the help and protection of her elder son when she most needed him. Alexander would attend school on the reserve, where conditions for learning and finding new friends were alike unfavourable. For Ethel, the agreement was to have serious consequences. She was committed to stay for an indefinite period in this isolated place, cut off from the companionship of young people of her own kind. She was denied the opportunity of furthering her formal education the lack of which was later to put barriers in her path. She would continue to be deprived of social and cultural advantages, and – probably as a result – she would find it difficult all her life to adjust with ease or grace to the exigencies of social events. She admired and emulated her mother's self-control and fortitude, but it is doubtful that she found a kindred spirit in her, or that Amy Johns fully understood the complex nature and needs of her sensitive, intelligent daughter.

But a strange occurrence was to open unexpected doors for Ethel Johns. It happened in the early Spring of 1896, a few months after her father's death. The ice on the lake was showing signs of melting when, late one evening, a horsedrawn sleigh came over the treacherous surface toward the log house. Ethel and Alexander were outside gathering wood when they were hailed by the driver, whom they recognized as a Swede, Rocke Olson. They were amazed to see that he had a passenger, a white woman, the first they had seen in more than two years.

Ethel Johns was to record this unforgettable moment in her autobiography: 'There she stood, a slight graceful figure, dressed in well-fitting riding breeches and a trim long-skirted coat. "My name is Cora Hind," she said, "and I'm writing articles about life in the lumber camps. Do you think your mother would take me in for the night?"' There was no doubt about her welcome. Alexander led her into the house, and when Ethel followed a few minutes later with Rocke Olson, Cora Hind had rolled up her sleeves and was helping her mother to prepare the supper. Of that memorable evening, Ethel Johns later wrote:

... Until after midnight, we listened spellbound to Cora Hind's story of her adventures as a free-lance journalist. This vivid young woman lived in a world of which I knew nothing and was free to come and go as she pleased. I had never seen anyone like her. The weather turned cold during the night and by morning the ice was firm enough to travel over. Rocke Olson wrapped his unwanted passenger in the buffalo sleigh robe and once more set off for the railroad. I watched them until the sleigh turned the point and went out of sight. Never had I felt so restless nor so lonely. What had I to look forward to if I stayed on the reserve? Yet this is what I had promised to do. When Cora Hind wrote to Mother to thank her for her hospitality, there was a bulky envelope for me, filled with exciting clippings from newspapers and magazines. The lively correspondence that followed was the beginning of a friendship that lasted more than forty years ...

The chance meeting with Cora Hind marked a turning point in the life of Ethel Johns. Her new friend, who had been so quick to detect the young girl's need for intellectual food and her yearning for knowledge, was to become her sponsor, adviser, critic, loyal supporter, and source of help in time of trouble. Miss Johns was habitually reticent about personal matters which touched her deeply, but after Cora Hind's death (in 1942), she was to express to Kennethe Haig her feelings about Miss Hind's unusual gift for friendship: '... E. Cora Hind had a quite extraordinary capacity for friendship. She had an immense faith in all those whom she held in affection and defended them against all comers. But if she thought you needed correction, you got it straight from the shoulder. If you were in trouble you could always count on her and she never failed you ...'[7]

To what extent Ethel Johns was influenced by Cora Hind can only be a matter of conjecture, but it is reasonable to assume that Cora Hind gave her young protégée the early guidance and encouragement she needed to begin to develop her own literary abilities. Much more than this, she undoubtedly opened up for the younger woman the broad horizons of a world she had not known before. A mutual friend of both Cora Hind and Ethel Johns in those early days, the late Dr Helen Stewart, once suggested that 'E. Cora Hind did more than anyone else at the beginning to influence E. Johns – and she was the kind of woman who could do it. There was a certain freedom about it (their relationship) that released E. Johns from some of the shackles of the old-fashioned ladylike behaviour. E. Cora Hind was a fine person and well worth while ...'[8]

Late in the Spring of Cora Hind's visit, prospectors started coming into the district. The town of Wabigoon, on the main line of the Canadian Pacific Railway, was also becoming a centre of navigation. Steamers left regularly from its harbour to go into the mining country, and for some years the lure of the gold fields was to draw men into this area. But as so frequently happened when reserves were located close to railway towns or to mining or lumbering settlements, unscrupulous white men started selling liquor to the Indians of the Wabigoon band. Normally industrious and law-abiding, some of the men had in the past occasionally lapsed into intemperance. The Johns family remembered all too well the evening that a group of intoxicated Indians pounded on the cabin door, then burst into the house. The children were terrified, but their mother kept on playing the piano and singing, and presently the men left. Now, however, the situation was growing worse and gradually more and more members of the band were becoming addicted to alcohol.

The Deputy Superintendent General of Indian Affairs, in his report for the year 1897, pointed out the seriousness of the offence of selling liquor to Indians: '... Undoubtedly there is no one vice as dangerous to Indians as that of indulgence in strong drink, for not only are they peculiarly predisposed by temperament to such indulgence, but they lack the stamina of constitution which enables white men longer to resist its deleterious action, and when under its immediate influence they more completely lose control of themselves in all directions ...'[9]

As conditions worsened, Amy and Ethel Johns realized that they would not be able to stay much longer on the reserve. The old Chief could no longer exercise control over the band. Mother and daughter agreed that Ethel would have to seek some other way of earning a living. She had always wanted to be a trained nurse, so she wrote to Cora Hind to enquire whether she might have a chance of being accepted in the Training School for Nurses of the Winnipeg General Hospital. She was now twenty years old, one year younger than the minimum age required for admission at the time.

When the application forms arrived, Ethel and her mother scanned them eagerly. The educational qualifications, it appeared, would not be hard to meet: 'Applicants are expected to write legibly, to understand simple arithmetic, and to be able to take notes of lectures. This amount of education is *indispensable,* but applicants are reminded that women of superior education and cultivation will be preferred.' A character reference from a clergyman was required. Ethel Johns had not seen a clergyman for more than two years, but Cora Hind assured her that a kind Anglican rector in Winnipeg would give the necessary endorsement. A medical certificate was also requested. The nearest doctor was one hundred miles away, but Ethel had acted as his interpreter when he paid a visit to the reserve: perhaps he would testify to her physical fitness. As a student nurse, Ethel would receive board and lodging plus an allowance of eight dollars per month, 'not in payment of any services rendered but to meet sundry expenses associated with the course of training.'[10]

Presently word came from the Winnipeg General Hospital that she had been accepted: '... A wave of exhilaration swept over me. This was romance – I was going to be a trained nurse.'[11] Records of the Department of Indian Affairs show that Mrs Johns remained as teacher on the reserve until 1903, a period of four years after her daughter left Wabigoon.

3

Ethel Johns – Pupil Nurse

It was perhaps fortunate for Ethel Johns that she had always wanted to be a nurse, for alternatives were few. Careers for women at that time were limited mainly to marriage, teaching, and nursing. Cora Hind was exceptional in choosing to work as a stenographer and free-lance journalist; her ambition to join the staff of the *Manitoba Free Press* was yet to be realized. For her young friend, preparation for teaching would have presented a financial hazard, but she could take training as a nurse under the prevailing system of apprenticeship, paying for her education through service to the hospital.

So it happened that on a day late in June 1899 a slim, fair-haired young woman set out for Winnipeg via the Canadian Pacific Railway. What her feelings were as she left Wabigoon can only be surmised: anticipation tinged with fear of the unknown, homesickness, perhaps comfort in the knowledge that Core Hind was in Winnipeg and would look out for her. She must have wondered anxiously whether she would be able to measure up to the requirements of the Training School, and what she could bring to nursing.

Despite the limitations of the secluded life she had led up to this time, Ethel Johns was not without some attributes that would stand her in good stead as a student nurse. She was older than her years in the ability to carry responsibility, and was self-reliant and independent. Her understanding and appreciation of the Ojibway language and culture were a sound foundation for nursing in a pioneer, multi-racial community. She had witnessed death and felt the sorrow of bereavement, and would therefore have some initial understanding of the sufferings of others under similar circumstances. She had learned to exercise self-control in adversity. She had doubtless assisted her mother, reputed to be a 'good medicine woman,' in giving care to the sick and injured on the reserve, and to women in childbirth. She had also served as interpreter for the doctor on his infrequent visits to the reserve. To these qualities must be added her intellectual endowment. Her bright, inquisitive mind had absorbed eagerly her father's instruction in the subjects of a classical curriculum: Latin, Greek, French, history, and literature. Of scholarly inclination, she had continued her education by self-directed efforts and wide reading. A retentive memory allowed her to draw with ease upon her storehouse of knowledge. For years to come, her writings were to be adorned with quotations from the classics, yet it was somewhat of a trial to her to be labelled 'literary' by her classmates. Now she was eager to continue learning. Motivation was high: not only was nursing a long-held ambition, but it also meant an escape from the narrow life of the reserve, one in which she could perceive no future.

Her choice of the Winnipeg General Hospital Training School was a natural one. It was within easy travelling distance of her home, was located in a thriving young metropolis, and – most important – Cora Hind was there. Despite the hardships, rigid discipline, and educational limitations of her training, Ethel Johns was never to regret her decision. For her alma mater she would always retain a deep loyalty and affection.

At the time of Ethel Johns' admission, the Training School was in the twelfth year of its history. In common with other early Canadian schools of nursing, its students were expected to carry the heavy load of nursing service in the hospital. Instruction was elementary, irregular, and given mainly by staff doctors. Posting of students to the various wards was influenced, if not dictated, by the needs of the institution. Hours of duty were long, living accommodation and food left much to be desired, and health hazards were severe. Military discipline regulated the lives of the students, a legacy of the system established forty years earlier by Florence Nightingale based on the exigencies of the situations in civilian and military hospitals. But the endowed school of nursing which she founded in 1860 in association with St Thomas's Hospital, London, exemplified a basic principle, the educational independence of the school. This important principle and precedent were not followed in the subsequent establishment of training schools by hospitals.

Yet the Winnipeg General Hospital Training School for Nurses was to provide a setting within which Ethel Johns would develop competencies that would stand her in good stead throughout the years of her professional practice. The School was attached to a hospital which was closely bound up with the community and had grown with it. At the time of Ethel Johns' admission, a new wing of seventy-five beds for surgical patients – including an operating room suite – was ready to be opened, and the total bed capacity of the institution was somewhat over two hundred beds. Thus it afforded a variety of clinical experience not only for its student nurses but also for students of the Manitoba Medical College. When the medical college was incorporated in 1883, the hospital became a 'teaching hospital.'

The significance of this association to the School of Nursing was later recognized by Ethel Johns in a graceful tribute to those who had influenced its development. Of the medical staff she wrote: '... For many years, most of the meagre theoretical instruction afforded to nurses was freely given by members of the attending staff who were also professors in the Medical School, all of them able practitioners and most of them good teachers. It was these men who created and maintained that indefinable atmosphere of dignity and good manners which prevails in hospitals where sound medical teaching is carried on ...'[1] Generally speaking, in the period of Ethel Johns' training, the relationship of doctor to nurse was paternalistic. Nursing students learned from their medical preceptors not only in lecture periods but also in the wards, particularly when the opportunity arose to assist at medical rounds. Although nursing books were few and elementary, the students, if motivated to learn, could gain access to medical texts. That some did so was later attested by a classmate and friend of Ethel Johns.[2]

Another circumstance that was to contribute in a unique way to the preparation of Ethel Johns for her future work, especially for the European phase of it, was the rich diversity of ethnic groups in the community served by the Winnipeg General Hospital.

The final section of Ethel Johns' autobiography concerned the years of her training at the Winnipeg General Hospital. The following account is a colourful commentary upon the life of a student nurse in a Canadian school of nursing at the turn of the century:

... There were nineteen pupils in our class – by far the largest ever admitted to the school. We entered in a somewhat haphazard fashion, usually two or three at a time, but the day I arrived there was no companion in misery to comfort me. I was taken to a bleak little bedroom in the nurses' home with two beds in it, one occupied by a tired night nurse who groaned audibly when her privacy was thus intruded upon.

Ethel Johns – Pupil Nurse

I unpacked my probationer's uniform and put it on as quietly as I could. The blue gingham dress had been made at home and, in accordance with instructions, the bodice was tight-fitting and the skirt swept the floor. I pinned on the little muslin cap, with its pleated border. My reflection in the cracked mirror that hung above the dresser was dazzling. At supper-time I was taken to the dining room and assigned to a seat at a table occupied by others of equally low estate.

At seven the next morning I was sent on full duty to Ward Three, a medical service for women. It was a relief to find that the head nurse seemed glad to see me and that she found no difficulty in giving me something useful to do. Evidently, my chief task was to respond with alacrity whenever any one of the thirty patients rapped loudly on her bedside table and demanded a variety of services that completely bewildered me. Ward Three was part of the old hospital and had not been constructed with a view to facilitating nursing service. Half-way down the corridor leading to the utility rooms were six steps up and down which all utensils had to be carried. By ten o'clock I began to wonder whether nursing was really my true vocation. The regular staff had vanished into the ward kitchen and were enjoying tea and toast. When they emerged, the kindly ward maid beckoned to me and gave me a thick slice of bread and butter, plentifully sprinkled with brown sugar. 'Get behind the door,' she whispered, 'and eat it as quick as you can. Never mind the raps. It won't do them any harm to wait a minute.' I gratefully gulped down the scalding tea and returned to the scene of my labours.

At the end of a rather grisly week, I managed to find my way around. The head nurse taught me to make a bed and how to bathe a patient. I learned to read a clinical thermometer and to feel for an elusive pulse that slipped away from my fingers and seemed very hard to count. I could set a tray and feed a helpless patient. It was still my principal duty to answer those raps, to disinfect the bedpans in the bath tub and then to scour them in the unspeakable little sink in the utility room. I even got used to taking those six steps on the run. The hours of duty were from seven in the morning until seven at night with one hour off and twenty minutes for meals. If we could be spared, we were given one afternoon a week beginning at two o'clock. On Sundays we were supposed to have four hours free so that we could go to church. Most of the probationers didn't avail themselves of the opportunity. Our feet were too sore and our backs too tired.

When I entered the school, the newly-appointed lady superintendent had not yet arrived and, when my probation was over, there was no one to decide whether I deserved to be accepted. At last, the harassed medical superintendent looked me over and said that since they were pretty busy on Ward Three he would take a chance on giving me my school uniform and cap ...

The arrival of the new lady superintendent naturally created considerable excitement. Adah Patterson and her assistant, Cassie Thompson, were graduates of The Johns Hopkins Hospital School of Nursing and when they appeared at morning prayers, clad in spotless white and wearing the distinctive Hopkins cap, one admiring pupil wondered whether the puffed sleeves and butterfly bows of her hard-earned uniform were really as stylish as she had imagined. A few days later, these doubts were confirmed when she was summoned to the training school office and gravely examined from all angles, especially from the rear. Nothing was said about the puffs and the bows, but she was told quietly that the 'rat' which supported her imposing pompadour must be removed forthwith. A nurse's hair must always be parted neatly in the middle.

From a teaching point of view, the new order was all to the good. The doctors had previously given their lectures in the dining room and clinical instruction had taken place at the bedside on an apprenticeship basis. A combined class and lecture room was now set up in what had been a stuffy old storeroom in the hospital basement and there, for the first time, systematic teaching could be carried on without being interrupted by the exigencies of the nursing service. There was still no library, no laboratory, no diet kitchen, and not much equipment.

At the end of my fourth month in training, I went on night duty. There were thirty patients, most of them suffering from typhoid fever and some of them very ill. Hours of duty were from seven in the evening to seven in the morning without even a 'float' nurse to lend a hand. My night meal was set out on a tin plate and usually consisted of a slice of tough meat, a cold gray potato and a dry bit of cake. Fortunately, there was always plenty of milk in the refrigerator and sometimes a can of tomatoes. Bowls of soup, thickened with soda biscuits, were hastily swallowed between raps. At four in the morning, the delicious aroma of hot coffee pervaded every corridor.

An assignment to night duty was never less than two months and frequently extended to three. During this time, there was no relief whatever from twelve-hour duty except for the purpose of attending doctors' lectures which were always given in the evening. This meant that pupils on night duty had to be relieved by those on day duty. The lecturers, all busy men, often arrived late and seldom kept within their allotted time. The night nurse did not get back to her ward until nearly ten o'clock and her exhausted 'relief' staggered off duty, more dead than alive. To me, the worst feature of night duty was being routed out of bed at two in the afternoon so that I could attend bi-weekly classes in nursing procedure. I could never sleep soundly in the daytime and even yet have not forgotten this recurring nightmare.

Miss Patterson made a gallant attempt to afford each of us some experience in all the various services but systematic rotation had to be subordinated to the need for staffing the wards. Senior nurses who displayed executive ability were put in charge of a ward and left there for months at a time, thereby avoiding the necessity of paying salaries to graduate nurses. However, it would be quite unjust to suppose that the authorities found much satisfaction in what amounted to an exploitation of the school of nursing. Adequate financial support was not forthcoming from governmental sources and the directors were obliged not only to find enough money for maintenance but also to raise funds for capital expenditure. Under such circumstances, they can hardly be blamed for regarding the school as a heaven-sent and perfectly justifiable source of cheap labour. Patients had to be nursed and nurses had to be trained – it was just as simple as that.

Before many months were over, it became evident that Miss Patterson was finding it increasingly difficult to adjust to a rough and ready Western environment. In an effort to obtain better working conditions, she even went so far as to challenge the authority of the medical superintendent by requesting that an independent advisory committee be set up with which she might discuss problems related to nursing service and education. The directors refused to permit any such infringement of the medical superintendent's absolute authority and Miss Patterson resigned. The announcement of her resignation was received with mixed feelings. We both feared and respected her and were dimly aware that she had our interests at heart. Brief as it was, her term of office had a considerable impact on the school. She had herself been exposed to the powerful influence exerted by such leaders as Isabel Hampton Robb, Adelaide Nutting and Lavinia Dock. The Johns Hopkins Hospital School of Nursing had left its mark on Adah Patterson and she left hers on us.

For a time, there were far too many changes among the graduate staff and the atmosphere of the school remained somewhat turbulent. An increasing number of students were put in charge of wards and, since their rank was arbitrarily based on seniority, they found it difficult to maintain discipline. The system was, in fact, absurd. If you had entered the school one day later than a classmate and happened to be assigned to a ward of which she was in charge, she automatically ranked as your superior officer and you were bound to obey her. You rose when she spoke to you and respectfully stood aside and allowed her to enter the elevator ahead of you. Strange as it may seem, this fuss and feathers had a certain value. Not only did it signify authority – it also fixed responsibility.

Nevertheless, it soon became apparent that a different spirit might prevail in this Western Canadian school of nursing. Among the members of my own class was a strikingly beautiful young woman, Isabel Maitland Stewart, who, after a brilliant career, was destined to become an international authority on the education of nurses. Far better educated than the rest of us, she was a qualified teacher and thus able to perceive the utter inadequacy of the instruction afforded us. Moreover, she had little respect for military discipline and even less for rank based on authority.

When we were both in our senior year, we became involved in a critical situation. Four members of the graduate staff were summarily discharged on what seemed to the students to be insufficient grounds. A written protest was prepared by the student body and submitted to the board of directors. Forthwith, Isabel Stewart and I were summoned to appear for interrogation. We were sternly asked why we had chosen to break the contract that we had signed when we were accepted as pupil nurses and in which we had solemnly promised to obey the authorities under all circumstances. Did we realize that insubordination could lead to instant dismissal? My heart sank for I did not know what would happen if I had to forfeit my three years of training. Rather to our surprise, the ordeal ended at this point and we were permitted to withdraw. The directors took no action and the unhappy incident was passed over in silence. Later on, we discovered that the harsh terms of the contract had been considerably modified.

It did not occur to me at the time (although it has since) that the directors may have been a little afraid of us. This must have been the first time that they had encountered an organized protest made on behalf of a traditionally submissive group. It was true that they had the whip hand for at the time there was no legislation in the Province of Manitoba governing the training and registration of nurses. The school did not even have an alumnae association to which we might appeal for support. But suppose that organized protest had led to organized action – what might have happened then? The directors knew only too well that if the student working force were to be withdrawn the hospital would be forced to close its doors. What the directors did not know was that the idea of calling a strike had never entered our heads. This was the romantic age of nursing.

The whole unhappy situation vanished in the excitement of the graduation ceremonies. A grand ball marked the close of these festivities and, as was their custom, officers of the board of directors were in attendance. Arrayed in the first evening dress I had ever owned – a pink flowered muslin with a long train – I fondly hoped that someone would ask me for a dance. Someone did – the president of the board (who happened to be the German consul) made a formal bow and led me to the dance floor. We waltzed in the Continental manner at furious speed until we became entangled in a window curtain that was blowing out into the room. After we extricated ouselves from my train as well as from the window curtain, I was sure that he had recognized me as one of the rebels who had been summoned before the board. When the dance was over, he

THE CLASS OF 1902
E. Johns, second from left, second row
I.M. Stewart, second from left, first row
A. McKay, lady superintendent, centre
(Courtesy of the Winnipeg General
Hospital School of Nursing)

offered me his arm and, with exquisite politeness, escorted me to a seat beside my chaperon. 'It was a great pleasure,' he said. But there was a twinkle in his eye.[3]

The *Manitoba Free Press* of 20 May 1902 gave a detailed account of the 'convocation,' held the previous evening, of the largest class yet to graduate from the Training School of the Winnipeg General Hospital. One is tempted to speculate whether this comprehensive news story may have been written by E. Cora Hind, then on the staff of the paper. That she was present is certain, since she was to refer to the occasion many years later, in a citation which she was asked to write about Ethel Johns: '... Looking back over the years, I recall her tall slight figure and grave intent face, on the night of her graduation from the School of Nursing of the Winnipeg General Hospital ...'[4]

Despite heavy rains in the afternoon and evening, a large number of people attended the ceremony, which was held in the auditorium of the Y.M.C.A. and was chaired by the Honourable William Hespeler, the president of the Hospital's board of trustees. In his opening remarks, Mr Hespeler drew attention to the growth of the Winnipeg General Hospital, 'now a very large institution, so much so that very few people know the extent of it.' One hundred and fifty-five patients were being nursed every day, he added, and the Hospital was working on a very small allowance, 'having no income except from kind-hearted friends, the local government and the city.' His congratulations to the graduating class gave no hint of the shock and dismay which these young twentieth-century rebels had so recently caused the board. He reminded the graduates that 1902 was coronation year, and that the evening's ceremony was their coronation, the reward for their three years of hard work, with the results of which they had every reason to be satisfied. He then called upon the speaker of the evening, Dr J.S. Gray, a graduate in medicine of McGill University, and Registrar of the College of Physicians and Surgeons of Manitoba.

In his wide-ranging address, as reported by the *Free Press*, Dr Gray spoke in turn to the graduating class, to those responsible for the selection and training of student nurses, and to the general public, the employers of nurses. To the new graduates, he gave some fatherly advice, touching first upon the relationship of the trained nurse to the physician, the public, the patient, and her profession. Her efficiency and the quality of her service, he said, would depend upon her general intelligence, special training, and appreciation of the responsibility resting upon her. The nurse was answerable, he added, to the patient, the doctor, and her own best self. She should carry out her orders with kindness. She should be courageous, gentle, prompt in action, thoughtful, brave under trying circumstances, never indifferent to the sufferings of the patient, of a cheerful disposition, but never flippant, should have control of her emotions, keep tender her sympathies, and never do anything unwomanly. Those responsible for selecting pupils, the speaker counselled, should seek to weed out those whose ideas rose no higher than the low level of easy living or pecuniary gain. Turning to the nursing curriculum, he gave the opinion that the 'course of reading' for nurses should include history, sociology, literature, and should extend well into biography, in order to give a broader sympathy with human need. He spoke of the need for a system of free nursing for those who in a large city could not or should not go into hospital. Finally, Dr Gray dwelt upon the obligations of employers of nurses: the claims of nurses were on their sympathy and help, he suggested. A sympathetic interest should be taken in their welfare as individuals. When on duty, their physical comforts, a just amount of recreation, sleep, and rest should be provided. In this connection, he complimented the president of the board of directors for his kindness in giving a beautiful summer resort on Coney Island for the use of the nurses of the Winnipeg General Hospital.

Dr Gray's ideas on curriculum were surprisingly progressive, even visionary, when viewed in the perspective of the prevailing apprenticeship system of nurse training. They may have been prompted by his observations of the complex demands upon nurses, and the understanding required of them, in the multi-cultural community of Winnipeg. Certainly these ideas anticipated by many years the broadening of the base of nursing education and the flowering of nursing as a profession. Members of the graduating class who had some insight into the shortcomings of their own training doubtless found the speaker's remarks of absorbing interest. Two of their number, Isabel Stewart and Ethel Johns, were destined to make significant contributions to the upgrading of nursing education.

The graduation ceremony concluded with the presentation of medals and diplomas and of awards to top-ranking members of the class. Isabel Maitland Stewart won a prize of fifty dollars for highest general proficiency, with aggregate marks of 448 out of a possible 500. A close second was her friend, Ethel Johns, with a score of 440; and she received a special award given by Dr R.J. Blanchard, who – according to Dr Ross Mitchell – had a high regard for Ethel Johns' ability, and later supported her appointment to the X-Ray Department of the Winnipeg General Hospital.[5] Dr Blanchard, a prominent staff surgeon of the institution, was one of the founders of the Manitoba Medical College, and in 1909 was to become president of the Canadian Medical Association.

For Ethel Johns and her classmates, the glow of the graduation festivities must have faded quickly into stern, cold reality, as they faced the necessity of finding employment.

PART TWO: 1902-1914

4

Early Practice of Nursing

Limited opportunities for employment were open to the Class of 1902. Choice was confined chiefly to administrative posts in hospitals and private duty nursing in patients' homes. District nursing was still in its infancy, and teaching had not yet become a distinct area of nursing practice.

Hospital positions open to trained nurses at the time were few, comprising chiefly the posts of lady superintendent, night supervisor, and head nurses. That these posts were coveted is shown by a letter of 4 June 1902 addressed to the long-suffering board of the Winnipeg General Hospital. The communication was signed by twenty-seven nurses, of whom sixteen were from the recently graduated insurgents of the Class of 1902. It goes without saying that the signatures included those of Isabel M. Stewart and E. Incledon Johns. The letter was incorporated into the board minutes:

SIRS:

We, the nurses of the Winnipeg General Hospital wish to protest against the filling of vacant posts by graduates of other schools.

We are told on graduation that our certificates give us an equal standing with nurses from any other Hospital and consider that we should be given a chance of applying for any vacancies that may occur in our own.

The last three appointments have been given to strangers, though some of our graduates were willing, and, with a competent Lady Superintendent should be able to fill them.

Respectfully submitted.

The board appointed a committee to look into the complaint. The committee duly reported at the July meeting of the board, but the minutes did not give the substance of its findings.

Private duty was the major occupational field for trained nurses at that time. It was not without its drawbacks and problems. Assignment to cases often depended upon the favour of individual doctors. Hours of duty were long: the nurse usually moved into the patient's home and was subject to call at night in addition to her duties during the daytime. Domestic work not infrequently fell to her lot. Fees were small: in Winnipeg, in 1905, eighteen dollars per week for 'ordinary' cases and twenty-one dollars for infectious cases. In that city, the private duty registry was operated by the College of Physicians and Surgeons. A letter to *The Canadian Nurse* explained how the system worked, and added: '... During the past fall and winter Winnipeg has suffered from a severe epidemic of typhoid, and we have not been able to obtain sufficient nurses to attend the calls so that the doctors, unfortunately, added an "untrained" nurses' list to the registry ...'[1] The necessity for the trained nurse to compete for work with the unqualified person was to become one of the factors motivating the fledgling profession to press for legislation to regulate nursing practice.

Ethel Johns was engaged in private duty nursing for about eight months during her first three years of practice. In the same period, she was in charge of the operating room at the Winnipeg General Hospital for one year. She spent a few months at Prince Albert, relieving the superintendent of the small hospital there, and was night supervisor for one year at St Luke's Hospital, St Paul, Minnesota. The chronology of these experiences is unknown, with the exception of that as head surgical nurse at the Winnipeg General Hospital. Ethel Johns' Biography File in the archives of the Department of Nursing Education, Teachers College, Columbia University, gives this period as October 1902 – October 1903.[2]

Of Ethel Johns' private duty nursing, E. Cora Hind wrote many years later: '... In the homes she entered there are still grateful memories of the comfort and aid she brought to them ...'[3] Miss Johns' recollections of her own achievements in this field are self-deprecating. During her private duty experience, she wrote, she had learned much that was of 'untold value' but it had not been easy:

... More conceit was knocked out of me during those brief months than I could have believed possible; for, if the sad truth must be told, I was not precisely a shining success. Never shall I forget the sinking feeling which became apparent in my epigastric region when I climbed the steps of a strange house, with my suitcase in my hand. I can yet feel upon me the gimlet eye of the maid who admitted me, and who, I knew instinctively, resolved to hand in her notice that very day. I can hear yet the carping criticism of the maternal grandmother concerning my ideas on infant welfare. I can remember the broken nights and the exhausting days. But there was another side to it. There was the night that one showed a proud young father his first-born son; there was the night when one came to know that the word 'comfort' meant 'to be strong with,' to go down into the 'valley of the shadow,' until at last the kind, strong hand that had been the breadwinner for the little family grew cold in yours. Oh! I would not have missed that year with all its failures. It is no light thing to hold the cup of life and death to the lips of others, even though you taste not of it yourself ...[4]

Through this early experience, Miss Johns gained a first-hand knowledge of the difficult conditions under which private duty nurses often carried on their work. She became concerned, too, about the plight of people who required twenty-four hour nursing care in their homes but could not afford to pay for it.

It may have been as early as the summer following her graduation that Ethel Johns' 'wandering spirit and a desire for adventure' drew her to the eighteen-bed hospital at Prince Albert to relieve for the superintendent who was going away for a three-months' rest. The experiences of that period of her career were still vivid in her memory when she wrote about them several years later.[5]

This narrative, brightened by flashes of humour, told of the experiences of the 'young and verdant substitute' and the lessons they taught her. The account is of historical as well as biographic interest: it gives a contemporary description of a small pioneer hospital of the Canadian West and the community it served. Vignettes are drawn with stark realism: the two probationers 'of a truly verdant greenness' who comprised fifty per cent of the nursing staff; the cook whose love affair with the grocery man completely disrupted the hospital kitchen; the unqualified assistant superintendent who 'was nevertheless a most admirable nurse'; the Mounted Police who stood not only for law and order on the lonely prairies, but for kindness and human charity as well; the country doctors going 'on their daily round quiet and uncomplaining, bringing God only knows what help and comfort to those who needed it sorely'; and the Ladies Aid whose 'feminine eyes found the weak joints in one's armor at once,' and who 'always managed to make tours of inspection on some particularly trying day when the overcrowded wards and the undernursed patients looked worse than usual.'

A severe outbreak of typhoid in the community strained to the utmost the capacity of the hospital and the strength of its small but valiant staff. Two student nurses contracted the disease and one died. At last Ethel Johns herself, overburdened and exhausted, became ill:

... When things were at their very worst the head of affairs contracted typhoid also and was retired from active service, but not from the scene of action. The walls were thin and sound carried easily, so that dire murmurs of tragedies, domestic and otherwise, were easily heard in her sick room. There was plenty to hear, for the epidemic did not abate, and it was two weeks before a nurse was found to substitute for the substitute! The nights were the worst, for then things got all tangled up, and the tired nerves revenged themselves and bred a host of nightmares ...

Recovery from the illness marked also the end of an appointment which had tested her competence and stamina to the utmost. In this brief period, she may well have passed from girlhood to womanhood. Twenty years later, addressing an international meeting of nurses, she recalled the experience:

... I remember very clearly one small hospital. It served a small northern community then in the early stages of development. Its board of directors was composed of farmers of the district and a business man or two. Its medical staff comprised the three over-worked general practitioners; its ambulance was the patrol of the Royal Northwest Mounted Police; its 'matron' a youngster of twenty-two just out of training;[6] its nursing staff a group of three pupils who had never seen the inside of a high school.

The financing of the institution was precarious to the point of absurdity, but its modest budget constituted a very serious problem for the few taxpayers of a scattered and struggling rural population. This hospital, like many another, made the training school the keystone of the financial arch. An epidemic of typhoid came along and the little school rose to the occasion with true gallantry. Better nursing has been done no doubt, but none more devoted than those three pupils afforded their patients under conditions of almost hopeless discouragement. From an educational point of view their training school, as they fondly called it – poor children – was a pitiful joke. But the community it served did not see it in quite that way. They were absurdly grateful. You see some of them would have died if the hospital had not been there ...[7]

Ethel Johns' private duty experience had confronted her with problems that left her with serious and lasting concerns. Her early contact with a small hospital and its training school brought her face-to-face with the conflicting needs of a pioneer community for nursing care it could afford and of student nurses for a proper education. She could not condone the educational deprivation of the students, but sympathized with the difficult situation in which the community and its hospital found themselves.

Shortly after Miss Johns returned to the Winnipeg General Hospital, she received a new appointment. The *Annual Report* of the hospital for the year 1902 noted that Miss E. Johns, head nurse of Wards E and F, had been appointed to the position of head nurse in the operating room in November, 'with the approval of Administrative and Surgical staffs which she continues to receive.'

By strange chance, Isabel Stewart had her training in the operating room during the early months of her former classmate's direction of the department. Although Miss Stewart had graduated with the Class of 1902, she had not completed the required three years at that time, since she had entered the training school only in February 1900. More than half a century later, Miss Stewart could recall the strain which her subordination to Ethel Johns had placed upon their friendship:

... The operating room was a holy of holies, you know ... My friend and classmate Ethel Johns was head of the operating room for a while. I never envied her her job. She was a crackerjack. An operating room nurse was a special kind of nurse, and she had to be a master of technique. She trained all the internes, really, as well as the nurses. She had to, because she was supposed to protect the operating room. If any infection developed, then there was always the question, was it the nurse or was it the physician ... She was a very, very good operating room nurse. But she ruled it with a rod of iron. I got my training under her, and we had our own troubles, because I couldn't see why E.J., who was my good friend outside, had to put on so many airs when she got in the operating room. So one day I said, 'E.J., just come off your high horse.' She said, 'Miss Stewart, you go off duty,' so off I went. I had to go off because I had not treated my head nurse with proper respect, you see, even though she was my classmate and very close friend. Well, you see, I couldn't put up very much with a lot of this. But these were some of the things you had to face. It was part of the system ...[8]

Fortunately the breach was healed. The friendship with Isabel Stewart was to grow with the years and to embrace other members of the Stewart family as well. Isabel's sister Jessie became a close friend; so too did her sisters Helen and Elizabeth, and her brother David. Dr

Helen Stewart recalled that David, while pursuing his medical studies in Winnipeg, supported himself by working for the *Manitoba Free Press*. Mr Dafoe was editor at the time, and E. Cora Hind was on staff. Miss Hind 'adopted' the Stewart family, thus further cementing the bond between Ethel Johns and its members.[9]

Of Ethel Johns' year as night supervisor at St Luke's Hospital in St Paul, little is known. Many years later, she wrote a whimsical column about this experience for *The Canadian Nurse*. No one seemed to value her very highly, she recalled. She came on duty at seven o'clock in the evening, took the day report, and 'carried on from there.' Usually she had not slept very well, and felt slightly seasick. Yet the year, in retrospect, was a good one, and when she left, the stern superintendent, 'with a frosty twinkle,' told her that she had earned a good night's rest.[10]

By the year 1905, Ethel Johns was back on staff at the Winnipeg General Hospital. Miss Frederica Wilson had been appointed lady superintendent in January of that year. The exact nature of Miss Johns' duties for the first two years following her return is not recorded, but she probably carried both teaching and supervisory responsibilities. Later she wrote about the situation in the hospital at the time of Miss Wilson's appointment: '... the nursing service was exceptionally heavy. Winnipeg now had a population of more than 30,000 and the daily average of patients had risen from 171 in 1903 to 256. Typhoid fever was still prevalent and in 1905 no less than 911 cases were admitted to the Hospital. At the peak of the epidemic, patients had to be turned away and in September the city erected a fifty-bed emergency annex on Emily Street to take care of the overflow ...'[11]

A graduate who entered the training school in 1904 recalls that Miss Johns came in to teach a lesson to her class. One of the students had her eyes closed, whereupon Miss Johns 'marched out of the room and over to the director of nursing' and told her that she was not going to teach students who were too tired to stay awake. The same nurse also remembers that Miss Johns would walk through the tunnel to the nurses' residence with eyes cast down, not looking at the students whom she passed on the way. But in those days, seniority was the thing, and head nurses were not sociable with students.

In 1907, a new category of nursing position was established at the Winnipeg General Hospital, that of staff nurse in charge of the X-ray department. Ethel Johns was its first incumbent. The opportunity to embark on such an entirely new undertaking could not fail to appeal to her venturesome nature. At this time, radiology was in its infancy. X-rays had been discovered only twelve years earlier by Professor

Roentgen, their use for therapeutic and diagnostic purposes was still highly experimental, and their hazards were not yet understood. In this connection, it is of interest to learn that Dr Harley Smith touched upon the subject of X-rays in an address which he gave to the Graduate Nurses' Association of Ontario on the general topic, 'Advances in Medicine,' published in the May, June, and July issues of *The Canadian Nurse*, 1907. In the section of the paper which appeared in the June number, Dr Smith spoke of the therapeutic and diagnostic uses to which X-rays were already being put:

... When living tissue is exposed for a sufficient length of time to these rays, peculiar changes are brought about in the cells, expressed first by increased cellular activity and afterwards by cell-death. Thus far this treatment has been chiefly successful in diseases of the skin, the mucous membrane and the tissues lying directly beneath them, as lupus, eczema, sycosis, favus, epithelioma, rodent ulcer, and certain forms of carcinoma. But it is rather in the domain of diagnosis that the Roentgen rays claim their greatest achievements ...

Ethel Johns cannot have failed to read this report, and to have been alerted by it to the dangers as well as the use of the Roentgen rays. Preparation for her new duties, in addition to instruction by Dr M.S. Inglis, head of the X-ray department, involved the study of physics. This is attested in her application form in the Ethel Johns Biography File at Teachers College.

During the years that Ethel Johns was nurse in charge of the X-ray department, the work load increased steadily. The *Annual Reports* of the hospital for that period give a detailed breakdown of the therapeutic and diagnostic procedures performed. Miss Johns' recognized competency in this new field was mentioned in a news item about her in the *Manitoba Free Press*: '... When the "x" ray equipment was put in, being ever keen for new things in her profession, she specialized in this work, and for three years had charge of the department under Dr Inglis, and was one of the first women in the world to occupy such a position. At the time of the visit of the British Association to Winnipeg her work received the warmest appreciation by the experts of that section of the Association ...'[12] This reference was to the British Association for the Advancement of Science, which met in Winnipeg in 1909.

Two doctors who were interns in the Winnipeg General Hospital knew Ethel Johns at the time she was in charge of the X-ray department: Dr Ross Mitchell, and the late Dr Fred C. Bell, who became medical superintendent of the same institution in 1910.

Dr Mitchell remembers Ethel Johns as capable and intelligent-looking rather than pretty. She was bright but firm, and direct in conversation. Although outspoken and decided in her views, she had a good relationship with the doctors. 'She certainly wasn't meek, and she stood up to the doctors about the regulations of the X-ray department.' She had a great interest in nursing, which was obvious to anyone who spent any time in her company. But off duty, her 'highly-developed sense of humour' found release. Dr Mitchell also recalls that Miss Johns took part with him and another intern (Dr Hudson) in a comedy held in the nurses' residence. The skit was called 'Box and Cox,' and concerned a landlady who rented the same room to two lodgers, one of whom slept at night and the other in the daytime. Miss Johns played the part of the landlady and thoroughly enjoyed the lark.[13]

Dr Bell got to know Miss Johns very well in the summers when he was working at the Winnipeg General Hospital. He was taking his medical programme at the time, and the summer work experiences were counted as internship. He graduated in 1909. He remembered clearly the formidable machine Miss Johns was running in the X-ray department, with its balls, mirrors, and flashing light. He thought that she was 'an exceptionally pleasing-looking person. She could work up some wrath, you know, at times, but there was always a good reason for it, and as far as personality went, I thought Miss Johns was a wonderful person. In after years, you can't follow everybody, but she is one of the outstanding women of my experience.' He added that Miss Johns must have had a good deal of cultural background, from the way she looked at things and the way she would speak of people. Dr Bell's mother was very fond of her, and she used to visit their home. His father, at one time a board member of the Winnipeg General Hospital, was secretary of the Grain Exchange in Winnipeg, and (Dr Bell stated) it was he who got Cora Hind settled in her work in the grain trade.[14]

The period of 1905–11, during which Ethel Johns was on staff at the Winnipeg General Hospital, saw her increasing involvement in two newly established nursing organizations, the Alumnae Association of Graduate Nurses of the Winnipeg General Hospital and the Manitoba Association of Graduate Nurses. Together with Isabel Stewart, she participated in launching the *Nurses' Alumnae Journal* of the Winnipeg General Hospital, and became its first editor. She started to write for publication in this magazine and in the new national quarterly, *The Canadian Nurse*. Her early intensive concentration upon her own work now began to develop into concern for the broad issues with which the emerging profession of nursing was confronted.

5

The *Nurses' Alumnae Journal* of the Winnipeg General Hospital

In April 1904 the first steps were taken to form the Alumnae Association of Graduate Nurses of the Winnipeg General Hospital. The proposed objects of the organization, as drafted by Mrs Ada C. (Newton) White, were comparable with those of similar bodies elsewhere: to provide for the mutual help and protection of graduates; to promote social intercourse among the graduates of the school, and to extend all possible help to those in trouble; to further the interests of the training school; and to place the profession of nursing on the highest possible plane. In addition, it was proposed that the association would establish a private duty registry, a club room for members, and a sick benefit fund.[1]

Ethel Johns was present at the inaugural meeting of the Alumnae Association, which was held in the Y.W.C.A. rooms in the Rialto Block on Main Street; but, as she later confessed, she was somewhat bored by the early meetings of the organization: 'During the first year of its existence,' she wrote, 'I, like many other young and giddy members, regarded it as a tiresome institution to which one was under the painful necessity of paying two dollars a year ... In some vague way I did understand that Mrs White and her faithful few were fighting a battle, but "what they killed each other for" remained a mystery. The Battle of the Registry was fought and won by these few women against great odds, and the right of nurses to manage their own business affairs without undue medical interference was established in Winnipeg for all time ...'[2]

By chance, Ethel Johns was awakened to the significance of association work, and she later told of the incident which led to her involvement. She wandered, one afternoon, into the reception room of the nurses' residence to find a group of four women waiting expectantly. She was startled to be hailed by one of them with cries of, 'Joy! Joy! Quorum! Quorum!' – and she realized in a flash that her arrival completed the minimum of five members required to transact business of the association. Without delay, 'the president proceeded, with her usual energy, to get through business which had been accumulating for some time on account of the meagre attendance at the meetings. It struck me then that there was something gallant about the attitude of these women, who met month after month only to find that few were interested enough to put in an appearance, and then and there the great upward surge of the woman's movement (for this was but a phase of it) dragged me unresistingly into its current.'[3] From that time, for close to half a century, Ethel Johns was involved in the work of nursing organizations, whether at the local, provincial, national, or international level.

Initial steps toward the provincial organization of nurses in Manitoba were taken in June 1905. Handwritten minutes of the preliminary meeting reveal that the nurses of Winnipeg had felt for some time that an effort should be made to obtain registration. An opportunity to broach the subject publicly presented itself when it was learned that Miss Margaret Lennox was shortly to pass through the city. She was a graduate of the Toronto General Hospital, and a worker for the cause of nurse registration in Ontario. She was prevailed upon to address a general meeting of graduate nurses in order to acquaint them with the registration movement in her home province, and notices of the coming event inserted in the daily papers included notification of the intention to call a further public meeting in order to form a nursing association for Manitoba and provide for the registration of nurses.

Following the visit and address of Miss Lennox, a well-attended meeting of graduate nurses was convened on 5 July 1905 in the Y.W.C.A. rooms. The brief minutes noted that the object of the meeting was 'to form a Provincial Association of Graduate Nurses which should bring forward the general movement for registration and other matters of vital interest to the Profession.' The Manitoba Association of Graduate Nurses was established forthwith and Miss Reid was elected president. The first vice-president was Mrs White – presumably the same person who had provided dynamic leadership one year earlier in founding the Alumnae Association of the Winnipeg General Hospital. The record of this historic meeting concluded with the observation that, 'At this time there were the following nurses' organizations in Winnipeg – The Winnipeg General Alumnae, The Trained Nurses' Association, The St Boniface Alumnae formed in July, 1905.'

The year 1905 also witnessed the birth of *The Canadian Nurse,* under the aegis of the Alumnae Association of the Toronto General Hospital School of Nursing. That the editor, Helen MacMurchy, was a doctor rather than a nurse promptly elicited a sharp editorial rebuke from the five-year-old *American Journal of Nursing.*[4] But in fact the organizational pattern of the new Canadian periodical provided for substantial nursing support: two associate editors, a business manager, a six-member Committee on Publication, and fourteen 'collaborators' located in various parts of Canada and the United States. The leading editorial in the first issue of the Journal (March 1905) set forth a concrete statement of its aims:

The Canadian Nurse will be devoted to the interests of the nursing profession in Canada. It is the hope of its founders that this magazine may aid in uniting and uplifting the profession and in keeping alive that *esprit de corps* and desire to grow better and wiser in work and life which should always remain to us a daily ideal. For the protection of the public and for the improvement of the profession, *The Canadian Nurse* will advocate legislation to enable properly qualified nurses to be registered by law ...

Following through on its commitment to the cause of nurse registration, *The Canadian Nurse* in its first issue gave prominence to an article which sounded a challenge to the nurses of Canada:

The subject of State Registration for Nurses has been discussed much of late by those prominent in the nursing world. In Great Britain and Ireland it is a burning question. In the United States they have succeeded in having bills passed in several States; and in a number more they hope to record a victory within the next few months. In South Africa legal recognition was given to nurses in 1891. In 1901 a good bill was passed in New Zealand. It is, we think, high time that the nurses of Canada began seriously to consider this most important subject. In nothing that concerns the best interests of our calling would we lag behind our sisters of other lands ...[5]

Ethel Johns was one of the Canadian nurses who heeded the call. Within the next six-year period, she sought vigorously to further the nurse registration movement. She also gave her support to the young national Journal. Both of these causes she was able to espouse the more effectively because of her connection with the newly established quarterly magazine, The *Nurses' Alumnae Journal* of the Winnipeg General Hospital.

The inaugural issue of the *Nurses' Alumnae Journal* appeared in February 1907. Ethel Johns was appointed its first 'literary editor' and Isabel Stewart the business manager. Of this unique team, both destined to become leaders and writers of note, Miss Johns later recalled that they by no means saw eye to eye: 'In private we fought, in the Irish phrase, "rings around," but on the whole and in public we managed to pull in double harness fairly well.' A never-failing source of dispute, it seemed, was the preferred placements in the magazine which the business manager chose to accord the advertisements which she herself had solicited. The literary editor received several 'severe shocks':

... Here in the middle of my cherished editorial was a blatant 'ad,' which proclaimed the virtues of 'Somebody's Stockings, three pairs for $1.00.' Following a dignified account of the annual meeting appeared a panegyric on hot water bottles. This was too much. The Business Manager and the Literary Editor met in mortal combat – one of many, alas! – in which the latter was dragged (still kicking vigorously) from the arena. The epic virtues of the stockings and hot water bags continued to be proclaimed from the 'inside' pages. The 'space' had been sold for a price by the soulless Business Manager, and Art, as ever, was ground under the heel of Commerce ...[6]

These lively encounters barely ruffled the surface of the deep pool of mutual understanding shared by the two friends. The small Journal flourished and before long it was progressing steadily toward the goals set forth by the literary editor in her first editorial: to provide a bond of union among the widely scattered graduates of the Winnipeg General Hospital; to chronicle the growth of the 'Old General'; to endeavour, through its personal column, to give news of its members; to enlist the interest and support of married members and superintendents of smaller Western hospitals in 'the wider issues which the profession must deal with at once – such as the movement for provincial registration.'

The editorial of the second issue (June 1907) was addressed to the graduating class. While recognizing that the new graduates were doubtless surfeited with congratulations and good advice, said Ethel Johns, the Journal could not resist the opportunity of doing a little preaching on its own account. A nurse's active life was short, at best;

there was no time to waste. Nursing was essentially a young women's profession, and to succeed they must keep young, not in years but in their enthusiasm, interest, and ideals, which should be kept as fresh as when they started. Black moods would come, she warned, as a result of physical fatigue, discouragement, and misunderstanding on the part of others. It would be all too easy to give way in cynicism, to ask, 'What's the use?' But these dark periods must be fought. A sense of humour would help, despite the fact that women were not expected to have one: '... still, most of us acquire one gradually as a protecting sheath from the buffets of the world ... It will not be easy for you to laugh, for often it will be for you, as for poor Punchinello, "He laughed because he might not weep."' The young graduates must keep their interest high:

... Sooner or later you will begin to rust, the unending monotony will begin to tell on you, the spirit of your work will be gone. There is but one remedy – change. If you are in a hospital position, try private duty and vice versa. Post graduate work is always available; reading will do much for you. But fight it with all your might, for remember the schools are turning out every year numbers of women younger, better equipped, better trained than you. You have but one thing that they lack, experience, and soon they will have that also. If you drop the torch a score of hands will snatch it and carry it on. You will be relegated to the vast army of incompetents ...

The editor then deplored the fault to which nurses, in common with other working women, were subject: a tendency to use their profession as a stepping stone to 'higher things' or as a stop-gap to fill in the years before marriage. A choice must be made, she asserted, between the profession of nursing and matrimony: 'Do not hope to conciliate both. They are quite incompatible. Like iron and whisky they are both most valuable – but you cannot take them in the same glass.' Although the graduates, in the light of their probation days, were now grown 'sadly old and wise,' they must try to keep their ideals as a guard, must set some goals to work toward, some prize to win. An appeal for a religious motive to permeate nursing ministrations concluded this unusual graduation message.

So Ethel Johns, herself prematurely 'old and wise' at the age of twenty-eight, proposed some exacting, rather forbidding tenets for the graduating class. Doubtless her advice to the young graduates reflected her experiences in and feelings about nursing at the time, and the situation in nursing as she observed it in the early twentieth century. The tone of the editorial betrayed a weariness of spirit that may have been related not only to the monotony, fatigue, hardships, and frustrations of her early practice, but also to the uncertainties which she felt about her future. Even then, Isabel Stewart was planning to enrol in the recently established nursing programme at Teachers College, Columbia University. Ethel Johns must have longed for a similar opportunity, acutely aware, however, of the almost insuperable obstacles in her path; lack of a high school education, financial inability, and family problems. It was little wonder that 'black moods' would have to be fought, for the future must have looked bleak indeed.

The question arises, too, as to whether Ethel Johns herself deliberately made a choice between marriage and nursing in favour of the latter. The answer to this query is unknown. Her lifelong reticence about personal matters has left a veil over this aspect of her life. A few clues suggest possible romances. Her graduation medal, now in the Woodward Library of the University of British Columbia, has the name, 'Jack,' scratched on its reverse side. Helen Franklin (Owen's daughter) recalls that her father told of a quarrel between his sister and a young man over Ethel's insistence that her brothers accompany the couple to a circus – whereupon she drew a ring off her finger and said that if he didn't want her family, he couldn't have her. From another source it was rumoured that she had had a romance but that the man had been killed in an accident. An unanswered question, too, concerns the identity of the man in the small framed picture which she had on her bedside table when she died. In any event, by the time she was in her late twenties, Ethel Johns had probably turned her back on marriage and decided to devote her life to nursing.

The September 1907 issue of the *Nurses' Alumnae Journal* carried an editorial by Ethel Johns on the subject, 'State Registration of Nurses.' The editor deplored the tardiness of the 'much-vaunted West' in seeking legislation to register nurses. She summed up the meaning and benefits of registration, and outlined in some detail the standards which should be legalized by Parliament, to which the nursing profession, hospitals, and the public would have to conform. She reported that the Manitoba Association of Graduate Nurses, during the past two years, had been struggling to frame a bill to incorporate the required provisions. Not much progress had yet been made, although a medical and legal advisory committee had been appointed. 'The path of legislation is by no means an easy one,' she warned. 'There are many lions by the way – the indifference of the majority of nurses to any interests other than their personal concerns, the possible opposition of the medical profession, and (largest and hungriest lion of all) the difficulty of banding women together for concerted action. These difficulties can all be overcome in time. What the nurses of New York can do, what the nurses of Ontario can do, surely we in Manitoba will not call impossible ...' Defeat might well be expected on the first attempt to secure legislation, and perhaps on a number of subsequent efforts. But with perseverance, she concluded, the law's delays would surely be overcome.

With the issue of December 1907 the first year of the *Nurses' Alumnae Journal* ended. The little magazine was well on its way to a fair future. It had elicited a good response not only from members of the Alumnae Association but also from doctors and other friends who were willing to pay the subscription fee of fifty cents per year. A commentary from one such subscriber so intrigued the editor that it won a place in the December number:

Canadian Pacific Railway Co.
R.M.S. Empress of India.

DEAR LITERARY EDITOR:

This is to be considered more for its value as a Literary Gem than that the envelope contains a sordid fifty cents. Send me the N.A. Journal for two hundred and seventy-nine years, – one year at a time. The fifty cents is for the first year. I'v [sic] got the other fifty centses for the other years, but won't send them to you just now for fear they should get mixed up about 2713 A.D., which would grieve me much.

To those who are too busy to write letters the news of your Journal is very interesting, but to those who are too lazy to write it is a veritable boon. Now we can sit with our feet over the side of the vessel with our lungs full of the fragrant atmosphere of the Pacific and our head full of nothing, not even the fear of an enraged head nurse whose faultless beds have been ruthlessly sat upon by students, and simply trust to Providence and the Journal and fifty cents that all the happenings worth while being recorded as having happened will be made known to us.

And tho' our doctorial mind is deeply interested in 'State Registration of Nurses,' etc., and our soul is fond of poetry, yet if you want our subscription to last longer than 1937 do not curtail the 'Personals,' at the end of the Journal, even for the sake of introducing a page on the latest fashion in nurses' caps.

Wishing the Journal every success, but in case you have already ceased to publish it, owing to the present unfavorable financial condition of our beloved country, why, then use the money to get three pink drinks, with which, I hope, the three editors will drink to the health of the surgeon on board,

THE EMPRESS OF INDIA.

The humorous 'Editorial Note' appended to this communication indicated that the editor had appreciated its contents:

The above letter was received by the Literary Editor just in time for insertion in the Journal. The writer refers to it, modestly, as a 'Literary Gem,' and the Editor has, accordingly, mounted it in the appropriate setting of the Journal. Her sentiments on receiving it were a little mixed. The Managing Editor immediately kennabled the fifty cents, the Personal Column Editor became wreathed in smiles, but the Literary Editor could only hide her diminished head. She has a hazy recollection of requesting Dr Thom and other members of last year's class of graduates in medicine, not to sit on the beds in historic Ward B. The request was proffered with becoming humility, indeed, it was more a tender appeal. But, as ever, she is 'misunderstood.' Dr Thom has amply revenged himself and his classmates. Not content with sitting on the beds, he has sat upon that article on State Registration, which was the apple of the Literary Editor's eye. He has even scorned the high-class poetry, which has decorated the Journal pages from time to time. But the Literary Editor, in spite of a rather unpromising exterior, is really not a bad soul after all, and she heartily hopes, with Dr Thom, that her successor in office will furnish a journal with a maximum of interesting gossip and a minimum of heavy weight ethics. Woman like, she must throw one Parthian shaft: the space devoted to Dr Thom's letter and her answer to it would otherwise have been filled up with 'Personals' of surpassing interest.

As it happened, the Alumnae Association re-appointed Ethel Johns to the office of literary editor for the year 1908. Isabel Stewart declined re-appointment. She was planning a trip abroad for the following summer, after which she would enrol in the Hospital Economics course at Teachers College. To her old friend and associate Ethel Johns paid tribute in the March (1908) issue of the Journal: 'A large measure of the success of the Journal has been due to her efforts, which were not confined to the Business Department alone, but were extended to the Literary Department as well. During Miss Stewart's regime the actual cost of the magazine to the Association was very small, almost the whole expense being covered by advertising and subscription fees.' Isabel Stewart, after completing her studies at Teachers College, remained on staff there in the department of nursing education for the rest of her professional life, finally becoming director of that department. But she always retained her interest in the Alumnae Association of the Winnipeg General Hospital School of Nursing, and in its Journal. To the latter she contributed a number of excellent articles throughout the years.

In the same issue (March 1908), Miss Johns gave warm support to *The Canadian Nurse*, pointing out that the periodical was in every way worthy of its name, and that it deserved loyal support from all Canadian nurses. Its price was low, she added, only one dollar per year, and its contents were of value: '... So far the articles published in it have been eminently practical, and must prove helpful both to nurses engaged in private work and to those who prefer institutional positions. In a new country such as our own,' she commented, 'where so much organization remains to be done, and where hospitals are situated at considerable distances from one another, a journal of this type can do much to bind our interests together and to give to East and West that union which means strength.'

A visitor to Manitoba in the fall of 1908 aroused Miss Johns' interest in a current social problem. Mrs Cran, a nurse from England, was brought to Canada by the Dominion government to undertake a study of the industrial conditions for women in this country. The findings of the survey, it was hoped, would serve as a basis for encouraging English women to immigrate here. Mrs Cran, upon her return to Winnipeg from a tour of the west, had given strong public expression to her opinion that women of the Canadian west, especially those in isolated areas, were not receiving adequate obstetrical care. Several factors were found to contribute to this deficiency. Small hospitals throughout the country refused, as a general rule, to accept maternity cases; there were no 'Maternity Homes' even in the larger towns; and the fees of graduate nurses precluded their employment by the very people who most needed nursing care.

In her final editorial (December 1908) for the *Nurses' Alumnae Journal*, Miss Johns called attention to Mrs Cran's visit and her well-publicized statements based on the findings of her survey. While recognizing the basic accuracy of these observations, the editor expressed indignation both about Mrs Cran's working procedure and some of her allegations. The visitor had interviewed the Premiers of the provinces but had not consulted with members of the medical or nursing professions. The picture she painted of Canadian nurses as being generally afflicted with gastritis and varicose veins was false, declared Ethel

Johns, pointing to herself, a battle-scarred veteran of ten years' experience, who had no such health problems. But it was Mrs Cran's proposed remedies that drew the heaviest editorial scorn: young English women should be given from three to six months' training in English maternity hospitals, after which they would be sent out to farming and ranching areas of Canada under government auspices. Miss Johns rejected this plan as providing totally inadequate preparation for the obstetrical care required, but she had an alternative to suggest:

... The Victorian Order of Nurses was not mentioned by Mrs Cran. A mere 'Colonial' enterprise, of course, 'a poor thing but our own.' Does it not seem possible that this service might be greatly extended beyond its present bounds so that it might supply the great and crying need for really efficient nursing at a small cost, or in really deserving cases, at no cost at all. Government aid might more reasonably be given to these women, Canadian by birth or adoption, trained for some time at least in Canadian institutions, having some knowledge of Canadian methods in medicine and housewifery. There is no just reason why nurses for the West should have obstetrical training only. A woman with three years general training, including obstetrics, would with all due deference to Mrs Cran, be of infinitely more use than one whose training was confined to one branch of the profession alone ...

The editor's sense of fair play re-asserted itself in the concluding paragraph: 'Nevertheless, she has shown us the core of the wound. She has said, and justly, "Thou ailest here, and here." If we do not like the prospect of her remedy for our ills, then it behooves us to be up and doing. For remedy there must needs be, and quickly.'

Her social conscience now thoroughly aroused, Miss Johns pursued the matter further. Three months later, an article by her on the same subject appeared in *The Canadian Nurse*.[7] An editorial in the succeeding issue urged readers to turn again to Miss Johns' article, 'A Nursing Problem of the West':

... We must not put the problem of caring for the mothers of Canada out of our minds. We hope it will be considered by the nurses of East and West alike. As Miss Johns says, 'We should take counsel together, East and West, and find out how best we can answer, and that quickly, the exceeding bitter cry of our pioneer sisters of the West for help and succor.' Miss Johns' suggestion, that all western hospitals be required by the Government to take obstetrical cases, and that the Government should give financial aid to such hospitals to enable them to take in every maternity case that applies is a good one and should be carried out ...

The editor went on to quote the opinions on the problem of Miss Mary Ard. MacKenzie, Chief Lady Superintendent (since 1907) of the Victorian Order of Nurses:

... The idea of Mrs Cran is to import midwives from England, which would be a most disastrous thing for the West – though I doubt if the West would consider employing it for a moment. The conditions are improving rapidly, young doctors are settling throughout the West, nurses are being placed in hospitals and in districts in the West, and in a few years there will be very few places where assistance cannot be procured on short notice. But meantime, there is a great deal of room for improvement and Miss Johns' suggestion about the small hospitals is a timely and good one. The people of Canada should solve this problem.

The editor of *The Canadian Nurse* had the final word: 'There are two sets of workers needed in this problem – the trained nurse and the domestic worker. The trained nurse problem can be dealt with by the V.O. throughout Canada.'[8]

Viewed in the perspective of history, it is understandable that Miss MacKenzie's response was somewhat guarded in regard to Ethel Johns' suggestion for extension of V.O.N. services to isolated rural areas. While the stated objectives of the Order[9] would readily encompass the enlarged sphere of work, neither its organizational procedure nor its resources at the time would permit rapid, widespread expansion of its programme. It should be noted that the Victorian Order of Nurses, in the early years of its history, assisted in providing a number of small Cottage hospitals throughout Canada. However, this action was never taken unilaterally, but at the request of the community concerned and its local committee. The financing of the Cottage Hospital Scheme was very difficult.[10] Despite Miss MacKenzie's non-committal published response to Miss Johns' article, a courageous effort was actually made in the same year, under her leadership, to bring V.O.N. services to one isolated area in Alberta.[11]

Ethel Johns relinquished the editorship of the *Nurses' Alumnae Journal* at the end of her second year in office, but she continued to contribute articles to the magazine and to write for *The Canadian Nurse*.

In light vein, a series of three 'Letters from a Nurse in Training' appeared in the March, April, and July numbers (1909) of *The Canadian Nurse*. Signed only 'E.J.,' they are unmistakably from the pen of Ethel Johns. At least some of the experiences recounted therein appear to have been based on those of her own student years. In June of 1909, her article on the history of the Winnipeg General Hospital was published in the same periodical.

Freed of her responsibility for the *Nurses' Alumnae Journal*, Miss Johns became more active in other affairs of the Alumnae Association, and early in 1909 was elected its president. She was also able to devote more time to participation in the business of the Manitoba Association of Graduate Nurses and continued to press for the cause of nurse registration. At the same time, she maintained her keen interest in community affairs and found time to include some recreational activities in her busy schedule.

6

High Adventure

In view of Ethel Johns' known devotion to her family, it may be assumed that she visited her mother and brothers whenever she could manage to do so. Little specific information is available about the activities of the Johns family during this period, but it is reported that when Amy Johns left the Wabigoon reserve (probably in the summer of 1903), she went with her sons to the town of Dryden, twenty-eight miles west of Wabigoon, on the main line of the Canadian Pacific Railway. There Alexander, then fourteen years of age, continued his schooling. Some time later, the family moved to Keewatin, which was conveniently close to Winnipeg. It is thought that Owen and Alexander may have worked in a mill there. Amy Johns evidently had a church affiliation at St Alban's Cathedral in Kenora.

Mabel Gray, who graduated in 1907 and became an instructor a year later in the Training School of the Winnipeg General Hospital, recalls that in 1909 her own mother and Mrs Johns spent a few winter months together in a cottage at Long Beach, California. The two women had a pleasant time, going for walks on the seashore, reading, and so forth.

Despite intense devotion to her work, Ethel Johns early cultivated interests outside the hospital and nursing, in which no doubt she was encouraged by E. Cora Hind. She became a member of the Social Science Club of Winnipeg, a group which concerned itself with a study of housing, city planning, taxes, and social affairs generally. Literature and poetry were also discussed.[1]

Although not much inclined to outdoor sports, Miss Johns enjoyed tennis, a game which she had played as a child in Wales, and she liked walking. Cora Hind's hospitable apartment was home to her, and there were a few other friends whose company she sought. Among these were Mrs H.J. (Elizabeth) Parker and her daughter Jean. Dr Fred C. Bell remembered Mrs Parker as 'a very erudite lady from the Maritimes, with a very solid idea about what Canadianism should be, and so on.' Mrs Parker, he added, wrote a column for the *Free Press*, called, 'Readers' Notes.' She and her daughter had a good deal to do with the formation of the Alpine Club of Canada (in 1906), and Ethel Johns, because of her friendship with them, was in the centre of the talk and planning about it. But it was not until the Club was three years old that Miss Johns decided to attempt to qualify for membership. Accordingly, she made plans to attend the 1909 Camp, at Lake O'Hara, from the second to the ninth of August.

This event was later reported to have been the most successful to date in the history of the Alpine Club of Canada. A number of factors contributed to this happy outcome. Attendance was high, nearly two hundred persons being 'under canvas' during the week's outing. Many of the Club's early members were becoming expert on rock and ice, and the campsite itself was ideal, accommodating in a large grassy meadow the large number of tents and other facilities required. Most important of all, in the opinion of the honorary secretary, Elizabeth Parker, was the presence of a group of British climbers, some of them eminent mountaineers, who contributed not only their assistance in the climbs but also delightful entertainment around the campfires in the evenings.[2] Many of the visiting climbers were delegates to the forthcoming meeting in Winnipeg of the British Association for the Advancement of Science. Members of various European and American alpine clubs, they had accepted the invitation of the Canadian club to attend the O'Hara Camp and the special events arranged for their entertainment.

From Hector, a flag-station on the Canadian Pacific Railway, access to the O'Hara Camp was by way of a delightful path through the valley of Cataract Creek, a distance of seven and a half miles. The memory of this trail was still fresh and vivid in the memory of Arthur O. Wheeler, the Club's president, when he wrote:

... It wound beside a rushing, rock-walled torrent; then through an old brule, brilliant with summer flowers; across the debris of a huge rock fall; up and down through the cool green forest of spruce, balsam, and fir, with glimpses of the swiftly flowing glacial stream now and again; along an old moraine and beside the blue-green Lake O'Hara, its surface broken by sparkling ripples, scintillating in the sunshine; and finally over a timbered hog's back to an open meadow and the city of white tents, looking as first seen like a glimpse of fairyland – all green and yellow, white and blue ...[3]

Ethel Johns' enjoyment of the walk and her appreciation of its beauties were doubtless somewhat dampened by her unexpected immersion in a mountain torrent, an incident of which she later gave an amusing account.[4] The disaster was compounded when she found, upon arrival at camp, that her outfit had been left behind at Hector: '... There was nothing for it but to drape myself about in blankets and seek the chaste seclusion of tent number five while my clothes were sent to the cook tent to be dried ...[5]

The day following her arrival, Miss Johns signed up for a walk of two and a half hours to Lake MacArthur. While the trip entailed 'no real climbing' she found herself suffering from acute shortness of breath. She realized that her distress was due both to the sudden transition from the low altitude of Winnipeg to the heights of the mountain country, and to her lack of training for such exertions. In fact, she had had no previous experience in either hiking or mountain-climbing; and she must have begun by now to question the wisdom of her impetuous decision to attempt the official climb, the prerequisite for full membership in the Alpine Club of Canada. But once she had set her sights on a goal, however lofty, it was not in her nature to turn back. Her British pluck and determination, coupled with strong family tradition, would have scorned such withdrawal as inexcusable weakness.

Mount Huber, height 11,041 feet, was the official climb for the 1909 Camp. The president later described the mountain in his report:

... Towards the camp Huber presented a bold rock face much broken by cliffs and far too steep to attempt an ascent. To reach the summit it was necessary to traverse along the west face and attack the mountain from the north and east. Here, the entire character changed and snow and ice predominated. At one point in the cliffs, at a lower altitude, it was considered advisable, though not absolutely necessary, to place a rope, which helped much those making their first climb ...[6]

According to the official report, Ethel Johns' graduating climb took place on 6 August, the fifth day of the meet. Dr Fred Bell clearly remembered the event. Then a young doctor just commencing his practice, he was one of the original members of the Alpine Club of Canada, and an experienced climber. On 5 August, he was engaged in the general work of the Camp when he observed that the Swiss guide, Edouard Feuz, was quite put out by the fact that the party assigned to him for the next day's climb included four novices. In addition to Miss Johns and another equally inexperienced person (a man), there was a fairly elderly couple who – in Dr Bell's opinion – did not appear fit for the exertion that would be required. So he went to the president, Mr Wheeler, and volunteered to go with Edouard on the morrow. The president accepted the offer with alacrity: '... He thought that would be a good idea,' Dr Bell recalled with a chuckle, 'because I was a doctor.'[7]

So it came about that Dr Bell was in the 'end man' position on the rope when the ragged little party ascended Mount Huber on the following day. A Church of England clergyman had joined the group, and Ethel Johns was later to comment, in a whimsical account of the climb which she wrote for a friend, that it was very comforting to feel that all the consolations of the Church and Medicine were present in the hour of execution.[8]

Ethel Johns would never forget the rigours, hazards, and exhaustion of the next fourteen hours, but the view from the summit of Mount Huber was well worth the price: '... After a few minutes I stood up and looked around. It seemed as though we were standing on the roof of the world. In every direction lay a sea of peaks, glittering in the cloudless blue. Far below us shone a chain of little lakes linked together by a mountain torrent, an emerald necklace fit for a queen. Then I was glad I had climbed Huber and for the moment counted not the stress and strain of it ...'[9]

Warm was the camp-fire that evening, and good it was to have earned a place in the noble company of mountaineers: '... Every separate bone and muscle ached; every time I closed my eyes I saw that knotted rope dangling down the rock face and my cheeks burned when I thought how cowardly I had been, but, in spite of all, I had made my climb, badly, falteringly, but nevertheless to the top, and I knew at last to the full why mountaineering may justly be called "a stern and noble sport."' While the week had tried her stamina to the utmost, she found in retrospect that the outing had brought significant benefits. She had gained, she felt, a new set of values, and the work and worries of the past year had slipped from her like an outworn cloak. Best of all, she concluded, it was 'good to have learned a little, a very little, of the secret of the mountains. You cannot wrest it from them ... you must live in them and with them for a space. Then suddenly some golden morning you will find that the green pines and the grey rocks and the white snow have whispered it to you. Then you are of the craft, and worthy to be a very humble member of the Alpine Club of Canada ...'[10]

Shortly after her return to Winnipeg, Ethel Johns wrote the account of her adventures for the September 1909 issue of the *Nurses' Alumnae Journal*. She also gave a sparkling address on the same subject at an anniversary dinner of the Alpine Club. This intriguing narrative, entitled 'A Graduating Climb,' was published in *The Canadian Alpine Journal*, 1910.

A third record of her climb was prepared by Ethel Johns as a Christmas gift for a friend, Mr Herbert Carpenter, for several decades the organist of St Alban's Pro-Cathedral, Kenora. Presumably this booklet was returned to Miss Johns after Mr Carpenter's death in 1938, for it was found among her personal papers when she herself died, thirty years later. On its faded, multi-coloured pages is inscribed, in her fine printing, an amusing account of the ascent of Mount Huber. Illustrated by snapshots of various stages of the climb and enlivened by cartoons from *Punch*, this unique memento of a great occasion clearly reveals her keen sense of humour and ability to laugh at herself, and evokes most poignantly that long-ago high adventure. Clipped inside the cover of the little album is a yellowed calling card inscribed, 'Miss E.I. Johns,' on which is written the following message: 'This publication will of course be a strictly private one. It is indeed limited to one copy. Do you mind letting mother see it – I think she would be amused. I feel guilty in a sense to think that I have jested with the mountains – because way down deep in my heart I feel that "They have not seen the Snowy Hills of God who have not seen the Rocky Mountains, – silent, serene, immeasurably great." '

7

A Champion for Nurse Registration

In the summer and early fall of 1909, the editor of *The Canadian Nurse* and Miss Margaret Lennox of the editorial board visited nursing associations throughout the west. A news item in the September 1909 issue of the Journal noted that in Winnipeg they were met and welcomed by Miss Johns, the president of the Winnipeg General Hospital Alumnae Association.

True to the commitment made at the time of its inception four years earlier, *The Canadian Nurse* had given steady support to the nurse registration movement, and its editor was well-informed on the subject. The leaders of the Manitoba Association of Graduate Nurses seized the opportunity of her tour to have her speak to the members about the need to press for legislation to control nursing education and practice. A special meeting was convened on 6 September, and the minutes recorded the names of the fourteen members who were present, including that of Ethel Johns. Illustrative of the difficulty encountered by the young organization in gaining the active support of its members is the fact that, following Dr MacMurchy's talk, it was decided to designate this as the annual meeting; the one called at the regular time had been unable to transact business because of the lack of a quorum. Two years earlier, Miss Johns had warned alumnae members of the 'lions' in the path of nursing legislation. It would seem that her concern about the disinterest of 'the majority of nurses' was not without foundation.

That the early leaders of the Manitoba Association of Graduate Nurses were well aware of the need to enlist the support of nurses, doctors, and the public, is shown by the organizational arrangements which they made. A meeting held as early as 27 March 1906 had established a committee on legislation. This was broadly representative of various nursing interests. Its membership comprised the eight officers of the Association (including Ethel Johns as third vice-president), eight members at large (one of whom was Isabel Stewart), and the superintendents of hospitals in Manitoba. It was reasonable to assume that the understanding and support of the latter group would be a critical factor in the struggle for nurse registration. At the same meeting, the decision was made to affiliate with the Local Council of Women. It was not until five years later that the organization appointed a medical-legal advisory committee; in the interim, several individual doctors had lent strong support to the registration movement.

An opportunity to place the issue of nurse registration before the public came early in the year 1910. With the co-operation of the Manitoba Association of Graduate Nurses, the Local Council of Women convened a meeting on Saturday afternoon, 26 February, to discuss the question of provincial registration for trained nurses. This was the second in a series of Lenten programmes conducted by the Council to explore matters of public interest. The well-publicized event was held in the concert hall of the Y.W.C.A., and featured a paper by Ethel Johns. Again, one is tempted to conjecture whether Cora Hind may have written the lucid, comprehensive account of the meeting which appeared in the *Free Press* on the following Monday. Almost certainly, she would have been present on this important occasion, which was reported to have been of exceptional interest.[1]

The situation underlying the movement for registration of nurses in Manitoba, as Miss Johns described it, was similar to that in other provinces and states, and in Great Britain. Approaching the subject positively, she spoke of the advantage to the public of having a legal standard established for the nursing profession as it had been for medicine, dentistry, pharmacy, law, and teaching. State registration, she explained, meant that, by an Act of the provincial legislature, standards would be established by which all women desiring to be professional nurses would be measured. Specific requirements under the Act, the nurses hoped, would include such matters as: a definite standard of preliminary education; a uniform length of training; a certain minimum number of beds for hospitals offering training facilities to nurses; a standardized curriculum; and provision for examinations 'on the theoretical side of nursing' to be controlled by a central provincial council. Nurses coming to the province from training schools outside of it would be required to show credentials from their own state board of examiners or they would be required to pass the examinations of the local board. No person would be permitted to call herself a registered nurse who had not first obtained a licence to practice from a provincial council; to do this, said Miss Johns, she must have gone through the full course of training and passed the required examinations.

Although these reforms appeared simple, the speaker added, in actual fact they involved a great deal. To begin with, the matter of an enforced standard of preliminary education could present difficulties. Some would say that a high level of education would not necessarily ensure that the woman possessing it would make a good nurse. While conceding this point, Miss Johns commented drily, '... still, we do not wish to train women who are absolutely illiterate, no matter what qualities of heart they may possess.' A way around this difficulty might be found, she suggested: '... Some of us hope that our new university may help solve this problem by establishing a short preliminary course for nurses which any woman of good moral character and physical fitness for the work may take, thus fitting herself to pass on to the training schools of the Province as a pupil nurse ...' But Ethel Johns could envisage an even broader sphere of influence for the young university in the field of nursing education: '... I hope to see a class of graduate nurses trained in Manitoba hospitals take their diplomas at the hands of the chancellor of the university ...' Implicit in this aspiration, it would seem, was the assumption that training schools would have to measure up to exacting educational standards, if their graduates were to win such recognition by the University of Manitoba.

Little difficulty was anticipated, Miss Johns continued, in regard to standardizing the length of training; but trouble could certainly be expected over the issue of demanding a certain number of beds before a hospital would be allowed to establish a training school. Some small schools in the Province, she noted, were turning out graduates who were a credit to them and to the nursing profession. But she regretted to say that there were a few hospitals, run mostly for private gain, which set up training schools simply as a cheap way of getting their nursing done, and which made no effort to give a systematic education, but turned out their nurses 'after a varying period of time to practice on a confiding public as trained nurses ...'

Miss Johns then turned her attention to the proposal which, she stated, had caused more misunderstanding and done more to militate against the cause of registration than had all the rest combined: no person would be permitted to call herself a registered nurse who had not obtained a licence from the provincial board of examiners. This clause, said the speaker, was not intended to prevent untrained women from practising. In fact, it would not be possible to do so: '... Nursing the sick has been from time immemorial the special privilege and labor of love of women. There will always be untrained nurses. Every mother is a nurse and often a very good one. No state registration bill ever framed has attempted to legislate against untrained nurses ...' She recognized that some of the untrained women were meeting a real need in the community, giving ordinary nursing care, taking care of the household as well, and charging smaller fees than those of the trained nurses. But there were limitations to their usefulness. Willingness to serve could not in itself suffice to meet situations requiring the knowledge and skill of the graduate nurse. Furthermore, the present uncontrolled practice was both hazardous for the public and unjust to the qualified nurse. In the absence of legislation, any person could don a uniform and call herself a trained nurse. Miss Johns cited an actual case of such an imposter. This was an uneducated woman, without a vestige of training, formerly a domestic in one of the local hospitals, who had assumed the uniform of the institution and was now calling herself a graduate nurse. State registration would prevent this at least. The legal provision would protect both the public and the members of the nursing profession.

A further advantage of state registration, Miss Johns continued, would be the disciplinary control it would permit over the trained nurse who had proved herself incompetent or morally undesirable. The local board could deal with such a case by either suspending or revoking the person's licence. Still another benefit would be elevation of the standards of training schools. With state registration would come inevitably a system of inspection of schools as well as hospitals, large and small alike: '... A good school need not fear inspection,' she said, 'A poor training school needs it in order that its faults may be pointed out and remedied.'

The *Free Press* report noted the speaker's spirited closing remarks:

... Miss Johns pointed out that it was high time for Manitoba to be up and doing in this matter if she did not want it to be made a dumping ground for the inefficient. The states to the south were adopting registration of nurses very generally, eastern Canada was making progress in that direction, and it was gaining ground in England; British Columbia was bringing in a registration bill at the next session of the legislature and both Alberta and Saskatchewan were taking up the question actively ...

Brisk discussion followed Miss Johns' paper. A question was raised as to the stand of the medical profession on the registration of nurses.

Miss Johns replied that no general canvass had been made, but that many doctors, especially the more progressive, had declared themselves in favour of it. Dr Mary Crawford (reported the *Free Press*) thereupon rose and gave her hearty endorsation of the scheme from the standpoint of the practising physician. Miss Bond, a nurse with wide experience, also gave strong support to the idea, pointing out its value to the public.

Manitoba was to be the second province in Canada to have a Nurse Registration Act, which won assent on 15 February 1913. But Ethel Johns was not to guide to its conclusion the movement which she had helped to promote, nor was the resultant Act more than a faint shadow of what its petitioners had hoped it would be. Bitter opposition was aroused in the Legislature on the part of some members representing rural constituencies in which there were small hospitals with weak schools of nursing. As a result, the Act enabled any hospital with a daily average of five patients to conduct a school of nursing.[2] A further disappointment was the non-inclusion of a compulsory educational qualification for admission to training. Provision was not made for inspection of hospitals or schools of nursing. On the positive side, the title 'Registered Nurse' was protected by law. Even more significant was the provision for 'all examinations and matters pertaining thereto' to be 'determined and conducted by and under the direction of the Council of the University of Manitoba, who shall appoint the examiners therefor.'[3]

These developments were still three years in the future on the February afternoon when Ethel Johns earnestly pleaded the cause of registration before the Local Council of Women. In the interim, much remained to be done. Consolidation of nursing groups was an essential first step. In May, Ethel Johns gave her presidential address to the annual meeting of the Alumnae Association. She was pleased to report that perhaps the most vital element in the work of the past year had been the growth of good feeling between the society and the Manitoba Association of Graduate Nurses, '... with increased possibilities of cooperation on the question of State Registration, which is now more and more recognized as an ideal to be striven after ...'[4] The president also commented upon the fact that the Alumnae Association had had the pleasure of entertaining Dr Helen MacMurchy and that the members had derived fresh stimulation from her visit. Other distinguished guests were expected in the future. At the close of the meeting, Miss Johns was re-elected president by acclamation.

A happy event of late August was Isabel Stewart's visit to Winnipeg, prior to her leaving for New York to take up the duties of her new position as instructor in the department of nursing and health, Teachers College, Columbia University. During her brief stay in the city, Miss Stewart attended an informal meeting of the Alumnae Association, and, upon Miss Johns' invitation, spoke to the members about the programme in which she had recently completed her own studies and was now to be a teacher. The information which she gave could not fail to excite her listeners. The report of her talk in the *Nurses' Alumnae Journal* concluded: '... Doubtless some of the members were fired with the ambition to seek the great metropolis with its varied advantages and opportunities for widening the outlook of the nursing profession.'[5] Ethel Johns' eagerness for further study must have mounted as she heard her old friend describe the opportunities to be found at Teachers College. Perhaps the goal seemed more attainable as Miss Stewart explained that some working scholarships were available for senior students wishing to defray part of their expenses by this means.

In the month following Isabel Stewart's visit, Ethel Johns had an opportunity to broaden her professional horizons. With another staff member, the head nurse of the operating room, she left for Chicago to observe in selected hospitals. Predictably – and promptly after her return – her graphic account of their experiences appeared in the *Nurses' Alumnae Journal*. The major focus of the tour for Miss Johns was to observe in departments of radiology and electrotherapy, but she did not restrict herself to these areas. With her travelling companion, she watched noted surgeons at work in the operating rooms of the Augustana and Mercy hospitals. She visited the Michael Reese Hospital and observed the programme of obstetrical care in that institution. But to her the highlight of the tour was a visit to Presbyterian Hospital and its school of nursing.

Ethel Johns was greatly impressed by the programme of nursing education which she found there. The students' first six months were devoted to a preliminary course, during which they had brief periods daily in the wards. The remainder of the time they spent in classes. The training school was affiliated with the Rush Medical School, and the students took certain subjects – chemistry, anatomy, and physiology – in college laboratories under college instuctors. During their preliminary course, they served a term as assistants in the hospital pharmacy, an experience which Miss Johns judged to be 'a most valuable training and one which makes for economy and safety when later they are entrusted with the actual administration of drugs ...' Training in the diet kitchen was arranged during this part of their programme, another experience which would contribute to their later efficiency in the wards. Miss Johns concluded that Presbyterian Hospital gave promise 'of that good time coming when the training school shall cease to be considered a convenient appendage of the hospital proper, and shall itself become an entity, separate and distinct, serving the hospital but not subservient to it ...' The affiliation of this school with the university, in Miss Johns' opinion, lifted the school onto a different plane:

... The very association, the University spirit, gives the pupils a different and better ideal of their work. They feel that they are in the training school primarily for the purpose of obtaining an education in nursing and not as cogs in some vast soulless machine, that on themselves depends the issue of the day, that directly in proportion to the efficiency of their work in the hospital will be the educational benefit to themselves. Will not the hospital be immeasurably the gainer as well as the nurses? This gives meaning to the repetition of duties which were formerly meaningless and objectless. It makes for better teaching methods, for less of the rule of thumb; it gives to those who have eyes to see, the vision and the dream. Not that this Elysian state of affairs has been reached in the Presbyterian Hospital or elsewhere. It comes, but it comes slowly. It is only when we look back that we see how far we have travelled. Thanks to the superintendents of the last ten years, the day of wretched housing and worse food for nurses is well nigh past. Every concession gained has been purchased with infinite pains. We take them lightly, not knowing the cost ...[6]

Ethel Johns' vision of the goal for nursing education was now fixed upon the university. Affiliation of the school of nursing with the institution of higher learning would place the school, she concluded, upon a firm educational footing. Home base for the school of nursing, she took for granted, would still be the hospital. It might appear that she did not perceive, at that time, the cross-currents and contradictions lurking within the concept that the school would serve the hospital but would not be subservient to it. But it is more likely that, being a realist, she could see no present alternative to a large measure of dependence upon nursing students for the care of the hospitalized sick. The precarious financing of hospitals sharply limited the numbers of staff nurses who could be engaged. Miss Johns herself would shortly be in a position in which she would find herself powerless to solve the agonizing dilemma of how to meet, at one and the same time, the needs of the patients for care and those of students for education.

8

The McKellar General Hospital

The year 1911 began auspiciously for Ethel Johns with her nomination for membership in the Canadian Women's Press Club, at a tea held on 26 January, in the home of Mrs H.J. Parker.[1] Three months later, she was elected president of the Manitoba Association of Graduate Nurses. The first vice-president was Miss Kate Cotter, a 1905 graduate of the Winnipeg General Hospital Training School for Nurses. Surprisingly, within a month of her election to the presidency of the provincial association, Miss Johns accepted the position of lady superintendent of the McKellar General Hospital, Fort William. Her resignation from the staff of the Winnipeg General Hospital took effect on 25 May.[2]

The news of her departure from Winnipeg, commented the *Nurses' Alumnae Journal,* came as a 'distinct shock' to Miss Johns' many friends in the Association, and the fact that she was going to a position of greater influence and responsibility scarcely compensated them for their loss:

... To say that she has been the mainspring of Association progress since her return to the staff of her Alma Mater some years ago is only a truism, and her name will be given a place among the pioneers whose names are honoured in the retiring Presidential Address, which we are glad to be able to publish in this issue. What makes Miss Johns' departure more regrettable at this juncture is the fact that, retiring after two years' strenuous service in the Presidency of this Association, she had been elected this year to the same office in the Manitoba Association of Graduate Nurses, and an aggressive campaign under her leadership was being planned in the interests of Provincial Registration ...[3]

Miss Cotter succeeded to the presidency of the provincial association, and gave able leadership to the organization throughout the critical two-year period which led to passage of the Registration Act.[4]

Miss Johns' position in the X-ray department, it appears, was more difficult to fill upon such short notice. The problem was aggravated by the impending absence of Dr Inglis. At a meeting in May of the Finance Committee, it was suggested that a student nurse, Miss Aikman, should take Miss Johns' position during the absence of Dr Inglis or until some other arrangement could be made. She was to receive a salary of thirty dollars per month, and was not to operate the X-ray machine. Meantime, Doctors Blanchard and Inglis would correspond with the English authorities to enquire on what terms a qualified, competent X-ray operator could be obtained. In August, the Finance Committee considered a communication from the lady superintendent to the effect that Miss Aikman was losing a great deal of training in the nursing departments of the hospital, and that she was anxious to be released. In November, the Finance Committee was able to recommend the appointment of Mr L.G. Simmonds as radiographer at a salary of $750 per annum, with room, board, and travelling expenses, the salary to commence on the day he left England.[5] Specialization was under way in hospital service and diverse categories of personnel were gradually to assume functions originally performed by doctors and nurses.

The question inevitably arises as to the reasons which motivated Ethel Johns to make this sudden change, particularly after having accepted the presidency of the Manitoba Association of Graduate Nurses at a critical juncture in its struggle for registration. The offer may have come at a time when she was beginning to find her work in the X-ray department monotonous, lacking in scope and challenge for the future. The opportunity to advance to a senior administrative post may have been one which she found attractive, and the new position probably offered economic incentives. Possibly, too, the need of the McKellar General Hospital was so urgent that the Winnipeg General Hospital was willing to release on short notice a member of its own senior nursing staff to fill the position which had been vacant since April.[6]

It is reasonable to assume, too, that Ethel Johns was attracted by the growing repute of Fort William as a dynamic young community of extraordinary promise. She may well have read the glowing two-page article on this city which had been featured two years earlier by the *Manitoba Free Press*.[7] At that time, Fort William had a population of twenty thousand. Strategically located at the head of the Great Lakes, it had a fine harbour on Thunder Bay and was also an important railway terminus. Grain from the western prairies flowed into its elevators and thence eastward by ship. Commodities from the east destined for the rapidly growing west were transported by ship and rail through Fort William. Rich deposits of iron ores in the district foretold a great industrial development. Electrical power was abundant and reasonable in cost. A tremendous asset was the unlimited supply of water brought by gravity from a large lake in the hills south of Mount McKay. The impetus to seek this excellent source of water came from the typhoid epidemic which swept the city in 1906. Subsequently, by an amazing feat of engineering, a tunnel one mile in length was driven through solid rock to tap the pure waters of Loch Lomond.[8] The economic health and vigour of this bustling community augured well for the strength of its hospital.

Civic improvements had difficulty in keeping pace with the needs of the expanding community, but in 1909 the city planned to build a Carnegie Library and two new schools. Under construction in that year was an addition to the McKellar General Hospital, at a cost of $100,000.[9] This was to increase the bed capacity of the hospital from thirty-five to one hundred and twenty. The following year, construction was started on the north wing, and a third floor was added to the original (1902) building. In 1911, at the time of Miss Johns' appointment, a Nurses' Home was under construction, and by November the first two floors were ready for occupancy.[10] A third floor was completed by 1913.

Prior to her departure from Winnipeg, Miss Johns was honoured at a number of functions.[11] The staff nurses of the hospital entertained for her at a reception and dance. On the following evening, the Alumnae Association was 'at home' in her honour, and presented her with a gold watch. This was engraved on the reverse side with her initials, and inside the back cover with the name of the Association and the date, 'May 24.' This gift she cherished all her life. When its usefulness as a time-keeper was at an end, the works were removed and, mounted on a silver stand, it became the repository for the small photograph that was beside her when she died. Miss Frederica Wilson presented the gift, and read the following address:

... On behalf of the Alumnae Association of the Winnipeg General Hospital, I have much pleasure in asking you to accept this watch as a very small mark of the high esteem in which you are held by the Association. It is in a large measure due to your efforts that the Association has reached its present state of efficiency. Too much cannot be said in praise of your able management of the Journal. As first editor your difficulties were many, but your untiring zeal and energy in establishing for it a sound foundation has launched it on its successful career: it is the great means of keeping our nurses in touch with each other. It was with much regret that we learned your decision to leave Winnipeg. We hope sincerely that your new field of work will prove both happy and interesting.[12]

Personally, as lady superintendent, Miss Wilson added that she would greatly miss Miss Johns from her staff and that the Winnipeg General Hospital would miss her also. The account of this event which appeared in *The Canadian Nurse* concluded: 'Miss Johns was too much overcome to more than bow her acknowledgments.'

The *Nurses' Alumnae Journal* added its tribute and good wishes: 'The Journal must join the Association in wishing Miss Johns greater usefulness (if that were possible) in her new sphere of labor, and every success and happiness therein. We believe the Journal may still rely on the kindly help which has always been available since the active management passed out of its founder's hands, and on those contributions from her gifted pen which have given so much literary grace to its pages ...'[13] The Journal then gave a passage from a favourite quotation used by Miss Johns, and suggested that she, too, had a place among the 'famous men' of whom Kipling had written.

The exact date of Miss Johns' arrival at McKellar General Hospital is unknown. In the absence of board minutes for the period prior to 1915, other information of an official nature concerning her superintendency is scanty.[14] However, an old register in the School of Nursing contains the records of the nursing students from 1904 (when the School started) to 1923, and those for the two years of Miss Johns' appointment are in her handwriting.

In later years, Miss Johns was to look back to this, her first major post, and to reflect that her qualifications for its responsibilities were inadequate:

... In my new position I was responsible for the direction of the nursing service and for the school of nursing – a task which gave me a practical (and painful) insight into the problem of making sure that patients were well cared for while at the same time avoiding exploitation of the student nurses. From the outset, I realized that I was not qualified for the job I had undertaken to do and, as the months went by, gave more and more thought to what was going on in the department of nursing education at Teachers College, Columbia University ...[15]

The problems which Miss Johns encountered at the McKellar General Hospital would have tested the skill and wisdom of a much more experienced superintendent. The needs of the rapidly growing industrial community had exerted steady, relentless pressure upon the young institution from the time of its existence, ten years earlier, as a Cottage Hospital under the supervision of the Victorian Order of Nurses. Overcrowding was a chronic state. This had reached a peak during the typhoid epidemic of 1906, when an annex to the hospital was erected in seven days, to house forty patients. The hospital board had been confronted with financial problems since its incorporation in 1902. Costs of constructing and operating the original building were succeeded by those required for the additions to it.[16]

Private individuals and societies gave generous assistance in furnishing the hospital, and from the beginning it enjoyed the remarkably generous and effective support of its Ladies Aid. Much of the money raised by this group went to the nurses' home, and in 1911 it supplied the furnishings for the first two floors of the new residence.[17] Ethel Johns recognized the importance of maintaining good relationships with this important body to whom the hospital owed so much.

Despite the dedicated efforts of the board members, the Ladies Aid, and private philanthropy, there were difficulties in financing the operation of the expanded hospital during Miss Johns' tenure as superintendent. It is recorded in the brief typed 'History of the McKellar General Hospital' that at the time of Miss Johns' arrival there was 'a staff of four graduates and seventeen pupils.' This was a pitifully small force with which to meet the needs of an active hospital of more than 120 beds, and one that would leave no possibility of providing an educational programme for the students. The old record book in the School of Nursing reveals that Miss Johns continued the practice of her predecessor in admitting pupils one by one throughout the year, as they presented themselves. From April to December 1911 ten students were enrolled in this way. Of these, four left in the same year: one for health reasons, another because of financial inability, a third as a result of several 'hysterical crises,' a fourth for unsatisfactory performance. In 1912, thirteen students were brought into the School, one at a time. A half-century later, Ethel Johns would recall her mounting anxiety as she found herself unable to protect the students' right to an education:

... As the months went by, I began to realize how severe the tension might become as a result of the conflicting demands of administering a nursing service and directing a school of nursing. Again and again, I was forced to sacrifice the educational needs of the students to the exigencies of the nursing service.

I knew enough of the financial problems with which the directors had to cope to understand why so little money was available to pay for graduate staff. I began to wonder whether there was any solution ...[18]

A graduate who entered the McKellar General Hospital School of Nursing in 1911, one of Miss Johns' first probationers, remembers that Miss Johns was very kind, but the work was hard and the hours of duty long – a twelve-hour day. So rugged was the training that of a class of sixteen who entered, only five finished.

As superintendent, Miss Johns was responsible not only for the nursing service and the School of Nursing, but also for all housekeeping activities. There were no interns at the time, and in an emergency she had to do the best she could until a doctor arrived. In view of the varied and heavy duties and responsibilities which she carried, she was concerned that she was denied direct access to the governing body of the hospital:

... There was a business manager who not only had the last word when expenditures were under consideration but also acted as secretary to the board of directors and attended meetings from which I was rigidly excluded. My only contact was through a small executive committee, and there was no way in which I could present and defend my own point of view before the whole membership. On Sundays and holidays the entire hospital staff calmly went off duty and I had to do the pinch hitting ...

The impossibility of stating her own case to the board of directors was difficult for Ethel Johns to bear, particularly since the business manager through whom she had to report had no insight into medical and nursing matters.[19]

One achievement during her regime at McKellar Hospital to which Miss Johns could later look back with satisfaction was the appointment of a dietitian. Of this innovation, she later wrote a lively account:

... One department in which the directors took a personal interest was the general kitchen. In the early days it had been the scene of conflict as one cook after another had departed. Then it was decided to employ a Chinese staff and Sam Lee entered the picture. He was paid a lump sum, engaged his own helpers and ruled them with a rod of iron. Fortunately Sam Lee and I got on rather well together. This was just as well for I had been given a broad hint by the president of the board that if any controversy arose between us their support would be given to Sam Lee rather than to me. The only time that any difference of opinion arose was over the appointment of a dietitian. The Ladies Aid had been persuaded to furnish a diet kitchen and a promising candidate had been found. When the news was broken to Sam Lee, there was such a great banging of soup kettles and roasting pans that no conversation was audible in my little dining room which adjoined the kitchen. The next morning Sam Lee appeared in my office and delivered an ultimatum. Unless he was assured that this interloper would never be allowed to set foot in his kitchen, he and his staff would depart immediately. It was so ordered but before long the gentle charm of that dietitian led to the setting up of a satisfactory if guarded working arrangement. But whenever there was need for consultation, he kept his word and met the dietitian at the threshold of his own domain ...[20]

In the summer of 1912, Miss Johns spent her month of vacation with her mother in Winnipeg. This item of news was noted in the August issue of the *Nurses' Alumnae Journal*. When Mrs Johns and her sons moved to the city is not known, but it may have been prior to her daughter's departure for Fort William. Ethel must have been reassured to know that Cora Hind was nearby. Kennethe Haig recalls that Cora Hind was devoted to the family; and that when Miss Johns was out of the city, she would keep an eye on its members and give assistance if problems arose.[21]

Miss Johns' second year at McKellar General Hospital was also her last in that position; she resigned in September 1913. The *Manitoba Free Press* later commented on the responsibilities which Ethel Johns carried at the McKellar General Hospital and the reason for her resignation: '... The nature of the work carried on in Fort William, namely, concentration of railways, shipbuilding, coal docks, elevators, and the like, makes the surgical work enormous, and the demands on the superintendent heavy and exacting. Miss Johns held this position for two years, and when, owing to her mother's health, she was obliged to resign and go to California, the board and citizens of Fort William gave her the most substantial proofs of their extreme regret in losing her ...'[22]

In Los Angeles, Ethel Johns accepted an appointment as head surgical nurse at the Good Samaritan Hospital, a position she held for somewhat less than a year. The institution has not been able to locate any record of Miss Johns' tenure in this position. Her mother was now resident in Los Angeles, and it is thought that her younger son, Alexander, may have settled there about the same time. According to information received from several sources, Ethel contributed substantially to the support of her mother throughout the years.[23] Because Miss Johns rarely spoke of her mother, even to close friends, the relationship which existed between mother and daughter is veiled in obscurity.

By the spring of 1914, the way had opened for Ethel Johns to realize her long-cherished ambition to study in the department of nursing and health, Teachers College, Columbia University. Though she was uncertain of her admissibility and financial readiness, she put all doubts behind her and sent her application to the University for admission in September 1914. The reply proved to be somewhat disappointing. Her irregular early education did not measure up to matriculation requirements; still, some valuable courses would be open to her if she were willing to forego any academic credit for taking them. On the positive side, she knew that Isabel Stewart, now a junior instructor on the staff of the department of nursing and health, could be depended upon to be her 'guide, philosopher, and friend.' In her courageous way, she resigned from her position, scraped up enough money to see her through a year of study, and set off for New York.[24]

PART THREE: 1914-1919

9

Teachers College, Columbia University

In mid-summer of 1914 Ethel Johns arrived in New York, only to be greeted by word of a family crisis. The nature of the emergency is unknown, but her small savings had to be diverted to meet the situation, and it seemed that the longed-for year of study at Teachers College was to be lost. Isabel Stewart forestalled disaster by giving her friend a letter of introduction to Clara D. Noyes, superintendent of nurses of Bellevue and Allied Hospitals.

In later years, Ethel Johns recalled her memorable meeting with this outstanding woman:

... Tall and stately in her black uniform, Miss Noyes received me very kindly. I was neither the first nor the last impecunious student to whom this distinguished administrator of nursing services held out a helping hand. At that time there were no nursing scholarships nor loan funds in Canada, and many of us came up the hard way. To my immense relief, Miss Noyes said that a part-time job in the central linen room was available, and that, in return, I might have a room in the nurses' residence in addition to whatever meals I could snatch in between lecture periods at the College. That same evening, I moved in, bag and baggage, and from my window caught my first glimpse of the beautiful St Gaudens statue of Diana, poised on tiptoe against the sky above Madison Square Garden ...[1]

The quiet bedroom was to prove an ideal place for study in the months ahead, while the pleasant environment of the linen room would scarcely interrupt her concentration upon academic work. She would never cease to be grateful for the assistance which Miss Noyes gave her so generously at a critical juncture in her life.

The weeks following Ethel Johns' arrival in New York were shadowed not only by family and personal problems, but also by a general atmosphere of foreboding as war in Europe seemed inevitable. Every evening she walked across to Herald Square to watch the news bulletins. Then the blow fell. War was declared and Canada followed Great Britain into the conflict. The United States remained neutral, and Ethel Johns – intensely patriotic – now felt herself to be an exile at a time when the Mother Country and the land of her adoption were entering into the agony of war. On 30 August, she dispatched to the *Manitoba Free Press* a poignant description of the impact which the outbreak of hostilities had upon the people of diverse national origins who, with her, anxiously peered at the flashing war bulletins along Broadway.[2] The *Free Press* later referred to this article as 'one of the best pen pictures of conditions in the neutral country to the south that has been written ...'[3]

The sense of exile and inner conflict engendered by enforced 'neutrality' grew within her as classes started at Teachers College in the third week of September:

... On the day that the College opened, all students were summoned to the noonday service in the Chapel and were told by the Dean that the President of the United States of America had declared that strict neutrality must be upheld, 'even in thought.' The Dean said that he knew that among us were students from countries involved in the conflict but that he was sure we would remember that we were the guests of a neutral nation and would conduct ourselves accordingly. The organist was an English student, and whether by accident or design, the closing hymn was, 'Fight the good fight with all thy might.' Some of us sang it with undue enthusiasm. In those Arcadian days, the tall elms on the campus were given distinctive names by various national groups gathered beneath them. In the shade of the British Empire Tree it was a relief to find Canadian, English, Irish, Scottish, and West Indian folk who found it difficult to be neutral 'even in thought'...[4]

As a 'special student' Ethel Johns was able to select courses to meet her felt needs. Doubtless Isabel Stewart advised her in the choice of offerings from two programmes, 'Training School Administration' and 'Teaching in Training Schools.' Records preserved in the archives of the Department of Nursing Education at Teachers College reveal not only the courses in which Miss Johns enrolled, but also their content, by whom they were taught, and the days and hours on which they were scheduled. In the skilful balance of physical, biological, and social sciences with nursing subjects, her programme was well-rounded and challenging. Her keen intellect, high level of motivation, and background of experience enabled her to make good use of the learning experiences which it offered. She later spoke of this as 'the golden year' and commented: '... The work at the College was profoundly satisfying. It can truly be said that in those days there were giants in the land. Adelaide Nutting, Annie Goodrich, Lavinia Dock – these were names to conjure with ...'[5] The three renowned nursing leaders were among the eminent teachers under whom Miss Johns was privileged to study.

Mary Adelaide Nutting was already almost a legendary figure in nursing at the time of Ethel Johns' first meeting with her. A Canadian by birth, and a member of the first graduating class of the Johns Hopkins Hospital, she was widely recognized for her achievements as an administrator, educator, author, and speaker. Her leadership in national and international nursing organizations was distinguished, and she was in the vanguard of the movement for reform in nursing education. Miss Johns later recorded her impressions of Miss Nutting as she observed her at Teachers College:

... It was in one of the bleak little Teachers College classrooms that I saw her for the first time. A tall slight figure, she stood on the low platform and looked us over as though wondering what we were seeking. There was something troubling about that cool, clear gaze. At first, I was afraid of this woman as well as fascinated by her. Here was a quality of mind far superior to any that I had yet encountered in the nursing profession. Her penetrating intelligence shed a disconcerting light on problems that nurses had been willing to ignore because we did not know how to deal with them. She was determined to free the school of nursing from its bondage to the hospital. For the first time, it was borne in upon us that the two were not one and indivisible. She was never overemphatic, indeed she seldom raised her voice. Yet in spite of this restraint a certain ruthlessness made itself felt – a driving force that would not be denied.

Adelaide Nutting had a deep sense of the past as well as an extraordinary insight in the future. She could grasp the significance of events while they still lay hidden below the horizon. It was this quality of vision, ranging over both the past and the future, that seemed to set her apart from all the rest. There were two gifts that she seemed to lack – understanding and sympathy. When, many years later, I came to know her better, I found that she possessed both but that they were hidden by the mask that those who exercise authority must wear in self-defence ...[6]

Ironically, Ethel Johns was often to convey the impression that she was a hard person, lacking in the same qualities that she missed in Adelaide Nutting, understanding and sympathy. Yet she, too, may have assumed a mask to conceal her true feelings because of her conviction that a position of command, in a militaristic system, required discipline of self and subordinates. The sensitive awareness of and compassion for human needs and suffering so often reflected in her writings contrasted oddly with her often stern expression and sharp speech.

Unwittingly, Miss Johns once gave offence to Miss Nutting. The late Dr Helen Stewart sadly recalled the incident: '... I think they were coming out from a class ... and E. Johns had made a remark to somebody next to her and behind Adelaide Nutting. Adelaide Nutting had heard just a section, but not enough to know what she was talking about, and thought that E. Johns was poking fun at her or something of the kind. That would be the last thing under heaven that E. Johns would do. She had a very smart tongue but she never made fun of anyone, let alone an elderly woman. So it was an entire mistake, but it just spoiled her for Adelaide Nutting ...'[7] Ethel Johns was often conscious of being misunderstood, but never, it seems, more tragically.

An 'important addition' to the regular staff of the Department of Nursing and Health for the 1914–15 session was Annie W. Goodrich, assistant professor, formerly inspector of Training Schools in New York.[8] Miss Johns thoroughly enjoyed her classes with Miss Goodrich:

... The course in administration of schools of nursing given by Annie Warburton Goodrich meant a great deal to me because it dealt with practical problems I had actually encountered. Her lectures were a bit discursive but there was something about the woman herself that caught and held attention. As an instructor she was most inspiring, her ready wit and sparkling sense of humour enlivened every discussion and she was quite as willing to laugh at herself as at us ...

Her previous career had been varied and somewhat stormy. In less than ten years, she had held three major positions and in each instance had courageously introduced and defended educational policies that were far ahead of the time. As a result, she was accused of exhausting her environment rather too quickly and it is true that by nature she was a rebel. Perhaps, as one observer has justly remarked, it was during those years of storm and stress that she acquired that 'toughness of spirit that enabled her to accept defeat without being overwhelmed by a sense of failure.'[9] In 1914 she was free from any responsibility for the direction of nursing services and revelled in the freedom afforded by the academic life. She had both the time and opportunity to read widely and she shared her reading with us – history, comparative religion, politics – no wonder so many of us caught fire from her unquenchable enthusiasm ...[10]

Inspiring as Miss Nutting and Miss Goodrich were, it was Lavinia Dock whom Ethel Johns most admired and who won her lifelong gratitude and affection:

... A number of distinguished nurses addressed us from time to time but to me Lavinia Dock was the most striking personality of them all. She had been secretary of the International Council of Nurses, was an ardent pacifist and took no pains to hide it. With Adelaide Nutting, she was author of the classic *History of Nursing*. She had a working knowledge of several languages. The campaign for votes for women was then at its height and together with other outstanding women from all walks of life, she had marched in the famous parade up Fifth Avenue, led by a beautiful young woman mounted on a white horse. Later on, she broke through the ridiculous inhibitions that prevented plain talk about venereal diseases and insisted that instruction should be given to student nurses in this subject as in any other ...

Early in her career, and while serving as night supervisor at Bellevue Hospital, Lavinia Dock had written a textbook, *Materia Medica for Nurses,* a task that most of us would have regarded as a full-time job. This book had run through several editions and while I was at the College, Miss Dock was engaged in revising it. She wanted help with the proof-reading and I was asked to lend a hand. It was a long, rather tedious process, but I enjoyed it because it gave me an opportunity to observe her at close range. There had been no definite arrangement about payment and when the work was done I was given an envelope that evidently contained a cheque. At first glance, I saw the figure '15' and my heart sank, for funds were at a low ebb and I had secretly hoped for a little more, perhaps twenty-five. Then, to my utter astonishment, I saw that the sum total was one hundred and fifty dollars. That evening, I pushed my tray along the cafeteria counter without even looking at the price list and bought a really satisfying dinner. Then I began to wonder whether the service I had rendered had really been worth so large a sum. Could this be the gift of a generous teacher to a student who she knew was coming up the hard way? I have always thought so ...[11]

A course in psychology was required of all students attending the College, and Ethel Johns enrolled in Professor Thorndike's Course, 'General and Educational Psychology,' together with about two hundred other students. Of this experience she retained one painful memory:

... He was then engaged in the preparation of a new textbook and, as usual, required a large supply of clinical material. One drowsy afternoon, his victims were assembled in one of the large amphitheatres and he put us through our paces. The teaching of elementary arithmetic seemed to be uppermost in his mind and we were asked to solve a number of simple problems. Some of these recalled my inability to grapple with seven times eight and I gazed helplessly at the blackboard. In a moment or two he asked those who had completed the test to stand, and a few smug individuals popped up. After another short pause, any others who were finished were told to rise. Practically everybody stood up. Then he looked around the room and asked whether there was any one student who had not completed the test. Four shamefaced individuals, myself amongst them, rose to their feet. 'Please come up to the blackboard,' said Professor Thorndike with a glint in his eye. Could we, he gently enquired, indicate diagrammatically on the blackboard how the figures 'looked to us in our heads.' One brave soul seized a piece of chalk and drew a rough circle with the numbers arranged clock-fashion. Two of the others said they saw figures that way, too. My arrangement wasn't like that at all. It started in a neat row from one to twelve, then a jog from twelve to twenty, then another jog from twenty to thirty, and after that a long line that faded out altogether. Professor Thorndike seemed quite pleased and beamed on his unhappy victims. The other students stared at us blankly – evidently their numbers were unhampered by any sort of pattern and could be summoned at will. We were hampered by what is called a number form and had to take time to go and get them off their hooks. It seemed that a brochure had been written on the subject and Professor Thorndike wanted to confirm its findings. Incidentally, there appeared to be more hope for the clockfaces than there was for me. It seemed that I could never look forward to being sure about seven times eight ...[12]

The courses in biology, especially the laboratory periods, were a joy to Ethel Johns. In her early teaching experience, she had given elementary instruction to student nurses, with the help of specimens obtained from the hospital's butcher shop. '... Now I learned not only to dissect a frog, but also to spread the living web between his toes under the lens of my microscope and to watch the corpuscles squeezing their way along the winding capillaries. I also picked up a working knowledge of teaching method and was much elated when a lesson plan came back marked with a large red "A" ...'[13]

Miss Johns' interests ranged beyond the confines of her courses. In the evenings she sometimes attended concerts and lectures at the College which were open to students. These made up, she later said, for the theatre and opera tickets that she could not afford. When the subject-matter of the lectures proved to be abstruse, she found it stimulating to study the personalities of the lecturers. On one occasion, however, the subject of the discourse struck her with the impact of a thunderbolt. The topic was, 'Dr Sigmund Freud,' and Ethel Johns recalled that the large audience listened with rapt attention, and that when the lecture drew to a close, lively discussion followed. '... Much of what the speaker said,' she commented, 'was beyond my comprehension. Some of it was plain enough and came as a distinct shock. It was as though a cold searching light had suddenly been shed over a landscape that had been veiled in a rosy mist. I was afraid to look at it ...'[14]

Nearly half a century later, Miss Johns summed up her reflections about the values of the year spent at Teachers College:

... Looking back on my brief academic experience, I realize how fortunate it was that it took place at that particular time. Among my fellow students there were several who later on became leaders in the national and international nursing world. No longer young, they already held responsible administrative positions. Yet they buckled down to the routine effort of daily study as if they were still in training. Students in other departments were a bit inclined to be rather condescending. A group of gay young things from the school of physical education passing by the open door of the bacteriological laboratory took a look at us as we fussed with our test tubes. 'My dear, who *are* those old crones?' asked one of them in a harsh whisper. 'Department of Nursing and Health,' said her companion, 'you can always tell them by their stiff upper lips.' The child was right – we had the fortitude to put in the foundation after the house had been built.

A few of the professors as well as some of the instructors were inclined to be disdainful. With some notable exceptions, we did not seem to be particularly alert or enthusiastic students. Yet they admitted rather unwillingly that there was a certain quality about us that their livelier students sometimes lacked – we were dependable, we knew what we wanted, and we were ready to work for it.

The spring term drew to a close and it was high time to look for a steady job, The position of superintendent in the Children's Hospital of Winnipeg was vacant. I was told that an application might be accepted, and it so happened that it was, provided I could report for duty immediately. I was grieved to think that my wonderful year was over. Like all students who were not returning to the College for further work, I was interviewed by Miss Nutting, who made it plain that she did not consider me equal to the task so rashly undertaken. It was not easy to defend my position and it was a relief when the question of my eligibility was dropped and she enquired whether I was satisfied with what the College had given me. Unhappy and confused, I tried to explain that I could never be sufficiently grateful. 'But *what* did we give you?' she said. 'A point of view,' I stammered and let it go at that. For some obscure reason, this artless reply seemed to please and amuse her and she smiled.

If only I had not been so much in awe of her, I could have told her that I had been shown aspects of nursing that were altogether new to me and I had been brought into touch with international affairs. Above all, I had acquired a rooted conviction, based on my personal experience, that it was in the university and in the university alone that nurses could hope to find the broader educational opportunities without which they could never meet the increasing demands being made upon them ...[15]

Ethel Johns carried away from Teachers College something much more significant than the diploma or degree denied her by her lack of matriculation standing.

10

The Children's Hospital of Winnipeg

Ethel Johns' imminent return to Manitoba was heralded by the *Free Press* in the issue of 12 May, 1915. The paper congratulated the Children's Hospital of Winnipeg upon securing the services of a superintendent of such wide experience, one of proven competence, and 'a woman of broad interests and many gifts.'

To Ethel Johns, the joy of homecoming was tempered by the anxieties of the war situation. But she was still in her prime, full of energy and enthusiasm, and eager to try out new ideas acquired during her year at Teachers College. Essentially a realist, she squarely faced the fact that military demands would limit the extent to which improvements could be effected in nursing education and legislation while the war lasted. Upgrading of standards would have to come gradually. Meantime, the nursing profession in Canada should seek to consolidate its ranks and its thinking. Perhaps the similarity of problems in nursing education across the country would serve as a catalyst to bring about this synthesis.

The next four years were to open up many opportunities for Ethel Johns to exercise leadership in both provincial and national nursing organizations. Even more significant, her appointment to the Manitoba Public Welfare Commission was to provide her with a unique channel through which to enlist the interest of government and the public in the existing problems of nursing and hospitals. These outlets for her professional dedication were to prove stimulating and satisfying. But the period was also to be a time in which her maturing political philosophy, at a time of crisis, would isolate her from her employers, friends, and associates.

The Winnipeg Children's Hospital was in its sixth year when Ethel Johns arrived in June 1915 to take over her responsibilities as superintendent and principal of the training school. The unique character and philanthropic orientation of the hospital were later described by Miss Johns:

> ... This institution had about a hundred beds and its patients were drawn for the most part from working-class families in the 'North End.' There was an extraordinary diversity among these people as to national origin, language and religion but the authorities of the Hospital never made any invidious distinctions as to race, colour or creed. The babel of tongues in the out-patient department on a busy morning gave ample proof of that fact.
>
> The board of directors was composed exclusively of women belonging to well known and prosperous families and, in addition, there was an advisory council of moderately wealthy men who kept a friendly eye on financial policy. The greater part of the revenue was derived from the payments made by the municipal and provincial governments in return for the treatment given to children of parents who were not able to meet the cost themselves. Relatively large sums of money were also obtained through the untiring efforts of the board of directors and these devoted women thus made it possible to give far better service than would have been the case if the hospital had been obliged to depend on governmental sources only. The directors were proud of their hospital and were anxious to help children who were so much less fortunate than their own. But they had not the faintest conception of the underlying economic causes of the suffering they were so genuinely eager to relieve ...[1]

It was a source of satisfaction to Miss Johns that here she had direct access to the board of directors. A review of the board minutes for the period 1915–18 conveys the impression that the relationship between the superintendent and the directors was harmonious and cooperative. The chairman of the board (Mrs Mary Walker), a British nurse (Mrs Annie Bond) through whose initiative the Children's Hospital had been founded,[2] and several 'Guilds' gave generous support to the hospital, and this doubtless made the superintendent's work easier and more congenial. Although Ethel Johns had had little previous experience with children, it is said that she related happily to them.[3]

A distinctive feature of the Children's Hospital was its active out-patient service, which yearly gave free treatment to thousands of underprivileged children. In addition, the hospital staff already included a social service nurse who visited the homes of patients when such contacts were indicated. That the new superintendent was in complete support of these community services was shown by the satisfaction she expressed in her annual reports as the numbers of patients visiting the out-patients clinics increased year by year. In 1917, she strengthened the programme by combining the out-patient and social service functions into one department under the competent direction of a registered nurse, Elizabeth Carruthers.

In her first year as charge nurse, Miss Carruthers reported that a total of 253 home visits had been made. Some of these were for the purpose of giving follow-up supervision and direction to the care of recently discharged patients. Other visits were made to assess the suitability of homes for reception of children about to be discharged from the hospital. In some cases, the nurse went to homes to obtain the consent of parents for operation. In still others, she visited to find out why patients had failed to report to the out-patient department for prescribed treatment. In her report to the superintendent, Miss Carruthers commented: 'The value of follow-up work in patients' homes cannot be over-estimated. It would be most desirable to extend this work still further, if at all possible, in the interest of both indoor and outdoor patients.' Surprisingly, more than half a century later, such close contact by hospitals with their patients' homes and families is still largely an unrealized ideal. The extension of this hospital's services into the community was probably an important factor in the reduction of the average days' stay for in-patients from 17.1 in 1915 to 10.66 in 1919.[4]

As principal of the training school, Ethel Johns was in charge initially of a student body of twenty-nine young women. By 1918, numbers had increased gradually to forty. A deterrent to more rapid growth of the school, so desirable in the war emergency, was lack of adequate residence accommodation. Students and staff lived on the top floor of the hospital. The board of directors had been aware for some time that this living arrangement was unsatisfactory, but their concern was sharpened by Miss Johns' reference to the situation in her annual report for 1916:

... The need of a nurses' residence becomes more pressing as our work increases. We are handicapped at every turn for want of proper accommodation in the nurses' sleeping quarters and dining room. The pupils have no opportunity for social intercourse whatever and are obliged to meet their friends outside the hospital. The crowded bedrooms have re-acted unfavorably on the health of the pupils. The night nurses particularly have suffered severely from lack of sleep owing to the unavoidable noise from the operating room and kitchens which are on the same floor. I must emphatically state that no further extension of our activities can be undertaken until this need is met as our present staff can hardly cope with the work in its present state of development. Furthermore, if a desirable class of pupils is to be attracted to our school we must be able to offer suitable and sufficient residence facilities ...[5]

Despite financial difficulties and the admonitions of the advisory council to the board that this was an unfavourable time to launch a building project, the board of directors proceeded to plan and erect the residence. The nurses' home was opened in December 1918.

Records for the period 1915–19 show that the nursing students at that time had eight months of the three-year training away from the home school. Six months were spent in affiliation at the Winnipeg General Hospital, where learning experiences were arranged in medical and surgical nursing of adults, obstetric nursing, and dietetics. Two months' affiliation at the King George Municipal Hospital provided the students with instruction and practice in communicable disease nursing. In the home school, teaching was done by Ethel Johns and her assistant, and by staff doctors. The records show that Miss Johns taught anatomy and physiology, practical nursing (theory), history of nursing, charting, and (in some years) materia medica, surgery, and gynaecology.

A graduate of the Class of 1919 recalls that Miss Johns was 'very clever and a wonderful lecturer – very easy, an outstanding lecturer.' A nurse who graduated a year earlier found that Miss Johns was firm but fair in dealing with students, and felt that she was a good teacher, but that she talked too quickly. In accordance with the custom of the day, Miss Johns reviewed all notes taken at class and helped with study problems.

One of Miss Johns' graduates had a vivid recollection of her appearance as superintendent and principal of the school: 'She always looked so smart – had a broad cap, and five or six curls up the back. Her hair was fair, sandy-gold. She wore a white uniform. Cap and hair were always immaculate. She had a birthmark on her hand, which was covered with hair.'[6] It should be added that Miss Johns was painfully aware of this blemish. Some time later, the area was apparently treated, leaving a large purple mark. People often wondered why she made a habit of keeping her gloves on at meetings.

Miss Johns exacted high standards from her students, who, it is said, regarded her as austere and (generally speaking) were afraid of her.

One graduate of the period recalls that Miss Johns did not communicate freely with the students, but that she was decisive in what she did say. The superintendent, too, lived on the top floor of the hospital, and the probationers occupied rooms adjacent to hers. She was aware of the noise and activity of the nurses off duty but never interfered. Prayers were said every morning and roll call was taken. If a student's appearance was not acceptable, she was asked to stay behind for a critique by Miss Johns. 'She saw everything – you would have thought she had eyes in the back of her head.'[7]

A member of the Class of 1919 has less happy memories of Miss Johns, who impressed her as being 'cold and unfeeling.' Two incidents she recalls in particular. On one occasion, she was summoned to Miss Johns' office to account for a mishap which had occurred. When the student started to explain, 'I thought...,' Miss Johns cut her off with a curt remark: 'A student is not supposed to think.' Evidently Miss Johns' point was that a nurse must be *sure*, not just *think* she knows what to do. At another time, Miss Johns came to her room to tell her that her brother had been killed in the war, and to say that she could go home for a few days. Miss Johns asked her room-mate to accompany her, to see that she got home all right. Nothing more was said, and the student construed this reticence as a lack of feeling. Miss Johns, no stranger to the anguish of bereavement, was unable to convey her understanding and sympathy to the young woman so greatly in need of both. Yet this graduate realized in later years that Ethel Johns was a 'remarkable woman' and that her manner as superintendent was the custom of the day.

Records in the archives of the Manitoba Association of Registered Nurses show that Ethel Johns renewed her active participation in the organization shortly after her return to Winnipeg. At the September meeting she gave an 'interesting and instructive' paper on her experiences in New York. Early in 1916 she became a new registrant under the provisions of the 1913 Act. In the spring of that year she was elected to the office of corresponding secretary, a commitment which involved a good deal of letter-writing, since the organization did not yet have a secretariat. The pressures of this undertaking were increased by the fact that the Canadian National Association of Trained Nurses and the Canadian Society of Superintendents of Training Schools for Nurses were to hold concurrent meetings (with some joint sessions) in Winnipeg, in June. This necessitated much correspondence on the part of the hostess association.

The local arrangements committee also asked Miss Johns if she would deliver a paper at the convention on the subject, 'The Power of the Professional Press,' the purpose of which was to motivate Canadian nurses to support nursing journals, especially *The Canadian Nurse*. The question of purchasing the latter had been under consideration for some time by the Canadian National Association of Trained Nurses, and a decision in the matter was to be one of the important items of business at the June meeting. Miss Johns accepted this fresh challenge. The cause was dear to her heart and she would have found it difficult to refuse. Her paper was subsequently published in *The Canadian Nurse*.[8] In this address, Miss Johns suggested criteria by which to evaluate a professional journal, taking as an example the values served by medical periodicals of the day. As a piece of writing, this paper lacked the careful editing and polish which were characteristic of Ethel Johns' work. It appears to have been done under pressure, but the content was excellent.

The Manitoba Association of Graduate Nurses shortly laid still another responsibility on the burdened but willing shoulders of Ethel Johns. In May 1916 she was appointed convener of the standing committee on legislation and education. The weak Registration Act of 1913 had been a bitter disappointment in its lack of provision for control and upgrading of training schools. Ethel Johns was later to refer to this frustrating outcome of years of struggle by the nurses of Manitoba:

... Licensing and inspection – here is a beginning at establishing standards. But before you can have either you must have legislation. Aye! there's the rub; because you can't have legislation of the kind you want until you have educated public opinion. You may prepare a bill which opens before you dazzling prospects of improved conditions, only to find that same bill emerge from the committee stage a total wreck. I don't know how much your bill in Alberta suffered from your legislators; but I do know that when we in Manitoba gazed upon the mangled remains of ours, after the brethren had done their worst, we felt that everything was over but sending a few flowers. However, we feel differently now. We realize that a bad bill is better than none; that amendments can be so skilfully formulated that, slowly but surely, the poorly-mangled thing will become a stout and efficient club to swing over the heads of the evil-doers. Only it will take time and patience, and the constant dropping which wears away a stone ...[9]

With a conviction that the cause was not lost, Ethel Johns assembled a five-member committee on legislation, including Kate Cotter who had taken over her presidential duties in 1911. Two members were from small hospitals outside of Winnipeg. Miss Johns assumed the responsibility of preparing a questionnaire to tap the opinions of hospitals throughout the province on certain points of critical significance in elevating standards of nursing education, with particular reference to the small training schools. In this task, she enlisted the assistance of a friend, the wife of Dr David Stewart, herself a graduate of a small hospital school, who also prepared a diplomatic covering letter to accompany the questionnaire. The response was disappointing: only five hospitals out of eighteen replied.

During the same year, Miss Johns was appointed by the Canadian Society of Superintendents of Training Schools to convene a committee on the Standardization of Training Schools. In an undated letter, written by hand, presumably in the spring of 1917, Ethel Johns invited Miss Jean I. Gunn, whom she greatly admired and respected, to become a member of the standardization committee. Miss Gunn, superintendent of nurses of the Toronto General Hospital, was also the secretary of the Canadian National Association of Trained Nurses. With her letter, Miss Johns enclosed a copy of the questionnaire which had been circulated recently to the hospitals in Manitoba. She expressed concern at the lack of response encountered: 'As usual, the replies are most dilatory and it is too early yet to decide what results we are going to get or whether we are going to get any. To my mind there will be but little hope of doing anything until we can get provincial chapters formed of the Superintendents' association with some possibility of personal contact in committee meetings. Correspondence is futile ...'[10] Miss Johns added that she proposed writing also to Miss Elizabeth Flaws (secretary of the Superintendents' Society) to invite her to become a member of the committee. Using the Manitoba questionnaire if they chose, Miss Gunn and Miss Flaws could look into the general attitude of the superintendents in Ontario. In conclusion, Miss Johns apologized for her delay in issuing this invitation, 'But the truth is I have had a most harassing winter and seemed to have no leisure for thought and reflection. I really should not have accepted the convenership at all.'

In mid-June of 1917, the two national nursing associations held concurrent annual meetings, again with some joint sessions, at the Windsor Hotel in Montreal. Miss Johns attended the conventions, with the approval of the board of directors of Children's Hospital: 'In view of Miss Johns' impending trip and in recognition of her devotion in the interests of the hospital it was decided to give her a bonus of one hundred dollars.'

The tenth annual convention of the Canadian Society of Superintendents of Training Schools opened on 12 June. In her presidential address, Helen Randal spoke of the trying time which all superintendents were experiencing due to the war. So many nurses had gone overseas that civilian hospitals were depleted of their graduate staffs. The president added that there would be no public recognition, no Royal Red Cross, for those left behind to carry on home duties, and yet they were 'as truly patriotic though not taking active part in the honors of war ...' She expressed satisfaction that women were becoming more and more recognized as 'leaders in the important spheres of our national life.' She then drew attention to the pressing need for standardization of training schools, and announced that a committee had been formed to discuss a standard curriculum.[11]

Miss Johns was then called upon to present her report as convener of the Committee on Standardization of Training Schools. Rarely had she faced a greater challenge than on this occasion when she stood before the company of her peers from across the nation and invited them to look upon the deficiencies of their training schools and the ills of the apprenticeship system of nursing education:

... It is unnecessary for me to emphasize to this audience the need which exists for the standardization of training schools. It is brought home to us every day of our working lives. The problem grows more acute as time goes on, for every year sees an increase in the number of small hospitals, and every year makes the economic struggle for existence on the part of these hospitals more acute. One cannot blame them for being tempted to maintain training schools when they are hardly prepared to offer proper teaching facilities. The hospital is needed, sick people must be nursed, finances are at a low ebb, pupil nurses form a cheap and fairly efficient working force; it all leads to one easy solution, does it not? Start a training school. Anyone may *start* one: all that is necessary is to gather some sick people under a roof and call it a hospital. No tiresome inspection of your educational methods is required. There are no impossible standards to which you must conform. There are no standards at all. You need not even put a graduate nurse in charge unless you wish. You just start a training school, and Providence and the patients do the rest.

That this state of affairs can exist in a country so advanced as Canada in educational matters is a crying shame. I will go farther and say that it is a disgrace to the nursing profession that we have made so little concerted effort to remedy it, for we could work out our own salvation if we would ...[12]

Miss Johns then gave a 'rough sketch' of what standardization of training schools would involve: a required daily average of patients; sufficient diversity of clinical experience to give a grounding in the main branches of nursing, or, failing that, supplying the lack by arranging affiliation with other hospitals; proper and adequate provision for the pupils in regard to food and lodging; a trained teaching staff and a supply of teaching material; such regulation of hours of duty as to allow time for theoretical work; a standard curriculum; a standardized system of training school records; standardized admission requirements; and inspection of training schools by a competent nurse inspector under provincial auspices.[13]

The speaker then turned her attention to the questionnaires which the committee had sent to superintendents throughout Canada. Many had not replied. Miss Johns analysed and commented upon the answers that had been received, and dwelt at some length upon the opinion expressed by a considerable number that it should not be necessary to have an instructress when the superintendent herself was available. To this argument, Miss Johns had a crisp rejoinder:

... I will ask those of you who, like myself, are captain, mate and bo'sun's boy of your respective institutions, what time you have to formulate curricula, to make lesson plans, to prepare for demonstrations? Have you not again and again had to postpone classes in order to attend to some detail of administration which admitted of no delay? Furthermore, not all of us can teach, and few of us are specially trained to teach ...

But, when all is said and done, it is a question of economics after all. Miss Nutting, the head of the Department of Nursing and Health of Columbia University, one of our greatest authorities on the question of the education of nurses, contends that until the Training School is financially independent of the hospital we cannot hope for better educational standards. Boards of directors still fail to recognize their responsibilities to the pupils of the Training School. They mistake a student body for a working force. The superintendents of hospitals have already gallantly done their best to meet these lions in the path. Slowly but surely 'concessions' (save the mark) have been wrung from them. Better food, better housing, better hours (some of us are content to stop there) – but there is more – better teaching and more of it ... These young women come to us for training, trusting that we will keep the faith with them. Are we going to be content to give them 'experience' more or less meagre, more or less uncoördinated, scattered, fragmentary? – or are we going to co-operate with one another to devise a true system of education founded on sound principles and bound together with the spirit of unity and concord? It is worth while, even though there be no tangible reward; for it is a strange and rewarding thing to kindle a flame ...[14]

There can be no doubt that Ethel Johns' impassioned plea 'kindled a flame' within many of those who heard her on this occasion. But a concerted attack upon the deficiencies of nursing education in Canada was to be delayed for more than ten years.

At this meeting, the name of the Superintendents' Society was changed to 'The Canadian Association of Nursing Education.' Miss Randal continued as president, while Miss Johns was elected to the office of second vice-president.

An important topic on the agenda of the convention of the Canadian National Association of Trained Nurses was the serious issue of midwifery. Papers on the subject were given by Mary Ard. MacKenzie and by Winnifred Tilley, the latter on behalf of the nursing committee of the National Council of Women. Miss Johns read the text of a speech which had been delivered by Mrs John McNaughton, president of the Saskatchewan Grain Growers Association, at a luncheon arranged in Winnipeg during a meeting there of the National Council of Women. Much discussion followed these papers and it seemed that the consensus was that qualified nurses, and not midwives, should give care to women in rural areas. Rural hospitals staffed by graduate nurses were needed, but it was acknowledged that it would be difficult to ensure that graduate nurses would be willing to serve in rural and outpost areas. A recommendation was carried that each provincial association of nurses should interview the government of the province and state that 'the nurses are willing to supply nurses for these fields if they will supply the funds and get the hospitals ready.'[15]

At this convention, Miss Gunn was elected president of the Canadian National Association of Trained Nurses. Miss Johns became secretary of the organization, an office which she was to hold for three years. In the absence of a national office or a paid secretariat, the responsibilities of this office were to grow steadily heavier as the volume of national business grew. The combined weight of this new work and that of corresponding secretary of the Manitoba Association of Graduate Nurses forced her to relinquish the latter at the end of November 1917.

In October 1917 Ethel Johns accepted still another commitment: she was appointed to the newly established Public Welfare Commission of Manitoba.

11

The Manitoba Public Welfare Commission

The Public Welfare Commission of Manitoba was appointed by Order-in-Council in October 1917 under the provisions of an Act, passed earlier in the same year, respecting 'Public and Other Institutions.' Ethel Johns was one of nine commissioners, seven of whom were men. Subsequently, a third woman was added to the membership.

The terms of reference of the new body were comprehensive: 'The Commission is by the terms of the Act under which it was appointed empowered, and required to investigate and report to the Lieutenant-Governor-in-Council on all phases of charitable and welfare work, both public and private within the Province. The field covered by the powers and duties of the Commission is, therefore, very broad ...'[1] At the first meeting of the Commission, held on 10 October 1917, the Honourable Thomas H. Johnson was elected chairman. Five committees were established for the purpose of accomplishing the assigned work: Child Welfare, Hospitals and Nursing, Prisons and Reformatories, Dependent Poor, and Methods of Finance, Supervision and Control. Miss Johns became a member of the Committee on Hospitals and Nursing, together with H.Y. Symington, K.C., and Dr A.T. Mathers (chairman). The latter was reputed to be a brilliant psychiatrist who later (in 1931) was appointed dean of the medical faculty at the University of Manitoba.[2]

The first public hearing of the Commission was held in Winnipeg on 30 November 1917. Delegations from twelve organizations were heard, among which were the Children's Hospital and the Manitoba Association of Graduate Nurses.[3] The provincial nursing organization presented the following resolution.

... RESOLVED that the Manitoba Association of Graduate Nurses respectfully direct the attention of the Public Welfare Commission of Manitoba to the conditions which exist regarding the establishment, maintenance and direction of Training Schools for Nurses in connection with Hospitals throughout the province. These institutions offering education to women in one of the most vital and difficult of arts are to-day totally unsupervised. They are under no obligation to maintain proper educational standards, nor to provide suitable teaching material or personnel. The directorates of many of our Hospitals endeavour to maintain good standards, but the nurses of Manitoba feel that the proper instruction of nurses is of such vital importance to the community that nursing education should be recognized, supervised, and controlled by the Provincial Government through and by the University of Manitoba under which body the Nurses' Registration Act is at present administered ...[4]

At a meeting of the Manitoba Association of Graduate Nurses held on 27 December 1917 the president reported that the resolution had been 'sympathetically received' by the Commission. Miss Johns, as a member of that body, was asked to report to the Association if any activity on the part of the organization were necessary.

Within the two-year period following their appointment, the members of the Committee on Hospitals and Nursing accomplished a formidable task. Investigations were launched into four major areas: hospitals, nursing, care of the tuberculous, and care of the mentally unfit. Data for the study of the care of the tuberculous were collected mainly by Dr David Stewart, medical superintendent of Ninette Sanitarium. Upon invitation, the Canadian National Committee on Mental Hygiene carried out an extensive survey of hospitals for the insane and institutions for mentally defective persons in Manitoba. Miss Johns surveyed nursing care and nursing education in the province and (presumably) wrote the report of her investigations. All three members of the committee signed this report and the other sections of their work.[5]

It is difficult to understand how Miss Johns, in view of the demands of her work at Children's Hospital and her commitments to provincial and national nursing organizations, was able to discharge the heavy duties of a commissioner. That she did so with distinction was doubtless due to her intense interest in nursing and the public welfare, her capacity for hard work, and sheer enjoyment of the stimulating contacts with a group of intelligent, community-minded men and women. It is evident that this assignment meant a great deal to her. A framed photocopy of the Order-in-Council which appointed the commissioners hung on the wall of the living room in her Vancouver home – the only visible sign of her active life in nursing. Neatly typed on the back of this memento was a summary of events in the life of the Public Welfare Commission and the single most significant immediate outcome of its work – the appointment of a Board of Welfare Supervision as a permanent body.

In her work for the Commission, Miss Johns visited hospitals and collected data on the status of hospitals and nursing in Manitoba. Her tours were financed by the Commission. When possible she stayed in private homes, but more often she had to resort to hotels which offered little in comfort or cleanliness. In the course of these trips, she often availed herself of the opportunity to speak to groups of nurses and to women's institutes on what constituted good nursing, and tried to develop an understanding of the Nurse Registration Act.

The University of Toronto was host to the two national nursing organizations at their concurrent annual meetings (with some joint sessions as heretofore) held from 4–8 June 1918. Ethel Johns was an active participant in both conventions. Isabel Stewart and Adelaide Nutting were among the distinguished guest speakers.

An important item of business on the agenda of the Canadian Association of Nursing Education was the matter of a standard curriculum for training schools. Miss E. MacPherson Dickson, convener of the Committee on Standard Curriculum, presented as a basis for discussion the suggested curriculum for training schools in Ontario which had been prepared in 1915 under the aegis of the Ontario Association of Graduate Nurses. This had worked out well, she said, and it had imposed little if any hardship on the very small institutions.[6]

Miss Johns opened discussion on the proposed standard curriculum. While conceding that the standards were 'reasonable and just,' and that they should be attained by hospitals in the large centres, she decried the idea that the same curriculum could be achieved by large and small training schools alike:

... To say that one and the same curriculum is possible for the Toronto General Hospital and for Dauphin, Manitoba, is as ridiculous as to say that the little red schoolhouse on the prairie can give as wide a culture as the great university in which we stand. And yet the little red schoolhouse serves its community as faithfully and as well as the great university, and is as deserving of recognition and assistance. In the West at least, the small country hospitals are going to maintain training schools for some years to come, whether we like it or not. That being the case, it is our duty as nurse educators to see to it that the teaching done in these schools is as good as we can make it. In other words, we must frame a curriculum planned on little red schoolhouse lines; remembering all the time that through that humble door the student may enter even the great university, if she has the courage and the will to learn.[7]

The large training schools, continued Miss Johns, must co-operate with the universities in training women wishing to prepare themselves for teaching in small hospitals. Before the curriculum of training schools, great or small, could be standardized, it would be necessary to standardize the training of nurse teachers:

... Nursing stands today in a splendid isolation as the one vocation which does not think it necessary to train its teachers as such. We still seem imbued with the idea that we are our own teachers. A woman may be a good administrator. She may wrestle with the cook; she may subdue the night fireman with her glittering eye; and at the same time she may be, and often is, totally incapable of teaching. In a small hospital you must be an administrator first and a teacher afterwards. Unless you look well to the ways of your household, you are no use in a small hospital; but neither are you of use in your training school unless you can teach ...

One evident remedy, Miss Johns suggested, would be for young nurse teachers to have their early practice in small training schools. A current problem, she admitted, was the lack of such instructors. The large training schools, in affiliation with the university, should fill this need: 'Let them see to it, it is their contribution to the common cause.' Further ways to strengthen the programmes of small training schools should be explored. Affiliation with larger schools was one such measure. Inspection of small training schools by a competent nurse inspector who could serve as adviser was another potential means: '... Such a woman, going about from place to place, could forge a connecting link which would bind city and country together. She would know the teaching resources of her province; she could advise with the individual superintendents concerning affiliation; she could check up the work of the instructors, and could do more to standardize teaching than a host of printed curricula ...' Finally, she admonished, a deadline must be established below which the training of nurses must not be allowed to sink. Some so-called training schools in the West were turning out only 'badly trained attendants for the sick.' The medical profession and the public were demanding cheaper nursing service. If the nursing profession did not undertake the training of attendants, other means would be found of doing so. Perhaps the small hospital could be used for the purpose. 'Personally,' concluded Miss Johns, 'I would rather graduate a well-trained attendant than a half-trained nurse; and if some of us here today would look our conscience straight in the eye we would acknowledge that some of the women whose diplomas we have signed as fully trained nurses hold no true claim for that honourable title.'[8]

Discussion following Miss Johns' remarks revealed that there was no place in Canada at that time where nurse instructors could be trained. It was expected that McGill University would soon introduce such a programme. Meantime, Columbia University, New York, was the only source of training Canadian nurses for teaching. Miss Gunn introduced the idea that the large institution might serve as the 'parent school,' and give the theoretical instruction during the first year of training. Pupils could then spend a certain time, during the second and third years, in smaller schools. It was the feeling of the meeting that at least three groups of hospitals should be considered in discussing standard curriculum: small, up to fifty beds; medium, fifty to two hundred; and large, over two hundred. Eighteen years were to pass before the Canadian Nurses' Association would publish a proposed curriculum for schools of nursing in Canada.

The report of the nominating committee proposed Miss Johns as first vice-president of the Canadian Association of Nursing Education. But the retiring president, Miss Helen Randal, was nominated from the floor for the same office, and was elected. It is a matter of conjecture whether Miss Johns' blunt speech concerning the standard curriculum and her proposal about the training of attendants may have influenced the outcome of the election. Her strong convictions and forthright statement of them may have alarmed and alienated some of those who heard her. In any event, she descended from the top rung of the ladder leading to the presidency and was elected instead as one of the councillors.

Ethel Johns' earlier stand against midwifery was evidently undergoing some change at the same time that her belief was growing that a trained auxiliary was needed to fill the unmet requirements of the people for nursing care. The wartime shortage of nurses probably contributed to her conclusion that another worker must be prepared for the field of nursing. Economic factors influenced her thinking, too: many people could not afford to pay the fees of graduate nurses. Graduates were not available for the smaller hospitals, or did not wish to take posts in rural areas. Measures attempted by the Victorian Order of Nurses to provide obstetrical (and other) care in outlying districts had been only partially successful. Visiting nurse and public health nursing services were not yet able to fill the gap. These considerations may have been in Miss Johns' mind when she addressed a group of public health nurses: '... Of all animals a dog in the manger is the most objectionable, and the sooner we realize that the modern graduate nurse is not meeting all the nursing needs of our community the sooner we shall face and help solve that knotty problem of trained attendants, and burning questions, such as midwifery and other controversial topics, which are agitating the public mind ...'[9]

Ethel Johns was ahead of her time. She inspired and challenged many: others she undoubtedly irritated or intimidated. Her strongly held views, strongly expressed, were probably not conducive to personal popularity. Her outstanding ability was recognized, her services were in demand by the professional organizations, but it has been said of her, 'She was not trumpeted.' She captivated many people through her speeches and writings, but in face-to-face contacts she was apt to draw into herself if she did not know or was disinterested in the person.

In her report to the 1918 convention of the Canadian National Association of Trained Nurses, Miss Johns noted that, as secretary, she had sent out approximately 250 communications during the past year. Most of these were with affiliated organizations. Miss Randal, editor of *The Canadian Nurse*, reported upon the financial difficulties of the journal. A good deal of time was devoted to the lengthy report of the Committee on Public Health Nursing, which had conducted an extensive survey of existing resources in Canada for the preparation of public health nurses. The continuing grave shortage of nurses due to the war was another topic of discussion at this meeting. Ways and means were considered of increasing the enrolment in training schools as a way of meeting the problem.

A joint session of the two associations on the final evening featured Adelaide Nutting as chief speaker. She reviewed the activities of the nursing profession in the United States in relation to the war, and gave a list of American universities that were co-operating with nurses in connection with teaching. She hoped that similar opportunities would be open to nurses in Canada through the great universities in this country.[10]

In the absence of Dr Helen MacMurchy who was ill, her sister read the paper which she had prepared, 'University Training for the Nursing Profession.' This contained the report of a survey which Dr MacMurchy had made of universities in Canada for the purpose of finding out whether or to what extent they were involved in the education of nurses. The reply from McGill had been most promising: the vice-chancellor had stated that steps were being taken toward the university education of the nursing profession, and that it was hoped the scheme would be in operation the following year. Dr F.F. Wesbrook, president of the young University of British Columbia, had expressed interest, and a copy of his reply to Dr MacMurchy is in the archives of the University of British Columbia:

... I may say that in this University we have as yet made no official arrangements in the matter of the teaching of nursing. The course as given in the University of Minnesota is one with which I am familiar, as I helped to inaugurate it, and it expresses my ideas of what might well be done. I was Dean of the Medical School at the time the course was established there. Miss Adelaide Nutting has kept in touch with the work, and I think she regarded what was then a new step in Minnesota as of potentially great importance. Here in Vancouver, Dr R.H. Mullin, who is head of our University Department of Bacteriology and of the Pathological Department of the Vancouver General Hospital, lectures to nurses, and it may be possible, in the future, to develop, not a course of lectures or a chair of nursing, but a Department or School of Nursing. At the present time, having no Medical Department, we have made no arrangements whereby our programme is complicated unwarrantably.[11]

The proceedings of this session, as published in *The Canadian Nurse*, recorded that 'Miss Johns opened the discussion in a very clever and delightful manner.' Before the meeting adjourned, Miss Johns brought forward the matter of the great need felt in the Association for some record of its founding and early history, and said that, in the minds of all the members, there was only one logical archivist, and that was its own mother, Miss Snively. Upon the enthusiastic endorsation of this proposal by the convention, the distinguished founder of the Canadian National Association of Trained Nurses accepted the newly established office.[12]

While in Toronto, Miss Johns visited the Hospital for Sick Children and enquired whether it would be possible to send her assistant for a month's course in their current nursing techniques. Miss Johns' board of directors subsequently approved the plan.[13]

Following the convention, Mabel Gray and Ethel Johns spent a happy weekend together at Niagara Falls. The big hotel was not yet open for the season, so the friends stayed at the adjoining small annex. The service had an old-world quality: night attire was carefully laid out for them on their beds, and containers of hot water were at their door in the morning. Miss Gray still recalls with pleasure the fine, smooth grass of the park, and the walk which they took beneath the falls.

Pressure of professional duties during this period can have left Miss Johns little time for family and friends. But a graduate of the Class of 1919, whose mother was a friend of Miss Johns, recalls that Mrs Johns relieved the housekeeper at Children's Hospital during one summer. She remembers her as a fair, nice-looking woman, short, not at all like her daughter in appearance. Alexander had enlisted and was overseas. Owen was married, living in Winnipeg, and having a struggle to earn a living. It is said that Miss Johns was devoted to her family and that she helped Owen financially at that time. When Alex returned from the war, he did not stay long in Winnipeg, but went to California, where he married.[14] His mother lived with him and his wife until failing health made it necessary for her to be cared for in a nursing home.

The end of the war, in November 1918, found Canada in the grip of an epidemic of Spanish influenza. By the first of November, there had been over 2100 cases of the disease in Winnipeg alone, with sixty-two deaths.[15] A news item in the *Free Press* of 6 November reported that 'incoherent calls for aid' were constantly coming in to the volunteer nurses' bureau at the Medical College. Nurses were urgently needed to care for those stricken by the malady.

The staff of the Children's Hospital rose to the emergency with commendable loyalty and devotion. A ward was set aside for the care of children suffering from the disease, and it was filled to capacity throughout the epidemic. About two-thirds of the staff became ill, Miss Johns later reported, but all made good recoveries. The number of outpatients visiting the clinics declined during this period, but the social service work increased. Miss Carruthers and a student nurse assigned to help her visited patients' homes, assisted with their care, and referred them as indicated to suitable agencies for aid.[16] The board of directors, at the December meeting, decided that the splendid spirit of the nursing staff, pupils, office and domestic staffs during this trying time 'was so deserving of praise that a letter of appreciation should be sent to Miss Johns and the staff ...'

December 1918 saw the opening of the new nurses' residence, followed closely by the graduation exercises. January 1919 was also a busy month. Among her other duties, Miss Johns was concerned with making up the students' classes which had been cancelled during the epidemic. At this time, she must have been completing her report for the Committee on Hospitals and Nursing, since the *Second Interim*

Report of the Public Welfare Commission was to be presented in February to the Provincial Secretary of Manitoba.

The next few months were to bring Ethel Johns no respite from the heavy pressures of her various professional responsibilities. Added to them would be the strain which the rapidly approaching general strike would impose upon the hospital and the community which it served. Stressful events arising out of this critical situation would cause Ethel Johns to sever her connection with Children's Hospital. Her life and work were to find an entirely new outlet.

12

An End and a Beginning

The 'Report of Hospitals and Nursing' to the Public Welfare Commission laid bare the ills of nursing in Manitoba and prescribed remedies. Nursing education came under sharp criticism:

... There can be no question that the student nurse is at present exploited to an unjustifiable extent in the interest of the economic exigencies of the various hospitals in Manitoba. This policy can only re-act unfavourably upon these hospitals and the patients whom they serve, and it is doubtful whether in the long run it can be justified even on economic grounds. Faulty nursing in many cases was obviously due to incompetent and insufficient teaching and supervision, and failure to recognize the proper use and apportionment of available clinical material. These faults are not confined to any one training school but exist to a greater or less degree in all ...[1]

Hours of duty for pupil nurses were found to be excessively long, and the resulting fatigue predisposed to mistakes and negligence. The cause of this 'crying abuse' was attributed to the unsound financial basis on which the whole hospital system rested: '... The governing bodies of hospitals admit that pupil nurses are the cheapest and most efficient working force available for their purpose, and apparently are tempted to force too much from it ...'

The report identified causative factors in the situation. Centralized supervision and control of training schools were lacking. There was no uniformity in standards of preliminary education, curricula, clinical experience, tests and examinations. It was not recognized that pupil nurses were a student body as well as a working force. Teaching material and personnel were not provided. Only one school had an instructress whose duties were confined to teaching. There was no comprehensive system of affiliation which would bind together the large and small training schools of the province. Adequate training facilities for nurse teachers were lacking. Teaching work undertaken by various hospitals in the same city was not co-ordinated. There was lack of recognition of the training school as a separate entity and of proper financial provision for it as such. Finally, there was no licensure of hospitals or of training schools.

The report stated that some universities now accorded recognition to the art of nursing, and either conducted departments of nursing, or offered instruction to nurses in certain aspects of their work, both preparatory and postgraduate, which could not be given by training schools in hospitals. The University of Manitoba 'could and should offer similar privileges to the nurses of this Province and thereby assist them in preparing themselves for one of the most vital and difficult of arts ...'

The recommendations for the reform of nursing education advanced by the Committee on Hospitals and Nursing struck at the roots of the hospital and training school system which it had exposed. Soundly conceived, they were far ahead of their time, and change was to come slowly over the next several decades. Some ten years later, the medical and nursing professions in Canada jointly launched a nationwide survey of nursing education which revealed substantially the same problems, but in greater depth and detail. Some of the main recommendations of the Weir Report were similar to those of this earlier study in Manitoba.[2]

The Committee on Hospitals and Nursing turned its attention, also, to problem areas in nursing care. Its findings about the usage of convalescent hospitals have a strangely contemporary ring:

... Difficulty has been experienced in getting doctors to discharge their patients from hospitals to convalescent hospitals. It has been suggested that the absence of a competent nursing force is one reason for this unwillingness. Convalescent hospitals have a very definite sphere of usefulness but they cannot render efficient service without competent nursing supervision. The temptation exists to retain patients in general hospitals after they are capable of being transferred to a less expensive service and any deficiency of personnel or equipment in a convalescent service will be seized upon as an excuse for so doing.

Here again the lack of close co-operation between institutions doing similar work is apparent but the plan which is suggested of operating convalescent hospitals in closer connection with the outpatients and social service departments of the various hospitals should increase the usefulness of the convalescent hospitals and effect a material financial saving to the community ...[3]

Nursing care in the homes of the people also came under the scrutiny of the Committee. Concerns which Miss Johns had voiced years earlier were now reiterated. Many people could not afford to pay the fees of graduate nurses. Services of visiting nursing organizations were filling the breach only to a limited extent. Especially among the foreign population, the 'practical nurse' was undertaking a great deal of nursing care, and this type of person, while willing and anxious to serve, was frequently 'deplorably ignorant.' Physicians and nurses were not employed, and the services of ignorant and superstitious midwives worked untold havoc among both mothers and babies, stated the report. There was a 'crying need' for the establishment of an auxiliary nursing force. The State Association of Nurses in Virginia had introduced a bill, which had been assented to recently, for the training, licensing, and supervision of trained attendants. Similar provision, in the opinion of the Committee, should be made in Manitoba:

... The promoters of the Virginia plan are convinced that the two types of nursing service must be closely correlated to be successful and the graduate nurses show a commendable spirit in initiating such a courageous experiment. The development of such a group of workers in this Province might go far to meet the need which unquestionably exists both in city and country of a less expensive attendant for sick persons. In the cities and larger towns the work of these women could be supervised by graduate nurse inspectors similar to the supervisors utilized in England to check up the work of licensed midwives. It would be the duty of such inspectors not only to see that the licensed attendant performed her duties properly but also to assist her in any emergency which required a higher degree of technical skill than she herself possessed. The same plan of supervision should be carried out in the rural districts or the provincial public health nursing service might co-operate along these lines ...[4]

The Committee's recommendation concerned with the training and licensure of attendants received prompt approval by the legislature. An amendment to the Act respecting the Manitoba Association of Graduate Nurses, assented to on 27 March 1920, provided for the registering of trained attendants by the association and the granting of 'A Trained Attendant's Certificate' to persons who received at least six months' training in schools approved of by the association or by the

Board of Welfare Supervision of Manitoba, or who were otherwise qualified in the opinion of the association.

In mid-February 1919 the Manitoba Association of Graduate Nurses faced a critical issue. This was a proposed amendment to the Minimum Wage Act of the province, which would bring pupil nurses under its provisions. The Association quickly rallied its forces to prevent this. The alarm which the proposal aroused in the nursing organizations was doubtless aggravated by the current unrest and growing aggressiveness of trade unions in Winnipeg.

At a special meeting of the Association held on 15 February, a resolution was drafted for presentation to the Law Amendments Committee of the legislature, signifying disapproval of the inclusion of pupil nurses for the following reasons: '... Pupil nurses are not a working force but are in the strict sense a student body. That while we recognize that at present the practical side of the pupil nurse's training is overemphasized and the hours of actual duty are too long, the fact remains that the student nurse comes to the Training School not for a wage, and not as a means of subsistence, but for education in her chosen calling or profession.' It was agreed that Miss Mabel Gray, recording secretary (and superintendent of nurses of the Winnipeg General Hospital) should present this resolution. Miss Johns, as secretary of the Canadian National Association of Trained Nurses, was asked to communicate with the president, Miss Gunn, and to represent the national organization in a delegation to the Law Amendments Committee.

According to a news item in the *Free Press*, the nursing delegation appeared before the Law Amendments Committee on 20 February. The group included Miss Gray, four student nurses, and Miss Johns. Also present to support the nurses' case were H.J. Symington, and Dr Jasper Halpenny. Miss Gray presented the Association's resolution, and added that this body hoped eventually to see a chair of nursing established at the University, with degrees awarded by the faculty. The hospital was a college of instruction, not a 'mere factory of labour.' Miss Johns noted that certain changes were pending in the various provinces concerning the status of nurses which might be adversely affected if the proposed amendment were passed. She read a telegram from national headquarters in Toronto protesting against the attempt to bring nurses under the control of any labour organization. If the amendment were placed upon the statute books, Miss Johns insisted, student nurses would become mere employees of the hospital – they would cease to be students. The nurses did not wish to be ungracious or ungrateful, but they must respectfully ask to be relieved from the effects of the proposed amendment.⁵ Following addresses by Mr Symington and others, the amendment was withdrawn.

Within the next few months, Ethel Johns addressed meetings of the nursing associations in the neighbouring prairie provinces. On 24 and 25 April, she attended the second annual meeting, in Moose Jaw, of the Saskatchewan Registered Nurses' Association. Miss Johns gave a paper on, 'Some of the Present Day Nursing Problems' and conducted a round-table conference the following morning at which the topic was explored further. The published account of this convention noted that no one else could have given such an interesting paper or led the discussion as well as Miss Johns. Those who had already met and heard her were delighted to have the same privilege again, while those who heard her for the first time were 'loud in their praises to know that Canada had such women in the nursing profession.' It was hoped that Miss Johns' visit would bring the nurses of Manitoba and Saskatchewan into closer relationship, and that it would also awaken the nurses of Saskatchewan to the realization of the need for their interest in national nursing affairs.⁶

Speaking to the annual convention of the Alberta Association of Graduate Nurses, Miss Johns chose as her subject, 'Nursing Education in Western Canada.'⁷ This remarkable address contained a distillation of her beliefs about nursing and nursing education, expressed in pungent prose and laced with humour. The speaker warned at the outset that her remarks would not be confined to western aspects of the problem, since 'nursing is not a thing of provinces, it is not even a thing of nations; it is as broad as civilization and as deep as human need ...' Not all problems in different parts of Canada could be approached in the same way, but there should be greater co-operation among the provinces, and in particular among the three prairie provinces. The speaker made a strong plea for state control and financial support of nursing education, and added:

... I have never been able to discover why nursing should be considered an outcast Cinderella in educational circles. I do not believe it is an outcast, really. It is simply that we have withdrawn ourselves from the common herd, and have been inclined to feel that no one must lay sacrilegious hands on our methods, because, in some mysterious way, 'nursing is different.' I fancy that, in educational matters, we are not so different as we think we are, and that our splendid isolation has lost us much of the help and inspiration we might have had from men and women engaged in other branches of educational work ...⁸

Pointing out the numerous areas in which reforms in nursing education must be effected by the nursing profession, Miss Johns enquired: 'What is to be our reward for the toil and struggle of today?' To this query she proposed an answer:

... To blaze the trail – not to make the crooked straight, not to make the rough places plain (the others who come after will see to that). Ours is the nobler, harder task: to find, peradventure, the right path, and to light our watch-fires on the mountains. So, at the very end, shall we not see of the travail of our souls and be satisfied? And those who follow us shall say they have fought a good fight, they have run a straight race, *they have kept the faith.*[9]

Ruby Simpson remembers that Miss Johns came to speak to the senior class of the Winnipeg General Hospital Training School of which she was a member: 'She spoke to us on a little of everything, you know, but especially on the importance of keeping on studying. That was her long suit – "Keep right on" – and although that is fifty years ago, I can remember what an inspiration she was to young students. At the time, she was a young woman – she would only have been forty. There was a certain spark of enthusiasm to her at that time that we found very interesting.'[10]

In May 1919 the labour unrest which had been smouldering in Winnipeg suddenly blazed into an open conflagration. Forewarning of the trouble ahead came in 1918, when a series of disruptive strikes in the city involved first some of the vital civic services, then workers in certain other key occupations. Settlement of the strikes did not signal peace in the labour movement. Unions were becoming more truculent under the leadership of some able, aggressive leaders. By spring 1919, the metal workers and the building trades employees were engaged in strikes which dragged on without settlement. On 13 May the Winnipeg Trades and Labor Council, as an indication of its sympathy with the cause of the metal workers, voted in favour of a general strike, to be called at eleven o'clock on the morning of Thursday, 15 May.[11]

The causes of the labour unrest which culminated in the Winnipeg General Strike were subsequently investigated by two royal commissions, one appointed by the federal, the other by the provincial government. Social and economic grievances of the workers were identified. A precipitating factor, it was found, was the situation in respect to unemployment, which was becoming worse in the spring of 1919. Post-war inflation was also making itself felt, and wages had not kept pace with the increased cost of living. As a result, many people were living in poverty, and by contrast the obvious wealth of the privileged classes was the more deeply resented. Housing was scarce and of poor quality. Many employers refused to use the process of collective bargaining. Political reasons for labour discontent included wartime restrictions against freedom of speech, the ban upon importation of literature of a radical type, the delays of government in the release of political prisoners, and the sending of troops to Russia.[12] The general strike dragged on for more than six weeks and was marked by increasing bitterness between the strikers and other members of the general public. A Citizens' Committee was formed at the outset, in order to keep the essential services in operation as far as possible.

Ethel Johns' sympathies were pro-labour, but the circumstances in which she lived and worked were not favourable to socialistic expressions. The board of the Children's Hospital was conservative, while Cora Hind espoused the political philosophy of the *Free Press,* which was liberal – and vehement in its denunciation of the strikers. One observer suggests that the misfortunes of Ethel Johns' brother influenced her political views. He was out of work much of the time during this period, and Miss Johns held the social influence of the privileged classes and the lack of protective labour laws responsible. On the other hand, it is said that Cora Hind took a more objective view; had the family not moved to an environment which deprived them of normal social intercourse and formal schooling, the children might not have had so many obstacles to overcome later in life.[13]

It appears that Ethel Johns' political philosophy at that time was influenced also by her observations of patients and their families:

... All through the long drawn out strike of the metal workers union, the children of these men had been brought by their gaunt mothers to the hospital for treatment. The diseases they were suffering from were chiefly due to starvation and after they had been properly fed for a few weeks they were sent back to their poverty-stricken homes as 'cured.' In due course they were visited by our social service nurse and it was she who first told me of the growing desperation of these people and that there was some wild talk of a 'sympathetic' strike ...[14]

In spite of this warning, Miss Johns recalled, the hospital was taken by surprise when the general strike was declared. The first indication of its effects came when the usual delivery of milk to Children's Hospital failed to arrive on Thursday morning. Some strikers had over-

An End and a Beginning 109

turned the delivery cart into the gutter. Miss Johns hastily consulted the president of the board and called City Hall. Shortly thereafter Mayor Gray summoned representatives of the various hospitals in the community to attend a meeting which he convened with the strike committee. Miss Johns joined other hospital officials in the council chamber. All were asked to specify the needs of their respective institutions and were assured by the strike committee that these would be met 'in due course.' Whe Miss Johns returned to Children's Hospital, she found that milk had been delivered, 'escorted by a guard of apologetic strikers,' and that the engine room and laundry staffs had been instructed by their unions to remain on the job.[15]

Carts in which essential supplies such as milk were delivered bore the inscription, 'By permission of the strike committee.' This later became a weapon against the leaders of the strike. It was alleged that the unions had arrogated to themselves the authority of government and that they were trying to set up a soviet form of rule. Concerning this development, Miss Johns later commented: '... At the time it did not occur to me that anything highly subversive was contemplated. My impression was that the hospitals were trying to keep their doors open and that the strikers, in their own interest, were anxious to give them a helping hand. Certainly my mind dwelt more upon milk than upon Karl Marx, and I think that the members of both groups felt the same way ...'[16]

As the days dragged oppressively by, the life of the community slowed almost to a halt, and tensions and bitterness mounted. Miss Johns now found herself unexpectedly in conflict with the board of directors of Children's Hospital:

... A few days later, I had to face up to a problem of my own. Naturally enough, the women on the board of directors felt that they had been betrayed in the house of their friends. They had tried to help the children of a working class which was now openly in revolt against constituted authority. There was talk of closing the out-patient department as a retaliatory measure. It was then that I knew that I could no longer remain silent. I reminded them that the Hospital drew the bulk of its support from public funds and that we were therefore obliged to keep all essential services going. The out-patient department did not close but it was borne in upon me that I had lost the goodwill and the confidence of women who in the past had always given me loyal support even when they thought I might be in the wrong ...[17]

Equally distressing to Miss Johns was her alienation from the nursing and medical staffs of the hospital and from her friends:

... Practically none of the nursing staff had any sympathy for the strikers and the medical men took the same stand. My friends outside of the hospital, most of them active in the Citizens Committee, thought I had taken leave of my senses. Never in my life had I experienced such spiritual isolation. In the evening there seemed little to do except to wander over to the open-air rallies held in Victoria Park and to listen to what Fred Dixon and James Woodsworth had to say. I did not know either of these men personally but I had a great respect for their courage and integrity. I began to read the books that they recommended and to do a little independent thinking on my own account. One Sunday, Mr Woodsworth closed his address with the words: 'They shall not sow and another reap ... they shall not build and another inhabit.' The strikers and their children were sitting about in groups on the grass and began to sing the labour hymn that I had never heard:

> When wilt Thou save the people, Lord,
> O God of Mercy, when?
> The people, Lord, the people,
> Not crowns and thrones, but men.

I went home through the Spring twilight knowing that I was no longer alone. There were other men and women who felt and thought as I did and who were making the same journey over the same rough road ...[18]

Further trouble was in store for Ethel Johns and for the hospital in her charge. In the late afternoon of 14 June, a violent wind-storm suddenly descended upon the city, tearing away part of the roof of Children's Hospital, and dumping it into the river:

... Live wires came down in all directions and we were plunged into darkness. Fortunately we had always had regular fire drills, so the usual alarm was sounded, emergency lanterns were lighted, and children were wrapped in blankets ready for removal if necessary. There was no panic and everybody behaved extremely well. My heart swelled with pride, we were over the worst of it. Then to our dismay we found that the chimney had been damaged and that inflammable portions of the uncovered roof structure were dangerously close to it. The fires in the engine room were drawn and a messenger sent to the nearest fire hall to ask for help. The substitute brigade provided by the Citizens Committee were of course utterly unable to cope with the situation. There were only a handful of them anyway and appeals were coming in from all sides. We had to shift for ourselves as best we could. No telephones, no police, no fire brigade. It was a long and anxious night ...[19]

The next morning, members of the board of directors and the men's advisory council arrived to inspect the damage. They were standing in the grounds with Miss Johns, when the latter noticed two shabbily dressed men approaching. Miss Johns went over to enquire what they wanted. They replied that they were members of the metal workers union, and that the union had given them permission to make any repairs which were necessary, free of charge, to the roof of the hospital. Greatly relieved, Miss Johns hastened to convey the good news of this offer to the hospital's officials. Before she had finished speaking, she was interrupted by one of the members of the men's council who told her sharply to advise the metal workers that their offer was refused:

... In ordinary life, this man was a kindly soul, devoted to children, who had always been a pillar of strength to us. The black hatred in his voice and manner so terrified me that I hardly knew how to respond. However, I went over to the men and gave them as gentle a refusal as I could. They turned and walked away without a word.

At this point there seemed nothing for me to do except to make it clear, that, since the hospital authorities had refused the proffered help, I could no longer be held responsible for the safety of a hundred sick children in a building which might be swept by fire at any moment. The Citizens Committee did obtain sufficient voluntary workers to make some rough repairs and we got the boilers going again. But my task had come to an end. As soon as the strike was over I handed in my resignation and it was accepted with unflattering speed ...[20]

In retrospect, a quarter of a century later, Ethel Johns was to reflect: 'Looking back over the years, I realize that I was hot-headed and probably rather naive. I realize now that there were faults on both sides. But the brutal measures taken to crush the strike, and the farcical trials of the leaders which followed its collapse, aroused a burning sense of injustice which has never left me. The solidarity of the unions, their willingness to share what little they had, their discipline and good humour in the face of great provocation were alike admirable. I still cannot understand why they failed to touch the imagination of the social group to which I belonged ...[21]

As one chapter in the life of Ethel Johns came sadly to a close, another opened – one which was to confront her with a challenge greater than any she had yet encountered.

PART FOUR: 1919–1925

13

The Hospital and the University

The year 1919 marked the birth of the Department of Nursing at the University of British Columbia and the establishment there of the first baccalaureate degree programme in nursing in the British Empire. The role of Ethel Johns in the event might be described as that of midwife. As the first director of the Department of Nursing, she was also to be the foster mother and interpreter of the programme during its precarious early years.

The need was evident at the time for nurses with advanced preparation in teaching, administration, and public health nursing. But it is unlikely that the Department of Nursing would have been established as early as 1919 had it not been for the initiative taken by Dr Malcolm T. MacEachern, the progressive medical superintendent of the Vancouver General Hospital. His efforts were backed by the board and the nursing department of the hospital, and by Dr R.E. McKechnie, Chancellor of the University of British Columbia. Another influential doctor, the Honourable Henry Esson Young, secretary of the Provincial Board of Health, also favoured the conduct of nursing courses by the University because of the existing dearth of graduate nurses prepared for the public health field.

Dr MacEachern's interest in nursing education stemmed from his commitment to improving the quality of hospital services in general and those of his own institution in particular. The Hospital Standardization movement, of which he was a recognized leader, was gathering momentum in both the United States and Canada. Under his management, the Vancouver General Hospital had attained an enviable reputation; but he recognized that achievement of excellence demanded high standards of nursing, which in turn depended upon the calibre of education which students received in the Training School. He visualized a potential role for the university in this area.

Nursing education had a prominent place in the programme of the first meeting of the hospitals of British Columbia, which was convened in June 1918 by Dr MacEachern and the board of his institution. In reply to a query from the floor as to whether the Vancouver General Hospital might set up a school to prepare nurses for teaching, Dr MacEachern commented:

... It has occurred to me that the University of British Columbia should establish a chair for nursing and that hospitals throughout this entire Province could affiliate their training schools with the University and the University (could) see that the hospitals were supplied with capable teachers in different places. In this way a uniform standard course could be given to all nurses in the various hospitals where they receive the practical experience necessary. When you analyse the ability and efficiency of different nurses from different schools, you cannot help but feel that there is something wrong, and that there is need for more uniformity, standardization, or centralization of training ...[1]

President Wesbrook, as he had stated in his letter of May 1918 to Dr Helen McMurchy, did not think that the time was opportune for establishing a department of nursing at the University of British Columbia. The war-time founding (1915) and early years of the institution had been difficult, particularly from the financial point of view. The recently elected Liberal government showed little sympathy toward the monetary needs of the University, and rigid economies were required in its administration. Lack of funds delayed both the initiation of new programmes and plans for erection of permanent buildings on the Point Grey site. Meantime, the University was housed in temporary quarters adjacent to the Vancouver General Hospital, where conditions for students and teachers alike were far from satisfactory.[2] In spite of the limitations of these facilities, the geographic proximity of the University and the hospital favoured co-operative arrangements between the institutions. As an example, Dr R.H. Mullin held a dual position as Director of Laboratories at the Vancouver General Hospital and Head of the Department of Bacteriology at the University of British Columbia. Each institution paid a part of his salary.

President Wesbrook died in October 1918, and Dr L.S. Klinck, Dean of Agriculture, became Acting President.[3] On 13 February 1919 the Senate considered a letter from Dr MacEachern in which he asked the

University to take over the instruction of students in the Vancouver General Hospital Training School for Nurses by the establishment of a Department or a Chair of Nursing. The minutes of this meeting note that the Chancellor, who was also chairman of the Education Committee of the Vancouver General Hospital, explained in some detail what the plan was expected to accomplish. The Senate thereupon appointed a three-member committee from among its members, to confer with the hospital's Education Committee and to report back to the Senate. Dr W.D. Brydone-Jack, a physician and surgeon, was the chairman, and the other two members were Dr H. Ashton, a faculty member in the Department of French, and Miss S.P. Clement, a graduate in Arts of the University of British Columbia.

Details of the proposal which the Vancouver General Hospital made to the University of British Columbia were subsequently set forth in an article which the superintendent of nurses, Maude McLeod, wrote for *The Canadian Nurse*:

... That a Faculty of Nursing, or Department of Nursing, should be established in the University of British Columbia, with a Dean of Nursing, who should be the Directress of Nursing of the Vancouver General Hospital. That, on completion of the requirements as laid down later, a degree should be conferred, the first degree suggested being Bachelor of Nursing.

That provision might be made to grant a degree to graduates on the fulfilment of the requirements as laid down by the University, Nursing Faculty, or the Nursing Department.

That the Department of Nursing keep supervision over the training of nurses in the Vancouver General Hospital.

That hospitals desirous of having their nurses in training participate in this scheme should fulfil the following requirements, as recommended by Miss Johns in a recent report on 'National Standardization of Training Schools' ... (The requirements were then listed in detail.)[4]

Reporting its findings to the Senate on 5 March, the Committee on Nursing – as a result of its meeting with the Education Committee of the Vancouver General Hospital – stated that the plan was practical and that it offered the University 'a desirable and legitimate field of activity.' The committee suggested that the Senate endorse the proposal and recommend it to the Board of Governors for immediate adoption.

Miss Clement halted this rapid action by stating that she was not in accord with the recommendation. If the University were going to grant degrees in Nursing, she said, it should demand something in the line of general education, at least a year in Arts, as was required of students in Applied Science. Taking note of this objection, the Senate enlarged the committee by adding five members and requested further study of the matter.

When Dr Brydone-Jack presented the report of the enlarged Committee on Nursing to a meeting of the Senate held on 14 May, 1919, the committee recommended that a Department of Nursing be established in connection with the Faculty of Science, leading to the degree of B.Sc.[5] The admission requirements were to be matriculation or its equivalent at the discretion of the Senate, and the committee outlined the University training (as distinct from practical work) as the first two years of Arts. Practical work could be taken in any institution that came up to the standard set down by the University authorities, and such institution or hospital would make formal application and submit evidence of fitness. Hospital graduate nurses might be awarded the degree by complying with such conditions as might be laid down by Senate. The Medical Council of British Columbia was to be asked to draw up a standard of qualifications for the guidance of the Senate in reference to the proposed hospital requirements. The Senate adopted the report and recommended the proposal to the Board of Governors.

No evidence has been found that the Graduate Nurses' Association of British Columbia was consulted or otherwise involved in the plans to establish a department of nursing at the University of British Columbia. In any event, the Association was fully occupied at the time, preparing to carry out the legal responsibilities delegated to it under the Registration Act of 1918. Under the circumstances, Miss Johns' impression was doubtless well founded that the Graduate Nurses' Association initially was 'aloof' in its attitude toward the degree course.[6]

Meeting on 26 May, the Board of Governors considered the recommendation of the Senate that a department of nursing be established, and reviewed the general statement about the proposed standard and curriculum of the course. The Board was advised that the Department would not involve any additional expense to the University. The minutes of this meeting do not add a fact of which the Board was aware: that the Vancouver General Hospital would pay the full salary of its director of nursing, who would also take charge of the University's Department of Nursing. The Board approved the recommendation that a department of nursing be established. A letter confirming this decision was forwarded to the Senate. The communication emphasized that the action was taken on the understanding that the establishment of this Department would not involve any additional expense to the University.

President Klinck made a public announcement of the plans to set up a department of nursing within the University when he brought greetings, on 30 June, to the opening joint session (in Hotel Vancouver) of the annual conventions of the Canadian National Association of Trained Nurses and the Canadian Association of Nursing Education. He stated that, beginning in the Fall, the University of British Columbia in co-operation with the Vancouver General Hospital would offer a course leading to a degree in nursing.

Ethel Johns was absent from the convention because of the problems which had arisen at Children's Hospital as a result of the wind-storm and the strike. Mabel Gray deputized for her and presented Miss Johns' report as secretary of the Canadian National Association of Trained Nurses. The report drew attention to the growing volume of the organization's secretarial work, and stated that considerable free assistance was given to the Association by the office staff in the hospital where the national secretary was employed. The Association, she suggested, would soon develop beyond the point where this would be either necessary or desirable. Miss Johns was re-elected secretary, and a resolution was passed authorizing her to engage assistance when necessary.[7]

Isabel Stewart, then Professor in the Department of Nursing and Health, Teachers College, gave a paper at an evening session of the two associations. She spoke on the advantages of an eight-hour day for student nurses. Later she addressed the Second Annual Convention of the British Columbia Hospitals Association of which the founder, Dr MacEachern, was president. It is reasonable to suppose that he discussed with Miss Stewart the developments in regard to the degree course in nursing at the University of British Columbia, and that she may also have met and talked with President Klinck during her visit to Vancouver. It would have been logical to seek her advice, since the Department of Nursing and Health, Teachers College, had initiated (in 1916) a five-year combined course in conjunction with the Presbyterian Hospital, New York. In the same year, the University of Cincinnati School of Nursing had developed a programme leading to a bachelor's degree. In both of these earlier experiments, a similar pattern was followed: two years of liberal arts and sciences, two years of basic professional preparation in a hospital, and a final year in which the student elected as her major focus either teaching or public health nursing.⁸ The programme established in 1919 by the University of British Columbia closely resembled this pattern.

At the convention in July of the British Columbia Hospitals Association, Dr MacEachern spoke about the 'University scheme' for education of nurses, and expressed pleasure that the University of British Columbia had accomplished it. He pointed out that it was not a plan for the large hospitals only. The University affiliation was open to every hospital in the Province and to nurses from various training schools. He added that the University would turn out teachers and superintendents who would go to the smaller hospitals of British Columbia. 'It is to put nursing on a higher plane,' he said, 'and to stimulate smaller hospitals to more efficient training schools.'⁹

But the evolving plan for the combined course in nursing was moving away from Dr MacEachern's original concept of centralization of nursing education under the University of British Columbia through a system of affiliation of the training schools with the institution of higher learning. For many years the Vancouver General Hospital was to be the only school of nursing to be affiliated with the University in the combined course, and the large majority of its students were deterred from taking the degree programme by the academic requirements for admission or by economic considerations and the length of the course. The influence of the Department of Nursing upon nursing education and practice in the Province would not become apparent until its graduates assumed responsibilities in teaching, administration, and public health nursing.

Once the establishment of the degree programme was assured, the Vancouver General Hospital started to seek a director of nursing who would be competent also to meet the demands of the position within the University. Miss Johns later wrote an account of the problems encountered in the search, a version of the events which may have been coloured somewhat by her tendency toward self-deprecation:

... An active search began but it was found that the rapid expansion of the public health field afforded so many attractive prospects that potential candidates preferred not to venture into pioneer territory. An appeal for help to the authorities of Teachers College led them reluctantly to put forward my name but they were careful to point out that I did not possess an academic degree, a qualification which they quite rightly held to be indispensable. I had no idea that all these measures were being taken and was greatly surprized [*sic*] when an indirect approach was made to find out whether I would take on the job.

I consented and was forthwith appointed director of nursing service and education in the Vancouver General Hospital School of Nursing and as coordinator of the academic courses to be given at the University. My only excuse for such temerity is that I was too brash and inexperienced to realize the implications of the task I had undertaken ...[10]

Miss Johns' application was accepted by the Board of Directors of the Vancouver General Hospital at a meeting held on 28 August, 1919, 'despite the fact that she did not have a B.A. degree as desired by the University.'[11] On 23 September, Dr MacEachern wrote as follows to President Klinck:

DEAR SIR: *Re: Details of Department of Nursing*
We have been fortunate in securing the services of Miss Ethel I. Johns of Winnipeg, who has been recommened to us by all authorities on Nursing on this continent. Miss Johns has the most intimate knowledge of Nursing Education and the relation of such to Universities, of any woman I know of in Canada, as she has made a complete study of this in recent years. She arrives here a week from today and will assume duties on October first. I feel sure that she is the right person in the right place, and trust the University of British Columbia will accept her for the Department of Nursing. She is a vigorous writer and speaker and one who will reflect credit indeed on any institution she is connected with.

Naturally there are many details in the Department of Nursing which can only be settled when you get the Department fully organized and personnel appointed. When Miss Johns arrives, if you are willing, I would like to have an interview with you and talk matters over if such is satisfactory to you ...

Dr MacEachern concluded by enquiring whether the academic education of a specific applicant who was interested in the degree programme would be accepted by the University. This young woman was to enter the Vancouver General Hospital Training School for Nurses on the first of October.[12]

At a meeting of the Board of Governors held on 29 September, it was announced that Miss Ethel Johns had been appointed by the Vancouver General Hospital in connection with the Department of Nursing of the University. Miss Johns arrived in Vancouver two days later and commenced her duties at the hospital. One of her first actions was to interview the three students whose qualifications indicated that they would be suitable candidates for the combined course. These young women were Beatrice Johnson, Margaret Healy, and Marion Fisher.

All were interested and their educational backgrounds made it possible to grant them second year standing in the combined course. The degree programme was now under way, although its organization was as yet incomplete.

As soon as she could do so after her arrival, Miss Johns called a mass meeting of the student body and of the graduate staff. Dr MacEachern and members of the Training School Committee were also in attendance. The text of her address was preserved in the files of the nursing department of the Vancouver General Hospital, was later handed to Mabel Gray, and is now in the Woodward Biomedical Library of the University of British Columbia. It is an extraordinary document that vividly evokes the occasion when she reached out and sought to establish rapport with the large group, and to interpret the aims and nature of the new degree programme.

In this initial meeting with the student body, Miss Johns announced that she would appoint a students committee composed of representatives from each class, with which she would hold conferences from time to time. The function of the committee, she explained, would be 'to carry the current from you to me, and from me to you, so see then that you choose live wires.'

The reason for this meeting, Miss Johns continued, was to place before them 'a brief outline of the aim and purpose of the new experiment in nursing education which is to be made in this Training School and in others throughout this Province in conjunction with the University of British Columbia.' She spoke of the responsibility which they (the graduates and students) would carry for the success or failure of the experiment. For this reason, she felt it only fair to give them information about the course, and what its outcomes were expected to be. For the future there would be two groups of students in the Training School, first the student nurses as then constituted, and second a much smaller group of students who would be enrolled in the combined course. The latter, after taking 'a certain number of years of University work and a certain number of years of training in a hospital' would be granted both a diploma and a degree.

In order to clarify the reason for establishing the degree programme, Miss Johns then traced at some length the long evolution of nursing and the progress which had been made in the past fifty years. 'But we are concerned with the here and now and with the future,' she said. 'Why dwell on the past? For this reason, we must study the future in the light of the past. We must judge of what is good in the past and see if by any means we may still hold to it, reaching out at the same time to the broader opportunities of the future ... one of these opportunities being the experiment we are undertaking to make here ...'

Miss Johns then referred to her recent experiences as a member of the Manitoba Public Welfare Commission, and to the task which had been assigned her to investigate and report upon the status of nursing and nursing education:

... To my sorrow and surprise, it began to dawn upon me as the sittings of the Commission progressed that the public at large were not so well pleased with nurses and nursing as we had been led to suppose by enthusiastic and complimentary gentlemen who addressed us at Graduating Exercises. Suddenly I found myself a prisoner at the bar with the other eight Commissioners, all men but one, ranged against me as prosecuting attorneys. What they said, summed up, amounted to something like this: 'We are looking to you nurses for leadership in health questions, we are looking to you for teaching, we are expecting you to prove yourselves a vitalizing force in our community life, but you don't lead. We push you in front of us. You give us service, yes, devoted, kindly, but not as intelligent as it should be. Now what are you going to do about it?' I cannot conscientiously say that all this was news to me. I had suspected a good deal of it for some time and furthermore, I had done a little thinking about it on my own account, and at a subsequent meeting of the Commission I asked my prosecuting attorneys the question they had asked me: 'What are *you* going to do about it? If the community expects the nursing group to carry the almost intolerable burden they are thrusting upon us, then let the community see to it that we are prepared adequately for our task. I have yet to hear of a single penny being spent by any government for the betterment of nursing education ...'

The war, continued Miss Johns, had effected an improvement in the status of women. The war and the epidemic which followed had focused public interest upon nurses in particular, and in the bright light of that scrutiny, both their virtues and shortcomings were revealed. The community at large, she added, had 'come to realize that life transcends property and that every conserving factor we possess must be pressed into service if we are to repair the monstrous waste of war.' In this task, nursing had an essential role:

... Now where do we come in? Is there a single phase of life from the cradle to the grave where we do not come in? We see the curtain rise on life, we serve at every succeeding stage from infancy and adolescence through maturity to old age, and at the very end we watch the curtain fall forever. There is no avocation, not even medicine itself, which transcends ours in its intimate association with life. Do you think any preparation too broad and deep for such a task as this? Do you think we can rest satisfied with what we have? It is good, yes, but not good enough. Now what are we nurses going to do about it?

Calls were being made upon the nursing profession for leadership, continued Miss Johns. Nursing was becoming highly specialized. Nurses were already seeking additional preparation in various clinical branches; specialists were now needed in nursing education. 'We are going to develop them here,' she asserted. '... We are going to see to it that women ... will be soundly and thoroughly educated so that a few years from now, when nurses possessing University training are needed for certain work, they will be forthcoming, and the demand for them will, judging from present indications, be overwhelming.'

In conclusion, Miss Johns appealed to the staff and students of the Vancouver General Hospital to give their full support to the new programme. The public, she said, would not be so much interested in the record of the special students in the University; they would enquire whether the patients in the Vancouver General Hospital were well cared for:

... This is where you come in. You have got to demonstrate to the University and to the public that work done in the wards of this hospital by the rank and file of the staff and pupils is so good that it is worthy of University recognition ... To retain even the measure of University connection which we now have, we have got to maintain the nursing service of this hospital on its present high level, and more than that, we have got to raise that level. No one can do that but you, and remember, you are not doing it for yourselves alone, you are doing it in a Canadian School for Canadian Nurses, in every part of this Dominion. If they can do this thing in Minnesota, in New York, in Ohio, and in Missouri, we can do it here. And we will.

A few days ago I attended a conference with the University authorities. It was not easy for me; I was a stranger, unproven, untried. They were very kind, but beneath their kindness they were critical and they had a right to be. As I sat there I happened to glance down at the University calendar in my hand and on the cover was the seal with its motto, two Latin words meaning, 'It is thine.' Somehow that comforted me: I took it as a sign. I think when I came here one of your papers stated I am a Canadian by birth. I cannot claim that honor – I am half Welsh and half Cornish and therefore, incurably superstitious, and I am going to accept that motto as an omen for good. 'It is thine.' The opportunity has come to you to lead the way for Canadian nurses. See that you prove worthy of it. If some day you come to feel that I am worthy of the great trust reposed in me, I will ask you to change that motto a little and to let me say, 'It is ours.'[13]

Eloquent as Miss Johns' appeal was, in all probability few of the students or graduates present grasped its full significance or were in complete accord with the idea of the degree programme. A situation in which there would be two groups of students, the 'rank and file' and the privileged few enrolled in the combined course, was to lead inevitably to tensions within the student body and the staff. It was also to throw Miss Johns into inner conflict, since she could not give equal protection to the learning needs of the two groups who were her responsibility. A balanced programme of clinical rotation could be planned for the relatively small number of degree students, but this was not to prove feasible for the students enrolled in the three-year programme. In other respects, she treated all students alike. They found her a strict director of nursing, one who required conformity with rules and regulations, was not disposed to allow students to make explanations or excuses, and meted out impartial discipline to offenders, in whatever programme they were enrolled.

14

The Department of Nursing of The University of British Columbia

Certain matters concerning the newly established Department of Nursing received the attention of the Senate at the meeting of 15 October 1919. Dr MacEachern's application was received for affiliation of the Training School of the Vancouver General Hospital with the University through the Department of Nursing. The request of the British Columbia Hospitals Association was noted, that the University make provision for registered nurses to attend courses on the principles of public health nursing. The Senate delayed action on these questions, and decided to appoint a committee to interview the different faculties and to prepare a report (on the Department of Nursing) to be presented to the Senate in two weeks' time. The minutes do not state why this action was considered necessary, but the reason for it may have been a general query in the academic community as to why the department had been set up. In this connection, Miss Johns later wrote:

... It was apparent that certain members of the faculty of the University disapproved of this intrusion by a group of students in nursing. What right had nurses to University privileges? And where did they belong? There was no medical school. There was no school of education. There was not even a department of home economics. It was at this juncture that Dr MacEachern and Dr Mullin came to our rescue. They maintained that our proper place was in the department of Applied Science. Fortunately, the Dean, Dr Reginald Brock, agreed with them. This decision heartened me considerably. I believed then, as I do now, that nursing *is* an applied science and that we had a right to be there ...[1]

The decision to place the Department of Nursing under the jurisdiction of the Faculty of Applied Science proved to be a happy one. Dean Brock was a sympathetic interpreter of the young department's needs, recommendations, and progress. To Miss Johns he gave steady support, encouragement, and guidance.

The Committee on Nursing presented a comprehensive report to the Senate at the meeting held on 29 October. The report detailed the subjects to be taken by the students in the combined course during the first two years and made a statement about the nature of the final year's work. It also dealt with the question of conditions under which graduates of hospital schools might qualify for the degree until the year 1925. In the absence of criteria for assessing the standards of nursing schools seeking affiliation with the University, the application of the Vancouver General Hospital Training School for Nurses was tabled again. The secretary of the Senate was asked to write to the Medical Council of British Columbia requesting that body 'to draw up a standard of qualifications for the guidance of Senate in reference to proposed hospital requirements.' At the same meeting, a letter from Dean Brock was read, submitting recommendations from the Department of Nursing regarding the appointment of a Committee on Standards for Training Schools for Nurses. This proposal can have come only from Miss Johns. The minutes record that Dean Brock's letter was ordered to be filed. The matter was not raised again in the Senate.

Meeting on 18 February 1920 the Senate considered the report of the Committee on the Department of Nursing, which recommended a curriculum for the fifth year of academic work in the combined course. The minutes do not record that the committee consulted Miss Johns in drawing up the fifth-year programme, but they must have done so. She must also have guided the planning of a proposed four-month course in public health nursing, an outline of which was also presented in the committee's report. Both plans were adopted and forwarded to the Board of Governors which approved them five days later. The Board also considered a request from the Library Committee for a grant of two hundred and fifty dollars with which to purchase books for the Department of Nursing. But the Board had a long memory. After some discussion, it was decided to direct the attention of the Library Committee to the undertaking of the Hospital authorities that the University would not be asked to assume any financial responsibility in respect to the Department of Nursing. It was decided that a sum not to exceed one hundred dollars should be granted for books for the proposed extension course in public health nursing.[2]

The Board of Governors, meeting on 29 March 1920, ordered (on motion of the President) that the status of Miss Johns in the Department of Nursing should be that of special lecturer.

In April 1920 the University of British Columbia accepted a proposal from the Provincial Branch of the Canadian Red Cross Society to the effect that a Red Cross Chair of Public Health be established. For a period of three years from date of acceptance by the University, the Red Cross Society would pay five thousand dollars toward the salary of the professor. The expectation was that 'the cause of Public Health, which everywhere is being regarded as of great importance, will be materially advanced throughout British Columbia.' The Senate approved the proposal.[3]

Dr R.H. Mullin was subsequently appointed Red Cross Professor of Public Health, and Mary Ard. MacKenzie (former superintendent of the Victorian Order of Nurses) was named Red Cross Instructor. Miss MacKenzie commenced her duties by directing the fourteen-week course in public health nursing which had been scheduled originally (as an extension course) to commence on 1 March 1920, but which actually started in mid-November of that year.

The Board of Governors, meeting on 27 September 1920 reached the decision, 'That Miss Ethel I. Johns, now in charge of the Department of Nursing, be appointed as Assistant Professor in Nursing. Miss Johns' salary is chargeable in full to the General Hospital and to the funds provided by the Red Cross.' Presumably, this arrangement recognized the contribution which she had made to the organization of the short course in public health nursing. She was also to be one of the lecturers in the programme.

Meeting on 20 October 1920, the Senate heard the reply from the College of Physicians and Surgeons, conveying the views of the Council of that body about the degree programme in nursing:

... So far as the Council has been able to ascertain, the consensus of opinion of Medical men is to the effect that the teaching of a large part of the curriculum of the Medical student to nurses is undesirable. The Council is further of the opinion that,

1 If nursing is to be taught in the University it should be as a post-graduate course.
2 That overtraining of nurses is not desirable and results largely in the losing of their usefulness.
3 Theoretical branches of nursing are of very little use in the sick room.

4 That a nurse can be sufficiently trained in two years to meet all requirements.[4]

The Senate directed that the letter be acknowledged and filed, and decided to ask the British Columbia Hospital Association for advice as to 'what they would consider a proper standard for a hospital carrying on the practical work of the nurses' course.' Six weeks later, the Senate received a reply from Dr MacEachern, then secretary of the Hospital Association, 'setting forth the standard considered proper for training schools desiring to affiliate with the University of British Columbia for the combined course in Nursing leading to the University degree.' The letter was referred to the Faculty of Applied Science, which subsequently notified the Senate of its approval of the recommended standard.

Through a combination of circumstances, Miss Johns was in a position to guide the development of the statement of criteria and their final approval by the Senate. She was a member of the Hospital Association's Standardization Committee and of its Sub-committee on Nursing; in fact, she had been appointed to these committees before her arrival in the Province. She was also a member of the Executive of the British Columbia Graduate Nurses' Association, to which the Hospital Association submitted a proposed statement of standards for a training school desiring to affiliate with the University's Department of Nursing. Miss Johns was present at the executive meeting (on 9 February 1920) at which this submission was considered and approved. She was able, eight months later, to signify her approval of the same statement when Senate referred it to the Faculty of Applied Science.

While the organization of the combined course was progressing steadily, Ethel Johns' major efforts were concentrated at the Vancouver General Hospital. The transition from a small, specialized institution to this complex, thousand-bed hospital must have been overwhelming, but in typical fashion she met the challenge head-on. As soon as possible after her arrival, she undertook a survey of the nursing situation in the hospital and the school, and submitted a report to Dr MacEachern. Some aspects of the nursing service, she stated, were good; others were open to criticism. She was impressed by the breadth of clinical experience which the hospital offered for students. The only thing lacking, she felt, was the opportunity for the students 'to gain experience in nursing in the homes of the people.' This could be arranged by allowing them to have a short period during their training with the nurse in charge of the social service department and with visiting nurse organizations in the city. At the present time, this was not possible, 'since our entire available supply of pupil nurses is not sufficient to staff our ever expanding wards. A marked shortage of pupils still exists and it will be necessary to offer every inducement of good teaching, comfortable living conditions, and short hours if suitable pupils are to be attracted in sufficient numbers to our school ...'[5]

The number of students in the Training School in 1919 was one hundred and seventy-seven, including five affiliates from other schools. Fifty-two graduate nurses were on staff, including the director of nursing and her assistant, a night supervisor, an instructor and a 'demonstrator,' fourteen supervisors and head nurses, seven staff nurses in special departments, twenty-two staff nurses in the Military Annex, and four in the Marpole Annex for Incurables. The establishment included also five 'post-graduate pupils' and thirty-two ward assistants in the Military Annex.[6]

It is said that a disciplinary problem existed in the Training School prior to Miss Johns' arrival. According to one source of information, Miss Johns was 'told to come in and clean it up.' If this report is accurate, the problem must have been uppermost in her mind as she undertook her new responsibilities. It might also explain why she proceeded without delay to set up a Students Council: a constructive means of opening up channels of communication with the students. In spite of this, the students were in awe of her. As she paced through the corridors of the hospital in her black uniform, with eyes downcast, she must have seemed a severe and remote figure to the students whom she passed without recognition. To one student at least, Miss Johns seemed to be 'suspicious.' But when she came to know her former director of nursing many years later, she found her approachable and easy to converse with. Miss Johns confessed that she was under great pressure during the time she was in charge of the nursing department of the Vancouver General Hospital.

A problem which caused Miss Johns considerable anxiety during the same period was the open hostility of some of the staff doctors toward the degree programme. She had never been a meek person, and this unexpected opposition roused her fighting spirit. Confrontations between Miss Johns and these critical doctors were inevitable as long as she held the dual positions of director of nursing of the Vancouver General Hospital and director of the Department of Nursing of the University. Advanced education for nurses found both its greatest champions and most vigorous opponents among the members of the medical profession.

The year 1920 brought many problems to the Vancouver General

Hospital and its nursing department. The number of patients was increasing steadily. They came not only from Vancouver and district but from other parts of the Province as well. The specialized services which the institution offered added to the complexity of its general and nursing administration. Staff shortages were serious, particularly in nursing, and the hospital continued to lack the required financial resources.[7] February and March brought a recurrence of the epidemic of influenza which had earlier swept Vancouver. In order to accommodate patients suffering from the disease, it was necessary to open four additional wards (a total of one hundred and twenty beds). Staffing these units required the employment of a large number of graduate nurses and ward helpers. Aware of the current difficulties in financing the hospital's operation, Miss Johns tried to increase the enrolment of students in order to release the temporary staff. But she was hampered by the lack of sufficient residence accommodation, and in the emergency she found it necessary 'to transform the bedrooms into dormitories and to overcrowd the bedrooms in the residences still further. As a result of this overcrowding, the health of the pupils has suffered with consequent impairment of the efficiency of the nursing service,' Miss Johns reported.[8] An attempt by the management of the hospital to secure money to build a nurses' residence was defeated at the polls in June.[9] The problem of insufficient and inadequate residence accommodation was to continue for some time.

True to her conviction that directors of nursing should not immure themselves within their institutions, Miss Johns quickly became involved in the affairs of the provincial hospital and nursing associations. She accepted willingly any and all tasks assigned to her. At the same time, she retained the office of secretary to the Canadian National Association of Trained Nurses, and continued as a councillor of the Canadian Association of Nursing Education. Dr MacEachern doubtless encouraged her to engage in these activities; more than this, he opened doors that enabled her to do so.

Miss Johns availed herself of every opportunity to interpret the degree programme in nursing. In June 1920 she accepted the invitation to address a joint session of the British Columbia Hospital Association and the Canadian Public Health Association, on the first day of their concurrent conventions in Vancouver. Dr MacEachern was then completing his third (and final) year as president of the Hospital Association, and Dr H.E. Young was president of the Canadian Public Health Association. Both men were firm supporters of the combined course, and it was therefore not surprising that Miss Johns' paper on 'The University in Relation to Nursing Education' was given a prominent place in the agenda on the morning of 23 June.[10] This unique occasion was one in which she could plead the cause of nursing education before an audience – many of them doctors – whose influence could either advance or retard its progress. Skilfully she depicted the existing weaknesses in nursing education. A major deterrent to improvement, she pointed out, was the lack of nurses who were prepared to assume leadership positions. The modern movement of nurses toward the university was evidence of their recognition that this was the proper institution to which they should look for education in leadership. The speaker briefly described the degree programme recently established at the University of British Columbia, and mentioned other Canadian universities which were 'swinging into line.' She then touched upon certain criticisms which were commonly made by detractors of higher education for nurses. Addressing herself to the medical men in the assembly, Miss Johns made a plea for their understanding and support:

... To those who are in opposition or are in doubt, one last word, if there are any of such here: Will you not listen to the appeal of those upon whose shoulders you yourselves lay such heavy burdens? You see so many faults, so many blunders in our nursing service. So do we; they are not hidden from us. You cannot imagine why things should not run more smoothly, but we can; we know it is because of insufficient teaching and supervision. You do not realize how complex your own profession has become. How can we expect you to realize how difficult it is for us, with few of your educational advantages, to keep up with the advance shown in medicine? And yet we have tried to keep up. Slowly but surely the routine processes of medicine are being delegated to us. We are expected to give acceptable service as anesthetists, as laboratory and X-ray technicians, as your field workers in preventive medicine. You have taken us for granted, as men always take their women folk for granted.

If we had not wished to develop ourselves you would have forced development upon us. Some years ago I stood and watched with a high heart the women's suffrage parade in New York City. Near the end of the long procession, in which women from every walk of life participated, came a group of young girls with a banner inscribed, 'All this comes of teaching girls to read.' Remember, you taught us our letters in nursing. You should not have set our feet upon the road if you did not mean that we should climb the hill. You should not have taught us our letters if you meant that we were not to read the chapter ...

Miss Johns asked her hearers to reserve judgment, to be patient, not to throw the weight of their great influence against higher education

UBC Department of Nursing 133

for nurses. 'Give us a fighting chance, a fair field, and no favor,' she besought them. 'There is a long, uphill struggle ahead of us.' The universities were sympathetic, but their sympathy was tinged with caution; they feared – and rightly so – the lowering of their standards. Once it was made clear to the University authorities that nursing students would be expected to meet the same standards as others, they became more friendly. But, she added:

... The fact must be faced that we constitute a serious educational problem to them. Suitably equipped personnel for the faculty of nursing is difficult to obtain. Few of us possess full academic standing – no precedents exist. Compromise is necessary. No one knows that better than the pioneers of this movement. But before long adequately prepared women, the output of the combined courses, will be available. Until then we must carry on as best we can ...

In conclusion, Miss Johns defined the ultimate goal of higher education for nurses as one which was identical with that to which the members of her audience were committed:

... You are met here to consider ways and means whereby the community may be better served in health matters. The educational phase of this gigantic task is continually emphasized in your discussions. Surely we can enlist your sympathy in support of a movement which has as its object the development of a nursing force worthy of the cause to which it and you alike are dedicated – the prevention of disease and the conservation of life lived to the full, active, healthy, and happy.

Later in the convention, Miss Johns presented the report of the Nursing Committee, one which reflected her influence, a position of compromise, and support of the small hospital with a training school:

... That, since the whole question of nursing education, especially as it affects the smaller hospitals, is in such an uncertain condition in the minds of those vitally interested in conducting these training schools, your committee feels that it would be exceedingly unfortunate if any hasty action should be taken in the matter. They therefore recommend that they be instructed during the coming year to assemble data and formulate plans for an improved teaching and affiliation scheme for training schools, attached to hospitals of less than fifty beds. On completion, such plans shall be submitted to the hospitals concerned for criticism.[11]

The report was adopted. At this time, both the Hospital Association and the British Columbia Graduate Nurses' Association were concerned actively with standards of nursing education. The relationship between them seems to have been amicable and co-operative. Gradually, the provincial nursing organization was to assume a full measure of the responsibility which now legally belonged to it.

Miss Johns was re-appointed to the Standardization Committee on Nursing Matters, and she was elected to the executive of the Hospital Association. Dr H.C. Wrinch succeeded Dr MacEachern as president, and the latter became secretary of the association.

Miss Johns next attended the conventions, in Fort William and Port Arthur, of the Canadian National Association of Trained Nurses and the Canadian Association of Nursing Education. These meetings were held from the fifth to the tenth of July 1920. In submitting her report as secretary, Miss Johns gave an account of the work of the past year. She stated that the need for a paid, permanent secretary was becoming more apparent every year, and that it was 'very difficult for a woman in the full tide of professional life to give to this Association the continuous and careful service which is really necessary if its secretarial affairs are to be carried on in an efficient manner ...' She added that a competent paid national secretary would be a valuable means of welding together the component parts of the Canadian National Association of Trained Nurses.[12] But the Association was not quite ready for this step. Miss McMillan (Edmonton) was elected secretary, and Miss Johns assumed the office of second vice-president.

The morning session of 9 July was devoted to private duty nursing. Miss Johns addressed the gathering upon the topic, 'The Challenge of the Future.' The focal point of the paper was an issue which had long been of concern to her: the fact that people of moderate means could not afford to pay for nursing service in their homes. Now she bluntly took the private duty nurses to task for failing to tackle the problem. As a group, she stated, they were usually inarticulate, except when it was a question of raising fees or reducing hours of duty. Some of them actively opposed the introduction of attendants. She admitted that the economic burden of the unmet need for nursing care in homes should not be laid upon the shoulders of private duty nurses, but they should take constructive action in making suggestions to doctors and the laity as to how the problem might be solved. Had the possibility been investigated of insurance against illness? Might the Government inaugurate such a plan? Had the private duty nurses concerned themselves with these matters, or tried to educate the public or themselves about the issues? 'Surely it is not impossible,' said the speaker, 'that some day the time will come when sick people during the acute stages of their illness, shall be cared for by highly skilled women working reasonable hours for a fair wage, and, when the stage of convalescence ensues, they shall transfer these patients to the care of properly licensed attendants, duly supervised by graduate nurses ...' Much of the opposition to the higher education of nurses, said Miss Johns, came from the fact that nursing care in the homes was so difficult to obtain: 'Physicians and the public accuse us of educating nurses away from nursing, and rendering them unwilling to perform ordinary nursing duties,' she continued, 'I leave it to you to say whether or not there is some truth in this accusation. They urge us to lower our standards, to give shorter courses, to do something to get nursing attendance for the people who need it ...' She expressed concern that the modern graduate nurse was trying to fill the need for both routine and highly skilled nursing care, and was not succeeding well in either. The same educational system could not prepare for both at one and the same time, but this was expected. There was an overwhelming demand for highly trained women for public health, for training school and hospital administration. She advocated the preparation and use of trained attendants for routine duties, and predicted that – should this occur – the graduate nurses whom they displaced would be absorbed immediately into the more difficult and highly skilled branches of nursing. The skilled private duty nurse would still be very much in demand. Miss Johns suggested that there was not so much a shortage of private duty nurses as of domestic help during illness, a need which the trained attendant could fill more acceptably than could the graduate nurse. Miss Johns ended her address with an exhortation to the private duty nurses:

... 'Increase the borders of thy habitation and enlarge the place of thy tent.' Organize among yourselves, and your leaders will appear. Educate the medical profession and the laity concerning your real attitude. Incidentally, you will learn much yourselves. Grasp every opportunity for developing a more skilful technique and a broader knowledge of the more highly specialized branches of private duty; be ready when the time comes to organize and direct an auxiliary force ...[13]

The Canadian National Association of Trained Nurses, a year earlier, had approved the principle of trained attendants whose preparation and practice would be controlled by law. But the proposal was not one with which all nurses were in accord. In particular, it was threatening to those in private duty nursing, at the time the largest field of employment for graduate nurses. On the face of it, Miss Johns' paper could not have been reassuring to many in this group. It was to provoke a bitter reaction on the part of one private duty nurse, which in turn would stir up a storm of controversy during the following spring.

Miss Johns also spoke at the convention of the Canadian Association of Nursing Education. She did not submit a written paper, but dealt briefly with the subject, 'Relation of the Training School to the Hospital.' Discussion followed her presentation. At the same meeting, the president, Miss Flaws, introduced Miss Kathleen Russell, the newly appointed director of the department of health nursing which had been established recently at the University of Toronto through the efforts of the Provincial Red Cross and the Graduate Nurses' Association of Ontario. The assembly went on record as approving the plan of having a training school committee connected with hospitals. A resolution to the effect 'That the C.A.N.E. become a section of the National Association of Trained Nurses' was lost.[14]

In addition to her administrative duties, Miss Johns participated in teaching activities during the year 1920. Subjects which she taught included: History of Nursing and Ethics, the Field of Modern Nursing (to senior classes), and Anatomy and Physiology. She also gave seven hours of instruction in Medical Nursing to the second-year students in the diploma course.

In the annual report of the director of nursing for 1920, Miss Johns noted the shortage of staff which had been a serious problem throughout the year. She commented that 'a careful analysis of complaints regarding the nursing service received during the year shows more than half of these to be due to under-staffing in the departments concerned.' Staffing statistics in this report show that the total enrolment of students for the year was two hundred and four, an increase of twenty-seven over the previous year. Of these, ninety-three were junior students. The position of assistant director of nursing, left vacant by the resignation of Miss Buttle, was not filled. An additional instructor and a 'demonstrator' were engaged, making a total of four teachers. Members of the teaching staff probably supplied relief in the training school office, an arrangement which was not unusual at that time. Miss Johns increased the number of head nurses from five to nine, appointed an additional supervisor, and cut down the number of graduates on duty in the Military Annex from twenty-two to seven, presumably replacing them by students.

On the positive side, Miss Johns was pleased to report that the director of nursing had held regular conferences with the Students Council. This arrangement made it possible for students to bring their difficulties or grievances to the attention of the authorities for adjustment. The Council had also 'interested itself in the maintenance of good order in the residence and in fostering social activities of a simple and healthy nature ...' The director of nursing also noted that an experiment in the training of orderlies had been initiated during the year; a six-months course given under the general direction of the Training School had shown gratifying results. A comparable six-months course was in progress at Infants' Hospital where six young women were being prepared to work as nursery-maids. A further achievement was the reorganization of the Social Service Department, bringing it into close co-operation with the Hospital in general and with the Out-patients' Department in particular. 'Pupil nurses are now assigned to duty in this department,' added Miss Johns, 'thus gaining valuable insight into conditions in patients' homes.' The connection with the University of British Columbia, she said, had undoubtedly added to the prestige of the Training School. Students enrolled in the degree programme who had entered for their period of hospital service were 'satisfactorily performing their duties.'

Some progress had been made, both in the nursing service and school of the Vancouver General Hospital and in the small but sturdy growth of the young degree programme. But the conflicting demands of the dual positions were now causing Miss Johns increasing anxiety. She knew that she could not continue much longer to cope with the difficulties of the situation.

15

A Time of Testing

Reaction to Miss Johns' speech, 'The Challenge of the Future,' was not long delayed. Within a month after the convention, an irate private duty nurse wrote to Helen Randal, Editor of *The Canadian Nurse*.[1] The letter was venomous; its target Miss Johns. Miss Randal was evidently in a predicament. Miss Johns was a member of the executive of the Graduate Nurses' Association. As an officer of the Canadian National Association of Trained Nurses, she was also a member of the editorial board of the Journal. But Miss Randal was an independent, strong-minded person, used to making her own decisions. She had encouraged nurses to write their opinions for publication in *The Canadian Nurse*. She held the letter for eight months and then inserted it in the March issue (1921). It was signed, 'Private Nurse.'

In rebuttal of Miss Johns' allegation that private duty nurses were usually inarticulate, the writer quoted some lines of Edmund Burke: '... Because half-a-dozen grasshoppers under a fern make the field ring with their importunate chink, while thousands of great cattle repose beneath the shades of the British oak, chew their cud, and are silent, pray do not imagine that those who make the noise are the only inhabitants of the field; that of course they are many in number, or that, after all, they are other than the little, shrivelled, meagre, hopping, though loud and troublesome, insects of the hour ...'[2] The writer went on to say that she had had ample opportunity, at nurses' conventions, 'to see how little the self-promoters really know about the actual work.' Seizing a phrase which Miss Johns had used in her talk, the writer hurled it back like a knife: yes, she did think it would be well for superintendents to 'clean their own steps.' She had never seen such 'mean, unprincipled things' as she had known to be done by superintendents. She cited the instance of a superintendent's peremptory dismissal of a nursing student, and left the reader to conjecture whether she was or was not imputing this action to Miss Johns.

Publication of the 'Private Nurse' letter triggered a general reaction of shock and dismay from individual nurses and provincial nursing organizations across the country. Miss Dickson, president of the Canadian National Association of Trained Nurses, wrote to Miss Johns without delay to express her concern.[3]

Miss Johns was absent in Kansas City, attending a convention of the National League of Nursing Education, and Miss Dickson's letter did not reach her for several weeks. When it finally arrived on her desk, Miss Johns made haste to reply, and enclosed the following letter, with the request that it be read at the forthcoming convention in Quebec City, and that it be published as soon as possible thereafter in *The Canadian Nurse*:

... The letter from 'A Private Duty Nurse,' which appeared in the March issue of the Canadian Nurse, was most certainly construed by me as a personal attack. It could not be regarded as anything else since it discussed none of the points of my article, answered none of the questions raised therein, and made no intelligible criticism of it whatever. To take notice of a letter couched in such language was, of course, impossible. I therefore made no reply and have taken no action whatever concerning it.

With regard to the propriety and wisdom of an editorial policy which permits publication of letters of this type in the National Nursing Journal, I have nothing whatever to say. I am content to leave this matter where it belongs, in the hands of the Canadian National Association of Trained Nurses.

May I, through you, offer my most cordial and heartfelt thanks to the various organizations and individuals, especially private duty nurses, who have protested against the publication of this unprovoked attack. It has touched me very deeply that such protest has been made, and I only wish I were more worthy of the kindly and whole-hearted defence of my fellow nurses ...[4]

Miss Johns' reply was read at the convention. The ensuing discussions focused mainly on the question of publishing letters anonymously in *The Canadian Nurse*. Miss Randal explained that, in the interest of free discussion by nurses in the pages of the Journal, she had given assurances that if contributors gave their names to the editor, she would not publish them without their consent. She did not look upon the 'Private Nurse' letter as a personal attack, although it did seem bitter. After further debate, a motion was made: 'That letters continue to appear in the magazine under a nom-de-plume, provided the name and address are in the hands of the editor, leaving it to her discretion to withhold any letters which, in her opinion, are of a personal nature.' At this point, Mabel Gray voiced concern about letters without signatures being inserted in the Journal; the published report of this session states: 'She thought we should be big enough to stand criticism and brave enough to write our names under it.' The motion, on a divided vote, carried.[5]

Miss Dickson was re-elected president of the national association, and Miss Johns retained the office of second vice-president. The post-convention executive meeting decided to set up a Publications Committee for *The Canadian Nurse,* and to ask Miss Johns to serve as convener. Understandably, she declined the invitation.[6]

Further letters to the Editor on the 'Private Nurse' matter appeared in the August (1921) issue of the Journal. Mary Catton (of Ottawa), who had strongly expressed her disapproval at the convention in Quebec, protested the publication of anonymous articles in *The Canadian Nurse,* or letters of such a nature that they 'did not allow open, honest professional expression.' Of Miss Johns, she said: 'I believe that I voice the sentiment of the majority when I say that no woman in the nursing profession is worthy of greater esteem and admiration.'

In the same year, the Board of Governors of the University of British Columbia indicated that the University was now prepared to accept a measure of financial responsibility for the Department of Nursing by voting to increase Miss Johns' salary as Assistant Professor of Nursing from six hundred to twelve hundred dollars per annum, part time. Of the total, half was to be paid by the Department of Nursing and half by the Department of Public Health.[7]

By mid-year of 1921, Miss Johns had finally decided that she could not manage her two positions successfully. Many years later, she wrote about the reasons for this conclusion:

... Like all other hospitals of the period, it (the Vancouver General Hospital) depended almost entirely on its pupil nurses for the care given its patients. The fact that 'these University students' had to be given special consideration with regard to hours on duty was resented by overworked head nurses. Quite naturally, it also created discontent among the pupil nurses who had to take the buffet and cushion the shock whenever an emergency arose which kept them on duty for unduly long hours. Worst of all, whenever anything went wrong with the nursing service (and plenty did), it was attributed [to the degree programme] by members of the medical staff who disapproved of the higher education of nurses, and argued that too much time and attention was being given to the development of the combined course and not enough to the supervision of the nursing service. All this led to such serious friction that it began to look as though the second year of the experiment might also be its last.

It was clear that something had to be done and done quickly. I confessed that I could not cope with the dual task I had undertaken and offered to withdraw from both of them. However, a plan was ultimately worked out whereby I should give up my duties at the VGH and devote my entire time to the academic aspects of the combined course as a very humble member of the Faculty of Applied Science. Miss Kathleen Ellis, a very able administrator and educator, became the director of nursing services and of the school of nursing at the VGH, and together we set about making a pattern for the co-ordination of our respective responsibilities.[8]

In July 1921 Miss Johns tendered her resignation as director of nursing, but continued in the position until the end of December. Miss Ellis commenced her duties in January 1922. By mutual consent, Miss Johns acted until May as director of the educational programme in the Training School. She then became a full-time member of the University faculty.

In April 1922 Dr MacEachern was granted leave by the Vancouver General Hospital in order to carry out a national survey for the Victorian Order of Nurses. His leave became permanent when he accepted the position of associate director in the Chicago headquarters of the American College of Surgeons. His departure was a loss to the hospital, the province, the combined course in nursing which he had fathered, and to Miss Johns who had always been able to count on his support.

Miss Johns became secretary of the British Columbia Hospitals Association in Dr MacEachern's place, an office which she retained for the remaining years which she spent in British Columbia. Released from the heavy responsibilities of director of nursing, she now threw herself with undiminished energy into her work at the University and the activities of hospital and nursing associations. She resigned from the council of the Graduate Nurses' Association, stating as her reason that she was no longer director of nursing of the Vancouver General Hospital. But a few months later, she accepted the convenership of the newly established Nursing Education Committee, and in this capacity (and later as a member of the Board of Examiners) was closely associated on a continuing basis with the affairs of the nursing organization.

Ethel Johns was absent from the annual meetings of the national nursing organizations held in Edmonton during the last weeks of June since she had accepted a commitment to speak at the convention in Seattle of the National League of Nursing Education. Jean Browne (Saskatchewan) was elected president of the Canadian National Association of Trained Nurses, and Miss Johns became first vice-president. A decision was made at this meeting that conventions henceforth would be held biennially and the terms of office would be for a corresponding two-year period. Miss Johns was also appointed a member of the new Committee on the Training and Education of Public Health Nurses, of which Florence Emory was convener.

In response to a request from Dean Brock, the Board of Governors agreed that the University should pay two-thirds of Miss Johns' expenses to the convention in Seattle, but stipulated that the sum should not exceed thirty-five dollars. The Board declined to approve a recommendation that her salary, as full-time Assistant Professor and Head of the Department of Nursing, should be increased from six hundred to nineteen hundred dollars per annum (plus a six-hundred dollars stipend from the Department of Public Health). Both decisions were indicative of the University's limited financial resources at the time.[9] It should be noted that her salary was raised one year later to twenty-five hundred dollars per annum, chargeable in full to the Department of Nursing.[10]

The League's convention brought Ethel Johns needed refreshment and inspiration. To her, the highlight of the impressive programme was the abstract, read by Annie Goodrich, of the report of the Rockefeller-sponsored study of nursing and nursing education in the United States. The abstract, prepared by Dr C.E.A. Winslow, chairman of the study committee, summarized the conclusions reached by that body.[11] They fully supported her own observations of the status of nursing and nursing education, and prescribed remedies which opened up exciting possibilities for the future. Her feelings upon this occasion she later described as a thrill which comes once in a lifetime.[12]

The Rockefeller study found that young women 'of high capacity' were required for public health nursing, hospital supervision, and nursing education. Special training beyond the basic course was necessary to prepare for service in these fields. A majority of the hospital training schools had serious shortcomings, a primary cause of which was 'the lack of independent endowments for nursing education.' With the necessary financial support, a separate training-school committee or board organized for educational purposes, and an entrance requirement of complete high school or its equivalent, the 'fundamental period of hospital training' could be reduced to twenty-eight months. State legislation should be enacted to provide for the licensing of subsidiary nursing workers and, following that, training courses under educational auspices should be set up to prepare them. University schools of nursing should be developed and strengthened for the training of leaders; this was of 'fundamental importance.' The final statement emphasized: 'That the development of nursing service adequate for the care of the sick and for the conduct of the modern public health campaign demands as an absolute prerequisite the securing of funds for the endowment of nursing education of all types; and that it is of primary importance, in this connection, to provide reasonably generous endowment for University Schools of Nursing.'[13] The complete report was published a few months later, and became a blueprint for improvements in nursing education in the United States for many years to follow.[14]

Miss Johns chaired the Friday morning session of the convention, the subject of which was administration of schools of nursing. Her introductory remarks made reference to the abstract of the long-expected report of the Rockefeller study:

... We have heard, but, mercifully perhaps, we have not comprehended its tremendous implications. Nevertheless we still live and move and have our being. We are not quite sure whether our elaborate structure of education has crashed about our ears, or whether, as we vaguely hope, though the foundations are shaken, it still stands four square to all the winds of controversy which sweep about it. The consequences of that report are quite incalculable. Much time must elapse before even its more immediate results make themselves apparent ...

For the purposes of this introductory statement, I propose to disregard the report insofar as it is possible to dismiss completely from one's mind the overwhelming significance of it. Prolonged and careful study will be necessary before it can be comprehended, much less acted upon. My aim, therefore, will be to afford a basis for discussion of existing conditions rather than to indicate future development, and to drive in more or less clumsily a few pegs upon which fruitful discussion may be hung ...[15]

Miss Johns identified questions which, she said, were fundamental to administration, and then proposed answers which were based upon her own experiences. The presentation must have been superb: her paper was soundly conceived, its conclusions logical, the style vivid, forceful, and witty. Miss Goodrich was present and (at the chairman's request) commented upon nursing school administration. She prefaced her remarks by a reference to the report of the Rockefeller Committee, of which she was a member. She stated that no matter how much each person – and even members of the committee – might differ on certain of the conclusions reached, 'In the main we are all, throughout this great convention, at one on two points, namely that our schools have not been what we want our schools of nursing to be, and secondly, that we believe the importance to the community of our work justifies the university school ...'[16] Miss F.M. Shaw, director of the McGill School for Graduate Nurses, described the courses in teaching, supervision, and administration of schools of nursing which were offered by that two-year-old university school. Discussion ranged over a variety of topics, and the verbatim report of the proceedings reveals Miss Johns' skill as chairman.

Miss Johns had an opportunity to revisit Saskatchewan in the summer of 1922. At the request of the Registered Nurses' Association, the University of Saskatchewan agreed to arrange a short course for nurses engaged in training school work. Miss Johns was invited to direct the course, in which eight graduates enrolled, the majority of whom were superintendents of nurses. According to the published report of the session, the lectures were most practical, and dealt with such topics as training school organization, principles of teaching as applied to schools of nursing, and a consideration of modern developments in nursing. The shortness of time for planning and the brevity of the course made it impossible to utilize various departments of the summer school to the extent that would otherwise have been done, but lectures and demonstrations were given in nutrition and bacteriology, and classes in both physical education and household science were observed.[17]

In September Miss Johns called each of the three members of the first class into her office and reminded them that they would have to decide whether to take administration and teaching or public health nursing in their final year. Each one settled immediately for public health, whereupon they had the distinct impression that Miss Johns breathed a sigh of relief.[18] Mary Ardcronie MacKenzie was in charge of the certificate course in public health nursing (which had now been lengthened to one academic year), and the final-year degree students followed the same programme of theory and field work as did those enrolled in the certificate programme. Miss Johns taught both groups (together) a course in Teaching of Nursing Principles and Methods and one in Contemporary Nursing Problems.

Miss Johns was delighted that one of the first degree class won the gold medal for general proficiency in the hospital part of her programme, but she was devastated when she heard that this graduate had failed in one of her examinations for registration. Beatrice (Johnson) Wood, the nurse involved, recalls the incident. Upon hearing from the Graduate Nurses' Association about the failure, she went down to the Provincial Office and told Miss Randal that she could not believe it. The Registrar rebuked her for questioning the judgment of the doctor who had set and marked the paper, and subsequently wrote her a 'scathing letter' which Miss Johnson took to Miss Johns. The latter's reaction was not comforting or supportive. She made the young graduate sit down, and put her through the whole paper, question by question. She was then convinced that Miss Johnson knew the subject. She took the matter to the Board, the doctor reread the paper and discovered that he had overlooked three pages. Not only did the graduate pass the paper, but she also scored the highest marks in the province on the total examination.[19]

Another member of the first class, Marion (Fisher) Faris, has vivid memories of Miss Johns as a teacher: '... She was a superb teacher. I do not have any record of her lectures, nor am I able to recall their content: but I shall never forget that slight figure, frail but commanding, forceful but restrained, pulling us up by the very intensity of her personality and desire to impart the ideas and ideals that poured from her. To me, at such times, she seemed inspiration personified, and nursing became the noblest of professions ...' Mrs Faris also recalls an unhappy incident, one which revealed Miss Johns in a less favourable light:

... One of my head nurses accused me of something for which I was not to blame and reported me to Miss Johns. Once again I crossed the threshold of her office. This time, instead of a smile, she showed her sternest face, and started berating me in no uncertain terms. I took it silently at first, but the injustice of not being given a chance to tell my side of the story seized me; my anger was on the boiling point when Miss Johns evidently became aware that enough was enough and dismissed me abruptly. As I recall this episode, it brings to mind something she wrote: 'We have to admit that the masculine side of our nature sometimes makes us explosive and unreasonable as well as heroic.'[20]

But Miss Johns could be kind and thoughtful as well as stern. When Marion Fisher's mother was very ill in hospital, Miss Johns visited her. Three weeks later, Mrs Fisher died, and Miss Johns arranged for representatives of the hospital to attend the funeral. Her interest in Marion Fisher continued after her graduation, and she kept in contact with her during the year that Marion was hospitalized at Tranquille Sanatorium and when she became a public health nurse at Kamloops.

At the Congregation Exercises in May 1923, the three members of the first class received their degree, Bachelor of Applied Science (in Nursing). Miss Johns' pride can be imagined.

Memoranda in the files of the University of British Columbia reveal that evaluations of the combined course took place while the students of the first class were in their final year. One of these was written by Miss Johns, presumably as a report to the Dean. The other, in the files of the President's Office, was part of Dean Brock's annual report of the Faculty of Applied Science. Miss Johns reported that the student body in the degree programme had grown steadily, and that it now numbered thirty; of these, three were working toward the double degree of Bachelor of Arts and Science. Students who had served for any length of time in the hospital, she said, had 'upon the whole demonstrated the truth of the contention that this type of education fosters the development of initiative and capacity for leadership.' Their influence in the Training School, she added, had been remarkable:

... They have succeeded in living down a certain jealousy which certain privileges they enjoyed excited in the minds of three year students ... At the same time, they have shown with one or two exceptions complete willingness to submit themselves to hospital discipline, and to share with the other students all disabilities imposed by hospital routine. They have formed an aggressive and forward looking Undergraduate society which makes its presence felt in the deliberations of the student body of the University at large and they take part in the social activities such as the Players' Club and the Musical Society on equal terms with other students. It is altogether too early to forecast their success or failure in the professional world, but one fact is amply demonstrated: The result of this course up until the present is the development of a group of students possessing initiative and capacity for leadership. These qualities have been developed in them by a sounder and broader type of education than was possible by means of the Training School alone ...

Miss Johns added that the opposition which the course had encountered at first, because its aims were not clearly understood, was dying down. The Graduate Nurses' Association, at first aloof, had recently requested an extension of the activities of the Department of Nursing, a short course in teaching and administration. But a serious problem remained to be faced:

... The financial position of the University is most precarious. The total budget of the Department for the last year was $1400 (fourteen hundred dollars). This was the total available for the salary of the director and all administrative expenses. The plan of having the director act in a dual capacity as Director of Nursing Service in the hospital did not and could not prove satisfactory. It involved certain conflicting elements and interests that were incompatible and precluded success.

The direction of the Department involves the articulation of the academic portion of the course with the professional training and necessitates considerable time throughout and effort that cannot be afforded by a woman upon whose shoulders is laid the crushing responsibility of the active direction of nursing service in a thousand bed hospital.

The main problem then is financial in nature. Fortunately no great expenditure is at present necessary over and above the salary of the director and office expenses but these must obviously be provided for more generously than at present if the course is to continue.[21]

The Dean's report on the Department of Nursing, dated 23 May 1923, gave detailed information about the courses and by whom they were taught. During the past year, Miss Johns had received twenty-five dollars per month for teaching anatomy and physiology to third-year students in the Vancouver General Hospital. The report stated that the course was fulfilling claims made by its originators, because the students were soundly educated, academically and technically. Relationships were improving with the Hospital, the Graduate Nurses' Association, and the Medical Association. With regard to the latter, the comment was made that, 'Active open opposition has practically ceased due probably to Miss Johns not being brought into contact with medical men and second to aims and objects of the course being better understood.' Miss Johns was secretary of the Hospital Association, continued the report. The Dean stated that uncertainty had militated against the course: it was probationary, experimental. The question of its continuance was raised. Withdrawal of the course would be serious for the students, but if it could not be carried, it should be dropped now. Similar courses elsewhere had justified their existence. Dr Young had said that to discontinue would be disastrous. The possibility of reducing the combined budgets [presumably Nursing and Public Health] was problematical. Under the section, 'Report of Work, Faculty of Applied Science, Year 1922–23,' the Dean mentioned Miss Johns' participation in the Seattle convention and the short course which she conducted at the University of Saskatchewan. He also spoke of her convenership of the Nursing Education Committee of the Graduate Nurses' Association, under whose guidance a survey of conditions in the schools of nursing in the province had been made; the Committee was now engaged in a revision of the Standard Curriculum. The report noted, too, that 'At the request of the authors, Drs Bliss and Olive, Miss Johns assisted in the preparation of the new edition of their text book, "Physics and Chemistry for Nurses."'

The combined course survived the evaluation. Apparently from this time forward, there was no question of its discontinuance.

16

Ethel Johns Reports

Luminaries of Canadian nursing were present at a four-day meeting in Toronto (June 1923) of the Canadian Association of Nursing Education. Fortunately, verbatim minutes of the proceedings were taken and have been preserved in the archives of the Canadian Nurses' Association. Flora Madeline Shaw presided, and the members present included Mary Agnes Snively, Grace Fairley, Jean Gunn, Mabel Gray, Ethel Johns, E. Kathleen Russell, Mabel Hersey, and the president of the Canadian National Association of Trained Nurses, Jean Browne. The major focus of discussion was the question of amalgamation of the two national nursing organizations. But certain aspects of nursing school administration received a fair share of consideration, as did the recently published report of the Rockefeller study of nursing and nursing education in the United States. Miss Johns was in her element; her keen sense of history must have told her that history was here in the making, as indeed it was.

Miss Fairley read the report of the Joint Committee of the Canadian National Association of Trained Nurses and the Canadian Association of Nursing Education which was appointed to bring in recommendations concerning the future plans of co-operation of these two organizations.[1] Upon invitation by the chairman, Jean Browne opened the discussion and paid tribute to the record of unselfishness and devotion which had characterized the Canadian Association of Nursing Education throughout its history. But she pointed out that, under Canadian political ideals, provincial autonomy was a cardinal principle. The Association was not a dominant influence in the progress of the nursing profession simply because all developments must come through provincial effort. On the other hand, the Canadian National Association of Trained Nurses was 'just a great co-operative organization which attempts to unify the work of the provincial committees ...' An educational section was needed in the organization, she added, and a solution of the problem would be to have the C.A.N.E. become a section within the larger body.

Miss Johns led off the ensuing discussion. The question of amalgamation, she confessed, left her somewhat uncertain:

... Suppose, for a moment, we amalgamate: I should then feel constrained to speak as convenor of the British Columbia Provincial Association's Special Committee. I should express myself very differently in one case than in the other. I should feel, and rightly I contend, that I should give as far as possible, not my personal views, but those of the majority of the group with which I am associated. Now, I submit that there is something to be said for complete independence of thought on educational matters on the part of everybody. That is why I am on the fence, why I cannot bring myself as yet to the point where I can speak definitely ...

Miss Johns added that the important thing was that the group begin to function, and that if this could be achieved by amalgamation in such a way as 'to safeguard independence of opinion, especially in our younger members,' and adequate voting power for the educational group in the large association, she thought that 'we should give this question of amalgamation our most hearty support.' After further discussion, a decision was reached that – on certain terms – the Canadian Association of Nursing Education should become a section of the Canadian National Association of Trained Nurses. This became an accomplished fact one year later.

Miss Johns also contributed to the discussion of training school records. From the viewpoint of her short experience in university work, she said, 'our negligence in this matter is becoming more and more apparent. Again and again the university authorities have asked for definite information concerning students, only to be met with the reply that the superintendent had changed since the student had been there ...' Citing a personal experience, she stated that when the time came for her postgraduate work, it was necessary to obtain a detailed statement from the hospital in which she had been trained. 'I wrote them,' she said, 'and all the information I could get was that they thought I had been there' (laughter). She endorsed a point made by Miss Gunn on the value of a record of practical work carried by the student. Such a plan had been instituted at the Vancouver General Hospital: the student was responsible for keeping her own record of experience, and for drawing to the head nurse's attention the kinds of experience she needed. The system was explained to the head nurses in advance, and they were pleased to co-operate.[2]

Miss Shaw gave her report as chairman of the Text Book Committee and called upon Miss Johns for her comments on the value of reference books to supplement texts. Miss Johns endorsed the committee's statement as to the wisdom of 'forwarding a highly selected group of reference books.' She commented that the possibilities had not yet been thoroughly explored of resources which might be available through the library programmes of the various provinces. She stated that Isabel Stewart's sister had suggested that if a set of reference books [for nursing students] could be recommended, it could be sent around very much as a travelling library was in other work. 'I think if our provincial libraries had recommendations put before them, they would be very willing indeed,' said Miss Johns. She went on to speak of the question of stimulating the students' desire to read, a far more difficult thing to do, and suggested that books should be easily available – that the open shelf method should be used. The time would soon come, she added, when a better and wider selection of references would be necessary, especially from the 'psychic' point of view: 'The young nurses are intensely interested in that phase,' she pointed out. 'They, far more than we, are going to be concerned in the psychic aspect of disease.'[3]

With regard to short courses for graduate nurses, Miss Johns reported with pleasure that, a week before she had left Vancouver to come to this meeting, members of the Private Duty Committee had approached her to ask whether the University could arrange a programme for their group. They expressed a wish that the content include cultural subjects as well as those related to their work. Tentative plans for the four-day course were prepared. It would include sessions on the history and ethics of nursing, special problems which private duty nurses encountered, guidance (by the University Librarian) in a course of reading on general cultural subjects and books that would be useful to bring to the attention of patients, occupation as a curative agent (using the resources of the therapy department of the Military Hospital), the question of finances, investments, and so forth.

Miss Johns chaired the session on the Report of the Committee on Nursing Education (Rockefeller Foundation). The time originally allotted to this subject had been cut in half, therefore the chairman said that she had decided to focus discussion on certain aspects of the report

– those which, it seemed, might be controversial or which would involve elements of more or less radical change. In view of the reduction of time available for this topic, she stated that she was imposing discipline upon herself by refraining from giving the introductory remarks she had planned, giving precedence to two other speakers, 'since I know when I get mounted on my rocking-horse there is no stopping me.' She warned that the full text of the report must be read, line by line and chapter by chapter, in order to get the sense of it. In any summary, she added, 'a certain degree of the spirit of the thing is kept out.' She then called upon Miss Gunn to discuss the conclusion that the nursing course, under certain conditions, might be reduced from three years to twenty-eight months.

Miss Gunn spoke at some length. With brilliant and convincing logic, she demonstrated that the content of the present three-year course could be given in eighteen months; that if additional experiences were added which were now recognized as necessary (communicable diseases, mental nursing, tuberculosis, public health and social service), the total time required would still only be twenty-six months. She recognized the economic loss to the hospital by shortening the training period, and the increased administrative difficulty in arranging special training in all departments in a shorter period of time. The school would also be a greater expense to the hospital. But one advantage would be that the shorter course would attract more candidates with university entrance. The nursing profession, said Miss Gunn, was so bound by tradition that the idea of shortening the three-year training was a shock. Even though action might be delayed, she added, much could be done to improve the present course: 'I think our greatest fault in the past,' she admitted, 'has been thinking in terms of hospital service rather than in terms of the student nurse. If we could equalize that a little by giving more sympathetic thought to the student than we have in the past, it would be of great benefit. Then, I think, we would be in a position to watch developments that will take place in the next few years with an open mind ...'[4]

Miss Johns remarked that in the experiment with the combined course, the time of practical experience in the nurses' training had to be cut to twenty-four months. This had been one of her most serious anxieties, she said. But, although it was too early to forecast the outcomes of the experiment, she stated that she was 'most emphatically up to the present an ardent advocate of the course, providing the student enters upon her course with sufficient education and that the hospital course is carefully divided and duly proportioned. Our students on the whole have managed their senior work fairly well ...' Miss Johns added that she thought that the Rockefeller Report was right in its contention that, under special conditions as indicated, the course could be reduced to twenty-eight months.

Miss Johns then called upon Mabel Gray to speak about the conclusion of the Report that a subsidiary nursing service should be established. Miss Gray, after resigning as director of nursing of the Winnipeg General Hospital in 1919, had studied public health nursing at Symonds College in Boston, and since that time had been in charge of a project in Saskatchewan to prepare nursing housekeepers. The programme was sponsored by the Provincial Red Cross and was assisted by both the University and the Registered Nurses' Association. Miss Gray was therefore well prepared to speak upon the subject when the chairman invited her to do so.[5]

The session on the Rockefeller Report was resumed on the final morning of the convention. Miss Shaw gave a delayed paper on 'Conclusion 7,' – that superintendents, supervisors, instructors, and public health nurses should in all cases receive special additional training beyond the basic nursing course. Miss Johns then asked permission to make a 'brief statement,' obviously that which she had refrained from making at the previous session. Now she spoke of her experience to date with the combined course, frankly revealed her feelings about the project, told of the difficulties she had encountered, and voiced her hopes for the future of the degree programme in nursing. Consideration of the Rockefeller Report, with its emphasis upon the need for university schools of nursing, now opened the door for Miss Johns to plead for the support of her peers in the programme for the direction of which she was responsible. Her sense of isolation in the undertaking stood revealed.

She remarked that she had felt keenly that the nursing association in Canada did not completely support the experiment. Yet she believed it to be the keystone of the arch for the future: 'From it, we must expect in the future to be able to develop the faculties of nursing in our universities.' She spoke of the difficulties which a woman without sufficient academic preparation encountered in establishing a school of this kind: 'Those who possess degrees have been kind enough to assure me that their possession does not mean anything; I venture to disagree with them. It opens to them many doors. It is my earnest hope that from the combined course we may assemble a group that will be admitted to the faculty of the university on an equal ground, with every other faculty – medicine, arts, and so forth ...' She warned of the need for caution in launching such a course:

... Ours was started without stopping, looking or listening. Those of you who know Dr MacEachern will know that the grass has not grown under his feet to any noticeable extent. You will know he carries positions by assault, and then leaves someone else to consolidate them. I was the one who was left to do that. I wish to pay tribute to Dr MacEachern. He is one of the few medical men who has a deep and true conception of what the higher education of nurses means, and we shouldn't have had the help we received from the University of British Columbia if it hadn't been for his efforts. Nevertheless, I am free to acknowledge that if I had known what the conditions were to be I would never have undertaken what I did. However, since we undertook what we did, there were distinct assets: a very good hospital, embracing everything in its service except adequate training – and there was even that. There was also a young, western, great big striding university, without too many traditions. Those were clear gains, both of them. There was no medical school. I am going to leave to your imaginations whether that was or was not an advantage. That, then, was the situation ...

Miss Johns then paid tribute to the students who were the pioneers in the combined course:

... The next thing was to establish a student body. I felt in the beginning that the conditions were, to say the least, difficult, and I made it my business to assure every student who entered that she was undertaking a pioneer piece of work, and the chances of failure or success were pretty nearly equal, that I didn't want her to come in unless she was a good sport and willing to bear her loss if we had to withdraw. I cannot speak with deep enough feeling of those students. During the last four years they have really kept me going. When everyone else failed me the students stood by me, and someday this nursing group should remember that devotion of theirs. There will come others, as Kipling says, 'Clever chaps who followed,' but these nurses were the pioneers. I know who the pioneers were, and some day the nurses of Canada will give them their due ...

With respect to the hospital part of the course, Miss Johns commented that in the beginning there was an advantage in the fact that she herself was in charge of the nursing service and could therefore outline an extensive course for the students from the outset, and could see that they got it. But the disadvantages of this arrangement far outweighed the benefits, and she sounded a warning against undertaking such a combination of administrative and educational responsibilities as she had attempted: 'Don't do it,' she urged, 'it is absolutely impossible. I shall never forget that year. It was the worst year of my whole experience, until the breaking point had to come and there had to be a separation of the administrative and teaching duties ...' Now, she added, the relationship with the hospital was most cordial, and she paid tribute to Miss Ellis for generously making the necessary arrangements and adjustments for the degree students' clinical programme. Miss Johns enunciated a principle based on her own experience: 'The ideal thing is to have the direction of the five-year course definitely in the university, with a happy relationship and close-co-operation with the head of the training school ...' The principle which she stated was sound, but the design of the combined course as initially conceived militated against its attainment from the time that the director of the University's Department of Nursing was no longer in charge of the hospital's nursing service.

Twenty-eight students were now enrolled in the combined course, Miss Johns reported. Briefly she described the arrangement of academic and clinical aspects of the programme. She expressed satisfaction that the degree students were active participants and leaders in the Students' Council. She added that, despite 'the statement, freely made, that the degree students could not possibly be good practical nurses, a member of the first class actually carried off the prize for practical work.' As to the future, it was too soon to predict the results of the combined course: 'It is certainly no time to boast, when we are setting out on our journey. Here I may make an acknowledgment – thirty-three per cent of the class is married already. Of course, that is regrettable,' she said, amidst laughter.

Miss Johns continued her remarks by reference to the point that she had found 'sorest and hardest': that the local nursing groups did not initially support the experiment. 'Medical opposition only stimulated me to greater villainy,' she admitted, 'but that undermined me in a way I cannot describe. The reasons for that were not altogether to be laid at the door of the nursing group. They were partly due to the method in which the course had been organized, which, as I said, was hurried and without deliberation.' But there had been a complete change of feeling in the past year, as the nurses were coming to see that the Department of Nursing in the University was an excellent focusing point for courses for graduate nurses.

Miss Johns concluded her remarks by making a fervent plea for close communication among all universities in Canada which were giving instruction of any type to nurses:

... There should be close co-operation. We should be willing, and we have been willing, I know, to help each other in every possible way. In a word, stop, look, and listen. If you do not, it will in the end redound to the disadvantage of the whole movement – if the universities see the thing is weak, that we are duplicating all over the place and we don't know what we want ...

... I do not feel like asking for grudging support in this work. I don't want to part with any of my pioneer stars, but if those who come later are going to do a better piece of work, I do ask them to get behind. It is a good work ... it is, I am sure! If you only saw the results I think you would bless me.

So concluded Miss Johns, on a rather breathless and impetuous note. She had said what she had come to say. An immediate and sympathetic response came from Miss Russell. The combined course must grow: 'We must have it," she affirmed, 'to put our work on a foundation at all ...' Both the three-year and the five-year programmes of nursing education were necessary, she asserted.[6]

Miss Johns may have stopped in Winnipeg for a visit with family and friends on her way back from Toronto to Vancouver. But the vacation, if any, was necessarily brief, as she was to direct courses for graduate nurses at the summer school of the University of British Columbia.

The summer courses were well attended and successful. Seven graduates registered for a six-weeks' course in teaching, four enrolled in the two-weeks' course in administration, and thirty-three private duty nurses attended the four-day institute which they had requested.[7]

Miss Johns went to Penticton in late August for the sixth annual convention of the British Columbia Hospitals Association. In her report as secretary, she noted that three executive meetings were held during the past year, and a total of twelve hundred and fifty communications were issued from the office of the secretary. Her report included a summary of replies received to a questionnaire concerning the effect of the amended Liquor Control Act on hospital finance and administration. Dr MacEachern was present and spoke on the hospital standardization movement. He was now the president-elect of the American Hospital Association. An associate director of the American College of Surgeons, he was directing the programme of hospital standardization in which Canadian as well as American hospitals participated.[8]

In the 1923–4 session of the University, the five members of the second class in the combined course entered their final year. Four students elected the public health nursing option, and joined the six graduates enrolled in the certificate course, taking the same programme of theory and field work. One degree student chose the focus in teaching and administration. A review of this student's record shows that she took six courses with the students in public health nursing: sociology (an introductory course), mental hygiene, history of nursing, nutrition, hygiene and sanitation, and teaching of nursing principles and methods. She enrolled also in courses in the history and principles of education, educational psychology, and philosophy. One of her professors was Dr George M. Weir, who had recently been appointed to the newly created post of Professor of Education in the Department of Philosophy.[9] Surprisingly, this student also studied anatomy and physiology (under Miss Johns) in her final year, an unusually late placement for that course. Miss Johns also supervised her practice teaching and her term paper.

In the early years of the combined course, not all of the individual students' programmes conformed exactly to the arrangement indicated in the Calendar. Miss Johns made adjustments as necessary, evidently in order to facilitate recruitment of desirable applicants. A member of the third class recalls her own experience in this regard. She planned to go in training at the Vancouver General Hospital, and was interviewed by Miss Johns. When the latter found that she had had one year of university study, she enquired: 'Have you ever thought of taking the combined course?' The young woman replied that she had not, but her mother (who was present at the interview) 'thought it would be wonderful.' The daughter remarked that she was minus two subjects, Chemistry II and Zoology, but Miss Johns said that she didn't think that mattered a bit. 'You can easily take those two subjects,' exclaimed Miss Johns. As it turned out, the student found it far from easy:

... I had to beg off from ward duty to get to labs and lectures in the Fairview Building, which was across from the hospital. And then I left the hospital for a year to get my second year of University, and when I came back I was expected to take my place with my class who had had a year's experience more. So this was very difficult and I didn't get confidence until I had had my second year of training ... That was my training experience, and I am just giving it to you because – well, it typifies Miss Johns. She wouldn't think anything of doing that herself ...

The same graduate remembers her first impressions of Miss Johns: 'She was a golden-haired woman, rather a little reddish, tall and thin;

rather opaque, hooded eyes – an odd expression in the eyes. But there was a fresh vitality about her, and all through my training, I thought she was a woman of *great* courage. This is the characteristic that chiefly stays with me ...'[10]

Miss Johns travelled to Calgary in October 1923, to address the annual meeting of the Alberta Association of Registered Nurses. Her subject was 'The Rockefeller Report.' According to a press report, she spoke particularly about the recommendations in respect to cutting the time of training, the formation of a subsidiary nursing group, and the need for insurance to cover the cost of nursing service.[11]

For Ethel Johns, the spring months of 1924 were eventful. The Board of Governors re-appointed her for a further term of three years and raised her salary to twenty-eight hundred dollars.[12] At the request of the Graduate Nurses' Association, the Senate and the Board approved a four-day refresher course for practising public health nurses. On 28 April, the Board approved the recommendation of the Senate that the Departments of Nursing and Public Health be combined.

The decision to combine the departments was one which Miss Johns whole-heartedly endorsed. She admired and respected Dr Mullin, the head of the new Department of Nursing and Health. From the outset he had been a supporter of the combined course. Upon being advised by the President of the decision, Miss Johns replied to him by letter: 'I am very glad that the amalgamation of the Departments of Nursing and Public Health has been approved and shall do my best to take advantage of this broadening of scope. I also very much appreciate the action of the Board of Governors in my particular case.'[13]

At the annual meeting, in April, of the Graduate Nurses' Association of British Columbia, the president referred to the 'splendid work' done by the Nursing Education Committee in revising the Standard Curriculum. She also paid tribute to Miss Johns when she stated that the outstanding work of the past year had been the six-weeks' Institute for Nurses held during the summer session of the University, and the refresher course for private duty nurses. She drew attention to the institute for public health nurses to be held at the University from the twenty-third to the twenty-sixth of April. In recognition of Miss Johns' 'splendid work' and the weeks of extra work which she had devoted to making the institutes a success, the president proposed an honorarium of one hundred dollars, which was 'heartily endorsed.'[14] Miss Johns was re-appointed convener of the Nursing Education Committee and was named a delegate to the forthcoming convention, in Hamilton, of the Canadian National Association of Trained Nurses.

The June 1924 conventions in Hamilton of the C.N.A.T.N. and the C.A.N.E. were eventful chiefly because amalgamation was achieved at last. The Canadian Association of Nursing Education became a section of the newly named Canadian Nurses' Association. One might have expected that Miss Johns, as first vice-president, would now have succeeded to the presidency of the national organization, but Miss Browne was elected for a further two-year term. Miss Johns became one of four councillors from British Columbia on the national executive. She was also elected vice-chairman of the new Nursing Education Section of the Canadian Nurses' Association, of which Miss F.M. Shaw was chairman.

One can only speculate as to why Miss Johns at this time was not elected to one or other of the top offices in the national association for which she was clearly in line. Perhaps some contributory reasons were her strongly held convictions and sheer intensity of purpose, her forthright speech (blunt upon occasion), and her espousal of causes with which many nurses were not yet in sympathy. She had antagonized 'Private Nurse.' There may have been others, less vocal, whom she had displeased equally. Her far vision cast a bright beam down a pathway into which many may have feared to venture too quickly. They may have been apprehensive that her leadership would bring about changes too rapidly.

It should be noted that the Canadian Nurses' Association now had a national headquarters, in Winnipeg, and a permanent executive secretary, Jean Wilson. In September of 1924 Miss Randal relinquished the editorship of *The Canadian Nurse,* and this responsibility, too, was assumed by Miss Wilson.

Following the convention, Miss Johns went to New York, to attend the summer session at Teachers College, Columbia University. Miss Ruby Simpson remembers meeting her there:

... Miss Stewart and Miss Johns were always interested in anyone from the Winnipeg General Hospital. So I met Miss Johns as a friend. I remember the first thing that Miss Johns said to me was, 'Now, would you like to go and see a night court?' Wasn't that typical of her? She wanted to go and see a night court! However, she went but I didn't, I can't remember why. She said she would tell me all about it. How many people would be interested in going to see a night court of really low-grade people? This was in 1924. Miss Johns was at Teachers College that summer, taking a little of everything. She took a course with me in health education. The teacher we had – a rather immature one – was showing how to test hearing with an alarm clock. Miss Johns couldn't get over that; she didn't suffer fools gladly. She said, 'I don't know anything about public health, but I want to know: *do* you test hearing with an *alarm* clock?' Lots of people who didn't know anything about it would have paid no attention – would have sat through it – but not Miss Johns. She wanted to find out about it ...

Through Miss Johns, the head of one of the courses asked Miss Simpson to help evaluate a course she had taken. Miss Johns persuaded her to do so – she thought that students should help in this way to improve courses.[15]

A tragic event of late August was the sudden death of Dr Mullin, in the midst of the annual convention of the British Columbia Hospital Association. Miss Johns later wrote of her feelings about this grievous loss: 'He had been such a staunch friend and wise counsellor that I almost lost heart. However, the wheels had to be kept turning and arrangements were made for me to take over additional responsibility for the time being. It was at this particular juncture that I realized more keenly than ever how good it was to be able to turn to the President of the University and the Dean of Applied Science for the direction and support I so badly needed.'[16]

Early in the fall term, Miss Johns had an 'unexpected and somewhat alarming visitor.' Of this visit and its sequel Miss Johns, many years later, wrote to Dr Muriel Uprichard:

... This was a representative of the Rockefeller Foundation who explained that he had been visiting some of the well-established university schools of nursing on the Pacific coast and would like to take a look at what was going on at the U.B.C. I did my best to tell him quite frankly about what we were trying to accomplish and he was so understanding and sympathetic that I lost all awe of him and quite enjoyed the brief conference. Afterwards, it did occur to me that the Foundation might be thinking of giving a little money to the U.B.C. to help us along. But this rosy dream soon faded. Several months later, however, I found a letter from the Foundation on my desk. It appeared that the Foundation was interested in the development of Schools of Hygiene in several countries of Central Europe. The physicians directing these institutions wished to establish schools of nursing which would provide basic instruction in the principles and practice of nursing to young women who wished to enter the public health field. They had asked the Foundation to assist them by selecting and supporting a nurse who would be capable of acting in an advisory capacity in the organization of such institutions. If I cared to apply for such a position, favorable consideration to my application would be granted by the Foundation. Why I should have been chosen for such a task was (and remains) a mystery to me. All that I was told was that the Foundation felt that what I had learned at the U.B.C. and the V.G.H. might come in useful in the Balkans ...[17]

The invitation was irresistible. The Board of Governors, meeting on 27 April 1925, accepted Miss Johns' resignation, effective as at 15 September. A few days later, she received a letter from the Honorary Secretary: 'The Board of Governors of the University of British Columbia in accepting your resignation wished me to express their regret that we are to lose such a valued member of our staff. We rejoice with you, however, in the opportunity that will be yours for enlarged service and wish you continued success in the work you have undertaken to do.'

Miss Johns recommended Mabel Gray as her successor, and President Klinck went to Regina to interview her about the position. Her qualifications in public health nursing and her wide experience in both general and nursing education and in administration made her a very acceptable choice. Miss Johns later wrote: 'To the satisfaction of all, she proved to be willing to take over the direction of the entire combined course ...'[18] This was particularly fortunate since Miss MacKenzie's term of office was at an end, and she did not wish to renew it.

Mr Charles Graham paid tribute to Miss Johns in his presidential address at the 1925 annual meeting of the British Columbia Hospitals Association. She was not present, as she had already left the province. The president said: 'I must express our very great regret at the departure of Miss Johns for new fields. I think I can say without fear of contradiction that Miss Johns was the greatest asset that the Hospital Association had. She filled the office of Secretary for several years in an exceptional manner, always giving her best to the Association. I am sure that I voice the sentiments of the members in expressing deep appreciation of her work and that our very best wishes go with her in her new field of endeavor ...'[19]

Prior to her departure, Miss Johns was honoured by the Graduate Nurses' Association of British Columbia at a reception, and was presented with a gift. But it is safe to say that she was most deeply moved by a gift from her students. During the time that she was a full-time member of faculty, relationships with her students were close and happy. It is said that they held her in affection. In the grey leather correspondence case which they presented to her, and which she cherished all her life, there was a small silver plaque on which these words were engraved: 'Miss E. Johns, from your girls at U.B.C., July, 1925.'

PART FIVE: 1925–1932

PART FIVE

17

Service under the Rockefeller Foundation

Miss Johns' first assignment for the Rockefeller Foundation was carried out before she left the University of British Columbia. Late in May, and again in June, 1925, she made exploratory visits concerning nursing education to Stanford University Medical School. On both of these occasions, she visited her mother and brother in Venice, California. On the twelfth of August 1925 her appointment was confirmed in a letter from Dr Edwin R. Embree, Director of the Division of Studies of the Foundation. She was to serve as a 'Special Member of the Field Staff in Nursing Education' for a term of one year.

Miss Johns had already left the University when Miss Gray arrived to take up her new duties. It is thought that she stopped off in Winnipeg to visit Cora Hind and to see members of her family, before leaving for the United States and Europe. Owen and his wife had two children at that time, Gertrude and Helen, aged twelve and eight respectively.[1]

Helen (Johns) Franklin, to whom Aunt Ethel was 'a Rock of Gibraltar,' remembers the contacts which she arranged for her young nieces in her absence, in order to give them cultural advantages of which they would otherwise have been deprived. Cora Hind took a particular interest in the children. She invited them to dinner regularly each month, had the table set correctly, and instructed them in the social graces. She talked with them about reading, and impressed upon them the importance of the editorial page in the newspapers. At the same time, she cautioned them that editors are human, and that their writings should not be taken 'as the Bible.' Also through Aunt Ethel's arrangement, her nieces visited Judge Paget and 'other learned people.'[2]

When Miss Johns reported to Rockefeller headquarters in New York, she was surprised to learn that she was not to leave immediately for Europe. Dr Embree was impressed by her ability when he interviewed her in Vancouver, and he had arranged to borrow her services from the Division of Medical Education. She was requested to make a study of the status of the Negro woman in nursing in the United States.

Miss Johns spent the fall months of 1925 in this work. Within a period of forty-seven days, she made field visits to sixteen cities and to schools of nursing in twenty-three hospitals. Her itinerary included New York, Chicago, Kansas City, St Louis, Philadelphia, Baltimore, Washington, Hampton, Richmond, Raleigh, Atlanta, Montgomery, Tuskegee, Birmingham, Nashville, and Louisville. She was entranced by her first visit to the south: '... I had never visited the south before and the landscape enchanted me – the red soil, the winding rivers, the giant live oaks, the Spanish moss, the fields of cotton and sugar cane. More, even, than the landscape, the people delighted me: their soft voices, their irresistible charm ...'[3] To write the report of her survey was a task of major proportions, but she completed it before the year's end.[4]

Brief as it was, the period in New York afforded some opportunity to see old friends. Isabel Stewart had now succeeded Adelaide Nutting as director of the Division of Nursing Education at Teachers College. Helen Stewart was just embarking on her doctoral studies at Columbia University. Elizabeth Stewart was married to Charles Sharp, and they lived close to New York. Dr Helen Stewart recalled that they saw 'quite a bit' of Miss Johns at this time, and that 'it was very pleasant for all concerned.'[5]

Miss Johns arrived in Paris on 4 January 1926. An upper respiratory infection contracted on board ship had worsened during her brief stopover in England, and she was wretchedly ill when she finally reached her destination. She found it frustrating to have to spend her first two weeks in Paris confined to bed. Hazel Goff, a nurse colleague of Miss Johns in Europe, recalls that Ethel declined to stay at the 'nice clean little hotel' where she herself lived. Miss Johns said that the ticking of the electric clock on the bedroom wall would disturb her. But she had another reason for her decision: she was anxious to acquire an understanding of the French culture and a working knowledge of the language. She found lodgings which suited her purpose admirably, an attic room in a French residential club on the rue de Bellechasse, in the Bohemian quarter of Paris. Not only was Miss Johns physically ill upon arrival; she was so homesick that she dared not even look at the sailing lists in the office of the American Express. Painful as it was, this experience was to prove of value to her later, in dealing with Rockefeller fellows from various countries.

In spite of her initial difficulties, Miss Johns quickly grew to love Paris. She delighted in the pageant of the city. As she accompanied the French visiting nurses on their rounds, she observed the people and their way of life. Morning and evening, when the weather was fine, she walked to and from the office, across the Place de la Concorde and the bridge to the Left Bank. She went to the opera and the Comédie Française, and savoured the French food and wine. She found the French language musical, and enjoyed the lessons with her tutor.[6] She was an adept student of the language and quickly acquired facility in French conversation.

Miss Johns, like other field workers, required a fairly intensive orientation before she could be assigned to any of the nursing projects with which the Rockefeller Foundation was giving assistance in Europe. The situation was complex. World War I had left devastation in its wake and the task of reconstruction was immense. The Treaty of Versailles had rearranged the map of Europe, creating new states and changing the boundaries of others, taking territories from the vanquished and giving them to the victorious allies. Now, eight years later, an uneasy peace lay over Europe, but political and inter-racial tensions were widespread. Not only did the staff members of the Division of Medical Education require an understanding of these factors, but they needed also an appreciation of the philosophy, goals, and limitations of the Foundation in respect to projects undertaken in support of medical and nursing education.

In Europe, as in other parts of the world, the Rockefeller Foundation was concerned primarily with programmes of public health and preventive medicine. As a means toward this end, the Foundation (in cooperation with the governments concerned) sought to support projects of medical education and research in university schools of high calibre. The philosophy and objectives underlying its programme were set forth as follows in the *Annual Report* of the Rockefeller Foundation for the year 1926:

... It is within this general field of medical research and teaching, training of health personnel, and organization of health services that the Rockefeller Foundation finds its chief opportunities to lend a hand. It deals almost exclusively with universities or with government agencies, local, state, or national, and with these only upon their invitation. The constant aim is to stimulate progress, to encourage experiment, to demonstrate new methods, to increase efficiency.

It takes no interest in merely quantitative expansion. Nor does it assume more than a part of the cost of a new experiment or demonstration. It wants to be a partner, not a patron ... The Foundation succeeds best when it can withdraw completely from a health project which continues, as it began, under official auspices and is supported wholly by public funds ...[7]

The Rockefeller Foundation recognized the need for well-prepared nurses as well as doctors in the field of public health. This concern had motivated the study of nursing and nursing education which the Foundation had sponsored in the United States. The nursing programme carried on in Europe during Miss Johns' period of service appears to have been based – in a general way – on the conclusions of that study, but it was adapted to the particular needs and situation of each country and institution.

Within the Division of Medical Education, F. Elisabeth Crowell was in charge of the European nursing programme. Her official title was Director for Europe, Education for Nurses and Public Health Visitors. Her appointment to this post followed a period of brilliant service under the Rockefeller's Commission on Tuberculosis (1917–22) in France.[8] She brought a high level of ability to her new work. In 1924, she decided to add two associates to her staff to assist in field work, one of whom would have special competence in nursing education, the other in public health nursing. Both nurses should be able, if necessary, to deal with problems in both fields.[9] These staff members were known as field directors, and their numbers were soon increased to four. Miss Crowell assigned them to various countries and projects as the need arose, and recalled them when she deemed this advisable.

Hazel Goff and Ethel Johns had their major assignments in the field of nursing education, which made for a bond of common interest when they happened to be in Paris at the same time. Miss Goff remembers Miss Johns as 'prim and proper, a nurse of the old school, with high ideals and standards of nursing. She was direct and had a keen sense of humour. She was a fine co-worker.'[10]

Miss Johns' relationship with Miss Crowell was not entirely happy. The latter's preparation and experience were in the field of public health nursing, and Miss Johns apparently felt that the Director gave preference to public health nursing aspects of the programme.

A few months after her arrival in Paris, Miss Johns made visits to

England and Scotland for the purpose of assessing the opportunities for fieldwork for foreign students (nurses from various countries who were recipients of Rockefeller fellowships). She was delighted to receive this assignment, but when she mentioned the 'joyful prospect' to an American member of the Foundation's staff, he cautioned her not to count on enjoying the experience very much. She reminded him that she had been brought up in England and that she spoke the same language. 'That's just the trouble,' he replied, 'you think you do but you don't. All you share is a common tongue. You don't really understand what is in their minds. They don't show it because you are really not one of them. I'm an American but I know how hard it is for a Canadian to break through. Go easy and don't take anything for granted.'[11]

Miss Johns soon found that her associate's admonitions were soundly based:

... Although this good advice did not sink in at the time, it came home to me rather forcibly before I had spent many days in my native land. In breezy Canadian style, I began by making telephone calls asking for appointments with various directors of nursing services, and was politely told that Matron would be consulted and would call me in a day or two. Nothing happened and I got a little desperate, and tried a more formal approach by letter. This worked better, but as my routine report to the Paris office dolefully admitted, in England no one seemed to be able to see you earlier than a week next Tuesday and they weren't particularly anxious to see you even then. My American mentor must have smiled grimly when he read that report.

At last the barrier was lifted and I was invited to visit the various training schools where from time to time nursing fellows had been admitted for special fieldwork. It had already dawned upon me that the English did not take kindly to foreigners and it was surprising to learn that the Foundation fellows were rather a problem. *Language* was of course the primary difficulty. The head nurses were naturally unwilling to trust the fellows with anything but the most elementary nursing procedures for fear that orders would not be clearly understood and serious mistakes might ensue. This led to boredom on the part of the fellows since some of them had been accustomed to performing more advanced procedures than were ever entrusted to English nurses ...

Other problems which foreign nurses encountered, Miss Johns discovered, were having meals at times to which they were not accustomed, the English climate, and unheated quarters. Night duty was particularly hard on them, but 'slowly they began to see why they had been sent to observe its excellence.'[12]

Miss Johns' orientation to the field was rounded out by a trip with another staff member through central Europe. She was now giving thought to the question of accepting a permanent appointment under the Rockefeller Foundation, but was not entirely convinced of her own suitability for the work. She missed the definiteness of institutional work, and wondered whether she would be able to succeed with the use of indirect methods. She was also concerned about her mother. She decided to remain in Europe, but only after much thought.

In mid-year of 1927, Miss Johns had her first assignment to Roumania, a country which she grew to love and which she was to visit several times while she was in the service of the Foundation. She later wrote an article for *The Canadian Nurse* in which she vividly portrayed the countryside and the people, and described the rural health centres developed by the Department of Health of Roumania.[13]

Miss Johns made initial visits to Bulgaria and Turkey following her assignment in Roumania. In June 1927 Miss Crowell asked her to take over the responsibility for all nursing fellows in Europe, an assignment which she was to find both challenging and enjoyable. The work involved giving assistance in the selection of candidates for fellowships, acting as adviser to nurses having fellowship programmes in Europe, and being available for consultation (as required) when they returned to their positions.

Miss Johns also gave assistance with specific projects in both Lyon and Brussels, the nature of which has been described as follows by the President of the Rockefeller Foundation:

... The Foundation at that time had a substantial program in the development of medical education in a few European universities, including the University of Lyon and the Free University of Brussels. An integral part of that program was the parallel development of nursing education, with the aim of establishing university nursing schools. Under this program, Miss Johns worked closely with nursing and medical educators in Lyon in the establishment and operation of a health center used as a teaching unit, as well as in nursing education generally. The medal from the Civic Hospitals of Lyon is undoubtedly in recognition of her services there. In Brussels, it was originally planned that the Edith Cavell School of Nursing would become the university school. This plan was not realized, due primarily to local reasons, but the Foundation continued its interest in the Edith Cavell School, where Miss Johns was closely associated with the development of teaching programs. In addition, she spent considerable time and effort in the successful development of university-connected nursing schools at Debrecen, Hungary, and Cluj, Roumania.[14]

The *Annual Report* of the Rockefeller Foundation for the year 1927 gives a picture of the broad programme in which Miss Johns was involved. In that year, preliminary surveys of nursing education were carried out in Germany, Czechoslovakia, Bulgaria, and Turkey. Visits were made in connection with current programmes and supervision of fellows in nursing, in Poland, Hungary, Yugoslavia, France, England, Belgium, and Austria. The Foundation invited eleven leaders of nursing education to make study visits under its auspices; these included Florence Emory, assistant director of the Department of Public Health Nursing at the University of Toronto, who visited nursing centres in Europe.[15]

The same report noted that fellowships granted by the Foundation were awarded 'primarily to train leaders and teachers for supervisory and administrative positions in connection with projects to which assistance has already been given in the form of either advisory services or financial aid contingent upon a plan of development ...' Forty-one such fellowships were granted during 1927, of which twenty-eight were awarded to nurses from various European countries.[16]

At the end of September 1927 Miss Johns was assigned to Hungary, for the purpose of assisting with the reorganization of the school of nursing at Debrecen. The project was an important one, since it was hoped that the programme in nursing education to be developed with Miss Johns' help would be a pattern for other schools of nursing in the country. Dr B. Johan, head of the State Hygienic Institute of Hungary, and Dr Csiky, Dean of Medicine at the University of Debrecen, conferred with Miss Crowell before Miss Johns' arrival. Little information is available about the period before or after she completed her task, but Hazel Goff visited the School for Bedside and Public Health Nurses in Debrecen a few years later, while making a survey for the Health Section of the League of Nations. In her report, Miss Goff noted that the school had been founded in 1922 by the Dean of the Faculty of Medicine, in the University of Debrecen; that it was now (1932–3) an integral part of the University Hospital of Debrecen, housed in one of the hospital buildings in a beautiful park, and that it gave a two year, six month course in which much stress was placed on public health and preventive aspects of nursing.[17]

In her old age, Miss Johns was to look back to this time in Hungary as one of the happiest periods of her life. Late in life she began to record the memories of her experiences there, but ill health made it impossible to complete the task.

From Hungary, Miss Johns went on to Roumania, where she visited Cluj. Before returning to Paris, she travelled to Bucharest, in accordance with instructions received from the head office. There, much to her surprise, she received a letter by special messenger, requesting her to present herself at the Palace: the Princess Helene would like to hear her impressions of the nursing school at Cluj. Arriving at the appointed time, she was escorted up a red-carpeted staircase into 'a drawing-room gay with chintz-covered furniture and bowls of flowers.' Her later account of the visit was as follows:

... The Princess rose and came forward and in a few minutes I felt less shy and awkward and ready to answer the questions she put to me. As a girl, she had gone to school in England, and it was easy to see that the English way of life still appealed to her. While I was describing the progress being made in the Cluj University School of Nursing, there was a commotion at the door and her little son, King Michael, appeared carrying a tray covered with little animals which he had modelled in plasticine. This he set down on a table for inspection and then gravely advanced to shake hands, before he was led away by his English nanny.

The prescribed half-hour had slipped by and I began uneasily to wonder whether I had missed the cue for my departure. Apparently I hadn't, for Princess Helene still wanted to know more about the possible opportunities for obtaining travelling scholarships for Roumanian nurses. When assured that her request would be submitted to the authorities at the Paris office, it was clear that the interview had come to an end. As I reached the door, I turned to make my bow. She was standing beside a table looking down at a bowl of flowers; the slight figure in the beautifully cut, simple dress was a model of elegance, her only ornament a necklace of pearls ...[18]

In September 1929 Ethel Johns' 'European adventure' ended. Her decision to leave Europe was based upon several factors. The programme of the Rockefeller Foundation was now entering upon a new phase in which the type of work she had been doing would no longer be necessary. Also, she feared becoming so fascinated by the European way of life that she would be unable to adjust to conditions in her own country. There was also the possibility that a piece of work which greatly appealed to her might soon become available.

Before leaving Europe, Miss Johns was given the opportunity of visiting the various projects with which she had been associated, in order to assess achievements and failures:

... Most of the time had been spent in Hungary and it was there that my roots had gone the deepest. Things were going well in Debrecen, and in Budapest a good start had been made in organizing a national public health service. A few Hungarian friends wanted to give me a farewell party and I felt as though I couldn't face up to it. One of the more discerning said to the others, 'Perhaps she would rather cry with the gypsies.'

As frequently happened, it was necessary to come to Budapest for a few days. When I came to Budapest to report, I avoided the garish tourist hotels and stayed at The Hunting Horn, a comfortable place built round a small open patio where there was good Hungarian food and an excellent small Zgigane gypsy orchestra. I got to know the head waiter, and nearly always I was given a little table in the corner, where I could enjoy the music. It used to be considered quite natural, in Hungary, if your spirits were low, to seek a retreat of this kind and to shed a quiet tear or two. Nobody noticed you or intruded. And that is the way I said goodbye to Hungary ...[19]

Hazel Goff remembers that when Miss Johns was leaving Paris, she accompanied her to the station: 'It was a gray, rainy, morning, which I deplored and commented that it was most unfortunate. EJ replied, "Oh, don't feel that way, I love it, to me Paris is so friendly in the rain! You see the skies are crying with me today that I must leave it all!"'[20] And so the European adventure came to an end, and she returned to New York, where an interesting new project awaited her direction.

18

New York Hospital – Cornell Medical College Association Project

Immediately upon her return to New York from Europe, Ethel Johns was appointed Director of Studies for the Committee on Nursing Organization of the New York Hospital–Cornell Medical College Association Project. The position was one for which she was well prepared by virtue of her broad experience, her intellect, judgment, and organizational ability. The magnitude and philosophy of the project kindled her imagination and challenged her with their potentialities for a high quality of nursing service and education. The conditions of employment were favourable: she had an office, a competent secretary, a good salary, and – most important – stimulating and congenial relationships with members of the Committee and other people with whom the work brought her in contact.

The project to develop a medical centre was under the direction of two venerable institutions of which the association was formed in 1927: the New York Hospital whose history went back to the 1771 Charter granted by King George III, and the Cornell University Medical College, which had been established in 1898. Plans for the medical centre comprised a main twenty-seven storey hospital and three special hospitals (pediatric, obstetric, and psychiatric), to provide a total of approximately one thousand beds, plus medical social service and out-patient facilities; a medical college; and an educational unit for the School of Nursing, together with a nurses' residence to accommodate five hundred nurses. The chief executive officer of the project was Dr G. Canby Robinson, dean of the Cornell Medical College and director of the association.[1]

A matter of concern in planning for the medical centre was the organization of the nursing service and the School of Nursing within the complex. The new director of nursing had not yet been appointed when construction began in 1929, nor was she to be named until more than two years later. Dr Robinson recognized the need for expert nursing guidance in the interim, and in April 1929 he requested that a Committee on Nursing Organization be formed. He invited Mary Beard to chair the Committee, and authorized her to select its members, with the sole proviso that they be graduates of the New York Hospital School of Nursing. Miss Beard was president of the Alumnae Association, and from this point of view as well as that of her personal and professional qualifications, the choice was a fortunate one. The regular and honorary members of the Committee, and the honorary advisers who were to be consulted as the need arose, included many whose contributions in the nursing field were outstanding.

Of the composition and calibre of the Committee on Nursing Organization, Miss Johns later commented: 'Not only was it truly representative of the New York Hospital School of Nursing, one of the oldest and most distinguished in America, but its membership included women whose professional background and experience is such as to command the confidence and respect not only of the authorities of the project, but of the nursing world at large. It is not surprising that the recommendations of such a group were characterized by a breadth and sanity which stamped them as worthy of sympathetic consideration.'[2]

One of Miss Johns' first tasks was to assist the Committee in formulating goals and drafting a programme for its activities. Six objectives were outlined as terms of reference for the Committee, and these were subsequently approved by Dr Canby Robinson:

1 To formulate sound guiding principles upon which the organization and administration of nursing service in the new hospital can be based.
2 To outline suggestions for a comprehensive educational program which will be in accord with the best modern thinking and which will meet the needs of graduate and pupil nurses, medical students, and all auxiliary workers.
3 To recommend such cooperation with related activities as will afford full opportunity for basic instruction in the principles of public health.
4 To give such advice and assistance in planning for the School of Nursing buildings as will ensure dignified and comfortable living conditions as well as adequate and suitable educational facilities.
5 To supply such information to the proper authorities as will assist them in

formulating a financial policy which will provide for meeting the actual costs of nursing service as well as the special requirements of the School of Nursing.

6 To foresee and to plan to adjust the special difficulties likely to be encountered during a period of rapid expansion from a relatively simple to a highly complex nursing service.[3]

With respect to the third objective, the Committee requested the National Organization of Public Health Nursing to undertake a study of ways in which health and preventive aspects could be integrated into the basic nursing curriculum, with the use of facilities within the hospital and in the local community. The report of this detailed study was later included in one of the publications of the Rockefeller Foundation.[4]

In relation to planning for the nurses' residence, Alice Shepard Gilman was asked to serve as consultant to the Director of Studies. Of this arrangement, Miss Johns later reminisced: 'We had never worked together before, and mutual friends expressed doubts as to whether two rather positive individuals would get along with one another. This rumour had reached both of us and at our first interview I said to her: "They say we won't last six weeks." She looked me straight in the eye and said: "Let's show them." And we did. We lasted until the job was over.'[5]

An examination of records in the files of the New York Hospital reveals the variety of tasks which Miss Johns undertook as Director of Studies. She prepared agendas and reports for meetings of the Committee and wrote the minutes. She co-ordinated the various aspects of the work, and served as liaison between the nursing group and Dr Robinson, his administrative assistant, and the architects. Upon request, she reviewed blueprints for the hospital building, and made suggestions to the architects from the point of view of nursing service. She worked closely with Alice Gilman and the architects in relation to the plans for the residence and school. She systematically collected materials and sought advice from administrative officials of local hospitals regarding nursing costs. At the request of Dr Robinson, she prepared a preliminary report summarizing this source material and suggesting how it might be used as a guide in making rough estimates of staffing and costs. When he had approved this as a 'sufficiently valid' basis on which to proceed, she prepared a detailed, thirty-six-page forecast of staffing and costs for the nursing service, encompassing: a summary of the various services in the new project; a 'rough estimate' of the numbers and types of nurses required, based on ratios determined in the preliminary report; the cost of nursing education as distinct from nursing service; the comparative value to the hospital of graduate and student service, and of various types of nursing personnel; and a summary and tentative budget. In making estimates of personnel requirements for the medical centre, Miss Johns refrained from advancing recommendations in this regard. She maintained that the new director of nursing, when appointed, should have the right and responsibility to do so. This piece of work by Miss Johns is surprising, in that it antedated by almost a decade the classic treatise by Pfefferkorn and Rovetta on cost analysis of nursing service and nursing education.[6] Even more astonishing, in view of her admitted difficulty with arithmetic, was the mathematical skill evidenced by her report. By now, it appeared, she had succeeded in mastering the intricacies of addition, multiplication, and division.

Dr Robinson requested Miss Johns also to make a preliminary inquiry as to the possibility of linking up the School of Nursing with Cornell University, and to ask the opinion of the Committee as to the basis on which this might be achieved. Reporting this matter to the Committee at a meeting held on 5 May 1930, Miss Johns was advised to seek the advice of Annie W. Goodrich, Dean of the Yale University School of Nursing and an honorary member of the Committee. The question received a good deal of consideration from the Committee on Nursing Organization during the months that followed.

Even in the early months following her return to the United States, Ethel Johns' thoughts turned toward Canada. She was aware that a survey of nursing and nursing education in Canada had recently been initiated under the joint auspices of the Canadian Medical Association and the Canadian Nurses' Association and the direction of Dr George M. Weir, Professor of Education at the University of British Columbia. This significant event prompted Miss Johns to write an article, 'Canada Looks at the Neighbours,' for *The Canadian Nurse*. Her job during the past five years had brought her into contact with nurses and nursing in many countries, and she had found that 'a questioning spirit is abroad, and a desire to know what nursing is and where it is going.' She emphasized the need for a survey to be 'a co-operative undertaking in which the surveyed play a part quite as important as the surveyors,' and she expressed the hope that 'in Canada as in other countries an intelligent, unprejudiced study of nursing service may not only lay a sound foundation for future policy, but, even in its early stages, pave the way for reforms which are its ultimate goal.'[7]

In June 1930 Miss Johns attended the four-day biennial meeting, in Regina, of the Canadian Nurses' Association, where she gave addresses at general sessions and spoke at a luncheon. To her the focal point of interest was the interim report of the Survey given by its director, Dr Weir: '... It was abundantly clear that Dr Weir commands the respect and confidence of Canadian nurses and that their professional and personal interests are safe in his hands. He did not hesitate to put his finger boldly on several sore spots, but his kindly and searching diagnosis was accepted in the spirit in which he made it, and will go far toward preparing the way for better things.'[8] Miss Johns' address at the evening session on 25 June, entitled 'A Sense of Values,' served as a graceful prelude to Dr Weir's detailed, scholarly paper, 'Fact, Fiction and Opinion Regarding Nursing Education.'[9]

In another address, 'A Study in Contrasts,' which she delivered at a joint meeting of the three sections (private duty, public health, and nursing education), Miss Johns drew a perceptive sketch of the differences she had noted in the ideals underlying nursing practice which were cherished by nurses of various countries. She concluded with a plea for ties of sisterhood among the nurses of the world:

... In spite of its diversities and its contrasts, or perhaps because of them, the practice of nursing constitutes a great international bond. Such ties are not altogether broken even in time of war. It is to be hoped that we shall continue to hold fast to our sisters in other lands so that we may preserve our common heritage. I cannot do better than to close with another quotation from one of the Fellows, from a Balkan country where frontiers were frontiers and hard to get by: 'When I did leave my country in order to study, I did think that the frontiers were very high. Now that I have worked and learned in countries which were our enemies, I am thinking that no frontier is so high or any language so strange that nurses cannot meet and speak together.'[10]

The third occasion upon which Miss Johns spoke at the biennial meeting was a luncheon given by the Regina and District Association. No trace of her speech has been found, but Ruby Simpson remembers that 'Miss Johns was very funny. If you had known her in her prime – she could be so funny, and not a smile on her face! Those doctors were almost rolling in the aisles – she certainly was merciless with them. They were highly amused.'[11] Referring to this luncheon, Miss Johns only commented: 'There is possibly no country in the world where medical men and nurses have developed such a happy and dignified professional relationship as that which exists in Canada. The spirit of comradeship which prevailed at this luncheon is typical of it. It is a precious possession which Canadian nurses will do well to foster during the difficult adjustments which must be made sooner or later in order to meet changing conditions ...'¹²

A number of important decisions were reached at this convention. Following Jean Gunn's presentation of the Report of the Joint Study Committee (Canadian Medical Association and Canadian Nurses' Association) for the survey of nursing education, it was agreed that the Canadian Nurses' Association should pledge itself to finance the study to completion. Another far-reaching step – one that concerned *The Canadian Nurse* – was the approval by the delegates of a recommendation, 'that the permanent policy should be the employment of a full-time Editor and that the Executive Committee be empowered to take action in the matter when it is deemed advisable.' A decision was also made that membership in the Canadian Nurses' Association should be through membership in the provincial registered nurses' associations. Expressing concern about the current widespread unemployment of nurses, the convention passed the following resolution:

... That the Nursing Education Section ... be asked to send a recommendation to all hospitals in Canada conducting schools for nurses, asking Boards of these hospitals to seriously consider the question of the supply and demand for graduate nurses within the boundaries of Canada before increasing the number of student nurses to meet the additional nursing needs of the hospital, and that the policy of the employment of graduate nurses to meet these demands be adopted until such time as the unemployment conditions have been readjusted ...[13]

Miss Florence Emory was elected president of the Canadian Nurses' Association, an office she was to hold with distinction for two terms, four critical years in the history of Canadian nursing.

Miss Emory wrote to Miss Johns on 2 October 1930 in regard to the editorship of *The Canadian Nurse*. The time that must elapse before such an appointment could be made, she said, would depend upon 'the length of time necessary to ensure a stabilized income under the new plan of organization, namely membership through the nine provincial associations.' Nevertheless, the Executive had asked the president to write to Miss Johns, requesting her to advise them in advance of her accepting any new post. Miss Johns replied on 6 October, stating that while her present commitment was of uncertain duration, she did not feel at liberty to accept any other engagement; but that she would communicate with the Canadian Nurses' Association should the necessity arise of her making any decision about her own future. She added 'The Editorship of *The Canadian Nurse* is a piece of work which I should very much like to undertake and I am honored that Canadian nurses should think me capable of doing it.'[14]

On 19 November Miss Johns came up from New York to address the Registered Nurses' Association of Ontario (District Five) in Toronto on the problem of the apparent over-production of nurses at a time of economic maladjustment, one which seemed to be as prevalent in Canada as in the United States. A claim was being made by some that the root of the trouble was not over-production of nurses but rather faulty distribution: '... Influential members of the public claim that if hospitals, public health agencies, and nursing organizations would get together and present their case, and show a willingness to make a few experiments, the economic situation would improve and the unemployment problem be alleviated ...' The speaker recognized the need for specialization of function in nursing, but raised the question as to whether the problem of making changes in both the system of nursing education and business methods should be tackled separately by groups of nurses in public health, private duty, and hospital fields, or whether they should all get together and seek a common ground. She referred to the occasion when, 'in the innocence of her heart,' she offered advice in public to private duty nurses: 'To say that I was properly chastened for my temerity is to put it mildly. You have only to consult the back numbers of *The Canadian Nurse* to see what happened to me. But even that didn't make me stop ...' Miss Johns went on to suggest that professional unity in the face of specialization of function could be obtained only by seeking common ground from the beginning, by developing an educational system in which the students would have not only a foundation of bedside nursing in hospital, but also an introduction to the fields of public health nursing and private duty. 'No branch of nursing is so firmly established,' she asserted, 'that it can be independent of all the others.' Much remained to be done before nursing could really claim to be a profession:

... Listen to what Dr Weir has to say about the quality of our teaching in schools of nursing. If you have courage, read his grisly comparative table, which puts the nursing group at the bottom of the list as far as intelligence tests are concerned. Better get together and do something about all that. No one group can do it by themselves. Those of you who know England will remember the open fields one finds even in London, which are spoken of as the Common. They are not parks, they are not gardens. They are a sort of wild land, open to the sky. Places where people have a common right to seek the sun and the air; ground which, because it is shared by all alike, becomes in some mysterious way not common but holy ground.[15]

At a meeting of the Committee on Nursing Organization held on 17 October the main item of business was a discussion of 'the general situation with respect to nursing organization on a permanent basis,' an analysis of which had been prepared by Miss Johns upon the request of Miss Beard. Miss Johns' concise minutes of this meeting do not indicate the content of the analysis or details of the discussion, but note that the members went on record as heartily approving the eventual reorganization, on a university basis, of the School of Nursing of the New York Hospital. While recognizing that a policy of separate administrative controls of nursing service and education might be deemed advisable at a later time, the Committee concluded that for the present it would be 'desirable to concentrate authority in the hands of one director, who shall be responsible for the carrying out of the educational program as well as the immediate direction of the nursing service.' The director should be appointed as soon as possible.

The early months of 1931 saw the Committee of Nursing Organization beginning to bring its various tasks to completion. One of the most important of these was the consideration of possible candidates for the position of director of nursing. The Committee recommended Anna D. Wolf for this complex post, a nomination which was accepted with pleasure by the administrative authorities of the New York Hospital–Cornell Medical College Association.

The Committee met on 5 June to deal with unfinished business preparatory to its dissolution. Miss Johns was to remain for several months longer for the purpose of providing continuity and acquainting Miss Wolf with the work that had been accomplished during the two-year period. Miss Johns took her leave of the group with whom she had been associated by reading a letter which she had addressed to Miss Beard, in which she said, in part:

... As this will probably be the last opportunity I shall have of appearing before the Committee on Nursing Organization of the New York Hospital, I should like ... to express my deep sense of appreciation of the unfailing support, the understanding, the patience and courtesy which have made my task of the past two years one of the most interesting and happiest of my professional career.

Perhaps better than anyone else I am in a position to evaluate at its true worth the contribution made by the Committee, not only to nursing organization in the new project, but to nursing progress in the broad sense. A quality of vision, of steadfastness, of unselfishness, has been displayed by its Chairman and by her Associates which is rare indeed and of which every New York Hospital nurse has reason to be proud ...

It has been an honour and a privilege to be allowed to do what I could to express and to interpret the thinking of this Committee, because, while doing so, I was myself touched by the fine tradition which, for so many years, has inspired the nurses of the New York Hospital. If I could think that my own share of the work has been worthy of that tradition, I should be proud indeed.[16]

It appears that Ethel Johns' contribution was adjudged worthy. In later years, the Cornell University–New York Hospital School of Nursing was to give evidence of its recognition that this Canadian nurse had played a significant part in its history.

At the end of September 1931 Ethel Johns again travelled to Toronto, this time to participate in the convention of the American Hospital Association. She gave the major paper in a symposium that was part of the programme for the Nursing Section on the first of October. Her topic was one about which she was enthusiastic: 'Preparing for Nursing Service and Education in the New York Hospital–Cornell Medical College Association Project: An Experiment in Cooperative Planning.' Three other speakers made commentaries about Miss Johns' paper from different points of view: Jean Gunn from that of a nursing service administrator, E. Muriel Anscombe from that of a hospital superintendent, and Elizabeth Smellie from the viewpoint of a public health organization.[17]

While in Toronto, Miss Johns had a pre-arranged meeting with Miss Emory, to talk informally about the likelihood of an appointment being made to the editorship of *The Canadian Nurse*. The president was unable to make a definite proposal at that time.

Early in November Miss Johns completed her work as Director of Studies for the New York Hospital–Cornell Medical College Association Project. Almost immediately, she was invited to assist in preparing the final report of the Committee on the Grading of Nursing Schools. Before the end of November she accepted this offer and was appointed nurse associate to the director, May Ayres Burgess. The initial term of her appointment was six months, but this was extended, and throughout 1932 she was attached to the staff of the Committee's headquarters in New York City.

The Committee on the Grading of Nursing Schools, established in 1926, comprised representatives of the national nursing, medical, public health, and hospital organizations in the United States, together with members drawn from the lay public and the fields of general practice and general education. The stated function of the Committee was 'The study of ways and means for insuring an ample supply of nursing service, of whatever type and quality is needed for adequate care of the patient, at a price within his reach.'[18] The Committee recognized that the quality of undergraduate nursing education was a critical factor in provision of effective nursing services, and therefore concentrated its major efforts in that area. Grading of nursing schools, it was expected, would improve the standards of nursing education. Studies carried out under the auspices of the Committee included one on nursing economics, two gradings of nursing schools, and finally an activity analysis of nursing. Miss Johns was involved in the latter study, in collaboration with Blanche Pfefferkorn, Director of Studies of the National League of Nursing Education.

The rationale underlying the activity analysis of nursing was to provide information for a functional approach to curriculum construction in nursing education. It sought to answer two basic questions: what is good nursing and how should it be taught?[19] In this study, Miss Johns and Miss Pfefferkorn received the direction and guidance of a subcommittee composed of Professor W.W. Charters, a distinguished authority and pioneer in activity analysis studies, Dr William Darrach, Chairman of the Committee on the Grading of Nursing Schools, Elizabeth G. Burgess, and Katherine Tucker. Isabel Stewart had done some work previously on an analysis of nursing activities, and she made this material available. The published report of the study by Johns and Pfefferkorn naturally gave no indication of the authorship of its various sections, but the first chapter, 'What Is Good Nursing?' was attributed to Miss Johns when it was incorporated into the final report of the Grading Committee.[20]

The biennial meeting of the Canadian Nurses' Association which was held in Saint John, New Brunswick, late in June 1932, was described as 'the most representative national gathering of nurses ever held in Canada,' and 'the most momentous in the history of the C.N.A.'[21] The major topic throughout the programme was the report by Dr George Weir of the Survey of Nursing Education in Canada, which had just been published. But an important decision on another matter was reached: that an editor be appointed for *The Canadian Nurse*, dating from 1 January 1933.[22] The initial appointment was to be for an experimental period of two years. Miss Emory immediately wrote to Miss Johns, offering her the position.

On the first of July 1932 Miss Johns wrote as follows to Miss Jean Wilson, Executive Secretary of the Canadian Nurses' Association:

MY DEAR MISS WILSON:

The President of the Canadian Nurses' Association has written to me on behalf of the Executive Committee inviting me to become the editor and business manager of The Canadian Nurse under certain conditions which are set forth in her letter.

The invitation is accepted with both pride and humility. There is no task to which I would rather devote myself, and I shall hope to prove worthy of the responsibility which the Canadian Nurses have asked me to assume.

It is not easy to find words which express my deep feeling about coming back to Canada. Perhaps later I shall be able to do better, but for the present, all that I have to say can be summed up in a single sentence: I am so very glad to come home.

Yours very sincerely,
ETHEL JOHNS[23]

PART SIX: 1933-1944

19

Ethel Johns, Editor
The Canadian Nurse

Ethel Johns came to her new position at a critical period. The recommendations of the Weir Report on nursing education in Canada awaited study and action. *The Canadian Nurse,* as the official organ of the Canadian Nurses' Association, was expected to play a key interpretive role in making the survey report effective, yet from the economic point of view, the times were not favourable for a reorganization of the Journal as a separate entity and for the enlargement of its sphere of influence. The depression was then at its height, aggravating the unemployment among nurses which the Weir Survey had found even in the relatively prosperous years of the late 1920s. Subscriptions to the Journal were declining, and in 1932 they totalled only 1995 out of a national membership of 9385 nurses.[1]

Miss Emory lost no time after her re-election as president in bringing to the attention of the membership these and other issues of current concern. She announced that the headquarters of the Canadian Nurses' Association would move from Winnipeg to Montreal at the beginning of November 1932, and that the new editor of *The Canadian Nurse* would commence her duties in January 1933. With this appointment, she added, the national office would be well prepared to care for the interests of the profession. The executive secretary would function in the development of professional matters through closer contact with groups within and outside the association, while the editor would be responsible for interpreting, through the medium of *The Canadian Nurse,* national and international nursing ideas and ideals.[2]

The meeting in Saint John had settled that the offices of the executive secretary and the editor should be adjacent, if possible, but that they should be under separate management. During the summer and fall months, Miss Johns conferred with Miss Wilson in Winnipeg and Miss Emory in Toronto about policies and procedures under the proposed reorganization. The president reported the points of agreement to the executive committee of the Canadian Nurses' Association, which approved the new editor's terms of reference before she took office.[3]

As editor and business manager, Miss Johns would be responsible to the publications committee (of which she would be a member *ex officio*), which in turn was appointed by and answerable to the executive committee of the Canadian Nurses' Association. To ensure continuity, the two members of the publications committee who had served during the preceding two years would continue to act until the biennial meeting of 1934. These were Miss Emory as convener and Jean E. Browne (Director of the Junior Red Cross Society of Canada) as secretary. The latter had also served from the beginning as secretary of the Joint Study Committee of the Canadian Medical Association and the Canadian Nurses' Association which guided the survey of nursing education carried out by Dr George Weir.

The executive committee proposed some broad guidelines respecting the content of *The Canadian Nurse*. The editor should investigate the desirability of including in each issue of the Journal one or more pages dealing with national affairs relating to nursing and written in the French language, with brief synopsized translations. A section should be devoted to the activities of the national and provincial joint study committees appointed to make effective the recommendations of the survey. When indicated, one or more pages should be assigned to a description of the current activities of the national office contributed by the executive secretary. Finally, a change in the format and cover of the magazine would await the recommendations of the newly appointed editor.[4]

At the meeting of the executive committee held on 22 September 1932, the president remarked that in her opinion the success of the experiment in having a full-time editor and business manager would depend largely upon the contacts which the latter could make with the provincial registered nurses' associations. As the Canadian Nurses' Association had no budgetary allowance for travel, the suggestion was made that the provincial associations might facilitate Miss Johns' field contacts by arranging for her to speak at meetings and paying her expenses. The favourable response to this proposal was to have a significant effect upon the new editor's activities during her first year in office.

In retrospect, it appears that all possible steps were taken in advance to ensure a cordial reception for Miss Johns, and co-operation with her efforts as editor and business manager of *The Canadian Nurse*. Announcing Miss Johns' appointment, Miss Emory drew attention to her sustained interest in the growth of the profession in Canada throughout the years, and to the contribution which she had made as secretary of the Canadian Nurses' Association. The president referred to the new editor's 'unusual personal gifts,' and spoke of her broad experience. Miss Johns had been absent from Canada long enough 'to have acquired a detachment of outlook and yet to have preserved a depth of insight concerning Canadian nurses and nursing.' She pledged to Miss Johns 'the warmth and loyalty of a united profession.' The experiment was to last two years, but Miss Emory expressed the belief that Miss Johns' ability and the response of the nursing group would result in the period being prolonged.[5]

In her final editorial, Jean Wilson extended a cordial welcome to her successor in the office of editor. She paid tribute to Miss Johns' facility in writing, her ability and unlimited energy, assets which were enhanced by her varied and valuable experience.[6]

Miss Johns arrived in Montreal on 2 January 1933. From the outset, she was attuned to her new environment: '... The streets of this ancient and picturesque city,' she wrote, 'and the sound of the French tongue recall experiences in other lands and add richness and colour to the familiar Canadian scene ...'[7] She was fortunate in finding living quarters well suited to her needs, a bachelor suite in the charming old Marlborough Apartments on Milton Street, within easy walking distance of the office.

Her quiet second-floor rooms overlooked a grassy inner courtyard, bounded on the far side by a row of Lombardy poplars. The living-room was enhanced by a small wood-burning fireplace, and bookshelves lined the adjacent wall. From this pleasant room, French doors opened upon a long, narrow balcony overlooking two acacia trees, which in summer was to prove an ideal spot for writing. At that time, the suite had no kitchen, but Miss Johns improvised some facilities which served her needs. She installed a hot plate, and purchased a small refrigerator in which she took considerable pride and satisfaction.[8] Despite her admitted lack of skill in housework and cooking, she settled down quite happily here. Some of her household adventures, to the amusement of her readers, found their way, from time to time, into the 'Off Duty' pages of the Journal.

In her first editorial, Miss Johns responded warmly to the kindness shown her by Jean Wilson. Her path was being smoothed at every turn, she said, by the latter's unfailing patience and courtesy, and nothing had been left undone to make the transfer easy and pleasant. Miss Wilson had carried the double load for more than eight years with characteristic modesty and quiet efficiency, and despite the recent move of national office, '... the direction of the Journal has been so orderly and systematic that the new editor ought to be able to carry on without loss of time or duplication of effort.' She announced that Miss Wilson would take charge of a department in the Journal which would report upon various activities associated with the work of the executive secretary and the developments of the provincial nurses' associations.[9]

In view of the initial expressions of mutual admiration and co-operation by Miss Wilson and Miss Johns, good rapport in the reorganized national office seemed assured. But this was not to be the case; strained relationships were soon apparent between the executive secretary and the new editor, and these did not improve during the many years they shared the same office suite. But it was a measure of the maturity and commitment of both officials that each was able to support the professional efforts of the other throughout the period of their association.

The March 1933 issue of the Journal, the second to be published under Miss Johns' direction, appeared in a bright blue cover. Hailing 'The Canadian Nurse in a New Uniform,' the president appealed for the support of the membership on behalf of the magazine. Individual nurses should not only subscribe, she emphasized, but they should also contribute articles for publication. 'A professional organ,' commented Miss Emory, 'cannot exceed in usefulness the spirit of adventure and research displayed by its members.'

In the same issue, Jean Browne wrote a guest editorial which evidently made a profound impression upon Miss Johns and influenced her direction of the Journal. Now that *The Canadian Nurse* had become a department in its own right, asserted Miss Browne, the subscribers looked forward to its becoming a first-class professional periodical, of which the characteristics should be: '... that it constantly maintains the highest ideals of our profession, that it constantly stimulates our interest in our work and that it constantly helps us to understand and appreciate our problems.' Informative articles were important, but facts were not sufficient; rather, analysis of the facts was required. 'Because of the very nature of their work, nurses, perhaps more than other professional people, are apt to let others do their thinking for them. *The Canadian Nurse* will fulfil its most important function if it educates its readers to think for themselves, to bring an analytical mind to their problems, to be guided by reason rather than emotion, and to be ready to make changes when a changing social order demands them ...' Miss Browne suggested integrated series of articles on related topics to provide up-to-date, authentic information on every phase of nursing. Where differences of opinion existed, both sides of the controversy should be given.

The March issue also contained a report by Marion Lindeburgh (assistant director of the School for Graduate Nurses, McGill University), convener of the Standing Committee on Curriculum of the Nursing Education Section, Canadian Nurses' Association. The Committee was charged with the task of preparing a curriculum for schools of nursing in Canada, as a way of helping the schools to implement the recommendations of the Weir Survey Report. The convener now explained the general order of procedure which the Committee had adopted as a way of organizing its work. Each provincial association of nurses had been asked to appoint a subcommittee to carry out an analysis of nursing service, a necessary first step in curriculum construction. A central curriculum committee had been appointed, including representatives from all fields of graduate nursing service, from general education, and from the medical profession. Listed in the membership of the central committee was the name of Ethel Johns, representing *The Canadian Nurse*. The latter's experience in nursing education and her editorial competence made her a valuable member of the committee, while the contacts which she made through this work were beneficial to her both personally and professionally. Her friendship with Eileen Flanagan commenced as a result of their association on the curriculum committee, and (probably through Miss Flanagan) she also met Norena MacKenzie and Suzanne Giroux. This small group of four congenial people, including herself, Miss Johns later designated 'The Creative Minority.'

March 1933 also marked the inauguration of the 'Off Duty' page in *The Canadian Nurse*, one which was destined to make a wide appeal to the nurses of Canada. In this kaleidoscopic series of whimsical essays published throughout the years of her editorship, Ethel Johns' literary ability found release. Her keen, sensitive observations of everyday scenes and events, and the memories of her past life, were recorded with grace and humour, and for a normally reserved person, she here revealed her inner self in a surprisingly uninhibited way.

During her first year as editor, Miss Johns travelled throughout Canada, visiting eight of the nine provinces. She delivered addresses upon a variety of topics at annual meetings of the provincial registered nurses' associations, and availed herself of opportunities to enlist the members' interest in *The Canadian Nurse*. She gathered papers delivered by noted speakers, for insertion in the Journal. She observed the contemporary scene in Canadian nursing and commenced, in her editorials, 'to reflect, interpret, and integrate' the thinking of nurses across the country. And she stirred to the vastness, the beauty, and the spirit of the country: '... It would be a poor heart indeed which did not respond to such a magnificent opportunity. It would be a dull imagination which failed to be stirred by such a journey, from sea to sea, and from north to south across Canada ...'[10]

In a series of seven articles entitled, 'The Canadian Scene,' which appeared in the Journal between December 1933 and June 1934, Ethel Johns gave a synthesis of the impressions which she had gathered in her tour across the nation. Her strong, confident voice carried a message of faith and hope. Despite suffering and deprivation, she asserted, nursing morale was still good. Nurses realized the need for solidarity in their ranks, for seeking and finding a common ground, for reaching out to make closer contact with the communities they served. Nurses were no longer trying to live by themselves in a vacuum, but were 'beginning to see nursing in its real setting as a public utility ...' Although there were some diversities of nursing viewpoint across the nation, Canadian nurses had reached substantial agreement on some basic questions, both economic and educational. The heaviest burden of economic maladjustment rested upon the private duty nurses, among whom unemployment was widespread, but the editor perceived a hopeful sign in the fact that this group now felt the need of sharing their burden with other nurses, who in turn seemed disposed to accept this responsibility.[11]

In succeeding articles in this series, Miss Johns explored in some depth, and from the perspective of her participation in the American Committee on the Costs of Medical Care, the problem of the economic gap between unemployed nurses and patients requiring care but unable to pay for it. Dr George Weir, in his Survey Report, had proposed ways of solving the economic dilemma. He had endorsed the principle of health insurance which would provide a complete health service: medical, nursing, and dental services, with hospitalization when needed, and the maintenance of public health services. These benefits would be subsidized by contributions from insured persons and from government (federal, provincial, and municipal). Health insurance should be mandatory for all persons whose income fell below stated levels, and voluntary for others. Dr Weir had recommended the establishment of provincial nursing councils to operate or control all nursing registries under such a plan. Private duty nurses would be paid salaries out of a central consolidated fund, would be assigned to cases in the same way as were visiting nurses, and would be subject to supervision and control. Nurses who did not wish to participate in the plan would be free to carry on independent practice. Miss Johns advocated that these questions should be fully discussed at the forthcoming biennial meeting of the Canadian Nurses' Association, and sounded a note of warning:

... That there will be widely differing points of view about such highly controversial questions goes without saying. Yet there is such a thing as compromise and reconciliation for the sake of the common good. One thing must be kept in mind. No nursing policy can possibly be sound which ignores the patient. Whether we realize it or not, the community at large will eventually take an active part in deciding this issue. Above the clamour of our professional debates the still small voice of public opinion will make itself heard. It may be well to listen to it.[12]

The Canadian Nurses' Association celebrated its twenty-fifth anniversary at the biennial meeting, which was held in Toronto during the last week of June 1934. Florence Emory presided over the convention, and in her opening address she set a keynote of action: '... Let us push out from the land of conservatism,' she urged, 'and put down our lines in the deep waters of experimentation ...'[13] Resolutions passed at the meeting reflected concern to implement some of the major recommendations of the Weir Report. It was decided that an effort should be made to have the provincial associations set up the kind of registries Dr Weir had recommended, governed by representatives from all groups of nurses, and enrolling both graduate and practical nurses; and that the Association would make a grant, to be matched by the provincial association, in the event that a registry experimented with the plan of putting a group of nurses on salary. Another resolution approved the principle of country-wide registration for nurses, and authorized the establishment of a central committee with provincial representation to explore this question and report thereon to the 1936 meeting. A further recommendation concerned the licensing of all who nurse the sick for hire: the Joint Study Committee in each province, it was agreed, should study and take action in this matter.[14]

A sad event of the previous year was the death in September of Mary

Agnes Snively, the founder of the Canadian Nurses' Association. At the time, Ethel Johns wrote of the tributes which were paid across Canada to this great leader and she added: '... The first letter to the new Editor was written by Miss Snively and remains a cherished possession. Its closing sentence is repeated here: *Into the future open a better way.* In humility and affection that watchword is accepted.'[15] The 1934 convention decided to establish a memorial to its founder under which '... three medals will be presented at each general meeting of the Canadian Nurses' Association to nurses whose work exemplifies Miss Snively's ideals of nursing and service.'

Miss Johns reported to the convention as editor and business manager of *The Canadian Nurse*. During 1933 the Journal had incurred a deficit of slightly more than two thousand dollars, which had been met by the Canadian Nurses' Association. During this experimental period, the Journal had sought to discharge the following functions:

1 To afford a means of dignified publicity for the interests and activities of the Canadian Nurses' Association ...
2 To interpret to nursing groups in other countries the aspirations and ideals of Canadian nursing ...
3 To act as a stimulus toward constructive thinking concerning all nursing problems, educational, technical, and economic, and to reflect, integrate, and interpret the thought of Canadian nurses.
4 To serve equally all the principal branches of nursing service, public health, institutional, and private duty, and to avoid sectionalism and narrowness.
5 To be of service to individual nurses and especially to those who practice in isolated parts of the country.

The task of the preceding seventeen months had not been easy, commented the editor, and the measure of success attained to date was due largely to the 'magnificent response of nursing organizations and of individual nurses in every part of the Dominion who, sometimes under conditions of extreme hardship, have given practical proof of their faith in the Journal.'[16]

Miss Emory, in her opening address, had emphasized the need to place the Journal on a self-supporting basis, in order that 'the organ which plays so basic a part in the development of the profession through integration of its ideals and practices, may do so with a feeling of freedom and security ...'[17] Presenting the report of the publications committee, she recommended extending the appointment of Ethel Johns to the general meeting of the Canadian Nurses' Association in 1936, at which time the situation and policy of the Journal should be reviewed. For the intervening period, the sum of $4700 yearly should be budgeted to cover the salaries of the editor, a bookkeeper and general assistant, and a stenographer. Miss Johns' salary was to be $2780 yearly, and she was to have one month's vacation in each twelve-month period. This report was adopted, and a resolution was passed to the effect that the sum of $2000 from the assets of the Canadian Nurses' Association should be designated annually to cover a possible deficit of *The Canadian Nurse* until the next general meeting of the Association.[18]

The salary agreed upon for the editor marked a reduction of seven hundred and twenty dollars per annum, which – it appears – she volunteered to take in order to facilitate the employment of other needed staff for *The Canadian Nurse*. In view of her family responsibilities, this sacrifice could not have been an easy one. Her mother was now an invalid, and Miss Johns continued to contribute regularly toward her care and support. Her brother Owen was able to obtain only part-time work during the depression years, and Ethel Johns assisted with the education of his daughter, Helen, who recalls the generosity of her aunt in ensuring that she was always well dressed and that she had a regular allowance.

The 1934 meeting marked the end of Miss Emory's presidency. Ruby Simpson, O.B.E., director of public health nursing services for Saskatchewan, was elected as her successor. Miss Emory retained the convenership of the publications committee, and Miss Browne continued her membership therein. Retention of these wise and loyal advisers must have been a source of deep satisfaction to Ethel Johns as the new biennium started. The buoyant tone of her editorials at this time indicated that she faced the future with confidence.

20

The Canadian Nurses' Association and the Journal

Under Ethel Johns' direction, *The Canadian Nurse* developed steadily according to plan. Its pages reflected provincial, national, and international nursing affairs. The editor sought conscientiously to 'integrate and interpret' the thinking of Canadian nurses on current issues. Contributions by nursing leaders of the day graced the Journal and still impress the reader with their logic, clarity, and wisdom. Addresses at nurses' conventions by distinguished members of the medical profession and by representatives of general education, government, and other fields appeared without delay in *The Canadian Nurse*. The editor confessed that she found it most difficult to obtain articles on nursing care written by Canadian nurses. She sought to stimulate her readers to think, and to challenge statements which were made. She often asked, after presenting a controversial subject: 'What do *you* think about it? Why not write to us and share your opinion with others?' Quite early in her tenure, to the indignation of some readers, Miss Johns discontinued the notices of marriages and births which had always been a feature of the magazine. She insisted that news items for inclusion in a nursing journal should deal with topics of professional interest. Descriptions of table decorations fell victim to the editor's blue pencil: 'Leave out the sweet peas,' she advised.

One of the objectives for *The Canadian Nurse* which Miss Johns evidently found largely unattainable was that relating to the inclusion of French-language content. In September 1934, however, she realized a 'long cherished ambition' through the publication of Miss Caroline Barrett's report, in French, of the biennial meeting in Toronto.[1] In her introduction to this article, Miss Johns drew attention to the existence in Canada of the nursing Journal, *La Garde-Malade Canadienne Française*, which was much appreciated by its French readers. Not wishing to encroach 'upon the legitimate field of our contemporary,' the editor commented, '... At the Biennial Meeting, particularly in the discussions of the three national sections, French nurses, lay and religious, made a valuable contribution. The French language, like the French mind, has a clarity and logic all its own. And it seems right and proper that upon certain important occasions our national *Journal* should be bi-lingual.'[2] During Miss Johns' tenure as editor, French-language content in *The Canadian Nurse* was infrequent. But this can be attributed to the limited resources of the magazine, which would have made its bilingual development difficult if not impossible. Almost a quarter-century was to pass before this goal would be attained, during the editorship of Miss Margaret Kerr.

As the year 1935 commenced, Miss Johns sounded an optimistic note. Looking back over the past twelve months, she commented that, despite the fact that there had been no respite from the 'crushing burden of the depression,' 1934 could still be called a good year. It marked the coming of age of the Canadian Nurses' Association:

... The slow, steady building up, over a quarter of a century, of the Canadian Nurses' Association has been a task which has had its difficulties and dangers. The Association must have unity, and the strength which unity gives, and yet must be sufficiently flexible to allow for differences in language and in religion. It must find ways of bridging great distances, and contrive to meet the varying needs of a scattered membership. Above all it must give full play to the energies and aspirations of the three groups which constitute its membership and, at the same time, avoid sectionalism and narrowness. At the Biennial Meeting it was clear that these ends have been achieved ...

Furthermore, we are meeting certain issues more courageously and frankly than we once did. We know that our stupid refusal, through the years, to face the problem of the competition of non-professional workers in the nursing field has had most serious results and now we are beginning to do a little constructive thinking about it. A term like 'socialized nursing' no longer conjures up horrid visions of Stalin in command on Parliament Hill, but seems quite compatible with our Canadian system of government and with the regular changing of the Guard at Buckingham Palace. We are less afraid than we were of 'goblins and ghosties and things which go "bump" in the night.' Yes, 1934 was a good year after all ...[3]

For the year ahead one of the most pressing tasks was to bring about a better understanding of nurses and nursing on the part of physicians, hospital administrators, and the public in general. Miss Johns reiterated a conviction she had often voiced. Neither nursing practice nor nursing education could be carried on in a vacuum: 'We are part of the social and economic life of our time.'

A constant source of anxiety was the difficulty of securing and retaining subscriptions and advertisements. The latter, she often pointed out, were contingent on the former: potential advertisers kept a sharp lookout on the magazine's circulation. Fortunately, the editor did not have to fight the battle alone. She enjoyed the support and confidence of the president and the executive committee of the Canadian Nurses' Association and of the publications committee. Also, periodic campaigns in the interest of *The Canadian Nurse* were carried on by the provincial nurses' associations, their Journal committees, and by interested individuals and groups.

In the May 1935 issue Miss Johns reported upon a vigorous campaign to increase subscriptions to *The Canadian Nurse* which was launched by the nurses of Toronto under the leadership of Jean Gunn. The four-month drive resulted in 'the magnificent total of four hundred and seventy new subscribers.'[4] Ethel Johns revered Miss Gunn as a leader and held her in affection as a friend. That this busy woman should have lent her influence and organizing ability to the campaign must have meant even more to Miss Johns than did its successful outcome.

In the early fall of 1935, the executive committee of the Canadian Nurses' Association launched a circulation campaign for *The Canadian Nurse*. The president, Ruby M. Simpson, sounded a 'Call to Action' in the November number of the magazine. She spoke of the first of January 1933 as a red-letter day in the history of the Canadian Nurses' Association, '... for on that day a long cherished dream came true: a full-time editor and business manager was placed in charge of the affairs of its official publication.' The step had not been taken lightly; it was the outcome of lengthy consideration and planning and the venture had proved to be successful:

... This statement is made with assurance and with pride. We now have a *Journal*, greatly improved in format and content, which we can justly claim integrates and interprets the thinking of Canadian nurses, keeps the members of the Association accurately and consistently informed on Association policies and activities, expresses and develops a national viewpoint on pertinent nursing questions, and perhaps most important of all, serves as an indispensable link between the provinces.⁵

The president reported that within less than three years the circulation of *The Canadian Nurse* had increased from two thousand to slightly more than three thousand, and that its deficit in 1934 was only seven hundred and fifty dollars out of a total expenditure of over ten thousand dollars. This was a noteworthy achievement, particularly in view of the difficult economic conditions of the time. But still more must be accomplished, if the magazine were to continue to progress. Increased revenue from subscriptions and advertising was required for its further development. The target for the present campaign, the president reported, was to secure one thousand new subscribers before June 1936.

'Pride of place' in the January 1936 issue of the Journal was accorded an article by Mabel Holt, superintendent of nurses of the Montreal General Hospital, in which the writer reported upon an innovation used in staffing the recently acquired Western Division of the Institution. Instead of increasing the enrolment of students in the school of nursing and thus adding to the numbers of unemployed graduates, the decision was made to staff the Division with graduate nurses on general duty, supplemented by ward aides, orderlies, and maids. An eight-hour day for graduate nursing staff was instituted at the same time. The plan had proved successful, reported Miss Holt, both in creating employment for graduates of the school and in stabilizing and improving the quality of the nursing service. Commenting editorially upon this venture, Miss Johns wrote:

... Viewed simply as a study in effective nursing administration this article has definite value, but its implications go much deeper than that.

Here is proof that the authorities of one of the oldest and best of Canadian hospitals have had the foresight and courage to seek a more excellent way. The easy and obvious solution would have been to increase the enrolment of the School of Nursing; the awkward fact that there was already severe unemployment among the graduates of the School could have been conveniently ignored. To their lasting credit be it said, the Board of Governors of the Hospital weighed carefully the issues placed before them by the medical superintendent and by the superintendent of nurses, and decided in favour of a policy which, only too often, has been thrust aside as unworkable without thorough investigation of its possibilities.

The decision, coming from men who are authorities in the financial world, ought to put courage into the hearts and steel into the backbones of nurse administrators who have ventured to advocate this policy even in the face of powerful though sometimes unreasoning opposition ...

The editor commended to the reader a study of the eight-hour day described by Miss Holt, and she drew attention to the use of ward aides to whom were assigned 'the household duties on which student nurses sometimes waste time which ought to be put to more profitable use.' Miss Johns admitted that this plan for nursing service would not be equally applicable in every hospital situation, since the factors which had contributed to its success in this institution might be lacking in another. But she drew a significant conclusion:

... One stubborn fact, however, cannot be denied: given able direction, loyal support, and suitable physical environment, a graduate nursing service can be carried on at a cost not greatly exceeding that of student service. Now that it has been shown that there are other and better methods of staffing hospitals than by student nurses, the tide of battle will turn. When it can be proved (and it will be) that student service does not always pay in terms of dollars and cents, the victory will be won. We need a few more large scale experiments such as that which is now being worked out with courage, patience, and skill at the Western Division of the Montreal General Hospital.[6]

The eighteenth general meeting of the Canadian Nurses' Association took place in Vancouver, from 29 June to 4 July 1936. By chance, the convention synchronized with the fiftieth anniversary of the city. '... There was therefore an atmosphere of gaiety,' wrote Miss Johns, 'flags flying, bands playing, fountains throwing themselves into the cool, sparkling air. There was a lovely spontaneity about the whole thing that somehow rang true. The city was at its best – what more can one say? Yet one more word must be said: *the flowers*. Fresh every morning they came, all dewy from the gardens where they grew. Roses and honeysuckles and syringa, magically replenished, thanks to nurses whom one never saw or had an opportunity to thank. But we do thank them – and we thank Vancouver, too ...'[7]

It was generally agreed that this was a happy meeting, one distinguished by the skilful chairmanship of Ruby Simpson and by mature debate upon important issues: Dominion registration, health insurance and its implications for nursing, community nursing service bureaux, the curriculum guide, and the further development of *The*

Canadian Nurse. Among the guest speakers were Dr George Weir (now Provincial Secretary for the Province of British Columbia), Mary Beard, and Professor Ira Dilworth (from the Department of English, University of British Columbia).

Edith MacPherson Dickson presented her report as chairman of the Committee on Dominion Registration of Nurses. The consensus was that further intensive study of the proposal was required, and a resolution was passed requesting 'that the Committee on Dominion Registration for Nurses in Canada be re-appointed and asked to clarify its report in the light of both the discussion and the resolutions referred to it at the general session of the Biennial Meeting, July 3, 1936 ...'[8]

A highlight of the convention was Miss Lindeburgh's presentation of *A Proposed Curriculum for Schools of Nursing in Canada,* the outcome of four years' intensive work by herself and the members of the central and provincial curriculum committees. By resolution, this was accepted and referred to the provincial nurses' associations for experimental use in schools of nursing.[9]

A further resolution authorized the appointment of a committee to discuss with the Victorian Order of Nurses for Canada the question of the establishment of community nursing service bureaux, and the executive committee of the Canadian Nurses' Association was authorized to make a substantial financial contribution toward the development of any such approved project. At the same time, the provincial nurses' associations were encouraged to proceed with their plans for the reorganization of registries.[10]

In her report as editor and business manager of *The Canadian Nurse,* Miss Johns expressed satisfaction with the success of the president's campaign to increase subscriptions. The financial picture of the Journal was improving, and the deficit incurred in 1935 was only two hundred and eleven dollars. But the content of the magazine had not shown comparable progress. This she attributed to the fact that 'the unceasing struggle to find money, either from advertising or subscriptions, wherewith to pay the monthly expenditure, has absorbed by far the greater part of the time and energy of the editor.' It was right and proper that the Journal should pay for itself as far as possible, but she suggested that it was even more important that *The Canadian Nurse* be worthy of the organization that sponsored it. The present format was so restricted that it was difficult to meet the 'quite reasonable demands' upon it of the national sections and the provincial units of the Canadian Nurses' Association. Suitable illustrations were needed to improve the magazine, original articles should be procured, and, in short, more time and money should be spent upon it.[11] The delegates passed a resolution requesting the publications committee to report to the executive committee on 'measures which might be taken to improve the format and content of the *Journal*, and ways and means by which such measures might, if approved, be put into operation.'[12]

The climax of this memorable convention was the presentation of the first Mary Agnes Snively Memorial medals to the three members of the Association who had been nominated for the honour by the provincial nurses' associations: Edith MacPherson Dickson, Jean I. Gunn, and Mabel F. Hersey. Miss Johns' pre-convention editorial comment upon the selection of these first recipients revealed her personal approval: 'Hearty congratulations are extended to the three beloved and respected Canadian nurses upon whom this high distinction has been conferred. No better choice could have been made.'[13]

As the busy week ended, Ethel Johns' need for solitude led her to Stanley Park:

... At the portals of Stanley Park we invested in a ham sandwich and a chocolate bar. We then made a bee-line for a pathway of which we remembered every turning though we had not trodden it for ten long years. It leads to a sanctuary where dwell the great trees – centuries old. There was a lovely and a healing silence broken only once or twice by the song of a bird ...

After we had listened to the counsel of the trees we went on to Second Beach. It was low tide and our favourite rock (the one with a back to lean against) was high and fairly dry. As we consumed our frugal repast we looked about for other old friends and, all of a sudden, one of them suddenly appeared. He is an elderly crow who, for many years, has maintained a querulous friendship with a melancholy gull. When we lived in Vancouver they used to scuttle along the water's edge together, looking for succulent morsels. With an expectant eye on the crumbs of our sandwich, the crow hopped nearer. We thought we saw a gleam of recognition in his cynical eye, but, having snapped up the last almond of our chocolate bar, he continued to gaze wistfully out to sea. No gull. We were afraid to ask any questions. One never knows. At last, to our relief, there came a flash of wings and a thin, eldrich scream. It was the gull, *his* gull, our gull.

Drowsing in the watery sunlight, we listened to their profane and vituperative conversation until the tide invaded our resting place. Presently the rain began to fall again and we tramped home, alone, beneath the friendly trees ...[14]

Viewed in historical perspective, the period 1936–8 in Canadian nursing was a time of evaluation and reinforcement of progress already made, and the further development of projects which had been initiated. As the new biennium started, the re-elected president, Ruby Simpson, wrote a stirring article for *The Canadian Nurse,* suitably entitled, 'Marching Orders.' She recapitulated the major decisions made at the recent convention in Vancouver, clarified the Association's objectives for the coming two years, and drew attention to the Congress of the International Council of Nurses which was to be held in London in 1937. With respect to *The Canadian Nurse,* the president reported:

... The experiment of employing a full-time editor and business manager of our *Journal* is at an end. A definite appointment of this official was authorized by the General Meeting, the appointee to be, of course, the present incumbent of the office, who has given such distinguished service during the time of the experiment. Much has been done in these three years to build up *The Canadian Nurse.* Much remains to be done, as we have been seriously and persistently informed by the editor. The circulation campaign brought in more than 1,800 new subscribers. Now the editor and publications committee, with your continued support and cooperation, plan to set about to consolidate the gains made and to make the *Journal* still better and more indispensable to you. You may count upon them. May they count upon you?[15]

Directing the attention of readers to the publication of Miss Lindeburgh's report as convener of the Curriculum Committee, Miss Johns advocated its study by every Canadian nurse, and she made several astute observations:

... This curriculum is not an academic abstraction conceived in a vacuum: it is a living force which will profoundly affect the life and work of nurses in Canada. The Curriculum is primarily intended for use as a guide in schools of nursing – yet its influence extends far beyond them. Upon it will be based certain standards which will be used to measure the qualifications of nurses aspiring to fill administrative, supervisory, and teaching positions. Critical appraisal of schools of nursing will be facilitated by using it. Plans for graduate study will be based upon it.

It stands to reason that although the Curriculum was accepted by the Canadian Nurses' Association it is not to be regarded as having been graven on tables of stone or cast in imperishable bronze – its very format is proof to the contrary. The binding, the blank pages for comment on the part of the reader – all these show that the use to which the curriculum is to be put is that defined elsewhere by the President of the Canadian Nurses' Association: 'Every school in Canada will now participate in the trial use of the Curriculum and be prepared to comment on it in 1938.'[16]

The Canadian Nurse devoted much space during 1937 to the Congress of the International Council of Nurses. The executive committee of the Canadian Nurses' Association offered both Miss Wilson and Miss Johns the opportunity to attend the Congress, but Miss Johns declined, doubtless because she was a poor sailor. She contented herself with saying goodbye to the departing travellers: 'We rather like seeing people off,' she wrote, 'especially when they are going down to the sea in ships. For one thing, our pleasure is quite untouched by envy. We are delighted to be left on the dock, and to be comfortably aware that the lift of the bounding billow will soon be experienced by our friends but not by us ...'[17]

The biennial meeting of the Canadian Nurses' Association which was held in Halifax from the fourth to the ninth of July 1938 is remembered chiefly as the occasion upon which the nurses of Canada rejected the proposed plan for Dominion registration. But the convention was noteworthy for the general excellence of its programme, the thoughtful appraisals of the Proposed Curriculum, the masterly address by the retiring president, and the presence of Effie Taylor, dean of the Yale University School of Nursing and president of the International Council of Nurses. Miss Taylor's remarkable paper, 'Nursing, a Profession and a Service,' had as its theme the need for a revival of spiritual values in nursing education and practice. At this meeting, recipients of the Snively awards were Jean E. Browne, Jean S. Wilson, and Elizabeth L. Smellie.

Ethel Johns' report as editor and business manager held more than a hint of discouragement. The Journal had paid its way in both 1936 and 1937, but this was achieved only as a result of 'rigid economies in business management.' The upsurge in circulation as a result of the president's campaign was followed by a sharp decline in subscription renewals. The editor conducted an investigation into the reasons for this, and discovered certain underlying causes. Some nurses complained that the Journal was too small in size and too slight in content. Others found that there was too much advertising and 'official directory' material, that too much space was devoted to nursing organizations and too little to nurses and nursing practice. *The Canadian Nurse*, alleged some critics, could not compare in value with *The American Journal of Nursing*, even though the latter cost more. Others said that the

Journal was too 'Eastern' in outlook, and did not reflect or report upon activities going on in all of the provinces.

Miss Johns accepted these criticisms as constructive. Most of them could be remedied, she thought, by an increase in the size of the Journal, although it was 'absurd' to think that *The Canadian Nurse* could compete with *The American Journal of Nursing* in any but one respect: it reflected a viewpoint which was distictively Canadian. The most serious criticism, she felt, was that the Journal did not serve all parts of the country equally well. This fault would also be the most difficult to overcome: '... Canada is a vast country, and distance is a barrier which the restricted resources of the Journal, both in terms of money and personnel, have not been able to break down ...'[18]

Miss Simpson, in her presidential address, emphasized the significance of the official journal in the life of the Association: '... Unity of purpose, unity of understanding, unity of effort are impossible without an easily available means of communication. *The Canadian Nurse* has been a real power in the Association's progress and it has itself, shown consistent improvement ...' She raised the question as to whether the Association should increase its investment in order to obtain greater returns in professional value. She wondered what the safety level was for circulation, and inquired whether the time had come for the Journal to be included in membership fees. These questions must be answered, if the Journal were to develop to the full extent of its potentialities.[19]

The delegates were responsive to the needs of *The Canadian Nurse* as presented by the editor and the president. A resolution was passed which provided that the Canadian Nurses' Association should finance *The Canadian Nurse* to whatever extent was necessary 'to give the editor the necessary assistance so as to relieve her as much as possible for editorial work; to permit the editor the use of her discretion as to the size of the magazine for each issue; to arrange, if possible, for more suitable office accommodation for *The Canadian Nurse*.' The delegates recommended that the provincial *Canadian Nurse* committees be strengthened and that they should be in direct contact with the editor but receive leadership from the publications committee. A further resolution stated: 'Whereas Miss Ethel Johns has brought *The Canadian Nurse* to the position of esteem it now holds, be it resolved, that the Canadian Nurses' Association take this opportunity of formally expressing appreciation of the valuable work of the editor and business manager.'[20]

Grace Mitchell Fairley, director of nursing of the Vancouver General Hospital, was elected president. The succession of outstanding women to occupy this high office during Miss Johns' editorship remained unbroken. She had every reason to approach the new biennium with renewed optimism.

21

A Time for Expansion

Assured of the Association's approval of her proposals for the improvement of *The Canadian Nurse,* Ethel Johns now directed her energies to this task. On the first of October 1938 the editor and staff of the Journal moved out of national office into an adjoining suite. Miss Johns' relief upon obtaining more adequate accommodation can only have been equalled by Miss Wilson's. Both executives had worked under increasingly difficult conditions which were a deterrent to efficiency and to the needed increase of staff and facilities.

The editor shared with the subscribers the good news that *The Canadian Nurse* now enjoyed a modest suite of its own, comprising a general office, an editorial office, and a storage room. She expressed her pleasure that she had a private place in which to think and plan. It would be necessary to work harder to cover the increased expenditure, but she was encouraged by the 'excellent promotion work' being done under the auspices of the provincial nurses' associations and their *Canadian Nurse* committees. She wrote with pride of the financial independence which the magazine had enjoyed since 1936, and trusted that it would continue to be self-supporting. From the beginning *The Canadian Nurse* had relied upon the pioneers, and she expressed the hope that the younger nurses would now begin to take hold. The time had come for expansion and that meant 'facing a new adventure.'[1]

The October 1938 issue of *The Canadian Nurse* featured 'The Student Nurses' Page.' By way of introduction, Miss Johns commented that there had been lively debate at the biennial meeting as to ways of making the Journal 'come alive,' and that everyone agreed that there should be a student nurses' page. But the editor now remarked that her previous attempts in this respect were unsuccessful: '... Sometimes we opened a fat and promising envelope only to find that it contained trivialities about Hallowe'en or Christmas parties, complete with costumes and table decorations. Very seldom did we ever receive anything which brought the challenge of youth with it. New ideas – a fresh point of view – we looked for them in vain.' The Journal wanted material which reflected 'the original thinking and the actual experience of student nurses,' preferably (though not necessarily) related directly to nursing. Among the examples she gave of the kinds of subjects upon which students might write were the following: 'If you were the head nurse what would you teach the students on your ward, and why? Why didn't the pneumonia case you worked so hard over get well? What are you going to watch for next time? Was there anything you missed? What do you think about student councils? Is there any form of student government which really governs? If not, why not? If the old discipline is to pass, what is to take its place?' The editor emphasized that articles should not exceed one thousand words. 'Sometimes you can say more if you boil it down to five hundred. Just one word more – no poems, please. Positively no poems. We just can't bear them.' The editor had forgotten, it seems, her own youthful addiction to poetry.

Following its reinstatement, the 'Student Nurses' Page' became a regular feature of the Journal, and both the quality of the articles and the range of subjects dealt with suggest that the young contributors heeded the editor's admonitions. Doubtless Miss Johns also gave a good deal of coaching to the individual students as required. Her skill as a creative teacher was revealed in the techniques which she used to arouse the students' interest (and that of their instructors) in using *The Canadian Nurse* as a tool for learning. The January 1939 issue contained two pages of provocative questions on information which had appeared in the magazine during the preceding twelve months. Students were invited to find the answers to such queries as these: 'If you had to visit a home in which there was poverty and unemployment, how would you go about it? What new methods are being used in the treatment of schizophrenia? Could you plan meals for a family of five on $5.87 a week? Who is the President of the Canadian Nurses' Association? What messages has she sent to its members since she took office? What remarkable social experiment is being carried on at Antigonish, Nova Scotia? What are the obligations of Canadian nurses to their country in time of war?'

In her New Year's message, the editor observed that 1938 was 'kind to us' in many ways. The biennial meeting was an outstanding success, and it had 'brought into prominence some of the younger nurses whose capacity for leadership guarantees the continued advancement of nursing in Canada.' Substantial progress was being made in nursing education, as schools of nursing sought to carry out the recommendations of the Proposed Curriculum. Furthermore, the link between the nursing profession and Canadian universities was growing stronger. During the past year 'three of our leading Canadian universities conferred high academic rank upon women whom we ourselves have delighted to honour.[2] Thanks to the tact and patience of the women who direct departments of nursing within universities, the authorities now have a sympathetic understanding of the aims of nursing education ...'[3]

Throughout the years of Ethel Johns' editorship, in keeping with the policy of the Canadian Nurses' Association, significant events in schools of nursing within universities were faithfully reported in *The Canadian Nurse*. Thus the Journal recorded the financial struggle of the McGill School for Graduate Nurses and gave publicity to the magnificent campaign for funds waged by its alumnae association under the convenership of E. Frances Upton, the secretary-registrar of the Association of Registered Nurses of the Province of Quebec. A number of reports and articles also appeared in the Journal concerning the University of Toronto School of Nursing, and the experimental three-year undergraduate programme established there, with the assistance of a grant from the Rockefeller Foundation, to prepare nurses for both general and public health nursing. In the January 1939 issue of *The Canadian Nurse*, the editor wrote about a further gift to the University of Toronto School of Nursing, an endowment by the Rockefeller Foundation in the amount of two hundred and fifty thousand dollars:

... A great University and its medical school, some of the best hospitals in the whole Dominion, excellent public health and visiting nursing services – all are here and all are now in full co-operation with the School. Furthermore, dynamic leadership of an exceptionally high order is assured. The Director of the School, Kathleen Russell, is herself the fortunate possessor of an original and penetrating mind and she has gathered about her a staff which is worthy of the new enterprise ... We now have, in Canada, everything that is necessary for the establishment of an independent School of Nursing which may serve as an inspiration and a pattern for the whole world. Let us have the courage to accept the challenge which this gift brings and thus prove ourselves worthy of our high destiny.[4]

As 1939 began, the threat of war was smouldering in Europe. The Munich Conference in the previous September had halted the outbreak of hostilities at that time, but there was a general foreboding of the conflict to come. The president of the Canadian Nurses' Association responded to the crisis by making an urgent appeal to Canadian nurses to enrol in greater numbers than heretofore for emergency service in war or disaster.[5]

Summer 1939 brought the long-awaited visit to Canada of King George VI and Queen Elizabeth. The president, Miss Grace Fairley, heralded the occasion by a message in the May issue of *The Canadian Nurse* which extended a loyal welcome on behalf of the members of the Canadian Nurses' Association. The editorial comment introducing the president's message concluded: '... As we go to press, the international situation is still tense but there is every reason to hope that the skies will clear and that the eagerly anticipated Royal visit will bring happiness to a loyal and united Canada.' The royal visitors did indeed call forth a warm and joyful response from the Canadian people throughout the Dominion, but shortly after they returned to England, war broke out in Europe.

Again the president of the Canadian Nurses' Association addressed a moving message to the nurses of Canada:

... 'For the second time in the lives of most of us, we are at War.' These words, spoken by his Majesty the King, could not fail to stir the emotions of all who heard him. The National Emergency that we had all so fervently prayed might pass is with us, and we as members of a profession so eminently prepared by training and experience are likely to be called to Service.

Whether that Service will be at home or abroad, one cannot, at this early date, foretell. The Canadian Nurses' Association will follow the paths of its members with deep interest and affection, knowing that whatever duty lies ahead they will do it.[6]

The editor's brief message which followed that of the president called attention to an article, 'The Crisis and the Nurse,' which appeared in *The Nursing Times* on 2 September 1939, the eve of the outbreak of war. Miss Johns wrote of the qualitites of steadfastness, courage, devotion, and discipline which the British nurses showed in the face of crisis. She reminded her readers that for many years the Canadian Nurses' Association, in conjunction with the Canadian Red Cross Society, had carried on an national enrolment of nurses for emergency service, as a result of which more than three thousand nurses were enrolled. But she emphasized that the roster must be increased *now*, and she asked: 'Is your name on the list? *Are you willing to guard the flame?*'[7]

Miss Johns' traditional Christmas message to the readers of *The Canadian Nurse* appeared, as usual, in the December issue (1939), but its tone was poignant. Nurses were aware, she wrote, that hospitals were happy places at Christmas; and the presence of the shadow of suffering only added a deeper significance to the day. The British Commonwealth of Nations must celebrate Christmas this year under such a shadow:

... Nevertheless the English, according to their ancient custom, will hang up holly and mistletoe, sing carols, greet their friends, and eat as much plum pudding as rationing cards permit. The overseas mails may be a bit late, but, thanks to the British Navy, will arrive in due season. There will be fewer trains than usual, but Aunt Mary will come in from the country for dinner, gas mask on one arm and knitting bag on the other. Tall young adventurers from the Dominions, wearing the uniform of the Royal Air Force, will be marched off to Early Service by proud hostesses, like so many captives of war ... We do not know what may happen between mid-November and Christmas Day but, if with gentle gaiety they keep the Feast in England, we surely can do no less in Canada. Although we are still too far away to feel the full impact of the terrific forces now let loose upon the world, every day brings a keener realization of their strength and magnitude. Nurses, better than anyone else, know that even in everyday life it takes courage to be gay. This is Christmas Day in 1939 – yes – but Christmas just the same.

The January 1940 issue of *The Canadian Nurse* appeared in an attractive new cover, featuring a picture of Old Cannon Gate, Bay Bulls, Newfoundland. From this time on, the cover was to display arresting photographs of a variety of subjects: typical Canadian landscapes, uniformed nurses on military service, and scenes of nurses giving care to patients in many different settings.

The president, in her New Year's greeting, spoke of the opportunity of service which the national tragedy offered to Canadian nurses. Her message was followed by the letter which she had sent, at the request of the executive committee, pledging to the Prime Minister of Canada, the Right Honourable W.L. Mackenzie King, the loyal support of the Canadian Nurses' Association in this time of crisis. The president advised the Prime Minister that the Canadian Nurses' Association was giving 'serious thought and consideration to the maintenance of all health services as well as to the preparation of nurses for overseas duty.' She expressed the hope that the Federal government would 'utilize the services of this Association in any matter relating to nursing or to community health, realizing that this declaration of loyalty is made at the request of the nine Provincial Nursing Associations of Canada.'[8]

Calgary was the locale of the biennial meeting of the Canadian Nurses' Association in the last week of June 1940. Through the medium of *The Canadian Nurse*, Miss Fairley announced in advance the names of the recipients of the Mary Agnes Snively medals:

... The Executive had particular pleasure in endorsing the recommendations of the Award Committee, as the three women who are to be so signally honoured are women who have contributed generously of their time and ability to the Canadian Nurses' Association and to the nursing profession. They have also given leadership, and it is interesting to note that their leadership has been along such diverse paths. Such is the opportunity for the varied personalities within our profession, and such our joy in having within our ranks women who have so faithfully portrayed these ideals. The names of Kathleen Russell, Rev. Mother Allard, and Ethel Johns are worthy recipients of this, the highest award that the Canadian Nurses' Association can bestow on its members.[9]

Biographical sketches of the three nurses followed Miss Fairley's announcement in *The Canadian Nurse*. The writer of the brief account of Miss Johns' life and work was E. Cora Hind, who prefaced her remarks with the comment: 'Having been invited to prepare an outline of the professional career of Ethel Johns, I do so with profound admiration of the vision she has cherished of what nursing might and should mean to the world ...' Her concluding statement showed insight into Miss Johns' concept of professional service and the nature of her influence upon nursing: '... What she has done for the advancement of nursing through the *Journal* is well known to Canadian nurses. Keenly aware of the public demand for nursing service on a broader scale, she has striven to show how this demand might be fulfilled. Always learning herself, she inspires others to learn more so that they may serve better.'[10] Of all the honours which Miss Johns received in her lifetime, probably none touched her as deeply as this tribute from her old friend and the Mary Agnes Snively award itself.

In her account of the biennial meeting, Ethel Johns wrote, in part:

... The president of the Alberta Association of Registered Nurses, Miss Rae Chittick, has already told us in the pages of the *Journal* that long before the white man came, the Indians chose the 'swift running water' at Calgary as a place of happy meeting – 'good for the making of bows and arrows and for the transaction of business affairs.' And so, indeed, it proved to be: although, because the sessions were held in the shadow of the capitulation of France, there was a deep and sorrowful realization of the peril in which our British Commonwealth of Nations stands.

Nevertheless, the Canadian Nurses' Association went about its work with calmness and courage, and rose to the level of its great destiny as never before ...[11]

A major topic on the agenda was the nature of the contribution which the Canadian Nurses' Association should make to Canada's war effort. The convention decided to send to the Prime Minister of Canada a further statement of loyalty and willingness to serve; to present to the Federal government three surgical units at a total cost of forty-five hundred dollars; and to invest in war bonds all surplus funds of the Canadian Nurses Association.[12]

Marion Lindeburgh presented the Supplement to the Proposed Curriculum, dealing with the education of the nursing student in the clinical field. Miss Johns, commenting editorially upon this significant event, wrote: '... Mention should be made of the genuine enthusiasm and profound gratitude which marked the acceptance of this valuable and timely addition to the splendid achievement already attained by Miss Lindeburgh. She was accorded a standing vote of thanks, and must have been touched by the sincere and spontaneous response to her unselfish and untiring efforts on behalf of nursing education in Canada.'[13]

Among these who took an active part in the discussion of the Supplement were two nurses in whom Ethel Johns had reason to be interested. One of these was Margaret Kerr, a former student of hers at the University of British Columbia School of Nursing, now a member of the faculty of that school, and chairman of the Public Health Section of the Canadian Nurses' Association. Another was Gertrude Hall, a graduate of the Winnipeg General Hospital School of Nursing, the progressive secretary-registrar and school of nursing adviser of the Manitoba Association of Registered Nurses, whose remarks on 'Administrative Aspects of Nursing Education in the Clinical Field' were reminiscent of those often voiced by Ethel Johns herself, and went straight to the root of the difficulty in ensuring adequate education for nursing students:

... As long as we must continue to think in terms of nursing service to the hospital as of major importance, and the preparation of the nurse always as secondary, can we ever hope to build a sound educational program? True, every effort is being made to reduce the hours of duty so that our students may be in a position to obtain the maximum benefit from the improvements in the curriculum, but the problem of providing a sufficient number of graduate staff to enable administrators to plan the clinical experience for the student according to her needs and not according to the demands of the hospital continues to be a major difficulty and, as I see it, will continue to do so until we can bring the general public to appreciate the fact that nursing education is not the financial responsibility of the hospital ...[14]

Ethel Johns and Gertrude Hall had much in common. Both were committed to professional ideals of education and service. Both believed that one should 'stand and be counted' in defence of one's convictions. Each admired and respected the other, and there was a bond of affection between them.

In her report as editor and business manager, Miss Johns noted the steps which had been taken to enlarge the Journal, to secure additional clerical assistance, and to obtain suitable office accommodation. The financial picture was favourable because of a steady rise in both circulation and in advertisements. She remarked again upon the significant contribution of individuals and groups under the auspices of the provincial nurses' associations, and acknowledged the 'enlightened leadership given by the Publications Committee' (now Ruby Simpson, Jean Gunn, and Grace Fairley as convener). Through the years, in her reports as editor, Miss Johns had drawn attention to the support given by the Alumnae Association of the School of Nursing of the Hamilton General Hospital, which had a firm rule that all members must be subscribers to *The Canadian Nurse*. The editor again recognized this group for its continued support of the Journal.[15]

An amusing postscript to the editor's report appeared in the October 1940 issue of *The Canadian Nurse*. Miss Johns described a project undertaken by the Registered Nurses' Association of British Columbia, to subscribe to the Journal on behalf of one hundred nurses working in outlying districts of the province and out of touch with nursing affairs. Miss Johns commented:

... In her report at the biennial meeting of the Canadian Nurses' Association, the editor mentioned the possibility that the R.N.A.B.C. might make this friendly and generous gesture, but added that she 'never counted the chickens before they were hatched.' Later in the session, Miss Duffield rebuked the editor for this want of faith by asserting that 'British Columbia never yet laid an egg that wouldn't hatch.' And so indeed it seems. The whole 'clutch' is now scratching vigorously for a living![16]

Miss Fairley and all of the other officers who had served the Canadian Nurses' Association so well during the 1938–40 biennium were re-elected by acclamation, thus helping to ensure stability and continuity in the direction of national nursing affairs in the war emergency.

Miss Johns was now completing the eighth year of her editorship. At sixty-one years of age, she was still deeply absorbed in her work, but her interests were not confined to nursing. Glimpses of her personal life are contributed by people who knew her during that period, and are revealed in her writings – particularly in the 'Off Duty' page in *The Canadian Nurse*.

22

Ethel Johns Off Duty

By her own admission, Ethel Johns was a solitary person. Occasionally she mentioned this fact in the 'Off Duty' page of *The Canadian Nurse*, as when she wrote: 'Like most solitary folk, we do not particularly enjoy festivals, but the Christmas season fosters a mellow and reminiscent mood in which we recall our "Christmas past" in England ...'[1] In another essay, she cheerfully recognized the same trait in herself:

... National festivals are grand, especially when they come at week-ends in the summertime. This happy combination has occurred three times during this year of the King's grace, and we have celebrated each of them in a spirit which a friend who is by way of being an expert in mental hygiene stigmatizes as morose and 'antisocial' (or perhaps it is 'asocial'!). Her harsh judgment is based on our stubborn refusal to sally forth on excursions and picnics, and our equally obstinate determination to stay at home in the shadow of our own vine and fig tree. She darkly surmises that this disposition to flock by ourselves is something which ought to be corrected with the aid of a psychiatrist ...

Miss Johns went on to say that she was simply 'compensating' for the long years spent in hospital work, when it was her 'sad fate' to stay on duty over holidays so that she might 'cope with the untoward situations which inevitably arise on days of public rejoicing.' Now, for the first time in her professional career, she knew 'the consolations of domestic joys. We wash and iron, we sweep and dust, we even cook in a gypsy fashion ...'[2]

Possible reasons for Ethel Johns' love of solitude are not difficult to find. The loneliness of her childhood and of life on the reserve threw her upon her own inner resources. Her early assumption of positions of authority and long years of executive work – in a militaristic era in nursing – thrust her into another kind of lonely isolation. She had an artistic temperament and tended to withdraw from human contacts during periods of creativity, and occasional moodiness to which she was subject had the same effect. She was basically a contemplative person, and needed seclusion in order to think. Another factor cannot be overlooked: she gave so much of herself to her writing or other work in which she was engaged that quiet periods alone were essential to her renewal. In any event, Ethel Johns accepted herself as she was and made no apologies, yet her acceptance was not without sadness. In one of the 'Off Duty' essays, writing about the sounds of various kinds of bells in the world, she concluded: 'A bell on a rocking buoy off a dangerous coast, "Shoal, beware shoal!" This is the bell for us, if there could be but one, this we would choose, lifting untiringly to every wave that batters it, solitary and defiant. "Would I change with my brother a mile inland? not I." '[3]

Reading had always been a joy to Ethel Johns, and it continued to be a favourite means of relaxation: '... We may as well confess that we read in bed. After a long day filled with what Stevenson called "irritating concerns and duties," nothing is more soothing than to adjust the pillows and the light at the right angle and then to escape through the gateway of another mind ...'[4]

Another source of pleasure was the radio which she acquired not long after her arrival in Montreal. By chance, the first programme to which she listened was one which transported her into another world:

... After sitting in the seats of the scornful these many years, we succumbed at last and bought a radio, a modest affair but our very own, to twiddle the dials as we please. The first thing which gushed from it was not, as we had feared it might be, a shrieking soprano or a nasal tenor, or intimate advice on personal hygiene from the vendors of toothpaste. Instead it was a flood of melody, the voices of men and boys, sustained by the deep notes of the organ from a church in a town in Poland, which once we visited on a clear and shining autumn day, in order to see the Crucifix, beautifully carved out of dark wood, which according to legend floated miraculously down the Vistula long centuries ago. We were caught up on a magic carpet which annihilated space and telescoped time, and for a fleeting instant we looked again upon the ineffable beauty of that ancient shrine ...[5]

Ethel Johns loved music, and occasionally went to symphony concerts. But she had little money to spare for such treats, and the radio sometimes provided an enjoyable substitute. One such occasion prompted Miss Johns to write:

> ... We have been getting into arguments lately about the right way to listen to music. Some of our acquaintances sit dutifully before their radios and write down every word which falls from the lips of the 'eminent American composer and critic, Deems Taylor.' Others have no patience with him and insist on studying the programme notes, which he so deeply scorns. We agree with Mr Taylor that, no matter how ignorant you may be about musical techniques, you have the right to wrestle with the music, like Jacob with his angel, and to interpret its meaning in your own way. We will even go a step further and assert that its emotional impact cannot be expressed in words with any degree of precision ... We realized this one evening when listening over our radio to a performance of 'Perpetual Motion.' Toscanini was conducting and only the stringed instruments were playing. As the music reached its terrific climax, we found ourselves standing in the middle of the floor, not quite sure whether we were in this world or the next, and quite incapable of logical thought. When the music ceased we were only certain of one thing, we had heard the morning stars singing together, and lived to tell the tale.
>
> The radio never did this to us, either before or since, because as a rule we are dependent upon seeing as well as hearing the music. We like to arrive early, in time to watch the musicians dropping in one after another. When the oboe player sounds the A from which the other instruments take their pitch, a preliminary tingle runs down our spine, and when the conductor lifts his baton, we take off grandly with the violins. We can still see Rachmaninoff sitting austerely at the piano, ready to begin his own concerto, with the full orchestra as a sombre background. That afternoon in Carnegie Hall, we remembered as though it had been yesterday the first music we ever consciously heard. We were seven years old, and it was a summer evening in North Wales. The men who worked in the slate quarries were singing on their way home. The song was 'Ar hyd y Nos,' which means 'All through the night.' Hearing it, we burst into a flood of tears, and refused to be comforted or to explain what we were crying about. We still don't know, but whatever it was, Rachmaninoff touched the same chord, which vibrated then and which will never quite cease trembling until the music dies out forever.[6]

The radio brought Miss Johns not only music, but news bulletins, political commentaries, and addresses by noted speakers. It was a never-ending source of interest to her.

Another leisure activity which Ethel Johns enjoyed was walking. One of her favourite haunts in Montreal was Mount Royal. Weather permitting, she took solitary hikes up the mountain and absorbed the beauties which lay around her. She loved nature, took delight in birds, trees, flowers, lakes, and rivers, and was able to recreate what she saw in glowing word pictures. Many of her 'Off Duty' essays were such mirrorlike reflections of her observations that the reader was able to picture the scene as if he were there. Even the walk to the office on a pleasant summer day could be an adventure for Miss Johns:

... A modern poet tells us that something is radically wrong if we can find no time to stand and stare. So on a glorious summer morning we made up our mind that we would stand and we would stare. We invited our soul to bear us company on the way down to the office, and our roving eye was first attracted by a large spider which dropped down on his silken cable and swung lazily to and fro against the sunny doorway of our little balcony. He was not spinning a web, he was doing it for fun. Presently he reeled in his line and disappeared from view. We dawdled through the grounds of McGill University, and stopped to stare at the gingko tree which shades the tomb of the Founder. The tender green of the graceful branches was spread out like a pagoda. It is a Chinese tree, and there are only five in Montreal, all too far apart even to whisper to one another about home.

Presently we came to a long shed, where motor cars come down, like elephants, to bathe. 'Ten minute wash one dollar,' which seems reasonable enough. The garage men were sky-larking about, and one of them turned a neat handspring, quite in the irresponsible spirit of the spider. In front of a forbidding Tourist Home was a green bed of lilies of the valley. The perfume mounted to our head and we found ourselves going up a mountain (which is certainly not the way to our office) until we came to a little blue lake with a mediaeval castle beside it. A soulless civic corporation calls this sylvan retreat the Municipal Waterworks, but across the rippling water the dome of Hôtel-Dieu rises like a silver bubble above the trees, and toward the south the great St Lawrence draws his shining chain towards the Gulf and the open sea. Presently we responded to the prickings of our uneasy conscience and returned to the path of duty. Just outside the office door we were accosted by an arrogant Pekingese with whom we have a nodding acquaintance. This pampered animal gazed at us so disdainfully out of its goggle eyes that we mounted hastily to our place of toil, knowing that we really have no time to stand and to stare. That privilege is reserved for spiders, and garage men, and Pekingese, and other members of the leisure class.[7]

Although a solitary person, Ethel Johns had a gift for friendship.

This she did not bestow lightly, but once given she held firmly and with unswerving loyalty. She enjoyed good conversation with a small group of congenial companions with whom she could match wits in lively discussions of subjects ranging from philosophy to politics, from current events to books. The French-Canadian point of view interested her, and Suzanne Giroux was expected to contribute this on the occasions when 'The Creative Minority' came together. Miss Giroux remembers that the four friends 'had a gay relationship, had fun together, and those evenings left you with a champagne feeling.'[8]

Miss Johns sometimes accompanied Eileen Flanagan on visits to the home of her brother and his wife. Dr Cyril Flanagan belonged to the C.C.F. party, and at one time during this period he ran for member of Parliament in the Westmount riding of Montreal. He and Miss Johns had long talks about politics. She (in the words of a friend who knew her at that time) was a 'true socialist.' Apparently her political convictions had not changed since the Winnipeg General Strike.

Mabel Hersey sometimes invited Miss Johns to supper on Saturday evenings in her suite at the Royal Victoria Hospital. Other guests, according to Miss Flanagan, were a few directors of nursing in Montreal who were friends and who used to take turns entertaining each other on Saturday evenings. Miss Hersey was a practical and progressive person, and she and Miss Johns got on well together.

Another friend in Montreal was Caroline Barrett, supervisor of the Royal Victoria Montreal Maternity Hospital, who (early in Miss Johns' editorship) had prepared the report in French of the 1934 biennial convention. Some years later, Miss Barrett wrote an article, 'A Hundred Years of Maternity Nursing,' for *The Canadian Nurse,* and she recalls that Miss Johns helped her to prepare it. She also assisted Miss Barrett with the manuscript of a book (which she wrote in collaboration with Dr John Fraser) commemorating the centenary of the Montreal Maternity Hospital.[9]

Miss Johns rarely entertained in her apartment, although Miss Flanagan recalls attending small committee meetings there and finding the suite very homelike. When friends came to town, Miss Johns apparently took them to a club for a meal. The late Mrs Georgina (Denmark) Stocker remembered Miss Johns entertaining her in this way when she was passing through Montreal.

A business acquaintance with whom Miss Johns had regular contact during these years was O.T. Leeman, at that time manager of the Canadian Division of the J.B. Lippincott Company. Mr Leeman recalls that his former chief at Lippincott's, Ellis W. Bacon, who had 'had a hand in publishing the first nursing text in the U.S.A., was impressed with the fact that some of the foremost nursing leaders in the United States were Canadian. He wondered what made Canadian nurses so good.' In the 1930s and early 1940s, Mr Leeman (for Lippincott's) was trying to see what they could learn from Canadian nurses. In those days, he says, it took a long time to produce a nursing text, so it was important to be able to forecast nursing trends. Miss Johns was very helpful to Mr Leeman in this regard: she gave him sound advice and was able to suggest whom he should see. They had luncheon meetings quite often, usually in a little French restaurant. In the early years of Miss Johns' editorship, Mr Leeman remembers, when *The Canadian Nurse* was having a struggle financially, it was suggested to her that the J.B. Lippincott Company might be permitted to give some temporary assistance, such as underwriting paper and helping with advertising problems. But Miss Johns was too independent to accept this offer.[10]

A contact which Miss Johns valued highly during her years in Montreal was with her cousin, the Right Reverend Philip Carrington, who was consecrated Lord Bishop of Quebec in Holy Trinity Cathedral, Quebec City, on 25 July 1935. He later became Archbishop, and then Metropolitan of the Ecclesiastical Province of Canada. Archbishop Carrington had a distinguished academic career at Cambridge University and the University of New Zealand, was the recipient of several honorary degrees, and from 1929-35 was Dean and Professor of Divinity at Bishop's University, Lennoxville, Quebec. He was also a writer of note.[11] His cousin Ethel found a congenial spirit in her illustrious kinsman. From time to time, she went to Quebec City to visit Archbishop Carrington and his wife.

When Miss Johns visited Toronto on business, as she had occasion to do from time to time, she sometimes had tea or dinner in the home of Dr and Mrs Harry Cassidy. Mrs Cassidy was a former student of Miss Johns at the University of British Columbia and had never forgotten her old teacher, of whom she was very fond. She recalls that Miss Johns enjoyed conversing with her husband, and that her young daughter was attracted to her. Miss Johns often showed her fondness for young people, and they for her. It is said that in gatherings where student nurses were present, they would often be seen clustering around Miss Johns, engaged in animated conversation with her.

A consideration of Ethel Johns' personal characteristics at this time would be incomplete without reference to her personal appearance of which (it is said) she was very conscious. She was aging, and dark shadows under her eyes gave her a haggard look. Her expression was normally serious, even dour, but when she was stimulated by interesting talk or when she smiled her face lighted up, and an observer would not have considered her unattractive. Like many British women, she looked her best in evening dress. She loved beautiful fabrics, but did not usually have the means to indulge her taste for them. She dressed well, if plainly, and evidently possessed an understanding of the rudiments of style. After reading Elizabeth Hawes' book, *Fashion is Spinach*, Miss Johns wrote:

... True style should be functional, which means that your dress is suited to your work. Even a nurse's uniform has style, all except her cap, which has degenerated into a vestigial remnant, like the vermiform appendix. Style means that your dress has good lines and is well sewn. It may cost five hundred dollars, or only five, if you happen to have brains and an eye for colour and can sew a straight seam. Style never gets shabby or stale, because it has nothing to do with age, and a woman of seventy may have more style than a girl of seventeen. We have no reason to suppose that Elizabeth Hawes found her conception of style in the pages of the Book of Common Prayer, but it is there for all that. Style is the outward and visible sign of an inward and spiritual grace ...[12]

Whatever fleeting regrets Ethel Johns may have felt during this period of her life that she had little claim to physical beauty, her common sense and ability to laugh at herself were excellent antidotes. Her intellectual gifts were more than a little compensation, and these she recognized and valued.

23

Full Flower

An astute observer, Dr Rae Chittick, suggests that Ethel Johns' influence upon nursing was of a catalytic nature. A study of her speeches and writings together with a review of contemporary events in Canadian nursing serves to confirm this view, particularly during the years when she was editor of *The Canadian Nurse*. She watched closely the national and international trends and events in nursing, pointed them up in her editorials, and gave her interpretation of their significance. If, as she often lamented, the 'rank and file' of nurses paid more attention to the 'Off Duty' page than to the editorials, the same could not be alleged of the nursing leaders throughout the country. The latter both read and heeded the editor's commentaries.

In October 1940 the executive committee named Ethel Johns to represent the Canadian Nurses' Association on the Nursing Council on National Defence, a body recently established by the American Nurses Association for the purpose of assessing and readying nursing resources in the United States in advance of a possible national emergency. Membership in this important Council was stimulating to Ethel Johns and proved to be a valuable means of keeping the Canadian Nurses' Association in touch with the progressive measures which it adopted.

In an editorial for the February 1941 issue of *The Canadian Nurse* Miss Johns stated that a review of nursing journals in Britain and the United States showed some important trends. 'In the United States the work of the Nursing Council on National Defence continues to go forward with plans for a national nursing inventory, extension of nursing school programs, and preparation for the expansion of nursing services in hospitals and public health agencies. A large increase in the Army Nurse Corps is anticipated, and the Nursing Service of the American Red Cross has undertaken an active program of recruitment ...' The editor drew attention to an article by Isabel M. Stewart in the December number of *The American Journal of Nursing* which dealt with nursing education in relation to national defence. The writer proposed that certain measures be taken: emergency nursing and first aid courses for all nurses in active service; refresher courses for nurses out of active practice and for those whose training was inadequate or out of date; specialized training to prepare nurses to work in special fields; and up-grading programmes for nurses who were being placed in positions of responsibility without adequate preparation. Miss Johns concluded:

... American nurses are fortunate in having time to look to their defences before the storm is upon them. In Britain the practice of nursing is being carried on literally under fire. Under such circumstances, there is neither time nor opportunity for making surveys or for long range planning ...
... In Canada we have much to learn from our British sisters who are so bravely enduring this ordeal by fire. We are only just beginning to take our places in the front ranks of the battle, but the pace is quickening from month to month. Already our hospitals are beginning to feel the effects of the withdrawal of 'key' nurses in increasing numbers as they enter military service; we might do well to note how our neighbours to the south are planning to deal with this particular situation.[1]

Several of the pioneers of Canadian nursing passed from the active scene during the year 1941, and their records of professional service were noted in the pages of *The Canadian Nurse*. Miss Helen Randal retired, and Miss Johns, recalling her long career and some of her experiences as an early editor of the Journal, wrote:

... The editorials written by Miss Randal were characteristic of her quality of mind: clear and trenchant, and shot through with her unfailing humour and quick sense of the ridiculous. An incisive debater and strong disciplinarian, there has never been any manner of doubt as to what Miss Randal thought on any subject ... It is the sincere wish of her colleagues and friends that her alert, critical faculty, and her wide experience in the nursing field, will continue to make themselves felt to advantage for many years to come.[2]

The same number of the Journal announced the appointment of Harriet Evelyn Mallory as registrar and educational adviser of the Registered Nurses' Association of British Columbia. Miss Mallory's career had followed some of the same pathways as that of Ethel Johns. She was a graduate of the Winnipeg General Hospital School of Nursing, studied at Teachers College, had held the office of president of the Manitoba Association of Registered Nurses, and prior to coming to her new position had been superintendent of nurses of the Children's Hospital of Winnipeg. She was destined to become the third director of the University of British Columbia School of Nursing, succeeding Mabel Gray, whose retirement was announced in the November 1941 issue of *The Canadian Nurse*, Miss Johns paid a warm tribute to Miss Gray and recognized her fine contribution to nursing education and to the work of nursing organizations.

In August of the same year, the editor of *The Canadian Nurse* sadly recorded in the Journal the death of Jean Isabel Gunn. Her eulogy commenced: 'The passing of great leaders is rightly marked by tributes to their worth. From the church, the press, the public have come many expressions of the affection, respect, and admiration in which Jean Isabel Gunn was held ...' The loss was one which Miss Johns must have felt deeply. Miss Emory remembers that she spoke of Miss Gunn as 'the noblest Roman of them all.'

A significant editorial by Ethel Johns in the September 1941 issue dealt with the shortage of nurses caused by the increasing enrolment in military service. In some cities and towns, she reported, it was difficult to find private duty nurses to take cases, and public health and visiting nursing groups were feeling the strain of constantly changing staff: '... The military authorities claim (and not without reason) that the best is not too good for them. On the other hand, many far-seeing nurses think that highly qualified supervisors and teachers should be kept at home to train competent rank and file workers to meet the increased demands which are certain to come from military and civilian sources. This involves a personal factor which should not be overlooked.' It was natural and right that well-qualified nurses should wish to offer themselves for overseas service, and due credit should be given them should they consent instead to serve on the home front. The editor suggested certain measures to deal with the current situation. An inventory should be made of available nursing resources in Canada, and an analysis made of its findings. This might well reveal, Miss Johns stated, that the shortage of nurses was more apparent than real, and that more intelligent distribution of nursing service might help to solve some of the difficulties. Boards of directors of hospitals and public health agencies should encourage their younger staff nurses to prepare themselves for responsible positions in their own organizations, and departments of nursing within Canadian universities could serve as training centres for these nurses. Futhermore, every superintendent of nurses should select and train potential substitutes for all key nurses on her staff. Finally, the editor called attention to the fact that, because of the far-sighted policies and activities of the Nursing Council on National Defence, the American Congress had voted a large sum of money to be used in building up and strengthening the education of professional nurses. In Canada, she suggested, financial assistance for nursing education would probably have to come from provincial rather than Federal governmental sources, but such grants should be sought. 'The community will accept financial responsibility for educating nurses,' affirmed Miss Johns, 'if we can prove we are indispensable to its health and welfare. But the onus of proof rests with us – and not by words alone. "In the handicraft of their work is their prayer," ' she concluded.

Because of the existing acute problems in nursing service and education arising out of the combined military and civilian demands, the executive committee of the Canadian Nurses' Association convened a joint three-day conference in Montreal, at the end of September 1941, with representatives of the departments of nursing in eight Canadian universities. Miss Johns was present, as were representatives of the provincial nurses associations. The meetings, chaired by the president, Miss Fairley, were held in the McGill School for Graduate Nurses. Of this conference, Miss Johns wrote:

... The occasion proved to be historic in more ways than one. For the first time, the Executive Committee of the Canadian Nurses' Association conferred, as a group, with representatives of various University departments of nursing in Canada. More significant still, these University representatives met, for the first time, to take counsel with one another. While it was to be expected that enlightened leadership would arise out of a joint conference of this kind, it was less easy to predict the salutary influence that the participating groups would exercise upon one another. The impact of the reality of things as they are, upon the dream of things as they ought to be, made itself felt in no uncertain fashion. This friendly clash of ideas had a thoroughly tonic effect, and helped to keep the debate on a sane and practical level. The haunting sense of unreality which sometimes hangs about theoretical discussion was refreshingly absent. Yet it was frankly admitted, by even the most incorrigible realists, that the dead hand of the past must no longer be permitted to block wise and courageous action in the future.

It was encouraging to note a growing realization that dignified publicity must be given to nursing (and sometimes to nurses) if we are to obtain financial support from public funds ...[3]

The far-reaching recommendations submitted by the representatives of the University schools, and approved by the executive committee, were designed to improve conditions of learning for nursing students, to assist schools of nursing to increase their enrolments, to make better and fuller use of existing postgraduate courses in universities and to initiate new ones as required, to extend and enrich inservice education, to recall married and inactive nurses and to ready them for active service, and to give general staff nurses better professional status and more adequate remuneration. To assist in implementing these measures, the executive of the Canadian Nurses' Association decided to appoint a senior member of the profession (who should be released temporarily from her position) to work with the president, the executive committee, and the provincial nurses associations. After the original appointment of such an adviser, staff should be named to assist her, for example, a French nurse. It was agreed that an immediate programme of publicity should be arranged, and that 'an appeal for funds be made to the Federal and Provincial Governments in order to meet the needs of nursing services which have expanded so greatly under war conditions ...'[4]

Kathleen W. Ellis, Professor of Nursing, the University of Saskatchewan School of Nursing, was appointed as national nursing adviser. Suzanne Giroux was named to assist her, and carried out this work until she enrolled for military service.

As was her custom, Ethel Johns offered a Christmas message in the December number of the Journal:

... In Coventry, this year as last, carols will be sung by candlelight in the ruins of a great cathedral. If the bombers come over, as they usually do on the eve of any religious festival, the candles will burn steadily and the boyish voices will not falter. If, in the busy English hospitals, the power is cut off and there are not enough flashlights to go round, the nurses will go about their work by candlelight. After all, the symbol of nursing is a flaming Lamp, and not a brittle glass bulb that, once broken, can never be kindled again.

Even in the midst of the turmoil and agony of war, we must have faith to believe that some day it will end. A Christmas eve will come when there will be no blackout and after a silence of years, the church bells will ring out over the peaceful English countryside. Then, nurses in every country will lift their lamps high and signal to one another across the world that the night is far spent and the day is at hand. We shall be proud to remember that even in the darkness we steadfastly kept one flame burning. Perhaps, even now, although we do not know it, all nurses, friends and enemies alike, are keeping a Christmas vigil together, waiting for the dawn.[5]

In April of 1942 Miss Johns attended the annual meeting in Quebec City of the Association of Registered Nurses of the Province of Quebec. She took part in a symposium of which the theme was the international, national, and provincial relationships of the Association, and delivered an address in French on this subject. Other papers were given by Suzanne Giroux and Alice Albert, and all three were published in a subsequent issue of *The Canadian Nurse*.[6] As far as can be determined, this was the only occasion upon which Miss Johns gave a speech in the French language.

The twenty-first General Meeting of the Canadian Nurses' Association was held in the Windsor Hotel, Montreal, from the twenty-second to the twenty-sixth of June 1942. The city reached its tercentenary in that year, and the Sisters of the Community of Hôtel-Dieu commemorated the arrival, three centuries earlier, of Jeanne Mance, the first Canadian nurse. General anxiety over the war situation caused a modification of the original plans for celebrating these anniversaries; still, Miss Johns wrote, Montreal was at its best for the nurses' convention:

... Montreal never looked more beautiful than it did during the last week of June. Mount Royal was a mass of living green and the gardens were a riot of colour. Under the stately elms of McGill University, the sailors of the Royal Canadian Navy went through their complicated drill and, against a cloudless blue sky, the great bombers roared by on their way overseas. The streets were gay with flags in honour of Army Week and, to mark the Tercentenary of this noble and historic city, the blue and white banner of the Province of Quebec floated the fleur-de-lys proudly in the summer air ...[7]

The editor commented that the outstanding feature of this convention 'was its unity in both the national and an international sense.' The French-speaking members participated fully and several of their number carried the responsibility for concurrent translation of the proceedings. Copies of some major reports were available in both French and English. Among the distinguished international guest speakers were Effie Taylor, president of the International Council of Nurses, and Julia Stimson, president of the American Nurses' Association.

The business of the meeting focused sharply upon a review of measures already taken and those now required to ensure an adequate supply and distribution of nursing services to meet military and civilian needs.

Recipients of the Snively awards were Grace M. Fairley, E. Frances Upton, and Eleanor McPhedran. Marion Lindeburgh was elected president, succeeding Miss Fairley.

Insofar as *The Canadian Nurse* was concerned, the editor was able to report a slow but steady increase in subscriptions and in the cash reserve of the Journal. She noted that 'The most difficult articles to obtain are those which deal with actual nursing procedure but, during the last six months, a rich source of such material has been drawn upon with gratifying results. At the Toronto General Hospital the editor was kindly allowed to make an appeal at a staff nurses conference for help in this connection. A committee was formed immediately and excellent material is now being sent in regularly by both supervisors and head nurses ... If this example could be followed throughout the country, a long step would be taken toward making Canadian nurses more articulate and the Journal more vital and interesting ...'[8]

One of the first duties of the new president was to announce, through the medium of *The Canadian Nurse,* that the Federal government had now made a grant of $115,000 to the Canadian Nurses' Association 'to encourage and aid efforts to meet urgent requirements for providing adequate national nursing service.' The grant was in response to the appeal which the Association had made to the government in the preceding November.[9] In the September issue of the Journal, Miss Lindeburgh was able to give particulars about the purposes for which the grant was to be allocated: recruitment of student nurses; a programme for provision of ancillary services; provision of facilities for schools of nursing increasing their enrolment; scholarships to enable graduate nurses to take postgraduate courses to prepare for teaching, supervisory, and administrative positions; and support of the work of the Emergency Nursing Adviser. The executive committee subsequently appointed a Government Grant Committee, chaired by the president, of which Miss Johns was a member.[10]

The summer and fall of 1942 brought significant events in the personal life and relationships of Ethel Johns. Her niece, Helen Johns, was married. She recalls that her Aunt Ethel made a visit to Winnipeg about that time, and asked Helen what she would like for a wedding gift. She enquired whether the young couple owed anything on their furniture, and admonished her niece, 'You shouldn't have unpaid bills, ever!' Helen replied that they owed fifty-five dollars. Her aunt, evidently not convinced of the size of their debt, emphasized that her gift would be no more and no less than the sum of what they owed. But when Aunt Ethel's cheque arrived, says Mrs Franklin, it was for an amount considerably in excess of that amount.

Ethel Johns' mother died in a nursing home in Glendale, California, on 22 September 1942. No details of the event have been found, except that her body was cremated and her ashes interred in a tree-shaded plot in Mount Royal Cemetery, Montreal.

Two weeks later, Miss Johns sustained the loss of her dearest friend. Cora Hind died suddenly on the morning of 6 October.[11] An unconfirmed report states that Miss Johns was on a train when she received the news, that she collapsed, and had to be helped off and conveyed by wheel chair from the station. If this is true, it seems probable that, upon hearing that her friend was critically ill, she set out for Winnipeg, and received word of her death either before the train left the station in Montreal or after its arrival in Winnipeg. Like so many other events in Miss Johns' personal life, this is veiled in obscurity. Cora Hind's bequest to Ethel Johns was a sum of money which helped to safeguard her retirement years. It was sufficient to enable Miss Johns to buy the small home in Vancouver in which she spent the last twenty years of her life.

Ethel Johns' brother Owen died suddenly on 9 December in the same year. Helen Franklin states that she does not know what she would have done in this crisis had it not been for the help given by her Aunt Ethel, since her mother was totally unable to cope with the situation. Miss Johns arranged for the funeral service in St Matthew's Church, Winnipeg, and had Owen's body brought to Montreal, where his ashes were interred in the same plot in Mount Royal Cemetery in which his mother's ashes had been buried so short a time before. Mrs Franklin adds that her Aunt Ethel met all the expenses of Owen Johns' funeral, and that when his widow died a few months later, she assumed financial responsibility for her funeral, too.[12]

The president of the Canadian Nurses' Association announced the impending loss of two officials in the March 1943 issue of *The Canadian Nurse*. Jean Wilson's resignation as executive secretary was to take effect on 30 September 1943, and Ethel Johns wished to be relieved of her duties on 31 December. The president invited applications for these important positions.

'Getting Down to Brass Tacks,' was the title of Miss Johns' editorial in the May 1943 issue. A critical turning point in British nursing had been reached recently, she reported, when the Minister of Labour and National Service decided to take special measures to deal with the shortage of nurses and midwives. He appointed a National Advisory Council for this purpose, composed of twenty-three members of whom only six were nurses. The Council would be responsible for 'working out plans for better distribution of existing nursing services and for carrying on a publicity campaign in aid of the recruitment of students.' Should persuasive measures fail (in effecting an adequate distribution of nursing services), the Minister made it clear that more drastic controls might be necessary. Miss Johns emphasized that the implications for Canadian nurses were clear:

... First of all it would be wise to face up to the fact that here, as in Britain, public opinion may force the Government to take action unless we can meet reasonable demands for nursing service under our own steam ... There is a growing conviction on the part of the public that we either cannot or will not assure a proper distribution of nursing service. What sort of defence are we prepared to make? It had better be a good one.

Another lesson we must learn is that he who pays the piper has the right to call the tune ... When the British Government decided to subsidize nursing service it also assumed the right to exercise controls. The same thing may happen here ...

The third and possibly the most important lesson we have to learn is that, like the nurses in Britain, we may have to fight hard to preserve our hard-won educational standards ...[13]

Miss Johns' editorial in the June issue gave a detailed account of the submission by the Canadian Nurses' Association to the Special Committee on Social Security of the House of Commons. The main topic was health insurance and its relationship to the nursing profession. The text of the Association's brief, as presented by Miss Lindeburgh, was given in full in the editorial. Miss Johns concluded: '... Never before have the nurses of Canada had such a fine opportunity of pleading their cause in the presence of so distinguished an audience. Our President and her associates rose to the occasion magnificently and we are indeed proud of them.'[14]

Upon Jean Wilson's resignation, Kathleen Ellis accepted the position of general secretary and national adviser, with the understanding that she would be released in one year's time to return to her post at the University of Saskatchewan. Miss Johns' successor, Margaret Kerr, could not leave her duties at the University of British Columbia earlier than the first of May 1944. Miss Johns agreed to remain until the end of the third week in June, thus allowing the new editor a period of orientation.

In her final editorial, Miss Johns commented on the stature which the Canadian Nurses' Association had now attained. She wrote of the important factor which *The Canadian Nurse* had been, from the earliest days, in the life of the Association and its growth. She reviewed the statement of the Journal's objectives which she had given at the 1934 biennial meeting, and added: 'While it is obvious that the *Journal* has not yet fully attained these objectives, the women who in turn have served in an editorial capacity have done their utmost to achieve them. I am happy and proud to have had the privilege of being one of that honourable company.' Miss Johns congratulated her successor. Young and vigorous leadership was called for and Miss Kerr was completely competent to provide it.[15]

Appreciation of the work of Ethel Johns as editor and business manager of *The Canadian Nurse* was expressed in the first issue published under the direction of Margaret Kerr:

... Nurses across Canada unite in a tribute to the editor and business manager of our *Journal* who resigned from her position at the end of June. It would seem unnecessary and inappropriate to eulogize Miss Johns, for her work speaks for her, as evidenced by the public and professional recognition which has been accorded her at home and abroad. During the past eleven years, Miss Johns has made a contribution to nursing which it is impossible to measure. Her broad interpretation of the ideals and practice of nursing, as reflected in the pages of *The Canadian Nurse,* has had a profound influence upon the lives of nurses, and upon the spirit and progress of nursing ...[16]

Miss Johns was not in attendance at the biennial meeting in Winnipeg in the last week of June 1944, at which the following resolution in her honour was passed: '... Whereas it has been announced that Miss Ethel Johns will shortly be relinquishing her present duties after a long and distinguished service as editor and business manager of *The Canadian Nurse,* and whereas under her efficient direction the *Journal* has reached its present high standard; therefore be it resolved: that this

Association record its deep appreciation of this and other outstanding contributions to nursing in Canada, and express its pride in her achievements in international nursing.'[17]

Viewing Ethel Johns' professional career in historical perspective, Dr Florence Emory suggests that it was as editor and writer that Miss Johns' career 'came to full flower.'[18] Abundant evidence supports this judgment. Another contemporary opinion is voiced by Dr Rae Chittick, that Miss Johns had the faculty of deciding what was transient and what was of lasting value. She had a sense of the fundamental things that influence nursing, and did not look at nursing in a limited way or from a narrow perspective. Her editorship was superb: she had the ability and skill, when editing materials for publication, of deleting the superfluous and tightening up the writing without in any way altering the author's meaning. She was a true editor, concludes this critic.[19] Throughout the arduous years of her professional practice, Ethel Johns had been conscious of nursing history in the making and had proudly accepted her role as one of the pioneers whose task it was to blaze the trail. Now she was ready to relinquish the burden and eager to begin her retirement. The happy years ahead were to afford her a new freedom. This period, full of activities and interests, was to be productive, particularly from the point of view of her writing, an occupation which she loved and which she now had the opportunity to pursue at will.

PART SEVEN: 1944-1968

24

New Horizons

At sixty-five years of age, Ethel Johns had not yet put down firm roots. She loved Montreal and had a few good friends there, but she found the winters difficult. Vancouver, she thought, would be a desirable place in which to spend her remaining years, but at the time of her retirement from *The Canadian Nurse* she had not made any definite plans to move west. Almost immediately she became involved in a number of special assignments in both Canada and the United States which delayed for several years her intended departure from the east.

While still editor of *The Canadian Nurse*, Miss Johns had become interested in the anticipated postwar problems of women, and was a member of the Committee on Postwar Planning of the Canadian Nurses' Association. The committee early recognized the need for a study of the factors to be considered in recommending nurses for service in foreign countries, and established a subcommittee under the convenership of Ethel Johns to look into this aspect of the total problem. The subcommittee met, presumably early in 1944, with officials of the United Nations Relief and Rehabilitation Administration who gave information about current plans for the rehabilitation of certain areas in Europe, and the need for and required qualifications of nurses to participate in this work.[1] In an editorial which she wrote for the February (1944) issue of *The Canadian Nurse*, Miss Johns had publicized the work of UNRRA and its need for workers. Her association with the Committee on Postwar Planning and her interest in UNRRA did not cease when she severed her ties with the Journal. Following the 1944 biennial meeting in Winnipeg, Miss Johns was appointed the official representative of the Canadian Nurses' Association to the Council of the Canadian Voluntary Agencies assisting UNRRA. In this capacity she attended a conference of the International Council of Nurses, in New York, on 6 and 7 October 1944. She was also present as an observer at the meeting, in Montreal, of the Council of the United Nations Relief and Rehabilitation Administration, and subsequently wrote a colourful account of the conference which appeared in the December (1944) issue of *The Canadian Nurse*.

At the end of October 1944 a special assignment brought Miss Johns to New York. Some eleven years earlier, the National League of Nursing Education had published a pamphlet, *The Nursing School Faculty, Duties, Qualifications and Preparation*. This was now outdated, and the League set up a Committee on Revision of the Faculty Pamphlet, under the chairmanship of Isabel Stewart. The membership of this committee comprised an impressive number of the foremost nursing leaders of the day and included (ex officio) Adelaide A. Mayo, the executive secretary, and Blanche Pfefferkorn, director of studies of the National League of Nursing Education. Miss Johns' task was to assist the committee with the work of revision, an undertaking which initially was expected to require two months, but which, it was soon apparent, would take half a year of her time.[2]

On 27 January, Miss Johns wrote to Amy Lee, who had been her student at the Children's Hospital in Winnipeg and later attended the short courses for public health nurses which Miss Johns conducted at the University of British Columbia. Since that time, Miss Lee had kept in touch with her old teacher, even after she became severely crippled because of a spinal condition. Now Miss Johns sent a letter to thank her for a remembrance at Christmas and to give news of her own activities:

MY DEAR AMY LEE,

I am ashamed to have delayed so long in thanking you for the exquisite little water colour which now adorns my room in (of all places!) the Nurses Residence of St Luke's Hospital. No, I haven't gone back into training – the director of nursing very kindly allowed me the privilege of 'living in' because there literally was not a place in this great city where I could get clean and decent accommodation. You may well ask, 'What are you doing in New York?' To tell the truth I hardly know myself – but after I resigned from the Journal one piece of work after another kept cropping up, first in Canada and then down here in the U.S.A. At present I am making a study for the National League of Nursing Education and it looks as though I may have to remain as a guest of Uncle Sam until some time in April.

It has been rather nerve-racking but very stimulating to be so close to the centre of things and to watch the strange cross-currents which are beating in upon nursing from every side. We are in for some pretty drastic changes, if my prophetic eye sees aright.

... I have stopped making any definite plans for settling down but still have British Columbia in mind as a desired haven. So don't be surprized [sic] if you find me stealing flowers from your garden one of these fine summer days! With every good wish,

Affectionately yours,
ETHEL JOHNS

On 28 January 1946, Miss Johns wrote to Amy Lee again, and the following excerpts from her letter reveal how she now felt about her departure from *The Canadian Nurse* and something of her activities during the past year:

... Your *beautiful* card and very welcome letter reached me while I was on my Christmas visit to Canada ...

I'm afraid that I must confess that my 'retirement' doesn't seem to have quite come off. However, it is a tremendous relief to be free from a regular job and, better still, to feel that I am no longer responsible to any organized group of nurses and therefore obliged more or less to reflect their way of thinking. I did miss the Journal for awhile but I found when I went back to Montreal at Christmas that, somehow or other, it no longer pulled at my heartstrings.

There have been several interesting pieces of work down here in N.Y. Two of them have been for the School of Nursing of St Luke's Hospital ...

Miss Helene Olandt, who was director of nursing of St Luke's Hospital while Miss Johns was there, recalls that she wrote a manual for head nurses, the first of its kind at St Luke's, and she reorganized and rewrote a handbook for student nurses. Miss Olandt has warm memories of Miss Johns: '... She was truly a great woman and a great nurse. It was a real privilege to have known her. It was inspiring and helpful to us as well as a pleasure to have Miss Johns at St Luke's ... I am very enthusiastic about the tremendous amount that Ethel Johns was able to do for nurses and good nursing, not only in local areas but internationally ...'[3]

Miss Johns returned to Canada in the spring of 1946 and took up residence in Toronto. She now became involved in a study under the auspices of the Church of England in Canada. A National Commission on the Indian Work of the Church, under the convenership of Archbishop Carrington, was charged with the responsibility of surveying the situation of the Indian missions and residential schools. The report of this investigation states: '... The Commission was fortunate in obtaining the expert services of Miss E. Johns, R.N., whose distinguished work under the Rockefeller Research Foundation and wide experience of Canadian conditions are well known. Miss Johns gave her services freely to the Commission and made a detailed report to the Chairman, based on visits to four selected schools ...' Miss Johns was present at the final meeting of the Commission, in Toronto, on 22 May 1946, at which her report was discussed.[4]

Because the names of the schools selected for survey were not divulged in the Commission's report, Miss Johns' itinerary is not known. However, using a fictitious place name, she referred to one of the visits she made and what she learned from it, in an address which she gave shortly after in Toronto. Her paper, 'Nursing Service in General,' was one of three given at a symposium, as part of the programme of the twenty-third biennial convention of the Canadian Nurses' Association. A section of Miss Johns' speech dealt with nursing problems of the north as she had observed them in the course of her recent trip:

... When I got off the mixed train at the whistle stop I had to wait until an ancient gentleman by the name of Mr Scroggie warmed up the outboard motor boat which was to take me seven miles down the lake to the Indian school. A seaplane was bobbing about in the water at the dock and the pilot let me look it over. He told me that in the ordinary course of business, he often flew a doctor in or a patient out. 'Any nurses yet?' I asked. 'Not yet,' he said, 'But I sure have carried patients who could have used one.'

Mr Scroggie was ready by this time and, as we chugged away in the teeth of a cold northwest wind, he told me that the north country was opening up fast: 'Mines all over the place and lumbering, too, but especially mines. They are using invasion barges to bring in equipment and supplies; men are beginning to bring in their wives and children, but it's a tough life when there is sickness. It ought to be easier to get a nurse or a doctor – some sort of a centre maybe, from which you could fly them in.'

This reminded me of talks I had had a few days previously with an Indian agent and a government doctor in charge of a number of Indian reservations scattered over a vast territory. Their ideas of a nursing service in the far north seemed to me to be conceived in a new dimension. Nursing centres in remote areas might be serviced regularly by planes with communications through the meteorological stations now being constructed in the north country. Each centre would have a few beds for emergency cases, a sort of clearing station.

Bedside nursing skill of the highest order would be necessary and certainly midwifery. Yes, they said midwifery. Apparently these men had the same ideas as Mr Scroggie and the seaplane pilot about nursing in the new north in the atomic age.

Those few days at Pelican Lake made me realize as I never had before what a profound change in direction is taking place in our Canadian national life. Until now, the main roads led us east and west and south. Now the thrust is towards the north. Mr Scroggie is right – the country is opening up. A dangerous country, a challenging country, a new frontier!

Perhaps that is just what is happening in nursing, too. It may be time for us to leave the beaten track and to break a new trail toward a new horizon.[5]

Miss Johns' address on this occasion reveals that she was at her commanding best. Her comprehensive review and analysis of current nursing problems was followed by an eloquent plea for closer collaboration between nursing organizations, hospital administrators, and the medical profession. With respect to nurse-doctor relationships, she had some practical advice for the nursing profession:

... We need a continuing joint council with the medical profession similar to that which we have already set up with the hospital council. The nurse members of that council will need the courage of the lion, the wisdom of the serpent, and the gentleness of the dove. About three parts of dove to one each of lion and serpent. In the early days, we hardy pioneers frightened the medical men by too much roaring and hissing. Above all, use simple language. There is nothing that irritates the members of the medical profession more than what one of them quite justly calls 'the preposterous fiddle-faddle of the verbiage of nursing education.'[6]

Miss Johns then spoke of the changing pattern of nursing service and nursing education as envisaged at the biennial meeting in 1944 of the Canadian Nurses' Association, which recognized the need for professional nurses educated in both university-based and hospital schools of nursing, and for nursing aides prepared in courses of six to nine months duration. The same convention, she recalled, concluded that the three-year nursing course, if properly organized, might be completed in 'not more than three and not less than two years.' Furthermore, it was agreed that all persons rendering any type of nursing service for hire should be licensed. Miss Johns now emphasized the crucial importance of preparing, encouraging, and rewarding skilled professional bedside nurses: 'Most of them,' she asserted, 'will continue to come out of the hospital schools, and, it is reasonable to suppose, could be prepared in less than three years if the curriculum were wisely planned. This can only be done if and when the school exercises complete control over the time of its students and can use that time to the best advantage. This implies that the hospital must be able to provide a sufficiently large staff of graduate nurses and auxiliary workers to assure the bulk of the nursing service ...'[7]

Several significant resolutions were passed by this general meeting of the Canadian Nurses' Association. One of these approved the proposal of the executive committee 'that a demonstration be undertaken to determine whether a professional nurse can be prepared in less than three years.' Other resolutions concerned ways and means of dealing with the problem of the acute shortage of nurses, and recommended various measures to the provincial nurses' associations with this aim in view, many of which Miss Johns had advocated in her address.[8]

The Committee on Postwar Planning was now disbanded, and an Exchange of Nurses Committee was established, of which Ethel Johns was named convener. A member of the committee, ex officio, was Gertrude Hall, who had succeeded Miss Ellis as general secretary of the Canadian Nurses' Association. Miss Johns was also appointed convener of the Canadian Florence Nightingale Memorial Committee, a major function of which was to raise money with which to assist the Florence Nightingale International Foundation to conduct international courses for graduate nurses at Bedford College for Women, University of London.

Following the biennial convention, the Canadian Nurses' Association enlisted the services of Ethel Johns for a piece of work which required her intensive application throughout the summer months at national office in Montreal. This was the preparation of a report which had been requested by the Department of National Health and Welfare for the information of the Interdepartmental Committee on Professionally Trained Persons. In the preamble, the purpose, scope, and limitations of the submission were stated:

... The main purpose of this report is briefly to describe the existing situation with respect to nursing service in Canada and to estimate the demand for and the supply of nursing service which seems likely to prevail during the next three years. Since the time allotted for the preparation of the report was only five weeks, it was obviously impossible to initiate any new studies. All that will be attempted here is to assemble available information and to integrate and interpret it as clearly as possible. No claim is made that the report presents the whole picture. Nursing service is so varied and far-reaching in itself and is so vital a part of other health services that a thorough exploration lies far beyond the scope of this necessarily superficial and incomplete enquiry ...

The clear, factual, forty-seven-page report indicated situations and trends in the demand for and supply of nurses in all fields of service, their distribution, and potential sources for augmentation of nurse power. The brief was submitted to the Department of National Health and Welfare in September 1946.[9]

The Christmas season (1946) brought a pleasant reunion with a friend of long standing. Isabel MacIntosh recalls that Miss Johns was in Toronto at the time, doing some 'free lance work,' and that she was staying at the Selby Hotel. Train connections between Toronto and Hamilton were excellent, and Miss Johns was Miss MacIntosh's guest at Christmas dinner. '... We probably had three hours after dinner, sitting before the fire in a dimly lighted room where the atmosphere was perfect for confidential conversation.' Miss Johns rarely spoke of her personal life, but on this occasion she reminisced about her early life in England and Wales, her coming to Canada, training at the Winnipeg General Hospital, the first university course for nurses in Canada at the University of British Columbia, and the years in Europe under the Rockefeller Foundation. Her hostess still thinks of that happy time as 'a legacy, an evening to remember.' She also recalls an earlier occasion when her 'budding admiration for Ethel Johns became full-blown.' This was at the biennial meeting (1930) in Regina, when Miss Johns gave 'a captivating address' on the subject, 'A Sense of Values.' Miss MacIntosh reflects that 'Miss Johns was blest with a voice that had the dramatic power to move an audience to smiles or tears but, better still, to think,' and she adds: 'Miss E.J. walked this world alone because that was the way she desired.'[10]

The year 1947 brought Ethel Johns into renewed association with the J.B. Lippincott Company. By this time, Mr Leeman had become an officer of the Lippincott Company of Philadelphia. During her years as editor of *The Canadian Nurse*, Miss Johns had been concerned by the disinclination of many general staff nurses, head nurses, and private duty graduates, to read this and other professional literature. Courses of study for graduate nurses given under the auspices of universities focused upon administration, supervision, teaching, and public health nursing, but not upon clinical nursing. Sources of professional enrichment for the large body of nurses engaged in the direct care of patients were therefore either lacking or were unattractive to these practitioners. Now Miss Johns determined to do something about the situation. While on a visit to New York, she spoke to Mr Leeman about the problem, and enquired whether the J.B. Lippincott Company would be interested in publishing, from time to time, a small informal pamphlet designed to attract the attention and meet the needs of graduates in general and private practice. The proposal met a favourable response, and the first issue of *Just Plain Nursing*, edited and written by Ethel Johns, appeared early in 1947.

In her first article for the new publication, Miss Johns explained why and how it came into being. Based on her experience as an editor, she had concluded that nurses engaged in the care of patients wanted 'something new' in professional literature, reading material which would relate directly to their work. Miss Johns wondered whether this missing ingredient might be more information about 'new developments in diagnosis, in therapeutics, in psychosomatic medicine.' She went on to explain:

... Then we began to play with the idea of a leaflet which might contain a brief digest or two, and perhaps some pointed references to articles in the nursing journals which would coax even the reluctant reader to turn to the original text. Obviously, no scientific subject could be treated at any length, but might it not be possible by means of wide reading, judicious selections and condensation, to afford a background against which the day-in-day-out task of a bedside nurse might take on new values and deeper significance? Such a leaflet could never take the place of professional journals but might help many nurses to make better use of them ...[11]

Miss Johns then wrote of the 'no man's land which lies between nursing and medical practice' which had not yet 'been traversed or even mapped out,' and she suggested that 'some of it may turn out to be nothing more or less than that "something new in just plain nursing." In any event, no one is better qualified to explore its possibilities than a thoroughly competent bedside nurse, provided she is willing to do considerable reading and otherwise to equip herself for a stiff pioneer job ...'[12]

So Miss Johns turned to medical journals and from them selected articles and reports dealing with trends and developments in therapy of which nurses should be informed. She made concise summaries of these, and skilfully brought out their nursing implications. As Lippincott published new nursing and medical books, Miss Johns reviewed them in *Just Plain Nursing*. The eight-page pamphlet, sound in content and intriguing in style and format, made a wide appeal and continued to be published under her editorship, two to four times yearly, until 1960.

On 13 May 1947, her sixty-eighth birthday, Ethel Johns addressed the Ninth Congress of the International Council of Nurses in Atlantic City, New Jersey. This assembly of the nurses of the world held a special significance: it was the first such gathering since 1937. The war had effectively prevented the holding of the congresses which would normally have taken place in 1941 and 1945. Miss Johns' paper, 'The I.C.N. Responsibility for International Education of Nurses,' was worthy of the great occasion. She identified and elaborated upon four specific responsibilities of the Council for the international education of nurses:

1 The establishment and maintenance of close and effective relationships with all international groups associated with the United Nations which are engaged in promoting the health and welfare of mankind.
2 The maintenance and improvement of the standards already set in relation to the basic education of nurses.
3 The formulation of acceptable standards for postgraduate education and the encouragement of the interchange of nurses between the member countries for purpose of study and observation.
4 The development of strong and fearless leadership which will ensure the preservation of the moral and spiritual values which are the very soul of nursing.

Over and above these, Miss Johns concluded, there was a further responsibility which, through the years, the International Council of Nurses had always fulfilled:

... We have demonstrated by force of example that it is possible for people of different races, creeds, languages, and political beliefs to work together and, in a measure, to understand one another. The ICN has steadfastly refused either to be influenced or dominated by any political ideology whatsoever. It has run a good race. It has kept the faith.

The links which bind us together have survived the atrocious tensions of two world wars and a whole series of economic depressions. Slowly but surely, we are becoming convinced that international unity and peace does not only depend upon formal treaties drawn up by the heads of governments but also upon the determination of certain groups to keep their international solidarity intact. Among these, nursing is one of the most powerful because the service which we alone can render is given in response to universal need. We have the high privilege of giving it to our enemies as well as to our friends. As we look upon the International Council of Nurses to which we all belong, we can claim in pride and in humility that we have brought the honour and the glory of the nations into it.[13]

Mr Leeman was present on the occasion of Miss Johns' historic address. He recalls that as she left the platform she was accompanied on one side by Mary Roberts and on the other by Annie Goodrich. They came down the aisle together, 'looking like queens,' and they received an informal accolade from the large assembly.[14]

An interesting postscript to Miss Johns' address was its publication in the Winter (1951) issue of the *International Nursing Bulletin*. The editorial comment which preceded it was as follows: 'We venture to publish a paper presented by Miss Ethel Johns at the ICN Congress in Atlantic City in 1947: and we are happy to think that some of the developments in nursing education envisaged by Miss Johns are now being realized ...'

In October 1947, Miss Johns received a letter from Mrs Guthrie B. McVicar, chairman of the History Committee of The Johns Hopkins Hospital Nurses Alumnae Association. Miss Johns' name had been suggested for the writing of the history of the School of Nursing. The committee felt that she was 'a very well qualified writer ... and exceptionally well informed in nursing history and in nursing education.' Would she be interested in undertaking this work?

Miss Johns replied, on 22 October, that she deeply appreciated the honour that The Johns Hopkins Hospital Nurses Alumnae Association had done her in thinking of her in connection with the preparation of the history of the School. She expressed some reservations about her ability to do this work successfully: '... My first reaction was to wonder whether any nurse who is not herself a graduate of the School ought to attempt so delicate a task. The recording of facts would be relatively simple but a sympathetic interpretation of them might well be beyond me. However, I was heartened to see that some of my old friends are members of your Committee and, while knowing my limitations, are apparently willing to overlook them. I am very much interested in the project and, if circumstances permit, would like to have a share in it ...' Miss Johns then mentioned that she was acting as consultant to the Canadian Nurses' Association in relation to a certain project, but that she could probably handle both tasks provided it would not require her absence from Montreal for too long a period at any one time. She assumed that the assembling and examination of the material would have to be done in Baltimore, but that the actual writing of the book could be done in Canada.[15]

Mrs McVicar became ill shortly after this, so the subsequent preliminary correspondence with Miss Johns was carried on by Mrs C. Bernard Brack, president of the Alumnae Association, and Anna Wolf, now director of the school and the nursing service of The Johns Hopkins Hospital. Arrangements were finally completed: Miss Johns would arrive in Baltimore ready for work by 16 February 1948, and would stay in the Main Nurses' Home. A new adventure was beginning for Ethel Johns.

25

The Johns Hopkins Project

Ethel Johns was captivated by the atmosphere of The Johns Hopkins Hospital and by the gracious welcome which she received. Mrs Brack introduced her to the Historical Library and the wealth of available source material, while Mrs McVicar – now fully recovered – sought an early opportunity to confer with Miss Johns about the initial steps to be taken in getting the project under way.

Since the preparation of the History would be a co-operative enterprise, one requiring the active collaboration of several persons, Miss Johns proposed that she participate as editor rather than as author. In an editorial capacity, she suggested, she would be responsible for assembling, examining, and making abstracts from source materials. She would interview persons from whom additional information might be obtained and prepare outlines of possible content for the book. Subject to the advice and direction of the Committee, she would prepare a first draft of the History, submit this to the Committee for analysis and criticism, make such revisions as the latter deemed necessary, and prepare the final draft for submission to the same group. She would also give whatever assistance might be required in getting the volume through the press.[1]

Miss Johns also recommended the appointment of an associate editor whose duties might include: examination and general control over all activities involving the expenditure of Alumnae funds; provision for secretarial assistance, supplies and equipment; arrangement for interviews which Miss Johns would undertake in order to secure first-hand information of historical value; selection and reproduction of illustrations (an important factor in costs); and sharing responsibility with the editor in arranging for the printing and publishing of the History. These responsibilities, Miss Johns added, should be regarded as purely tentative and subject to modification or amplification as the situation developed.² The Alumnae Association accepted this proposal, and appointed Mrs McVicar as associate editor.

The History Committee of the Alumnae Association was broadly representative of older and younger graduates of the School of Nursing, ranging from the Class of 1895 to that of 1933. An Editorial Subcommittee was set up to which Miss Johns was directly responsible, an arrangement which proved somewhat confusing in the organizational stages of the work, since the editor was responsible also to the parent committee. The problem, however, was resolved satisfactorily as functions and lines of authority became clarified.

Early in March 1948 Miss Johns wrote a cheerful letter to Eileen Flanagan, with news of her arrival in Baltimore. '... My lines have fallen to me in pleasant places, and I'm quite enjoying my excursion into the nineteenth century. After all, that is where I really belong.' For the information of the 'Creative Minority,' she enclosed a lively description of her new environment:

... This is the Historical Library of the School of Nursing and has a plate over the door to prove it. Room shaped like a half-moon with three windows looking out over the Hospital grounds, nice lawn and a few grand old trees. On the walls hang the portraits of the directors of the School from 1889 on. In one corner is a little cabinet containing a replica of the Bonham Carter statuette of Nightingale which adorns the Sisters' dining room at St Thomas's. Somewhere along the line the Lady has lost her lamp. I hope this isn't a sinister portent of what is happening to nursing on this side of the Atlantic. Don't mention it to our medical critics. They might be tempted to make invidious remarks. Incidentally, the JHH nurses don't like to be teased about it.

The pièce de résistance is a wheel chair which once was used by Florence Nightingale. This is roped off so that I shan't be tempted to profane it by wheeling myself along the corridor on my way to the cafeteria. All round the walls there are bookcases containing one of the best libraries of the Nightingale era that I ever did lay eyes on. The one at TC isn't comparable to it. This was collected and presented by the Famous Kelly of Kelly pad fame. When I plumped my rattling little typewriter down in the middle of all this I felt as though I had been asked to write in a cathedral. Miss Nutting's desk was on one side of me and Isabel Hampton's chair on the other. Talk about ghosts of the past. And then one morning I came in and suddenly realized that the ghosts didn't mind my being there at all. Perhaps they were tired of being roped off and put in cabinets and felt the old fire stirring in their ashes. And there was plenty of fire, believe me. Nothing like getting a look at the original records to prove it ...

Miss Johns added that she was very comfortably housed in the Main Nurses' Residence, the original building, which, she felt, had 'far more atmosphere than the shiny one across the street.' The corridor in which she lived 'ought to be called Little International House or Foreigners' Rest,' and there she met and sought interviews with visitors from other countries, for the purpose of gaining information which might be helpful to the Exchange of Nurses Committee.[3] Miss Johns told of one of these encounters: '... My prize catch so far was Dr Yang, said to be one of the greatest obstetricians in China, and now head of the midwifery schools for all China under the Chinese Government. Oh, oh, what a woman. One of the wisest and best I have ever met. And a delightful bubbling sense of humour. Believe it or not, she was genuinely interested in the Exchange of Nurses Committee of the CNA. But she was mildly amused when she heard that we have no school of midwifery in Canada ...' Miss Johns then listed in full the practical guidelines which Dr Yang (at her request) had given her for 'handling Chinese young women' who might come to Canada under a plan for the exchange of nurses between the countries.

Most of Miss Johns' time during the four months of her first visit to Johns Hopkins was spent in examining, sorting, and classifying historical materials of which there was an abundance in the keeping of the Alumnae Association and the School of Nursing. These included a collection of biographical data about Isabel Hampton (superintendent of nurses and principal of The Johns Hopkins Hospital Training School from 1889 to 1894), which had been gathered some years earlier by Dr Edith Ware. Miss Johns interviewed Dr Ware, in Washington, D.C., in April, and learned that she had discontinued the Hampton project when she discovered that there was not enough material available for a full-scale biography. However, the information which she had gathered in her preliminary research, now in the files of the Alumnae Association at Johns Hopkins, was to prove very useful in writing the history of the early years of the School of Nursing.

Miss Johns felt a reverence for the original source materials which were temporarily in her keeping. She listed each document, and every scrap of paper, with meticulous care. With the help of Mrs McVicar, she worked out a system for filing the materials which were the property of the Alumnae Association, and placed them in steel files secured for the purpose. She also conferred with Miss Wolf about the disposition of documents which belonged to the School of Nursing.

During this period, Miss Johns also carried out nineteen interviews with available graduates of the School of Nursing who graduated between 1891 and 1911. With most of them she conferred only once, but a few of the older graduates were interviewed as many as three or four times. Miss Johns made careful notes of each interview, with copies for the files of the Alumnae Association. Because the actual writing of the book was to be done in Canada, she required – and gathered – a large quantity of well-documented data which she sorted into numerous files, each one clearly identified for ready reference.

As Miss Johns proceeded with research into the history of the School, she began to have misgivings about her qualifications to handle the whole assignment. It was necessary for her to return to Canada in advance of the time when her visitor's permit would expire. On the eve of her departure, 19 June 1948, she wrote a letter to Mrs McVicar in which she expressed her hesitancy about continuing and offered her resignation as editor of the project:

... You will recall that in preliminary correspondence I expressed some doubt as to whether anyone who was not a graduate of your own School ought to attempt to interpret its spirit and aims. I am now convinced that this doubt was justified as far as I am concerned and must ask to withdraw as editor. I do, however, feel a distinct responsibility regarding the exploration and organization of material related to the earlier years of the School – that is to say, from 1867 to 1907. If your Committee wishes me to complete the task which I undertook in this area I shall be glad to do so ... I quite realize that you may prefer the incoming editor to take over the project as a whole and in that event I shall be quite in accord.

I shall always look back with pleasure to the unique privilege which I have enjoyed in being permitted to examine source material which few Schools are so fortunate as to possess. I am most grateful to your Committee and to the School of Nursing for affording me so happy and stimulating an experience.

Cordially yours,
ETHEL JOHNS

Shortly after her return to Montreal, Miss Johns left for Sackville, New Brunswick, to attend the biennial meeting of the Canadian Nurses' Association at Mount Allison University, from 28 June to 3 July. There a special honour awaited her, an event which was later reported as follows by the editor of *The Canadian Nurse*: '... The outstanding occasion of the opening day was the special convocation held by Mount Allison University for the presentation of Miss Ethel Johns for the degree of Doctor of Laws (*honoris causa*). Resplendent in the beautiful robes which had been presented to her by her own alumnae association, the Winnipeg General Hospital group, Miss Johns received the scarlet and blue hood symbolic of her doctorate ...'[4] The accompanying citation reviewed the achievements of Miss Johns' professional career, spoke of her as an 'outstanding writer,' and concluded: 'Miss Johns' great contribution to the nursing profession makes her most worthy of the degree which the Senate of this University has asked her to accept.'

In her convocation address entitled, 'The Nurse Seeks the University,' Miss Johns traced the development of schools of nursing within universities. She spoke about the difficulties which nurses had encountered in attaining professional status within the university and the community at large, and attributed this to the persistence of the 'ancillary concept' of nursing as the handmaiden of medicine: '... If I seem to stress this point unduly,' she said, 'it is because failure to comprehend it has led to the mistaken impression that the movement towards the university on the part of nursing is an attempt to usurp the functions of the physician. Nothing could be further from the truth. Our own field is so vast, so challenging, our own imperfections so great, that we have no need and no desire to explore any other ...' Another obstacle, she continued, was the 'uncompromising attitude of some university authorities towards special (or vocational) education as distinct from liberal (or general) education.' Miss Johns foresaw an expanded role for universities in the education of nurses, and their continuing responsibility in helping to prepare women for leadership in the profession. Summing up, she stated that Canadian nurses looked to the university for staunch support when they strove to interpret to the community what professional nursing is and should become; for the firm, wise guidance in educational policy and practice which only the university could give; and for a share, no matter how small, in the creative and cultural values which it was the duty of the university to cherish and protect.[5]

Ethel Johns was the guest of honour at a reception which followed the convocation ceremony. The convention week which she spent in the congenial atmosphere of Mount Allison University, now her alma mater, must have been a happy time for Ethel Johns. She saw and talked with old friends, and on occasion acted as the hostess in the lounge provided by the J.B. Lippincott Company for the rest and relax-

Ethel Johns Receives the Degree of Doctor of Laws (*honoris causa*),
from Reverend William T.R. Flemington,
President of Mount Allison University, 1948
(Gift of J.B. Lippincott Company)

ation of the nurses. At a business session of the general meeting, she presented the report of the Exchange of Nurses Committee, and spoke with appreciation of the work of its individual members and of the subcommittee in Montreal, convened by Norena Mackenzie.[6]

Upon her return to Montreal, Miss Johns received a letter from Mrs McVicar, on behalf of the History Committee, conveying appreciation of the 'splendid work' which she had accomplished and urging her to reconsider her resignation as editor and to return to Baltimore at her convenience to complete the work she had so ably started.[7] Miss Johns replied to Mrs McVicar on 22 July:

... I am so sorry that there has been an unavoidable delay in answering your very kind letter. At the Canadian Nurses' Association convention in New Brunswick, it was decided that an immediate approach to our Federal Government would be necessary in connection with the new health programme which is soon to be initiated on a national-wide scale. I was asked to prepare the necessary brief and, as this had to be done at top-speed, I have hardly had a moment to devote to personal affairs. However, we were well received by the Minister of Health yesterday and hope that all will now go well so far as nursing is concerned ...

Miss Johns then expressed her thanks for the 'very encouraging vote of confidence which was passed at the last meeting of the History Committee. It touched me very deeply, and I am most grateful.' She still felt that the question of the editorship required further consideration, but she stated that she would return to Baltimore in September to continue with the organization of the source material which she had already assembled and classified. This plan was approved by Miss Margory Upham, the new president of the Alumnae Association, and Miss Johns left for the United States on 23 September 1948.

With the authorization of the chairman of the History Committee, Miss Johns spent a week in New York for the purpose of gathering further data about Isabel Hampton and Mary Adelaide Nutting. She visited Bellevue Hospital, was given access to the original records of the School of Nursing, and secured reference material about the conditions during the period of Miss Hampton's training, 1881-3. She spent some time with Isabel Stewart, examining folders in Miss Nutting's personal files of which Miss Stewart, as executor, had custody. With her permission, Miss Johns made excerpts from the records which pertained to Miss Nutting's early life and education, her career at Johns Hopkins Hospital, and other relevant information.

Following her return to Johns Hopkins, Miss Johns conferred with Mrs McVicar, and discussed the next steps to be taken in the project. It was agreed that Miss Johns would concentrate on the Hampton and Nutting periods of the School's history, begin to draft the manuscript dealing with this era, and continue at the same time to explore the pre-Hampton years. Miss Johns suggested that she now seek interviews with Dr Alan Chesney, Dean of the Medical School of Johns Hopkins University, and with the Director of the Welch Library. Mrs McVicar made arrangements for these conferences, and also for interviews with graduates of the School of Nursing.

Dean Chesney was very helpful. He expressed interest in the project, loaned her some original source material, gave her permission to quote from his own History, offered to advise and assist her, and suggested the names of several persons whom she might see. The Director of the Library issued a guest card to Miss Johns. In a letter to Mrs McVicar of 18 October 1948, Miss Johns wrote: '... I hope you had a pleasant sojourn in New York. I have been as busy as a beaver. Dr Tamkin has kindly admitted me to his course and I am also taking Dr Richards' teachers course. All this ought to stimulate my mental processes. Also I have started to work in the Welch Library. They have given me a cubicle and have been kindness itself.'

During the five months which followed, Miss Johns continued with the collection, classification, and filing of data. Mrs McVicar, as associate editor, worked closely with her, giving assistance as requested. By early December, Miss Johns had completed a rough draft of the proposed content of the manuscript for the period 1867–1907. She spent four days in New York at the end of December, for the purpose of further examining the Nutting files.

Mrs Brack had now succeeded Mrs McVicar as chairman of the History Committee, and served with distinction until the book was finally published. The congenial and understanding relationship which Miss Johns enjoyed with Mrs Brack undoubtedly meant a great deal to her and facilitated the ultimate completion of the complex undertaking.

On 23 February 1949, Miss Johns submitted a progress report to the chairman of the History Committee in which she detailed the work which she had undertaken since her return to Baltimore and that which she hoped to complete before her imminent return to Canada. She recommended that a search be made for a graduate of the School to undertake the writing of the period of the School's history following 1907. She expressed her thanks to the associate editor 'for establishing such helpful and pleasant contacts with many persons who either allowed me to examine documents in their possession or to interview them,' and she acknowledged her indebtedness to the School of Nursing in permitting her to use the Historical Library as a workroom.

Miss Johns returned to Montreal from Baltimore on 17 March 1949. She wrote to Mrs Brack without delay, thanking her for the 'fragrant farewell and for that *wonderful steak*.' She mentioned that she hoped to explore one or two possible sources of information at McGill University, and expected to be in Montreal until the middle of May.

On 6 July, Miss Johns wrote again to Mrs Brack, this time from Vancouver, and she enclosed a light-hearted memorandum to be shared with Mrs McVicar about 'The Adventures of EJ since last heard from':

... Fortunately, a good friend allowed her to use her home as a base of operations while EJ looked about for a place to live. After looking at some of the world's most dismal and expensive apartments, EJ discovered a little cottage with a lawn the size of a pocket handkerchief in front and a strawberry patch and a rose bush at the back. To make a long story short, she signed on the dotted line and is now the proud owner of A Little Grey Home in the West. She is to get possession within a week or two, has ordered her furniture out of storage ... and, incidentally, is financially broke but happy.

On 24 August, Miss Johns wrote to Eileen Flanagan who had recently returned from a trip through Europe, and described her newly acquired home:

... It is grey stucco with a red trim, three rooms and bath, plus what they call a utility room for storage purposes. The catch is that there is no basement which complicates the heating problem but there is an honest to goodness fireplace and I have put in an oil-burning cookstove which is also supposed to serve as a heating unit. We shall see what we shall see but, if the worst comes to the worst, I have had the piping put in for an additional oil heater. Here's hoping I won't need it.

At the time I bought the place it had been raining and misting for a solid two weeks and I had thought that there was no view except a rather pleasant though weedy back garden but when I woke up in my own bed, the very first morning, I looked out of the bedroom window and there, against a blue north sky, were the summits of the Hollyburn Ridge and the Sleeping Beauty range. I've never had a bigger thrill. Even if they only show up once in a blue moon, at least I know they are there and that they are mine free gratis and for nothing. My household gods, such as they are, are now somewhere enroute from

Toronto. At present, I am sitting amid a wilderness of unpacked trunks and am the prey of plumbers, heaters, odd-job men and so on ...

Miss Johns added that she had been going about socially more than she had the time for. The Johns Hopkins project was on her mind, and she was starting 'to hammer away at it like mad.' She had spent a very interesting afternoon at the University, and was surprised to find that the general outlines of the (nursing) course had not changed as radically as she might have supposed. The coming of the Medical School, she expected, would create new situations. She set down in one descriptive paragraph her initial impressions upon returning to the west:

... The difference in tempo both in daily life and in general thinking (as compared with the east) strike me very forcibly. I can best illustrate it by a rather homely simile: on the way out, I noticed that as soon as the train began to descend toward the Western littoral, every blooming cow was lying down, placidly chewing its cud and no stravenging about like the energetic animals on the prairies. The local press seems to me to be pretty provincial in its outlook. You have to comb the back pages for foreign news while the dresses of local brides are described with resounding headlines to point them up. The correspondence columns are given over to debates between Seven Day Adventists and Bible Fundamentalists rather too often. And yet I love the soft air and the soft water. The view from the Faculty Club is breath-taking. All up Howe Sound. Blue water and snow peaks. I always thought it would be a good place to watch the sun set. And I think it is going to be ...

Ethel Johns was home and utterly content to put down roots at last.

26

Full Circle

Soon after her return to Vancouver, Miss Johns was proposed for membership in the University Women's Club, an affiliation for which her lack of a degree had previously rendered her ineligible. An old friend recalls that she was 'childishly pleased' to be admitted to the Club. She attended meetings regularly, usually in the company of her friend Janet Greig, who had been an instructor in the Department of French at the University of British Columbia when Miss Johns was in charge of the Department of Nursing. She also joined l'Alliance Française and enjoyed attending meetings of that group.

Miss Johns' former students who lived in Vancouver welcomed her at social affairs arranged in her honour. Good neighbours presently took an interest in the new householder on West Fifteenth Avenue. Mr and Mrs Mayhew and their daughter Emily, who lived across the street from Miss Johns, made friendly overtures. This was the beginning of a friendship which was to deepen with time and bring support and solace to Miss Johns in her declining years. The circle widened when Lucille Blayney (Emily's sister), with her ailing husband and her daughter Ann, came home to live. Mr Blayney had to spend some time in hospital, and after he was discharged he required hypodermic injections on a continuing basis. Miss Johns taught Ann, then thirteen years of age, to administer them, and her instruction was so thorough, Mrs Blayney recalls, that Ann was able to carry out the procedure without difficulty. From that time, her mother says, 'Ann had such a nice relationship with Miss Johns, and they used to have long talks together.' For a year before Mr Blayney's death (in June 1953), Miss Johns often visited him, and they would discuss books by the hour. Mrs Blayney adds, with gentle amusement, 'Miss Johns really liked men. She could bat her eyes with the best of them.'[1]

Esther Paulson, Provincial Director of Nursing for the Division of Tuberculosis Control, with headquarters in Vancouver, had some contact with Miss Johns following her return to the city. Long an admirer of Ethel Johns, Miss Paulson met her personally for the first time at the convention in Sackville. As the only member of the Exchange of Nurses Committee in western Canada, she was now asked to help Miss Johns with reports and correspondence, an experience which she remembers as a 'rare privilege,' one which afforded an opportunity to know her better as a person:

... Her struggles to become a householder amused her. We conferred about her various domestic problems including the heatilator fireplace for which I brought a bag of briquettes for her to try out. I can recall instances that revealed facets of her personality – spurts of gleeful enthusiasm and humour that flashed out from time to time. One was when she told me of reading about some verbal encounter that Aneurin Bevan had with a conservative. His retort pleased her immensely and she felt Bevan had got his innings for previous rebuffs and said it showed his great spirit and courage ...[2]

While renewing old friendships, making new ones, and getting settled in her new home, Miss Johns was working on the manuscript of the early period in the history of the Johns Hopkins Hospital School of Nursing. She was in continuous touch with Mrs Brack by letter, keeping her informed of progress in the writing and being advised in turn of developments in the project as a whole. Early in September 1949, Mrs Brack wrote Miss Johns to say that Blanche Pfefferkorn had expressed an interest in continuing the History and that she would soon visit Baltimore to look into the matter further. Miss Johns' reply left no doubt of her relief and approval:

... There were many reasons why I was glad to get your letter of September 10 but the chief of them all was the thrilling possibility that my old friend and collaborator Blanche Pfefferkorn may perhaps be induced to tackle the 1907–1950 epoch of the famous history. No better choice could be made. She is one of your most distinguished graduates, she is a recognized authority in the whole field of nursing education, she has historical sense and can write good English. I shall eagerly await word of her acceptance ...[3]

This word reached Miss Johns a few days later, and she hastened to write to Mrs Brack expressing her pleasure: 'Good news for everyone concerned and especially for EJ ...' She added that progress in her writing had been slow and household matters troublesome:

... After a miserable week of sitting in front of my typewriter, 'heart of me, head of me, dull as a stone,' I have at last begun to feel that before long I may really get rolling. The advent of Blanche Pfefferkorn has acted as a catalyzing agent and I shall count on her for stimulus to keep me going.

In a subsequent letter to Mrs Brack, Miss Johns proposed that her title be changed from editor to author, since Miss Pfefferkorn would be writing the second half of the History. The History Committee readily accepted this recommendation.

On 16 May 1950, Miss Johns wrote to Mrs Brack that she had now forwarded the draft manuscript of that part of the book dealing with the period 1867–94. Arrival of the parcel in Baltimore elicited a jubilant telegram from Mrs Brack: 'Announcing the safe arrival of your "baby." Its parentage assures a wonderful future. Congratulations.'

A report on Miss Johns' progress with the remainder of the manuscript was contained in her letter of 19 September to the chairman of the History committee:

... All summer long, Heaven help me, I have wrestled with the spirit of Adelaide Nutting, like Jacob with his angel. Whenever, for a moment, I feel that I have seized that elusive essence, she flings me off and sends me flying. It will not be for me to pluck the heart out of her mystery but perhaps I shall be able to show what she meant to the JHH and what the JHH meant to her. The draft manuscript will, if all goes well, be ready for you and the committee towards the end of October ...

The draft manuscript on the Nutting era was despatched on 30 October. Upon its receipt, Mrs Brack immediately wired Miss Johns: 'Manuscript arrived this morning and has been avidly read. If this be not the woman herself the loss is hers for you have evoked a spirit splendid and clear cut. Thank you, thank you.'

Now came a period of anxious waiting for Miss Johns during which the manuscripts were under review by the members of the History Committee and a new Editorial Committee convened by Mrs McVicar. The stated responsibilities of the latter group were: 'To act as liaison with the authors in relation to matters of content; to carry out such editorial functions as may arise in connection with re-drafting of the manuscripts; and to make recommendations concerning publication of the manuscripts.'[4]

A composite statement of the comments, criticisms, and suggestions for revision of the manuscripts which had been made by the two committees reached Miss Johns in March 1951, a few days in advance of a meeting in Vancouver with Blanche Pfefferkorn. Evidently the four-day conference was strenuous but productive, as Miss Johns explained to Mrs Brack:

... Our Vancouver weather was most unkind – two feet of wet snow and a biting north wind – and even if British Columbia had lived up to its proud boast of being 'Canada's Evergreen Playground' I doubt whether Miss Pfefferkorn or I would have had time to do more than look out of the window. A mass of intricate detail had to be gone over as thoroughly as time permitted and this proved to be a tedious and time-consuming process. Nevertheless, I am convinced that as a result of this ordeal, the revision of my manuscripts can now go forward more rapidly and that my deadline at the end of September may yet be attained with a quarter of an inch to spare ...[5]

The rather stiff and formal correspondence between the co-authors which followed the conference in Vancouver was in sharp contrast with the informal and affectionate exchange of letters which preceded it. For both of these strong-minded and self-directing women, the resolution of inevitable differences in procedure could not have been easy.

On 16 August 1951, Miss Johns wrote to Mrs Brack giving a progress report on the revision of her manuscript: '... All summer long, I have been toiling at the oar and, as a result, the entire manuscript is practically being re-written. The content and sequence are substantially the same but there is considerable amplification and a general loosening up of the style which I hope will make the blooming thing more readable ...' She said that she hoped to deliver the revised version to the Editorial Committee by the end of September.

It was actually mid-October before Miss Johns mailed a bound copy of the revised manuscript to the chairman of the History Committee. The accompanying letter sounded as if the author were now exhausted by her labours and could brook no further requests for changes: 'In its present form, it represents the best work of which I am capable, and, therefore, I cannot undertake any further extensive revision or amplifications. I am perfectly willing, however, to correct any errors or to make any minor alterations which the Committee may deem necessary ...' She asked that the History Committee accept or reject the manuscript 'as it now stands.' In conclusion, she stated: '... No matter what the decision of the History Committee may be, I should like to thank its chairman and members for the privilege of being allowed to assemble and classify source material of such unique interest to the nursing profession at large. The task has indeed been its own reward.'

Mrs Brack once again sent a warmly worded telegram acknowledging receipt of the manuscript, and followed this with a letter in which she assured Miss Johns that the Committee was unanimous in its acceptance of the manuscript as it was, and had directed that an honorarium of two thousand dollars be awarded Miss Johns as a token expression of their gratitude and appreciation. In conclusion, Mrs Brack expressed an understanding of what the project had meant to Miss Johns in terms of the investment of herself in it. Mrs S. Ralph Mason, president of the Alumnae Association, added her thanks: '... All who have read it agree that it is a splendid account of our early years. We are very proud to have this history written in such beautiful form by so distinguished an author.'

Miss Johns requested that the honorarium be paid in four annual instalments. Acknowledging the receipt of the first cheque, she wrote to Mrs Brack on 21 February 1952, and attached a statement, which, if Mrs Brack approved, she might include in her report to the History Committee at a forthcoming meeting:

... It was a real pleasure, and in some sense a great relief, to receive the assurance of the History Committee that my manuscript in its present form appears to be historically correct as well as reasonably satisfactory in the manner of its presentation. Considerable work obviously remains to be done before it is ready for final submission and in the light of criticisms and suggestions recently received from the Editorial Committee, I am now engaged in further revision of certain parts of the text.

It will perhaps be remembered that from the outset I have contended that no one but a member of the School could acceptably describe and interpret the events and the policies which from 1907 until the present time have affected its development and it is most fortunate that one so eminently qualified as Miss Blanche Pfefferkorn has been willing to undertake this delicate and difficult task. For myself I can only say that, as a wilful and totally unreconstructed mid-Victorian, it has been a strange and profoundly moving experience to trace the history of the School during the earlier years and to reflect as faithfully as I could something of what went on in the hearts and minds of the men and women who then guided its destinies. Although I did my best to be sternly objective, it must be freely admitted that by reason of birth I share the spiritual and national inheritance of two of the principal protagonists and that, therefore, the detachment rightly required of the historian may not always have been strictly preserved. At least I can justly claim that I have shown these men and women, in their habit, as they lived and worked, for I have drawn heavily upon the records which they themselves set down – they not only made history, they wrote it.

In a further communication, Miss Johns advised Mrs Brack that because of an unexpected development in her personal life, she would be in the vicinity of Baltimore early in October (1952). She would like to take this opportunity of checking her manuscript with the aid of some of the original sources not available to her elsewhere. She had also suggested to Miss Pfefferkorn that the two authors confer informally about several matters affecting the History as a whole. In a letter of 1 July, Mrs Brack replied: 'How wonderfully exciting and pleasant to have E.J.'s "descent" to look forward to in the fall.' A meeting of the committee could be arranged for that time. The name of the Editorial Committee, she added, had now been changed to that of the Committee on Review.

The 'unexpected development' in the life of Ethel Johns was an invitation to give the address at the forthcoming graduation exercises of the Cornell University–New York Hospital School of Nursing. The occasion was significant: it would mark the seventy-fifth anniversary of the New York Hospital School of Nursing and the tenth year of its affiliation with Cornell University. Virginia M. Dunbar was now dean of the School, and Dr S. Bayne-Jones was president of the Joint Administrative Board of the New York Hospital and the Cornell Medical Center.

En route to New York, Miss Johns spent the weekend of 26 September in Old Bennington, Vermont, visiting Alice Shepherd Gilman, her former colleague in the New York Hospital–Cornell University project. She then went to New York, where she was a guest in the nurses' residence which she had helped to plan.

The commencement exercises, held in the auditorium of the School of Nursing, were attended by approximately four hundred and fifty persons. In her address, 'Blazing the Trail,' Miss Johns gave a colourful account of the activities of the Committee on Nursing Organization with which she had been associated. She spoke of the vision and the courage of graduates of the School of Nursing whose leadership had brought the institution to its present position of eminence, and recalled her encounter with one of the foremost of these:

... On a hot summer afternoon, I was having another go at it when the office door opened and there stood a slight figure, dressed in black except for spotless white at the throat and wrists. Although I had never seen her before, I knew instinctively who it was – Irene Sutliffe. The crown of silver hair, the deep eyes, the air of dignity and grace. It could be no one else. She who had first blazed the trail, as we say in Canada. Not broken the trail – that was for those who came after to do – just blazed it. Marking a tree here and there, alone where no one had passed before her, hoping that the blaze might show white for a time – long enough to serve as a guide. She was a member of the Class of 1880, she had been head of the School of Nursing. She had been at the heart of both School and Hospital in one capacity or another for fifty years and I had only touched the fringe of either. I was hot and tired and discouraged and at first did not know what to say to her. It was she who took the initiative and before long we were going over the troublesome draft together. I shall never forget her as she stood there in the dusty office looking down at the blueprints of the new School – the old School – her School ...

Miss Johns traced the events leading to the major proposals which the Committee on Nursing Organization had made some thirty years earlier – the establishment of a relationship with Cornell University and the endowment of the School of Nursing – and she said, 'The first of these objectives has now been attained – the Class of 1952 is a living proof of that. A beginning has been made so far as endowment is concerned but you young women must put your shoulders to that wheel ...' Miss Johns' concluding remarks reached out to the members of the graduating class:

... Observing the Committee on Nursing Organization, as I did, with a certain detachment, I was impressed by its stubborn conviction that world events would soon force an immense expansion of the nursing field on both a national and an international scale. Its members were less concerned with the preservation of a noble tradition than they were in ensuring the development of a School of Nursing in which leadership might be fostered – leadership capable of meeting the demands which these women foresaw would be made upon nurses in a catastrophic age. How proud you must be that the School as it now stands so amply justifies the faith of those indomitable pioneers. You are happy, indeed, that your leaders of today who so gallantly break the trail share the ability, the courage and the vision of those who blazed it.

It may well be that when your School celebrates its centenary, a member of this Class of 1952 will deliver the Commencement Address to the Class of 1977, and it is to her that I say my last word. Try to remember the picture I have given you of Irene Sutliffe looking down at the blueprints of this great School and Hospital. If only you will do this I shall feel as though I – a pilgrim and a stranger – have in some sense linked the old tradition with the new. If I had ever dreamed that I should stand here tonight I should have asked her to give me a message for you – but I did not. And yet I feel as though I know what she might have said to you: 'The roots of this School go deep into the soil of this Nation and its influence may yet be felt all over the world. Something hidden – go and find it – lost and waiting for you – go!'[6]

Miss Johns was profoundly moved by the unexpectedly warm response to her address. She was often to remark later that on that evening, for her, the wheel had come full circle. Dr Bayne-Jones's immediate reaction to her speech was conveyed in a hand-written note which he sent to Miss Dunbar on the following morning:

... Congratulations on the Commencement! I felt that it was the best of all – and fitting in every way to this Anniversary Year and year of promise.

Miss Johns' address was one of the most moving and factually interesting that I have ever heard on such an occasion. It was wonderful the way she wove recollections into the present and brought out general truths. She impressed me as a great person, and I felt inspired not only by what she said, but by merely being near her. I hope she will kindly lend us her manuscript – even if some of her most eloquent statements were made without reference to it. Also – please give me her address – I should love to write to her.

It was all very fine.

Sincerely yours,
S. BAYNE-JONES[7]

True to his stated intention, Dr Bayne-Jones wrote to Miss Johns, congratulating her on the address. He then asked if she would lend her manuscript: '... I realize that your manuscript may lack those eloquent, witty, and perfectly-constructed passages that you spoke from time to time without reference to the typed page ...'[8] The significance to Miss Johns of this tribute from so eminent a physician can only be imagined.

The week which Miss Johns spent in Baltimore after the commencement exercises was both pleasant and productive. Her meetings with Miss Pfefferkorn and with the History Committee were fruitful, and no doubt facilitated the completion of the project. It must have given her a good deal of satisfaction, from both professional and personal points of view, to see and talk with Mrs Brack whose continuous support had been a source of encouragement and strength to her.

On her way home, Miss Johns spent a few days in Montreal seeing old friends, and a week-end in Quebec City. From all points of view, the trip had been memorable. She left for Vancouver on 20 October.

In her Christmas greeting to Miss Flanagan, dated 9 December, Miss Johns mentioned that she had sent off what she hoped was to be her final streamlining of her share of the History, and that now 'only the perils of getting it through the press remain.' She also said that she was 'toying with the idea' of starting something on her own, and that a publisher was nibbling, adding that 'The old girl (and the publisher) ought to get their heads examined.' The visit in Montreal was a happy one, she said in conclusion, and the evening at the Themis Club 'was a high light that still flares away nicely ...' Ethel Johns' interest in life and work still burned brightly, too. She was not yet ready to rest.

27

Another Task for Ethel Johns

The Stewart family had long ago accepted Ethel Johns as one of themselves. They were fond of nicknames and all called her 'E.J.' During her retirement years, Vancouver was the rallying place for the clan on both sad and festive occasions, and she was always included in these functions.

A member of the family remembers that, from time to time, when Miss Johns' energies were drained by intensive concentration upon her writing, she would go to visit Helen Stewart at her home on Vancouver Island. There she could do whatever she wished. She lay in bed (a self-indulgence which she rarely permitted herself at home), had her meals in the garden, read, and walked in the woods. When her friend was expected, Helen (whom Miss Johns always called 'H.G.') made sure to provide books of the kind she liked best – history and biography. After a week of this therapeutic regime, she felt refreshed and could go on with her work.[1]

Isabel Stewart and Ethel Johns were firm friends, but it is said that, on the occasion of their infrequent meetings, 'there was a confrontation, they did battle, both were very stubborn and would not yield.' When Isabel Stewart came to Vancouver, she always wanted to see Ethel Johns, but not alone.[2] No doubt the vigorous encounters which, in their younger days, were stimulating and enjoyable, were now too tiring for Miss Stewart and she tried to avoid them.

Of all the Stewarts, Isabel's youngest sister, Jessie, was probably the dearest to Ethel Johns. Their friendship reached back to the years when the latter was superintendent of the Children's Hospital in Winnipeg, and Jessie's apartment was a refuge to which she could go when she was depressed or perturbed. A gifted artist, she gave Miss Johns a number of her paintings which later adorned the walls of her home in Vancouver. A rift occurred in the friendship when Jessie married. Miss Johns disapproved of her marriage and when the Pierces moved to Vancouver, she did not see as much of Jessie as she would have done under different circumstances. Despite this, when the latter died suddenly, in 1953, Ethel Johns was overcome with grief. Writing to Mrs Brack about this tragic event, she said:

... It has been a strange, sad summer for me. I think I told you that my nearest friend (a good deal younger than I) had died after a short and tragic illness caused by some stupid dentistry. It has taken me a long time to get squared away again. Without knowing it, I had come to depend on her as a younger sister, almost, and it never occurred to me to think that she might go first. Destiny plays strange tricks on us. She was the least morbid of souls, and I have tried to take the blow as she would have done. Next week, I am going over to her sister, who lives on Vancouver Island and is a passionate gardener. Long ago, while she was still in full career as one of the most brilliant librarians Canada ever produced, she, like a thrifty Scot, bought acreage not far from Victoria. Later on, she sold most of it and retained for her own use a lofty, craggy site on which she built her eyrie, rather like the falcon she reminds me of. She has a cliff covered with curious lichens and at its foot a nice stand of several Douglas firs. You can lie in bed and hear them soughing all night long in the sea wind ...

Once again, Miss Johns sought sanctuary and healing in the home of her friend, Helen Stewart.

A younger Stewart also took an interest in Miss Johns. Isabel's niece, Betty, was a graduate of the combined course of the Vancouver General Hospital and the University of British Columbia Schools of Nursing. After her marriage to Dr W.S. Maddin in 1946, they went to New York and lived there for six years. Betty wrote to Miss Johns at intervals, giving her the news of the members of the family who lived in that city. The Maddins moved to Vancouver in 1952 and lived a few blocks from Miss Johns' home. Betty saw Miss Johns quite often at that time. Sometimes when she called her knock was not answered, although she was aware that Miss Johns was looking at her through the window. This did not discourage her; she was 'accustomed to the ways of old people,' accepted the fact that Miss Johns did not want company at that time, and did not feel rebuffed. Betty Maddin recalls that Miss Johns did not enjoy social life, did not care to go out to dinner (unless to a gala affair at the Faculty Club), and preferred to be invited to afternoon tea. Features which Betty vividly remembers about 'E.J.' were her 'most vital eyes' and her 'tremendous sense of humour.'

The year 1953 brought satisfaction as well as sorrow. In the early fall, Mrs Brack wrote Miss Johns to say that final arrangements had been concluded with the Johns Hopkins Press for the publication of the History. In her reply, Miss Johns commented: 'It was a distinct relief to hear that the contract with the Johns Hopkins Press had been signed, sealed, and delivered. I was also glad to hear from Mrs McVicar, before she left for Scotland, that "the editors of the J.H.P. are to deal directly with the respective authors with respect to proof-reading." This means that we shall have the benefit of the advice of experts and that certain values which mean a good deal to me will be preserved.'[3]

That same year the J.B. Lippincott Company published a small bound volume of the collected issues of *Just Plain Nursing* which had been edited by Miss Johns over the six-year period since its inception. In a foreword to the book, the editor explained why and how the series came to be inaugurated. The same publishers now sought Miss Johns' help in adapting a British text on geriatric nursing for publication in the United States.[4] The task proved to be more time-consuming than she expected, but judging by her later comments to Mrs Brack, she enjoyed the assignment:

... My latest exploit was the 'Americanization' of an English text about (of all things) the 'Care of the Elderly Sick.' It was written by an English geriatrist and is a darned good little book – intended for nurses, of course. He was awfully nice about having his text chewed up a bit, and even submitted like a lamb to having an introduction written by a mere nurse. As a result, I am revelling in a brand new electric range purchased with my well-meant efforts ...[5]

For the first few months of 1954, Miss Johns was caught up in the final details preceding the publication of the History. The book, *The Johns Hopkins Hospital School of Nursing, 1889–1949*, appeared in May. At a ceremonial in Baltimore, Effie Taylor presented a copy to the School of Nursing on behalf of the Alumnae Association. The book was favourably reviewed and well received, and Ethel Johns expressed her satisfaction in a letter to Eileen Flanagan:

... To my immense relief, the bally thing has sold far beyond expectations and a second printing is being talked of. I had horrid visions of what in the trade are known as 'publishers' remainders' piled up in a dusty unsold heap. It even went on television in Baltimore when the chairman of the Alumnae Committee (very chic and pretty) was interviewed and an announcer with a good voice read extracts in a really noble manner – or so I am informed. As always happens with me, anything I have written is completely externalized as soon as it appears in print and I don't even want to read it. More experienced authors tell me that this is a common happening, and that a year or two later you read the thing with interest but complete detachment and wonder how (and why) you sweat so much blood over it. Anyway it was a tremendous help with the mortgage and the other day I gave a party at which the mortgage was burned with appropriate libations ...

Miss Johns went on to speak of the recent structure study of the Canadian Nurses' Association, and she commented: 'For the last year or two my life seems to have cut a new channel and the nursing aspects (in the narrow sense) seem increasingly remote. But I can't help being glad that I knew *nursing* in the heroic age. Much of it I saw and part of it I was – and this I say in all humility. One can only hope that the present phase will give rise to something better. Incidentally, I spoke at the RVH annual dinner here and am flatteringly informed that "even the younger nurses enjoyed it ..." '[6]

Writing again to Miss Flanagan a few months later, Miss Johns thanked her for sending *The Road to Mecca*. She had enjoyed the book, she said, although she did not necessarily approve of parts of it: '... the gentleman's attitude toward women, for instance. By the way, did you happen to read the review of it in a recent "Atlantic"? The reviewer (like yours truly) was put off by the rather lush sensuousness and yet (again like EJ) ended up by feeling that it was a great book ...' To pass from the sublime to the ridiculous, she added, she was sending a copy of her own 'magnum opus,' hoping that her friend would deal with it gently. It had been a mixed-up summer, with more illness than she liked among friends and contemporaries, but on the cheerful side, her literary earnings had encouraged her in 'horrid extravagance,' with the result that she had both an electric stove and an oil heater. 'Didn't enjoy getting them put in and on one occasion when there were three stoves and five large men all present in my little house, I felt that the world was too much with me late and soon and that things were getting a little too much for me.' Miss Johns continued: '... Not as many intellectual sprees this year as last but a week or so ago we did have W.H. Auden out at the University. He spent a whole hour reading his own poetry – most of it recent and pretty abstract. Not food for babes, either. But the students gave him a whale of a reception even though he did not really read very well. I had hoped he might touch upon his own philosophy by way of explanation. But no, he was austere and left us to struggle alone ...'[7]

A source of continuing enjoyment for Miss Johns was her attendance at symphony concerts on Sunday afternoons. For years she accompanied Mrs Blayney and Miss Mayhew to and from the auditorium, but she did not sit with them: she preferred to keep the same seat year after year. Emily Mayhew comments that she and her sister did not always want to come home immediately after the concert, but they did so because Miss Johns expected it. She was a little imperious, it seems, with these good friends.

In late December 1954 Jean Whiteford (president of the Alumnae Association of the Winnipeg General Hospital School of Nursing) was in Vancouver, and she telephoned Miss Johns to let her know that the Association was considering the possibility of publishing a history of the School. She wondered whether Miss Johns would make some suggestions relevant to such a project, based on her experience with the history of the Johns Hopkins Hospital School of Nursing. Miss Johns agreed to do so, and on 4 January 1955 she wrote to Miss Whiteford setting forth specific guidelines for her information.[8]

A special issue of *The Canadian Nurse* (March 1955) marked the golden anniversary of the Journal. Among the greetings which it contained from former editors and executive secretaries was a message from Ethel Johns:

... With this issue, *The Canadian Nurse* celebrates its Golden Jubilee. Fifty years is a long time in the history of a young nation and it is in this first half of the twentieth century that Canada has come of age and has taken her rightful place among the nations of the world. The ceremonial observance of a fiftieth anniversary goes back to Biblical times and was marked by rejoicing that had a deeper spiritual significance than mere exultation. According to the Book of Leviticus, the year of Jubilee was also a time of emancipation and restoration – a time to look forward as well as back.

The Canadian Nurse will continue in the future, as in the past, to serve as a living link between the nurses who live and work in the widely scattered communities of this vast land. More and more, it will afford free expression of many different points of view and help to reconcile them. Above all, it will strive to interpret the spirit of Canadian nursing, not only to ourselves but to nurses in other countries. 'All round the world – and a little hook to fasten it.'

Also in March 1955, the Alumnae Association of the Winnipeg

General Hospital School of Nursing accepted the recommendation of a special committee that the organization sponsor the publication of a history of the School and that Miss Johns be invited to write the book. Upon being approached, the latter agreed to do so, stipulating that she would accept no remuneration other than for her out-of-pocket expenses. Upon her recommendation, a small committee was appointed for the purpose of reviewing draft manuscripts and making suggestions to the author, as they deemed advisable, about changes in content. Miss Margaret Cameron, director of nursing of the Winnipeg General Hospital, was named the convener of the committee.[9]

Miss Johns spent the month of June in residence at the Winnipeg General Hospital School of Nursing, where she searched for, examined, and classified available source materials. As had been the case at Johns Hopkins, she found the research exciting. Jean Whiteford recalls Miss Johns showing her some very old files which Dr H. Coppinger had unearthed, and exclaiming, 'These are pure gold!'

While in Winnipeg, Miss Johns (now seventy-six years old) addressed the annual meeting of the Canadian Home Economics Association. The theme of her address was the common ground shared by the two professions, dietetics and nursing. 'Both our professions,' she said, 'stem from motherhood – to protect, to nourish, to nurse. That is our high calling, which we follow each in our own way. In an age of blind violence and wanton destruction, we belong to what Toynbee calls "the creative minority." We take hold on life itself. What we share is common ground – yes, but holy ground.'[10]

Miss Johns returned directly to Vancouver with the source material which she had collected. She was too weary to accept Gertrude Hall's invitation to stop off in Calgary, where the latter was now director of nursing of the Calgary General Hospital. As a member of the Alumnae Association of the Winnipeg General Hospital School of Nursing, Miss Hall had given strong support to the project to publish a history and to the appointment of Miss Johns as the author.

In a letter to Miss Flanagan written on 26 August, Miss Johns mentioned that Miss Hall had recently spent a day with her at her home, and that they had had 'a grand palaver over the Winnipeg General source material.' In the same letter, she expressed her thanks to Miss Flanagan for lending her Ellen Glasgow's recently published book, *The Woman Within*:

... They say it is a good deed to bring a worthy book to a mind capable of profiting by it so you see you are right up the Boy Scout alley. To say that I was fasci-

nated is to put it mildly. I could not put it down when I first read it and have returned more than once for a more analytic study. The closing paragraphs I have copied out and kept. They reflect my own life experience to such an extraordinary degree that I might have written them myself if I'd the capacity to do it, which I haven't. All through the book there are the most astonishing flashes of insight and above all the courage to face disillusionment ...
... This book is by far the best portrait that I have yet seen of the women of my own generation – that is to say, the intellectuals among them. It seems strange that she should have wanted to delay the publication of the book at all for its reticence is just as characteristic of the epoch as the frankness. And yet most of us would have done likewise. I must turn to her books now that I have the key. At that time, I was probably not ready for them ...

The task of recording the history of her own school of nursing was one to which Ethel Johns addressed herself with evident enjoyment. She herself was a part of its story, and from her recollections of people and events she was able to supplement the information gleaned from other sources. The writing must have been accomplished with relative ease, since the manuscript was completed in little over one year. In a letter to Eileen Flanagan 16 October 1957, Miss Johns said that she was sending her a copy of the book (*The Winnipeg General Hospital School of Nursing, 1887–1953*) and she confided that 'the writing of the earlier chapters was sheer joy. It was such a satisfaction to get the story of the early Red River days down before the original documents crumbled into dust. The sale has gone very well – they have an excellent young committee working on it.' In the same letter, Miss Johns added:

... It gave me a nostalgic pang to hear that you and Suzanne are setting up housekeeping in my old stamping ground – the Marlborough of happy memory. Quite a lot happened to me in that little bachelor suite where, incidentally, I was almost suffocated one night by ammonia fumes coming from the refrigerator. Don't be surprised if you encounter my astral shade still hovering around the little pool in the courtyard where an ancient turtle used to live ...

On 23 May 1958, Miss Johns wrote to Mrs Brack, presumably in reply to a letter stating that she and Dr Brack expected to be in Vancouver and hoped to see Miss Johns:

... After my long silence, I wonder that you can find it in your generous Southern heart to invite me to breakfast. A bright star has been placed opposite the proposed dates, June 24th to 28th, and I shall eagerly await further word as to which morning will be most convenient. Other plans can perhaps be made to fit in with the official festivities that are in store for the distinguished visiting firemen and their ladies. This is Vancouver's centenary and the welcome mat will be out.

Now for a little tale of woe which I hope will explain E.J.'s recent unresponsiveness. Just after Christmas, I had a bad attack of influenza, and, as an aftermath, turned a bright yellow. There were alarums and excursions, I was whisked off to hospital for a check-up. All the tests were negative and to my immense relief the golden glow faded away of its own accord. Now that I am back on my feet, I have to submit to some grisly dentistry which at the moment makes me look like an elderly serpent. I am assured however, that by the middle of June I shall be more presentable ...

While all this has been going on, more demands have been made than I could have coped with even in a state of rude health. Adelaide Nutting had her centenary, Isabel Stewart her eightieth birthday, the Vancouver General Hospital School of Nursing its fiftieth anniversary, and for every blessed one of them, 'something vital and interesting' was requested. Last week, the Canadian Nurses' Association, now celebrating its Golden Jubilee in Ottawa, said that they would like me to come along for the doings, all expenses paid, of course; but a speech or two 'in your light amusing style' would be much appreciated. What a relief it was to be able to say quite truthfully that my dentist thought it would be better if I kept my mouth shut for a while. However, here's hoping that the old girl will be on hand, equipped with a spoon, ready at least for a bowl of porridge and a grand and glorious talk ...

At the Fiftieth Anniversary Meeting of the Canadian Nurses' Association, Ethel Johns (in her absence) was awarded an Honorary Life Membership in the association to which she had given so much of herself.

She was now giving some thought to writing her autobiography, and may have made a tentative start on the task in 1958 or 1959. An event of the same period was a visit from her brother Alex, who came up from California to see her. According to Dr Helen Stewart, Miss Johns arranged for him to stay in a place near to her home, since she could not accommodate him there. The reunion with the brother whom she had seen so rarely was a joy to her, and it was probably the last time she saw him.

In her Christmas message (December 1960) to Miss Flanagan, Miss Johns mentioned that the year had been a sad one for her: '... More than one contemporary has departed. Hard as it is to lose old friends, it is even harder to reconcile oneself to the loss of those who are younger – especially Gertrude Hall – ... What I so admired in her (as in yourself and Norena) was that all three of you faced up to the problem of nursing service rather than dodging it after the manner of some of our more academic pundits. No one knows better than I do how much courage it takes to maintain sound educational standards in the middle of (and in spite of) the everyday turmoil in the wards ...'

October 1960 marked the publication of the final issue of *Just Plain Nursing*. Mr Leeman had now retired from Philadelphia and he and his wife were living in Montreal. For the next three years, he and Miss Johns carried on a leisurely correspondence. The latter wrote to him about the plans for her autobiography, while Mr Leeman sought her critical review of an 'Epitome' which he was writing of Burton's *Anatomy of Melancholy*. With typical thoroughness, Miss Johns undertook to delve into the classic work before venturing an opinion upon Mr Leeman's treatment of it, and her detailed notes on this exercise (preserved in her personal files) are not only intriguing in themselves but indicate the clarity of her thinking at the time.

Miss Johns submitted a 'sample chapter' of her autobiography to Mr Leeman and he encouraged her to go on with the writing of it. But personal problems intervened, and she was unable to concentrate on the task. She literally exhausted her energies in worry when her brother became ill; throughout 1962, she was in a state of constant anxiety about him. Emily Mayhew remembers that she would not even go to the symphony for fear that news of her brother might come in her absence. Mabel Gray, too, attests to Miss Johns' preoccupation with this family problem. For several years, Miss Gray had been accustomed to invite Miss Johns and one or two other friends to have dinner at the home which she shared with her brother. The latter died in 1962, and Miss Gray did not feel up to having the little group for Christmas dinner at home, so she and Miss Johns, with Margaret Duffield and Janet Greig, arranged to have a 'no hostess dinner' at the Devonshire Hotel. It was apparent throughout the meal that Miss Johns was uneasy: she wanted to get home as quickly as possible, since she was expecting a call from Alex's stepdaughter (in California) about his condition. He was critically ill at the time and died shortly thereafter.

Miss Johns' strength was failing now, but she was determined to remain in her home as long as she could manage to do so. She loved to sit in the garden when the weather was fine, and had a number of interests which kept her occupied. Her vision was good, she continued to be an avid reader, and fortunately was kept well supplied with books by Eileen Flanagan, Helen Stewart, and Lucille Blayney. She looked forward to the daily paper and read periodicals such as *The Atlantic Monthly* and *Maclean's*. The radio was her link with the outside world and was her constant companion. Mrs Blayney and Miss Mayhew were a mainstay to her, and each had a well-understood role: the former conversed with her about politics, books, religion, and other weighty matters, while Emily's task (like the Biblical Martha) was to take charge of practical affairs. Miss Johns called Emily's car 'the instant taxi.' For both of these friends she had a deep affection, and she grieved with them when their parents died, Mr Mayhew in June 1960, and his wife in March 1961.

Miss Johns had never been much interested in food, and she was unskilled in cooking. By 1964, her appetite was poor, and she was eating so little that she finally had to be hospitalized because of severe malnutrition. It is reported by close friends that she was critically ill, but in a subsequent letter to Miss Flanagan which she wrote on 25 August, she made light of the incident: 'Toward the end of April I had a return of that detestable hepatitis, complicated this time by a terrific anemia. This landed me in the VGH for three weeks or so and later on for a prolonged period in a convalescent hospital. Now, thank heaven, I am back at the old stand and with the help of a part-time housekeeper who is a pretty good cook, I am getting a more respectable blood count and making up for lost weight. Well, enough of that. Let us talk about something more interesting ...' She then went on to speak about politics, always a favourite subject with her.

A heavy blow fell upon Miss Johns shortly after her return from the hospital. Mrs Blayney and Miss Mayhew told her that they were going to move to West Vancouver. Mrs Blayney had suffered a heart attack in the spring, and it was essential for them to have a house with only one floor. Lucille Blayney says: 'She was so disturbed that we were moving, but she accepted that as she accepted so much else in her life.' A basic tenet of Miss Johns' philosophy was to endure afflictions without complaint, and she did not complain now, but she must have had a foreboding of loneliness to come.

28

The Setting Sun

Miss Johns was now alone a great deal of the time. Several people who would have liked to see her stayed away because they heard that she did not want visitors. She made no secret of the fact that she disliked having friends come unannounced. 'I'm not a drop-in person,' she once remarked. Mrs Mayall, her part-time housekeeper, was a continuing source of help and comfort. Although somewhat in awe of Miss Johns, she was loyal and devoted to her, and Miss Johns always referred to her – quite justly – as 'The Pearl.'

Dr William Stewart, the younger brother of Betty Maddin, had come to Vancouver in 1959, after he completed his medical course. He and his wife took an interest in Miss Johns, and it was he who arranged for her hospitalization in 1964. His presence in the city gave her a feeling of security, and since she worried when he went away on trips, the Stewarts tried to keep this knowledge from her whenever possible.

A regular monthly visitor was one of the priests from St James Church who (he said) quite enjoyed the contact with this elderly, alert, and witty member of the congregation. By her own admission, Miss Johns was not an entirely orthodox member of the high Anglican community. In a note to a friend, she referred to herself as a 'Darwinian Anglican with a touch of mysticism,' and she once wrote to Miss Flanagan:

... Now, about 'Honest to God.' It is a sincere and courageous statement that comes at the psychological moment. No sooner had I read it a couple of times when it was literally snatched from my hands by a friend who is closely in touch with several UBC groups who are having some rare tussles about it. After that, she wants to hand it on (indirectly) to members of St James Church (very high) who, in her opinion, stand in need of an antidote for some pretty narrow 'churchiness' – to quote the Bishop of Woolwich. Whether (as the owner of the book) I shall be disciplined by one of the young 'Fathers' remains to be seen ...[1]

A close friend observes that 'It was a real sorrow to Miss Johns in later life that she had only the shell of her earlier beliefs left.' The same friend adds; 'E.J. was a mystic – it was the mystical side of religion that appealed to her. But if there were question of a miracle, E.J. would be the first to require meticulous documentation.'

Of Miss Johns' political convictions in later life, a friend comments: 'In her later years, Ethel Johns was often browned off with the N.D.P. In this as in other areas, she had a struggle between expanding consciousness of change and the world of ancient loyalties. Loyalties usually won. She felt things so deeply – she couldn't brush things off as most people could.'

After they were settled in West Vancouver, Mrs Blayney and Miss Mayhew brought Miss Johns over to see their home and garden. Following that visit, she could picture them in their new surroundings and was content. From time to time, they came to see her; their visits usually followed the symphony concerts on Sunday afternoons which she was no longer able to attend. Should they plan to be out of town, Miss Johns wanted to know when they were leaving and the expected date of return. Both dates were entered into her calendar. Her two friends were in regular communication with Miss Johns by telephone. By arrangement, they called her at exactly a quarter to eleven each Tuesday morning. If they were not punctual, she declined to answer. The day and time may not always have been convenient for them, but they did not question Miss Johns' plan. Mrs Blayney recalls that she always prepared in advance for these conversations; not infrequently the agenda included discussion of the annotated clippings which the friends regularly exchanged by mail on a wide variety of topics related to books, current events, and politics. Mrs Blayney was always conscious of the fact that Miss Johns had a list of these topics in front of her as she talked, and that she ticked them off one by one.

In the late summer of 1965, Miss Johns had an interesting visitor. Dr Muriel Uprichard, at that time a member of the faculty of the University of California School of Nursing, was planning to write a history of nursing, and wished to secure information from Miss Johns about her own life and the founding of the University of British

Columbia School of Nursing. She spent the whole afternoon with Miss Johns, and recalls the visit as having been both stimulating and enjoyable. The latter promised to write to Dr Uprichard, giving the information which she requested. Judging by a draft of her reply which is among Miss Johns' papers, she composed this letter with great care, and on 16 September 1965 she typed it (double-spaced) on seven sheets of letter paper. She then sent if off to Dr Uprichard in Los Angeles.

Shortly after this, the School of Nursing of the University of British Columbia had occasion to seek the help of its first director. The Library Committee of the School (convened by the writer) decided to ask Miss Johns for her advice regarding the development of a nursing collection for the Charles Woodward Memorial Room of the recently opened Woodward Biomedical Library. The convener wrote to Miss Johns enquiring whether she would be willing to serve as adviser, and Miss Johns replied promptly expressing her interest. She invited the convener to visit her for the purpose of discussing the subject. The faculty of the School had been unaware of Miss Johns' serious illness in 1964, and the writer was shocked, at the time of the visit, to find her looking so frail and ill. However, her warm welcome was reassuring, and she showed a keen interest in the progress of the School of Nursing and the activities of the Woodward Biomedical Library. The quiet chat by the fireside that afternoon was the first of many such occasions throughout the remaining years of Miss Johns' life.

Miss Johns told the convener of the Library Committee that, because of her age and infirmity, she could not serve actively as a consultant, but that she would be glad to give guidance 'behind the scenes' regarding the building of the nucleus of a nursing collection for the Charles Woodward Memorial Room. She spoke of the times which she had spent in the Historical Library of The Johns Hopkins Hospital School of Nursing, and recommended that the initial focus of attention in building up the collection should be threefold: writing the history of the School of Nursing of the University of British Columbia; undertaking some research into the international influence of nurses from the Canadian West; and securing the histories of other Canadian schools of nursing, including that of the McGill School for Graduate Nurses, which was to be published shortly.

Miss Johns spoke of the recent visit of Dr Uprichard and about the brief manuscript which she had prepared in response to the latter's request, dealing with the initial period in the School's history. Subject to Dr Uprichard's approval, she would be willing for the School to have a copy of this material.[2] (Dr Uprichard subsequently agreed to give the

School of Nursing a copy of Miss Johns' letter, and wrote to Miss Johns to say that she had gladly done so.)

Miss Johns then gave further guidance, including the need for and urgency of obtaining information from early graduates of the School of Nursing. She advocated the use of a tape-recorder in interviewing, and spoke of the historical value of such tapes. She recommended that a start be made in collecting manuscripts and letters relating to this School in particular, but also to nursing in Canada as a whole and other countries. She cautioned that letters which might be regarded as having little value now might well be very valuable in fifty years' time.

At the conclusion of this first visit, Miss Johns gave the convener of the Library Committee (presumably for the Memorial Room) a collection of her medals and medallions: her graduation medal (1902) and its silver chain; the Mary Agnes Snively award; a medallion of l'Institut Edith Cavell-Marie Depage, Brussels; and a medallion (dated 1845) of the Conseil Général d'Administration des Hôpitaux Civils de Lyon. Miss Johns did not volunteer any information about these awards, either then or later; she simply said, 'Take them away quickly.' When asked, on subsequent visits, to tell something about her life, Miss Johns replied, 'That will come later.' She probably still hoped that she would complete her autobiography, but in fact was never able to go beyond the three chapters covering the early years of her life, and the sketchy notes for later periods up to 1929, some of which have been incorporated in this book.

Neighbours across the street and at the back of her house kept a watchful eye on her and stood ready to help her. She gave two or three friends keys to her back door, so that they could gain entry in the event that she needed help. As an added security, she prepared several small cards, one for each of a small group of friends, on which she listed the names and addresses of each one, and of her executors. She wanted these people to get to know one another and took steps to facilitate their doing so. With at least one friend – and possibly with all of the group in turn – she carefully reviewed the arrangements she had made for her funeral, cremation, and burial. This she did briefly and in a businesslike way; she wanted to leave nothing to chance. Her foresight proved to be sound; when it became necessary, the small group was able to swing into action like a well-rehearsed unit, and each member found no difficulty in identifying and assuming his or her role.

Miss Johns wrote to Miss Flanagan on 1 September 1966 to thank her for a copy of the history, *In Caps and Gowns*, of the McGill School for Graduate Nurses. She commented that the book was 'a well-documented history which gives a clear and authoritative description of the founding and early development of the School. The brief sketches of the pioneers are admirable, but leave one wishing that they could have been extended ... The format of the book is worthy of its content: simple, attractive and dignified. The material in the appendices is very well arranged and comprehensive ...' She then mentioned that the School of Nursing of the University of British Columbia was starting to collect materials on which to base its history. Returning to the McGill School's history, she wrote: '... There is one suggestion I should like to make, based on my Johns Hopkins experience. It might be worthwhile to retain as much of the original documentary material as you can find space for. Fifty years from now, it may come in handy to researchers.' Miss Johns told of a reunion which the Stewart family held in Vancouver during the previous month, and she added:

... EJ in her capacity as an honorary member of the Clan got caught up in the festivities, a delightful if rather exhausting experience. Some of the members of the Clan I have known for sixty years! I was the only 'outsider' at the various events and had to hold up my end with two other octogenarians who were really *family* and not honorary! On the whole I think all three did very well and were the life of the party to a limited extent. Fortunately for me, several members of the Clan live in Vancouver and have been a grand stand-by in various emergencies ...

Miss Flanagan was not only a faithful correspondent and provider of books, but occasionally she telephoned Miss Johns from Montreal, much to the latter's delight: not only did she find it stimulating to talk with her old friend, but (as she observed to Mrs Blayney) it made her feel so *expensive*. Miss Johns had had little luxury in her life, and she was impressed by this profligate expenditure on her behalf.

Writing on 24 August 1967 to thank Miss Flanagan for Gabrielle Roy's *The Road Past Altamont,* Miss Johns was in a conversational mood:

... The very day you called me up two good friends had spent the afternoon describing *their* visit to Expo. They had been overwhelmed by the experience ... the beauty of the setting, the grandeur of the whole concept, the noble architecture, the imaginative display – above all, perhaps, by the courtesy shown on every side ...

I am still holding out in my funny little house in spite of continued well-meant advice to the contrary. 'At your age, etc. etc. etc.' I must admit that I find it more difficult to get about. The spirit is willing but THE LEGS are weak.

However, I thoroughly enjoy doddling about with my housework and the untidy back garden is a joy. I still have my good helper who comes up twice a week and sets the house to rights.

What do *you* think about this strange and terrible world in which we live and have our being? What do you think of the men who aspire to leadership in our country? Ten of them are contesting with one another for the right to do so. Not one of them much more than mediocre.

Just as I was ready to burst into tears, the teen-ager from next door arrived with a gift of luscious corn on the cob. He has watered my lawn all through this long hot summer for a modest sum. He plays excellent hockey in winter. He is doing well at school and is going to specialize in electronics when he goes to University. When I look at him I forget the scruffy hippies who infest a street not very far away. Perhaps we shall come through safely after all ...

Miss Johns fell and injured an ankle shortly after this, and thereafter had increased difficulty in moving around the house. She was visibly failing now, and could remain in her home only because her housekeeper came in more frequently. Miss Johns – and her friends – became more anxious when winter brought heavy snowfalls. On Christmas Day, friends could not get to her home because of the snow. Despite this, she had quite a happy day. She spent the afternoon reading with delight some photocopies of the Jean Moore Collection of original Florence Nightingale letters loaned to her by the Woodward Biomedical Library. By strange chance, the librarian who selected and arranged these for her pleasure was Margaret Leighton (also a nurse), the niece of her faithful old friend and former student, Amy Lee. Once again the wheel had come full circle for Ethel Johns.

Time was running out now. On Victoria Day in 1968, a few days after her eighty-ninth birthday, her doctor arranged for her admission to a private hospital. She knew that she would die soon, and confided this to a friend while requesting that she not tell Mrs Blayney and Miss Mayhew: she wanted to spare them the distress as long as possible. These friends came to see her twice weekly during the long summer of her decline, and Emily went on endless messages at her request. Others of her small circle visited as well. She did not wish to have Miss Flanagan told of her illness, nor would she permit her niece to come from Winnipeg. She had a task to accomplish, and she faced it resolutely alone. She died quietly on the morning of Labour Day, 2 September 1968. She had directed that her funeral be private, but a small group, including her niece, Helen, attended the service at St James Church. According to her wishes, her ashes were taken to

Montreal for interment, with those of her mother and brother, in Mount Royal Cemetery.

At the request of Miss Johns' executors, Mrs Blayney and Miss Mayhew sorted and packed the contents of her home. They found a small piece of paper in the bedroom, on which were inscribed in her handwriting the following words:

The road,
You shall follow it.
The fun,
You shall forget it.
The cup,
You shall empty it.
The pain,
You shall conceal it.
The truth,
You shall behold it.
The end,
You shall endure it.

Epilogue

On the afternoon of Sunday, 12 January 1969, the University of British Columbia commemorated the Golden Jubilee of the School of Nursing and honoured the memory of its first director, Ethel Johns. The simple ceremony was held in the Charles Woodward Memorial Room of the Woodward Biomedical Library, and was presided over by the Chancellor, John M. Buchanan, attired in the black and gold robes of his office. Many faculty members and other university officials were present, as well as representatives of various nursing associations, former friends, and associates of Miss Johns. An honoured guest on this occasion was Mabel Gray, the School's second director. Evelyn Mallory, the third director, who now lived in Vernon, British Columbia, could not be present because of inclement weather and difficult travel conditions.

After the invocation by the Reverend Stewart Forbes and introductory remarks by the Chancellor, Professor Elizabeth McCann paid tribute to the 'three special people,' Ethel Johns, Mabel Gray, and Evelyn Mallory, who in succession guided the destinies of the School of Nursing for the greater part of its first half-century. She reported that 'from the initial "combined programme" of 1919, when three intrepid pioneers embarked toward the first baccalaureate degrees for nurses in Canada, to the ninety-seven students anticipating graduation this year from one of the four undergraduate programmes now offered, the University will have recognized two thousand three hundred and seventeen nurses as qualified to receive either baccalaureate degrees or diplomas in nursing. Six more pioneers joined the ranks this year,' she added, 'to forge the link between the first and second halves of this century of nursing as they enrolled in the graduate programme leading to the degree of Master of Science in Nursing ...'

Dr Rae Chittick then gave an address, 'In Appreciation of Ethel Johns,' in which she reviewed the story of her life and the achievements of her professional career. Of Miss Johns' contribution as editor and business manager of *The Canadian Nurse,* Dr Chittick remarked:

... In 1933, Miss Johns was welcomed back to Canada and to a new position – the first full-time Editor and Business Manager of *The Canadian Nurse*. It was a particularly happy appointment, for Miss Johns brought to this new position a world perspective on nursing, a hospitality of the mind from her rich experience, and unusual literary talent. She set new goals for the Journal which did not stop at informative articles, but reached out to challenge nurses to think for themselves and to create a body of nursing opinion on the changes essential to meet the health needs of a rapidly expanding nation. She travelled extensively and observed the contemporary nursing scene at first hand. The Journal began to reflect the opinions of nurses from many parts of Canada and from a wide variety of positions. The editorials were read for their pungent comments as well as their thoughtful analysis of prevailing practices. When Miss Johns retired after eleven years as Editor of Canada's national nursing journal, she had made *The Canadian Nurse* a potent force in uniting the nurses of Canada in a truly professional organization ...

Dr Chittick referred to Miss Johns' historical research at the Johns Hopkins and the Winnipeg General Schools of Nursing and of the histories which she had written: '... To read these histories,' she said, 'is to gain insight into the many vicissitudes and courageous leadership that marked the valiant struggle of nursing to become a profession in this century. Although one history is centred in a sophisticated medical seat and the other in a pioneer settlement on the harsh Canadian prairies, the difficulties remained the same.'

Of *Just Plain Nursing*, Dr Chittick commented: 'Each issue was a surprise with its warm, intimate discussion of pertinent nursing questions, suggestions for improving nursing skills, intriguing book reviews ...' In her *Off Duty* writings, the speaker continued, 'Miss Johns took a mellow look at human frailties and pretensions and displayed her genius for gathering into one varied impressions of the external world, that quality which Santayana called the amalgamating imagination.' Dr Chittick concluded: 'To this gifted woman whose remarkable contribution to nursing spans more than half a century, we are proud to pay tribute on this historic occasion.'

The faculty member to whom Miss Johns had handed her medals three years earlier now presented them, in turn, to the Librarian of the University of British Columbia. The Chancellor spoke of the symbolic significance of this gift and its value as a source of inspiration to nursing students and faculty alike.

The ceremony was over and the people departed, but the spirit of Ethel Johns lingered awhile in the quiet room.

Notes

CHAPTER 1

1 Ethel Johns, manuscript of unfinished autobiography
2 Charles Kingsley, *Glaucus, or the Wonder of the Shore*. Cambridge: Macmillan and Company, 1855, pp. 163–4
3 Letter to the writer from Archbishop Philip Carrington, 1 February 1969
4 'An Account of the North Wales Hospital Written by Dr J.H. Roberts (Medical Superintendent) and S.L. Frost (Hospital Secretary) in 1948 – on the Occasion of the Hospital's Centenary.' Sent to the writer, with letter of 24 October, 1969 by Dr Lewis Miles, Department of Social Institutions, University College of North Wales, Bangor, North Wales
5 Letter to the writer from Archbishop Carrington, 1 February 1969
6 Government of Canada, Department of Indian Affairs, *Annual Report, 1890*, p. 229
7 Government of Canada, Department of Indian Affairs, *Annual Report, 1895*, p. 363
8 Ethel Johns, manuscript of unfinished autobiography
9 Ibid.

CHAPTER 2

1 Ethel Johns, manuscript of unfinished autobiography. Unless otherwise indicated, quotations of Miss Johns' writings in this chapter are from the same source
2 Government of Canada, Department of Indian Affairs, *Annual Reports*, Savanne Agency and Manitoba Superintendency, years 1885–8 inclusive. Ottawa: Queen's Printer
3 Ibid., 1885, p. 127
4 This issue of the paper is in the archives of *The Dryden Observer*, Dryden, Ontario
5 In 1897 Amy Johns purchased the island on which her husband was buried. Many years later, Ethel Johns had her father's grave moved farther up on the island, to prevent its being inundated by the rising waters of the lake. In October 1970 Chief Paul Pitchenese of the Wabigoon reserve told the writer that Mr Johns' grave is in good condition, is clearly marked, and that

Indians, too, are buried on what is known as 'Graveyard Island.' It is located one and a quarter miles over open water from the reserve. The Indians had not been aware, he said, that Mrs Johns had bought the island. It reverted to the Crown in 1937
6 Ethel Johns, manuscript of unfinished autobiography
7 Kennethe M. Haig, *Brave Harvest* (The Life of E. Cora Hind, LL.D.), chap. 16, 'Her Friends,' Toronto: Thomas Allen, Limited, Publishers, 1945, pp. 132–3
8 Tape-recorded interview by the writer with the late Dr Helen Stewart, Victoria, 7 June 1969
9 Government of Canada, Department of Indian Affairs, *Annual Report*, 1897, p. xxiv
10 Ethel Johns, manuscript of unfinished autobiography
11 Ibid.

CHAPTER 3

1 Ethel Johns, *The Winnipeg General Hospital School of Nursing, 1887–1953*. Winnipeg: The Alumnae Association of the Winnipeg General Hospital School of Nursing, 1957, p. 80
2 *Reminiscences of Isabel M. Stewart*. New York: Oral History Research Office, Butler Library, Columbia University, 1961
3 Ethel Johns, manuscript of unfinished autobiography
4 E. Cora Hind, 'Ethel Johns,' *The Canadian Nurse*, XXXVI (June 1940), 350
5 Interview by Miss Kathleen Ruane with Dr Ross Mitchell, Winnipeg, February 1970

CHAPTER 4

1 A. Maud Crawford, 'Letter from Winnipeg, February 6th, 1905,' *The Canadian Nurse*, I (March 1905), 19
2 Frederica Wilson, lady superintendent of the Winnipeg General Hospital, supplied this information in a statement which she made on 14 February 1914 in connection with Ethel Johns' application for admission to Teachers College, Columbia University
3 E. Cora Hind, 'Ethel Johns,' *The Canadian Nurse*, XXXVI (June 1940), 350
4 Ethel Johns, 'The Challenge of the Future,' *The Canadian Nurse*, XVII (January 1921), 5–6

5 Ethel Johns, 'Western Hospitals,' *The Canadian Nurse,* IV (May 1908), 207–11
6 Miss Johns was actually twenty-three years of age at time of graduation
7 Ethel Johns, 'Administration of Schools of Nursing,' an address to the Twenty-eighth Annual Convention of the National League of Nursing Education, *Annual Reports and Proceedings, 1922.* New York: National League of Nursing Education, 1922, p. 257
8 *Reminiscences of Isabel M. Stewart.* New York: Oral History Research Office, Butler Library, Columbia University, 1961, pp. 42, 53–4
9 Interview by the writer with Dr Helen Stewart, Victoria, British Columbia, 7 June 1969. (*Note*: Dr Stewart died in April 1971.)
10 Ethel Johns, 'Off Duty,' *The Canadian Nurse,* XXXVII (May 1941), 362
11 Ethel Johns, *The Winnipeg General Hospital School of Nursing, 1887–1953.* Winnipeg: The Alumnae Association of the Winnipeg General Hospital School of Nursing, 1957, p. 37
12 'New Head Has Had Wide Experience' (news item), *Manitoba Free Press,* 12 May 1915
13 Interview by Miss Kathleen Ruane with Dr Ross Mitchell, Winnipeg, Manitoba, February 1970
14 Interview by the writer with Dr Fred C. Bell, Vancouver, British Columbia, 12 July 1969 (Dr Bell died in June 1971)

CHAPTER 5

1 Ethel Johns, *The Winnipeg General Hospital School of Nursing, 1887–1953.* Winnipeg: The Alumnae Association, 1957, p. 44
2 Ethel Johns, 'The Alumnae Journal,' *Nurses' Alumnae Journal of the Winnipeg General Hospital* (June 1914), 9
3 Ibid., 9–10
4 'A Canadian Nurses' Journal' (editorial comment), *American Journal of Nursing,* V (March 1905), 354–5
5 Charlotte Eastwood, 'The Meaning and Benefits of State Registration,' *The Canadian Nurse,* I (March 1905), 14
6 Ethel Johns, 'The Alumnae Journal,' *Nurses' Alumnae Journal* (June 1914), 12
7 Ethel Johns, 'A Nursing Problem of the West,' *The Canadian Nurse,* V (March 1909), 117–20
8 'Nursing Canadian Mothers' (editorial), *The Canadian Nurse,* V (April 1909), 201–2

Chapter notes 289

9 John Murray Gibbon, *The Victorian Order of Nurses for Canada, 50th Anniversary, 1897–1947*. Montreal: Southam Press, 1947, p. 8
10 By 1922 the Order had withdrawn from all but two of the Cottage Hospitals.
11 Despite many difficulties, by 1916 eleven County Districts, mostly in Saskatchewan, had been organized by the Order.

CHAPTER 6

1 Interview by Miss Kathleen Ruane with Miss Kennethe Haig, Winnipeg, 15 August 1969
2 Elizabeth Parker, 'Report of the Honourary Secretary,' *The Canadian Alpine Journal*, vol. II, no. 2 (1910), 207
3 Arthur O. Wheeler, 'Report of the 1909 Camp,' *The Canadian Alpine Journal*, vol. II, no. 2 (1910), p. 212
4 Ethel Johns, 'A Graduating Climb,' *The Canadian Alpine Journal*, vol. II, no. 2 (1910), 160
5 Ibid.
6 Arthur O. Wheeler, 'Report of the 1909 Camp,' 218
7 Taped interview by the writer with the late Dr Fred C. Bell, West Vancouver, 12 July 1969
8 Handwritten album prepared by Ethel Johns for Mr Herbert Carpenter, Christmas 1909
9 Ethel Johns, 'The Alpine Club of Canada,' *Nurses' Alumnae Journal of the Wimmipeg General Hospital* (September 1909), 13–14
10 Ibid., 15

CHAPTER 7

1 The full text of Ethel Johns' paper was published fourteen months later, in the April 1911 issue of *The Canadian Nurse*, 156–9. Unless otherwise noted, quotations from the paper in the paragraphs which follow are from this source.
2 Ethel Johns, *The Winnipeg General Hospital School of Nursing, 1887–1953*. Winnipeg: The Alumnae Association, 1957, pp. 46–7
3 An Act respecting 'The Manitoba Association of Graduate Nurses,' III, CAP. 114, 3 Geo. v, 15 February 1913, sections 10 and 11
4 'Annual Meeting of the Alumnae Association,' *Nurses' Alumnae Journal* (June 1910), 14–15

5 'Higher Education for Nurses,' *Nurses' Alumnae Journal* (September 1910), 9-11
6 Ethel Johns, 'A Glimpse of Chicago Hospitals,' *Nurses' Alumnae Journal* (December 1910), 3-4

CHAPTER 8

1 Information secured from Mrs G.E. Butler, archivist, Winnipeg Branch, Canadian Women's Press Club
2 Statement by Frederica Wilson, 14 February 1914, in connection with Ethel Johns' application for admission to Teachers College, Columbia University. *Ethel Johns Biography File*, archives, Department of Nursing Education, Teachers College, Columbia University
3 'Presentation to Miss Johns,' *Nurses' Alumnae Journal* (July 1911), 7
4 Ethel Johns, *The Winnipeg General Hospital School of Nursing, 1887-1953*. Winnipeg: The Alumnae Association, 1957, p. 46
5 Minutes of meetings of the Finance Committee, Winnipeg General Hospital, May, August, and November, 1911
6 'History of the McKellar General Hospital,' a five-page typed account of the institution's early years and growth, states on page 3 that in April 1911 the lady superintendent, Miss Elizabeth Davidson (Mrs J.W. Cook), resigned and was in turn succeeded by Miss Ethel Johns.
7 Rowe Lewis, 'Fort William's Advantageous Commercial Position: A Prosperous Young City Destined by Nature to Occupy a Commanding Place in the Commerce and Industry of Canada,' *The Manitoba Free Press*, 19 June 1909
8 Ibid.
9 Ibid.
10 'A History of the McKellar General Hospital,' pp. 3-4
11 'Tribute for Splendid Service Rendered' (news item), *The Canadian Nurse*, VII (August 1911), 409-10
12 'Presentation to Miss Johns,' *Nurses' Alumnae Journal* (July 1911), 7-8
13 Ibid.
14 Letter of 4 November 1969 to the writer from Miss C. Browne, director of nursing service, McKellar General Hospital, Fort William
15 Excerpt from letter of 16 September 1965 from Ethel Johns to Dr Muriel Uprichard
16 'History of the McKellar General Hospital,' p. 3

Chapter notes 291

17 'McKellar Auxiliary Story: Over 56 Years of Service' (news item), *The Daily Times-Journal,* Fort William, 3 June 1958
18 Ethel Johns, preliminary draft of section 'Fort William Unit' for proposed autobiography
19 Ibid.
20 Ibid.
21 Interview by Miss K. Ruane with Miss K. Haig, 15 August 1969
22 'New Head Has Had Wide Experience,' *Manitoba Free Press,* 12 May 1915
23 One of these sources is Mrs Helen Franklin, Miss Johns' niece, interviewed in Winnipeg by the writer, 14 October 1970
24 Ethel Johns, preliminary draft of section 'Teachers College Unit' for proposed autobiography

CHAPTER 9

1 Ethel Johns, Preliminary draft of section 'Teachers College Unit' for proposed autobiography
2 Ethel Incledon Johns, 'War Bulletins Along Broadway: An exile from Winnipeg writes about her New York experiences,' *Manitoba Free Press,* 5 September 1914
3 'New Head Has Had Wide Experience' (news item), *Manitoba Free Press,* 12 May 1915
4 Ethel Johns, 'Teachers College Unit'
5 Ibid.
6 Ibid.
7 Tape-recorded interview by the writer with Dr Helen Stewart, Victoria, British Columbia, 7 June 1969
8 Report of the Department of Nursing and Health, 1914–15. Archives of the Department of Nursing Education, Teachers College, Columbia University
9 Virginia Henderson, 'Annie Warburton Goodrich,' *American Journal of Nursing,* LV (December 1955), 1490
10 Ethel Johns, 'Teachers College Unit'
11 Ibid.
12 Ibid.
13 Ibid.
14 Ibid.
15 Ibid.

CHAPTER 10

1 Ethel Johns, Memorandum to Donald C. Masters, 'The Winnipeg General Strike,' 17 October 1945
2 Johns Murray Gibbon in collaboration with Mary S. Mathewson, *Three Centuries of Canadian Nursing.* Toronto: Macmillan Company of Canada, 1947, p. 193
3 Mabel Gray, conversation with the writer
4 Statistics from *Annual Reports of the Superintendent,* archives of the Children's Hospital of Winnipeg
5 Ethel Johns, *Report of the Superintendent, December 1, 1915–November 30, 1916,* archives of the Children's Hospital of Winnipeg
6 Interview by the writer with the late Mrs M.V. Stocker, White Rock, British Columbia, 3 May 1969
7 Interview by Miss K. Ruane with Miss D. Jenner, Winnipeg
8 Ethel Johns, 'The Power of the Professional Press,' *The Canadian Nurse,* XII (September 1916), 488–91
9 Ethel Johns, 'Nursing Education in Western Hospitals. An address to the annual convention of the Alberta Association of Graduate Nurses,' *The Canadian Nurse,* XV (June 1919), 1788–9
10 Undated letter from Ethel Johns to Jean I. Gunn, archives of the Canadian Nurses' Association, Ottawa
11 Proceedings of the Tenth Annual Convention of the Canadian Society of Superintendents of Training Schools, 12 and 13 June 1917, *The Canadian Nurse,* XIII (September 1917), 571–89
12 Ibid., 581–2
13 Ibid., 582
14 Ibid., 585–6
15 Proceedings of the Sixth Annual Convention of the Canadian National Association of Trained Nurses, 14 and 15 June 1917, *The Canadian Nurse,* XIII (August 1917), 439

CHAPTER 11

1 *Second Interim Report of the Public Welfare Commission of Manitoba,* February 1919. Winnipeg: Provincial Library of Manitoba
2 Dr Ross Mitchell, *Medicine in Manitoba.* Winnipeg: Stovel Advocate Press Ltd., 1954, p. 88
3 *First Interim Report of the Public Welfare Commission of Manitoba,* 5 February 1918. Winnipeg: Provincial Library of Manitoba

Chapter notes 293

4 Manitoba Association of Graduate Nurses, Minutes of meeting, 27 November 1917. Archives of the Manitoba Association of Registered Nurses
5 *Second Interim Report*, Appendix B, 'Nursing: Report of Hospitals and Nursing'
6 Canadian Association of Nursing Education, Minutes of meeting, 4 June 1918, *The Canadian Nurse*, XIV (July 1918), 1135-7
7 Ibid., 1137
8 Ibid., 1138
9 Ethel Johns, 'Ideals in Public Health Nursing,' *The Canadian Nurse*, XIV (March 1918), 911
10 Canadian Association of Nursing Education, Minutes of meeting, *The Canadian Nurse*, XIV (July 1918), 1146
11 Letter of 15 May 1918 from President Wesbrook to Dr Helen MacMurchy
12 Canadian National Association of Trained Nurses, Proceedings of Seventh Annual Convention, 1918, *The Canadian Nurse*, XIV (August 1918), 1239
13 Children's Hospital of Winnipeg. Minutes of meeting of board of directors, September 1918
14 Interview by the writer with the late Mrs W.V. Stocker, White Rock, British Columbia, 3 May 1969
15 *Manitoba Free Press*, 1 November 1918
16 Ethel Johns, Annual Report for the Year 1 December 1917 to 30 November 1918; and Elizabeth Carruthers, *Report of the Outpatient and Social Service Department*. Archives of the Children's Hospital of Winnipeg

CHAPTER 12

1 Government of Manitoba, *Second Interim Report of the Public Welfare Commission*, February 1919, Appendix B, 'Nursing.' Winnipeg: Provincial Library of Manitoba
2 G.M. Weir, *Survey of Nursing Education in Canada*. Toronto: University of Toronto Press, 1932
3 *Second Interm Report*, Appendix B, 'Nursing'
4 Ibid.
5 'Nurses Are Opposed to Dixon Proposal' (news item), *Manitoba Free Press*, 21 February 1919
6 'Saskatchewan Registered Nurses' Association,' *The Canadian Nurse*, XV (May 1919), 1764
7 *The Canadian Nurse*, XV (June 1919), 1785-92
8 *The Canadian Nurse*, XV (June 1919), 1787

9 Ibid., 1792
10 Taped interview by the writer with Ruby Simpson, Victoria, B.C., 7 June 1969
11 D.C. Masters, *The Winnipeg General Strike*. Toronto: University of Toronto Press, 1950, pp. 11, 40
12 Ibid., 128
13 Interview by Kathleen Ruane with Kennethe Haig, Winnipeg, 15 August 1969
14 Excerpt from memorandum to Donald C. Masters on 'The Winnipeg General Strike,' 17 October 1945. The first two sentences in this excerpt were quoted by Professor Masters in *The Winnipeg General Strike*, p. 128.
15 Excerpt from Ethel Johns' memorandum to D.C. Masters on 'The Winnipeg General Strike'
16 Ibid.
17 Ibid.
18 Ibid.
19 Ibid.
20 Ibid.
21 Ibid.

CHAPTER 13

1 *Proceedings of the First Annual Convention of the Hospitals of British Columbia.* Vancouver: The British Columbia Hospital Association, 1918, p. 45
2 Frederic H. Soward, *The Early History of the University of British Columbia,* 27 March 1930, p. 140. Transcript in the Special Collections Division of the Library, University of British Columbia
3 Dr Klinck was appointed President in May 1919.
4 Maude McLeod, 'The University and the Training School for Nurses, Vancouver General Hospital,' *The Canadian Nurse,* XV (November 1919), 2100–2103
5 The final decision was to place the Department of Nursing within the Faculty of Applied Science, and the degree conferred was Bachelor of Applied Science (in Nursing).
6 Memorandum by Ethel Johns, presumably written in 1923, in the files of the School of Nursing, University of British Columbia
7 Minutes of the General Meeting, June 1919, of the Canadian National Association of Trained Nurses. Archives of the Canadian Nurses' Association
8 Isabel Maitland Stewart, *The Education of Nurses: Historical Foundations and Modern Trends.* New York, Macmillan Company, 1953, p. 226

9 *Proceedings of the Second Annual Convention of the Hospitals of British Columbia.* Vancouver: The British Columbia Hospital Association, 1919, p. 47
10 Letter of 16 September 1965, from Ethel Johns to Dr Muriel Uprichard
11 Excerpt from 'Features from Board Minutes,' Archives of the Vancouver General Hospital
12 Letter in the archives of the University of British Columbia
13 Text of address in the Woodward Biomedical Library, University of British Columbia

CHAPTER 14

1 Excerpt from letter of 16 September 1965, from Ethel Johns to Dr Muriel Uprichard
2 Minutes of meeting of Board of Governors, University of British Columbia, 23 February 1920
3 Minutes of meeting of Senate, University of British Columbia, 20 April 1920
4 Letter of 3 May 1920, from A.P. Procter, Registrar of the College of Physicians and Surgeons of British Columbia, to Stanley W. Mathews, Secretary, The Senate, University of British Columbia
5 Report of the Director of Nursing for the Year Ending 31 December 1919. Archives of the Vancouver General Hospital
6 Ibid.
7 Report of the General Superintendent for the Year 1920. Archives of the Vancouver General Hospital
8 Report of the Director of Nursing for the Year Ended 31 December 1920. Archives of the Vancouver General Hospital
9 Report of the General Superintendent for the Year 1920. Archives of the Vancouver General Hospital
10 The full text of Miss Johns' address was published in the *Report of the Third Annual Convention of the Hospitals of British Columbia*, 23, 24, 25, and 26 June 1920. It was published also in *The Modern Hospital*, xv (August 1920), which issued reprints of the paper.
11 *Proceedings of the Third Annual Convention of the British Columbia Hospital Association*, pp. 30–7
12 Report of the Secretary of the Canadian National Association of Trained Nurses for the Year Ending 6 July 1920. Archives of the Canadian Nurses' Association
13 *The Canadian Nurse*, XVII (1 January 1921), 5–10
14 E. MacP. Dickson, Report of the Thirteenth Annual Convention of the Canadian Association of Nursing Education, *The Canadian Nurse*, XVI (August 1920), 454–7

CHAPTER 15

1. Miss Randal was also Registrar of the Graduate Nurses' Association of British Columbia
2. Edmund Burke, *Reflections on the Revolution in France,* 1790
3. *The Canadian Nurse,* XVII (July 1921), 433–4
4. Ibid., 434–5
5. Report of the general meeting of the Canadian National Association of Trained Nurses, 4 June 1921, *The Canadian Nurse,* XVII (July 1921), 416–17
6. Minutes of meeting of the executive committee, C.N.A.T.N., 6 January 1922. Archives of the Canadian Nurses' Association
7. Minutes of meeting of the Board of Governors, 25 April 1921
8. Letter of 16 September 1965, from Ethel Johns to Dr Muriel Uprichard
9. Minutes of meeting of the Board of Governors, 9 June 1922
10. Minutes of meeting of the Board of Governors, 30 April 1923
11. Dr C.E.A. Winslow, 'A Recent Study of the Education of the Nurse,' Proceedings of the Twenty-Eighth Annual Convention of the National League of Nursing Education, June 26–July 1, 1922. New York: The League, pp. 175–7
12. Verbatim minutes of Sixteenth Annual Meeting of the Canadian Association of Nursing Education, Toronto, June 6–9, 1923, p.163. Archives of the Canadian Nurses' Association
13. Proceedings of Twenty-eighth Annual Convention of the N.L.N.E., p. 177
14. Committee for the Study of Nursing Education, *Nursing and Nursing Education in the United States.* New York: Macmillan Company, 1923
15. Ethel Johns, 'Administration of Schools of Nursing,' Proceedings of Twenty-eighth Annual Convention of the N.L.N.E., pp. 255–6
16. Proceedings of Twenty-eighth Annual Convention of the N.L.N.E., pp. 271–2
17. 'Summer School for Nurses, University of Saskatchewan,' *The Canadian Nurse,* XVIII, (September 1922), 541–3
18. Interview by the writer with Mrs F.G.C. Wood, Vancouver, 24 June 1969
19. Ibid.
20. Quotation from: Ethel Johns, 'The Man Within,' *Just Plain Nursing,* vol. 10, no. 1. Philadelphia: J.B. Lippincott Company, 1956, p. 2
21. Ethel Johns, Memorandum concerning the development of the Combined Course in Nursing given by the University of British Columbia, Canada, in conjunction with the Vancouver General Hospital Training School for Nurses. Undated, but presumed to have been written in the fall of 1922 or the spring of 1923.

CHAPTER 16

1 Minutes of meeting of the Canadian Association of Nursing Education, 6–9 June 1923, p. 9. Archives of the Canadian Nurses' Association
2 Ibid., pp. 47–9
3 Ibid., pp. 59–60
4 Ibid., pp. 129–38
5 Article by Mabel Gray describing the Saskatchewan Nursing Housekeepers project in *The Canadian Nurse*, xx (May 1924), 286–9
6 Minutes of meeting of the C.A.N.E., 6–9 June 1923, pp. 163–70
7 Report by Ethel Johns to the Council of the Graduate Nurses' Association of British Columbia, contained in minutes of meeting, 17 September 1923. Archives of the Registered Nurses' Association of British Columbia
8 Sixth Annual Report of the British Columbia Hospital Association (Vancouver: The Association, 1923), pp. 14–17, 24
9 A few years later Dr Weir undertook a survey of nursing education in Canada.
10 Taped interview by the writer with Mrs Charles Vater, Vancouver, 16 July 1970
11 'Much Routine in Nursing Might Be Done Away With' (news item), *The Calgary Daily Herald*, Tuesday, 16 October 1923, p. 5
12 Minutes of meeting of the Board of Governors, 1 April 1924
13 Letter of 6 May 1924, from Ethel Johns to President Klinck
14 Minutes of twelfth annual meeting, 21 April 1924, of the Graduate Nurses' Association of British Columbia. Archives of the Registered Nurses' Association of British Columbia
15 Taped interview by the writer with Miss Ruby Simpson, Victoria, 7 June 1969
16 Letter of 16 September 1965, from Ethel Johns to Dr Muriel Uprichard
17 Ibid.
18 Ibid.
19 Eighth Annual Report of the British Columbia Hospital Association (Vancouver: The Association, 1925), p. 6

CHAPTER 17

1 Gertrude died three years later, in 1928.
2 Interview by the writer with Mrs Helen Franklin, Winnipeg, 14 October 1970
3 Fragmentary autobiographical note in Miss Johns' personal papers

4 Unpublished report of Ethel Johns' 'A Study of the Present Status of Negro Women in Nursing, 1925' is in the archives of the Rockefeller Foundation, New York, but it has not been released yet for scholarly research.
5 Interview by the writer with Dr Helen Stewart, Victoria, 7 June 1969
6 Fragmentary autobiographical notes in Miss Johns' personal papers
7 *Annual Report of the Rockefeller Foundation for the Year 1926*, p. 14
8 Mary M. Roberts, *American Nursing, History and Interpretation*. (New York: The Macmillan Company, 1954), p. 617
9 Letter of 18 December 1924, from F. Elisabeth Crowell to Ethel Johns
10 Interview by the writer with Miss Hazel Goff, Glenside, Pennsylvania, 4 September 1970
11 Autobiographical notes in Miss Johns' papers
12 Ibid.
13 Ethel Johns, 'In Transylvania,' *The Canadian Nurse*, XXXII (October 1936), 455–7
14 Letter of 26 November 1968, from Dr J.G. Harrar to the writer
15 *Annual Report of the Rockefeller Foundation for the Year 1927*, pp. 268–70
16 Ibid., pp. 270, 273
17 Hazel A. Goff, 'Nursing in Hungary, 1933.' Report for the Health Section of the League of Nations, p. 11
18 Autobiographical notes in Miss Johns' papers
19 Ibid.
20 Letter of 18 February 1970, from Hazel A. Goff to the writer

CHAPTER 18

1 'Huge New York Hospital–Cornell Medical Centre Opened,' *Hospital Management* (September 1932), 26–9
2 Ethel Johns, 'Preparing for Nursing Service and Nursing Education in the New York Hospital–Cornell Medical College Association Project: An Experiment in Cooperative Planning,' *American Journal of Nursing*, XXXI (November 1931), 1295–1302
3 Ibid.
4 'Report of a Study Made by the National Organization for Public Health Nursing for the Committee on Nursing Organization of the New York Hospital,' in *Methods and Problems of Medical Education*, Twenty-first Series. New York: The Rockefeller Foundation, 1932, pp. 1–18
5 Ethel Johns, 'Blazing the Trail,' address given at the 1952 commencement

Chapter notes 299

exercises of the Cornell University–New York Hospital School of Nursing. Archives of the School of Nursing

6 Blanche Pfefferkorn and Charles A. Rovetta, *Administrative Cost Analysis for Nursing Service and Nursing Education*. Chicago, Illinois: American Hospital Association and New York, New York: National League of Nursing Education, 1940
7 Ethel Johns, 'Canada Looks at the Neighbours,' *The Canadian Nurse*, XXVI (January 1930), 11–13
8 Ethel Johns, 'The Biennial Meeting, Canadian Nurses' Association,' *The Canadian Nurse*, XXVI (August 1930), 395–6
9 Both papers were published in *The Canadian Nurse*, XXVI (September 1930), 483–92
10 Ethel Johns, 'A Study in Contrasts,' *The Canadian Nurse*, XXVI (October 1930), 519–22
11 Taped interview by the writer with Miss Ruby Simpson, Victoria, 7 June 1969
12 Ethel Johns, 'The Biennial Meeting, Canadian Nurses' Association,' *The Canadian Nurse*, XXVI (August 1930), 396
13 'The Canadian Nurses' Association General Meeting, 1930,' *The Canadian Nurse*, XXVI (September 1930), 452–6
14 Correspondence between Miss Emory and Miss Johns in the archives of the Canadian Nurses' Association
15 Ethel Johns, 'Common Ground,' *The Canadian Nurse*, XXVII (April 1931), 177–81
16 Copy of letter from Ethel Johns to Mary Beard in the files of New York Hospital
17 The four papers were published in the *American Journal Of Nursing*, XXXI (November 1931), 1295–1311
18 *Nursing Schools Today and Tomorrow: Final Report of the Committee on the Grading of Nursing Schools*. New York City: Committee on the Grading of Nursing Schools, 1934, pp. 12–17
19 Ethel Johns and Blanche Pfefferkorn, *An Activity Analysis of Nursing*. New York City: Committee on the Grading of Nursing Schools, 1934, p. 11
20 *Nursing Schools Today and Tomorrow*, chap. III, 'What Should a Professional Nurse Know and Be Able to Do?' pp. 61–81
21 'The Biennial Meeting,' *The Canadian Nurse*, XXVIII (August 1932), 397–8
22 Florence H.M. Emory, 'Report of Publications Committee,' *The Canadian Nurse*, XXVIII (September 1932), 481–2
23 Letter in the archives of the Canadian Nurses' Association

CHAPTER 19

1 Florence H.M. Emory, 'A Critical Period,' *The Canadian Nurse*, XXVIII (October 1932), 525
2 Ibid.
3 Minutes of meetings of the executive committee, Canadian Nurses' Association, 22 September and 8 December 1932. Archives of the Canadian Nurses' Association
4 Ibid.
5 Florence H.M. Emory, 'The Appointment of an Editor,' *The Canadian Nurse*, XXVIII (October 1932), 527
6 Jean S. Wilson, 'Ourselves,' (editorial), *The Canadian Nurse*, XXIX (January 1933), 6–7
7 Ethel Johns, 'The Editor's Desk,' *The Canadian Nurse*, XXIX (February 1933), 79–80
8 Through the courtesy of Miss Eileen Flanagan, arrangements were made for the writer to visit this suite, 30 September 1970.
9 Ethel Johns, 'The Editor's Desk,' *The Canadian Nurse*, XXIX (February 1933), 79–80
10 Ethel Johns, 'The Canadian Scene,' *The Canadian Nurse*, XXIX (December 1933), 621
11 Ibid., 621–3
12 Ethel Johns, 'The Canadian Scene,' *The Canadian Nurse*, XXX (June 1934), 269–70
13 Florence H.M. Emory, 'Yesterday and Tomorrow,' *The Canadian Nurse*, XXX (August 1934), 349–52
14 Resolutions Formulated and Passed at the General Session,' in 'Notes from the National Office,' contributed by Jean S. Wilson, *The Canadian Nurse*, XXX (November 1934), 532–5
15 Ethel Johns, 'Hail and Farewell,' *The Canadian Nurse*, XXIX (November 1933), 570
16 'The Canadian Nurse,' in 'Notes from the National Office,' contributed by Jean S. Wilson, *The Canadian Nurse*, XXXI (February 1935), 76–7
17 Florence H.M. Emory, 'Report of the Publications Committee,' in 'Notes from the National Office,' *The Canadian Nurse*, XXXI (February 1935), 77–8
18 'Resolutions Formulated and Passed at the General Session,' *The Canadian Nurse*, XXX (November 1934), 532–5

CHAPTER 20

1 Caroline V. Barrett, 'Impressions sur le Congrès Biennal,' *The Canadian Nurse*, XXX (September 1934), 413–14

Chapter notes 301

2 Ethel Johns, 'The Editor's Desk,' *The Canadian Nurse*, xxx (September 1934), 417
3 Ethel Johns, 'The Editor's Desk,' *The Canadian Nurse*, xxxi (January 1935), 19
4 Ethel Johns, 'The Editor's Desk: What Toronto Did,' *The Canadian Nurse*, xxxi (May 1935), 207
5 Ruby M. Simpson, 'A Call to Action,' *The Canadian Nurse*, xxxi (November 1935), 485
6 Ethel Johns, 'The Editor's Desk,' *The Canadian Nurse*, xxxii (January 1936), 11
7 Ethel Johns, 'We Come of Age,' *The Canadian Nurse*, xxxii (August 1936), 350–1
8 'Resolutions from the General Meeting of the Canadian Nurses' Association – 1936,' in 'Notes from the National Office,' contributed by Jean S. Wilson, *The Canadian Nurse*, xxxii (September 1936), 414
9 Ibid., 413
10 Ibid., 414
11 'A Report Submitted by the Editor and Business Manager, for the Two-Year Period Ending May 1, 1936.' Archives of the Canadian Nurses' Association.
12 'Resolutions from the General Meeting,' *Op. cit.*, 415
13 Ethel Johns, 'The Editor's Desk,' *The Canadian Nurse*, xxxii (June 1936), 257
14 Ethel Johns, 'The Editor's Desk,' *The Canadian Nurse*, xxxii (August 1936), 357–8
15 Ruby M. Simpson, 'Marching Orders,' *The Canadian Nurse*, xxxii (September 1936), 393–5
16 Ethel Johns, 'The Editor's Desk,' *The Canadian Nurse*, xxxii (September 1936), 401
17 Ethel Johns, 'Off Duty,' *The Canadian Nurse*, xxxiii (June 1937), 292. *Note*: The format which Miss Johns used for the 'Off Duty' page was distinctive: italics were used throughout, and groups of words were interspersed with three dots. For the purpose of this quotation and others to be included later in this book, the sentence structure and punctuation are normalized.
18 'A Report Submitted by the Editor and Business Manager for the Two-Year Period Ending May 1, 1938.' Archives of the Canadian Nurses' Association
19 Ruby M. Simpson, 'Thirty Years of Growth,' *The Canadian Nurse*, xxxiv (August 1938), 411–16
20 'Resolutions,' in 'Notes from the National Office,' contributed by Jean S. Wilson, *The Canadian Nurse*, xxxiv (September 1938), 520–1

CHAPTER 21

1 Ethel Johns, 'A Room of One's Own,' *The Canadian Nurse,* xxxv (February 1939), 71–2
2 The July, August, and November, 1938, issue of *The Canadian Nurse* reported the granting of honorary degrees to Mabel F. Hersey by McGill University, to Sister Allard by the University of Montreal, and to Jean I. Gunn by the University of Toronto.
3 Ethel Johns, 'The Editor's Desk,' *The Canadian Nurse,* xxxv (January 1939), 19
4 Ethel Johns, 'A Gift and a Challenge,' *The Canadian Nurse,* xxxv (January 1939), 14
5 Grace M. Fairley, 'Preparation and Peace,' *The Canadian Nurse,* xxxiv (November 1938), 637–8
6 Grace M. Fairley, 'A National Emergency and a National Service,' *The Canadian Nurse,* xxxv (October 1939), 561
7 Ethel Johns (editorial), *The Canadian Nurse,* xxxv (October 1939) 562–3
8 Grace M. Fairley, 'A Letter to the Prime Minister of Canada,' *The Canadian Nurse,* xxxvi (January 1940), 10
9 Grace M. Fairley, 'The Mary Agnes Snively Medal,' *The Canadian Nurse,* xxxvi (June 1940), 346
10 E. Cora Hind, 'Ethel Johns,' *The Canadian Nurse,* xxxvi (June 1940), 350
11 Ethel Johns, 'The Time and Place of Meeting,' *The Canadian Nurse,* xxxvi (August 1940), 471
12 Ibid., 474
13 Ibid., 473
14 Gertrude Hall, 'Administrative Aspects of Nursing Education in the Clinical Field,' *The Canadian Nurse,* xxxvi (September 1940), 555
15 'Report Submitted by the Editor and Business Manager to the President of the Canadian Nurses' Association for the Period Ending May 1, 1940.' Archives of the Canadian Nurses' Association
16 Ethel Johns, 'The R.N.A.B.C. and the Journal,' *The Canadian Nurse,* xxxvi (October 1940), 699–700

CHAPTER 22

1 Ethel Johns, 'Off Duty,' *The Canadian Nurse,* xxxi (December 1935), 564. *Note*: In this and other excerpts from the 'Off Duty' essays in this chapter, the format has been normalized.
2 Ibid., xxxi (July 1935), 326
3 Ibid., xxxii (February 1936), 80

4 Ibid., xxxi (March 1935), 132
5 Ibid., xxx (June 1934), 276
6 Ibid., xxxv (February 1939), 110
7 Ibid., xxxiii (July 1937), 344
8 Interview by the writer with Eileen Flanagan and Suzanne Giroux, Montreal, 28 September 1970
9 Interview by the writer with Caroline V. Barrett, Montreal, 30 September 1970
10 Interview by the writer with O.T. Leeman, Montreal, 1 October 1970
11 *Crockford's Clerical Directory*, 1969–70
12 Ethel Johns, 'Off Duty,' *The Canadian Nurse*, xxv (January 1939), 42

CHAPTER 23

1 Ethel Johns, 'The Shape of Things to Come' (editorial), *The Canadian Nurse*, xxxvii (February 1941) 83–4
2 Ethel Johns, 'A Fine Record,' *The Canadian Nurse*, xxxvii (April 1941), 257–8
3 Ethel Johns, 'Breaking a New Trail' (editorial), *The Canadian Nurse*, xxxvii (November 1941), 743–4
4 Jean S. Wilson, 'Notes from the National Office,' *The Canadian Nurse*, xxxvii (November 1941), 761–3
5 Ethel Johns, 'A Christmas Candle,' *The Canadian Nurse*, xxxvii (December 1941), 815–16
6 'Travaillons Ensemble,' *The Canadian Nurse*, xxxviii (May 1942), 330–8
7 Ethel Johns, 'Meeting in Montreal,' *The Canadian Nurse*, xxxviii (August 1942) 533
8 'A Report Submitted to the President of the Canadian Nurses Association for the two-year period ending May 1, 1942.' Archives of the Canadian Nurses' Association
9 Marion Lindeburgh, 'Response from the Federal Government,' *The Canadian Nurse*, xxxviii (August 1942), 543–4
10 Jean S. Wilson, 'Notes from the National Office,' *The Canadian Nurse*, xxxviii (December 1942), 930
11 Kennethe M. Haig, *Brave Harvest* (Toronto: Thomas Allen, 1945), p. 273
12 Interview by the writer with Mrs Helen Franklin, Winnipeg, 14 October 1970.
13 Ethel Johns, 'Getting Down to Brass Tacks' (editorial), *The Canadian Nurse*, xxxix (May 1943), 323–5
14 Ethel Johns, 'A Friendly Hearing' (editorial), *The Canadian Nurse*, xxxix (June 1943), 387–91

15 Ethel Johns, 'A Turning Point' (editorial), *The Canadian Nurse,* XL (June 1944), 387–8
16 'An Expression of Appreciation' (editorial), *The Canadian Nurse,* XL (July 1944), 468
17 Florence H. Walker, 'Notes from the National Office,' *The Canadian Nurse,* XL (September 1944), 703
18 Interview by the writer with Dr Florence Emory, Toronto, 6 October 1970
19 Interview by the writer with Dr Rae Chittick, Vancouver, 3 July 1970

CHAPTER 24

1 Marion Lindeburgh, 'Report of the Committee on Post-war Planning,' *The Canadian Nurse,* XL (September 1944), 684
2 Minutes of meeting of Board of Directors, National League of Nursing Education, 25 January 1945. Archives of the National League for Nursing, New York
3 Letter of 8 August 1970, to the writer from Miss Helene Olandt
4 Indian Work Investigation Commission, 1946: Report to the General Synod of the Church of England in Canada, *Journal of Proceedings of the Sixteenth Session,* Winnipeg, 4–13 September 1946, 1–2
5 Ethel Johns, 'Nursing Service in General,' *The Canadian Nurse,* XLII (September 1946), 749–53
6 Ibid., 752
7 Ibid., 753
8 'Resolutions from the Biennial Meeting, 1946,' in 'Notes from National Office,' *The Canadian Nurse,* XLII (September 1946), 797–9
9 'Nursing Service in Canada – A Submission to the Department of National Health and Welfare by the Canadian Nurses' Association, September, 1946.' Ottawa: Archives of the Canadian Nurses' Association
10 Letter of 20 May 1971, to the writer from Isabel MacIntosh
11 Ethel Johns, 'Something New,' *Just Plain Nursing,* vol. I, no. 1 (Philadelphia and Montreal: J.B. Lippincott Company, 1947), pp. 2–3
12 Ibid.
13 Ethel Johns, 'The ICN Responsibility for International Education of Nurses,' *International Nursing Bulletin,* no. 7 (Winter 1951), 20–3
14 Interview by the writer with O.T. Leeman, Montreal, 1 October 1970
15 Letter of 22 October 1947, from Ethel Johns to Mrs Jessie McVicar. Ethel Johns' personal papers

Chapter notes 305

CHAPTER 25

1 'Points for discussion with Mrs McVicar, chairman of Committee, February 20, 1948,' Ethel Johns' working papers
2 'Points for discussion with Mrs McVicar, February 25, 1948,' Ethel Johns' working papers
3 The members of the 'Creative Minority' were members of the Exchange of Nurses Committee, of which Miss Johns was chairman.
4 'Campus Convention' (editorial), *The Canadian Nurse*, XLIV (August 1948), 618
5 Ethel Johns, 'The Nurse Seeks the University, *The Canadian Nurse*, XLIV (September 1948), 720–4
6 'Exchange of Nurses Committee,' *The Canadian Nurse*, XLIV (June 1948), 476–7
7 Letter to Miss Johns from Jessie B. McVicar, 14 July 1948

CHAPTER 26

1 Interview by the writer with Mrs Lucille Blayney and Emily Mayhew, West Vancouver, 10 July 1970
2 Memorandum from Esther Paulson, West Vancouver, following an interview with the writer, 9 July 1970
3 Letter of 19 September 1949, from Ethel Johns to Mrs C. Bernard Brack
4 Letter of 15 December 1950, from Mrs Brack to Miss Johns
5 Letter of 19 March 1951, from Miss Johns to Mrs Brack
6 Ethel Johns, 'Blazing the Trail: The Commencement Address Delivered to the Graduating Class of 1952 on September 30, 1952,' files of the Cornell University–New York Hospital School of Nursing
7 Letter in the files of the Cornell University–New York Hospital School of Nursing
8 Letter in the files of the Cornell University–New York Hospital School of Nursing

CHAPTER 27

1 Telephone conversation by the writer with Mrs W.S. Maddin, West Vancouver, 7 June 1971

2 Ibid.
3 Letter of 11 September 1953, from Ethel Johns to Mrs C.B. Brack
4 T.N. Budd, M.D. *The Nursing of the Elderly Sick, A Practical Handbook of Geriatric Nursing* (Philadelphia: J.B. Lippincott Company, 1954)
5 Letter of 25 October 1954, from Ethel Johns to Mrs C.B. Brack
6 Letter of 2 August 1954, from Ethel Johns to Eileen Flanagan
7 Letter of 16 November 1954, from Ethel Johns to Eileen Flanagan
8 Information contained in file on the history project, Department of Nursing, Winnipeg General Hospital
9 Ibid.
10 Ethel Johns, 'Common Ground,' *The Canadian Home Economics Journal* (September 1955), 9–10

CHAPTER 28

1 Letter of 1 August 1963, from Ethel Johns to Eileen Flanagan
2 In a subsequent letter to the convener of the Library Committee, Miss Johns expressed some concern about the use of this letter, in view of the long lapse of time between the events and her recording of them. But a comparison of the statements which she made in her letter to Dr Uprichard with accounts found in contemporary sources verify the accuracy of Miss Johns' narrative in 1965.

Bibliography

A WRITINGS BY ETHEL JOHNS

Books

Johns, Ethel. *The Winnipeg General Hospital School of Nursing, 1887–1953*. Winnipeg: The Alumnae Association of the Winnipeg General Hospital School of Nursing [1957]

Johns, Ethel, and Blanche Pfefferkorn. *An Activity Analysis of Nursing*. Prepared under the auspices of the Committee on the Grading of Nursing Schools. New York City: Committee on the Grading of Nursing Schools, 1934

– *The Johns Hopkins Hospital School of Nursing, 1889–1949*. Baltimore: The Johns Hopkins Press, 1954

Articles and Editorials

a In the *Nurses' Alumnae Journal of the Winnipeg General Hospital:*
Johns, Ethel, Editorial (February 1907), 1–2
– Editorial (June 1907), 1–3
– Editorial, 'State Registration of Nurses' (September 1907), 2–5
– Editorial, 'Valedictory' (December 1907), 2
– Editorial (March 1908), 2
– 'Ourselves as Others See Us' (March 1908), 3–5
– Editorial (September 1908), 2
– Editorial (December 1908), 2–5
– 'The Alpine Club of Canada' (September 1909), 9–15
– 'Confesio Medici' (April 1910), 10–12
– 'A Glimpse of Chicago Hospitals' (December 1910), 3–8
– 'Association Life and Work – A Retrospect' (July 1911), 4–6
– 'The Alumnae Journal' (June 1914), 9–13
– 'Twenty Years On' (March 1925), 3–7
– 'Off Duty,' *Nurses' Alumnae Annual* (1937), 22–24

b In *The Canadian Nurse*
Johns, Ethel. 'Western Hospitals,' IV (May 1908), 207–11
– 'A Nursing Problem of the West,' V (March 1909), 117–20
– 'Letters from a Nurse in Training': V (March 1909), 135–8; V (April 1909), 181–3; V (July 1909), 352–6; V (December 1909), 741–4
– 'The Winnipeg General Hospital,' V (June 1909), 298–303
– 'Power of the Professional Press,' XII (September 1916), 488–91

- 'Christmas – With a Difference,' XII (December 1916), 662–3
- 'Ideals in Public Health Nursing,' XIV (March 1918) 908–12
- 'Nursing Education in Western Hospitals,' XV (June 1919), 1785–92
- 'The Challenge of the Future,' XVII (January 1921), 5–10
- 'The Practice of Midwifery in Canada,' XXI (January 1925), 10–14, 33
- 'Isabel Maitland Stewart – A Biographical Note,' XXI (September 1925), 457
- 'Canada Looks at the Neighbours,' XXVI (January 1930), 11–13
- 'The Biennial Meeting of the Canadian Nurses Association,' XXVI (August 1930), 395–6
- 'A Sense of Values,' XXVI (September 1930), 483–4, 501
- 'A Study in Contrasts,' XXVI (October 1930), 519–22
- 'Common Ground,' XXVII (April 1931), 177–81
- 'Down by the Sea,' XXIX (Aigist 1933), 401–2
- 'Hail and Farewell,' XXIX (November 1933), 570
- 'The Canadian Scene,' a series of seven editorials which appeared in the following issues of *The Canadian Nurse:* XXIX (December 1933), 621–3; XXX (January 1934), 5–8; XXX (February 1934), 57–8; XXX (March 1934), 108; XXX (April 1934), 155–6; XXX (May 1934), 202–3; XXX (June 1934), 269–70
- 'A Lost Leader,' XXXI (January 1935), 18
- 'The Editor's Desk: What Toronto Did,' XXXI (May 1935), 207
- 'We Come of Age,' XXXII (August 1936), 350–1
- 'In Transylvania,' XXXII (October 1936), 455–7
- 'New Wine in Old Bottles,' XXXIV (March 1938), 135–7
- 'A Gift and a Challenge,' XXXV (January 1939), 14
- 'A Room of One's Own,' XXXV (February 1939), 71–2
- 'A Valiant Heart,' XXXV (August 1939), 459–62
- 'Let Us Take Counsel Together,' XXXVI (June 1940), 339–41
- 'This Heritage of Freedom,' XXXVI (July 1940), 401–3
- 'The Time and Place of Meeting,' XXXVI (August 1940), 471–6
- 'The R.N.A.B.C. and the Journal,' XXXVI (October 1940), 699–700
- 'The Shape of Things to Come,' XXXVII (February 1941), 83–4
- 'A Fine Record,' XXXVII (April 1941), 257–8
- 'Breaking a New Trail,' XXXVII (November 1941), 743–4
- 'A Christmas Candle,' XXXVII (December 1941), 815–16
- 'Travaillons Ensemble,' XXXVIII (May 1942), 330–8
- 'Meeting in Montreal,' XXXVIII (August 1942), 533–40
- 'Getting Down to Brass Tacks,' XXXIX (May 1943), 323–5
- 'A Friendly Hearing,' XXXIX (June 1943), 387–91
- 'UNRRA Takes Command,' XL (February 1944), 87–9
- 'A Turning Point,' XL (June 1944), 387–8

- 'UNRRA Comes to Canada,' XL (December 1944), 925–7
- 'Off Duty,' a series of essays which appeared in *The Canadian Nurse* throughout the years of Ethel Johns' editorship as follows:
  Vol. XXIX (1933): March, 158; April, 204; May, 270; June, 326; July, 383; August, 439; September, 496; October, 550; December, 659
  Vol. XXX (1934): January, 39: February, 94; March, 142; April, 190; May, 230; June, 276; July, 336; August, 386; September, 448; October, back cover; November, 536; December, 588
  Vol. XXXI (1935): January, 28; February, 80; March, 132; April, 182; May, 230; June, 273; July, 326; August, 374; September, 422; October, 470; November, 518; December, 564
  Vol. XXXII (1936): January, 38; February, 80; March, 134; April, 182; May 230; June 280; July, 330
  Vol. XXXIII (1937): January, 37; February, 90; March, 138; April, 192; May, 240; June 292; July, 344; August, 398; September, 454; October, 510; November, 574; December, 627
  Vol. XXXIV (1938): January, 46; February, 102; March, 158; December, 724
  Vol. XXXV (1939): January, 42; February, 110; March, 170; April, 230; May 290; June, 354; July, 414; August, 474; September, 538; October, 598; November, 658; December, 727
  Vol. XXXVI (1940): January, 54; February, 118; March, 182; October, 710; November, 788; December, 844
  Vol. XXXVII (1941): January, 62; February, 134; March, 206; April, 286; May, 362; June, 434; September, 650; October, 722; November, 794; December, 860
  Vol. XXXVIII (1942): February, 134; March, 206; April, 278; May, 350: August, 582; October, 814; December, 964
  Vol. XXXIX (1943): January, 74; February, 154; March, 226; April, 294; May, 362; June, 426; July, 492; August, 552; September, 618; October, 700; November, 772; December, 832
  Vol. XL (1944): January, 72; February, 144; March, 206; April, 288; May, 364; June 438
  NOTE: In addition to the editorials, essays, and articles listed above, which Ethel Johns wrote during her editorship of *The Canadian Nurse*, numerous editorials appeared in the Journal under the caption, 'The Editor's Desk,' and under other titles
- 'Nursing Service in General,' XLII (September 1946), 749–53
- 'Exchange of Nurses Committee,' XLIV (June 1948), 476–7
- 'The Nurse Seeks the University,' XLIV (September 1948), 720–4
- 'The First Ten Years,' LIV (June 1958), 521–4

c In Other Periodicals and Publications

Johns, Ethel. 'A Graduating Climb,' *The Canadian Alpine Journal*, vol. II, no. 2 (1910), 158–64
- 'The Training of Superintendents of Small Hospitals,' *The Modern Hospital* (October 1915), 241–2
- 'The University in Relation to Nursing Education,' *The Modern Hospital* (August 1920), 1–5 (Reprint)
- 'Administration of Schools of Nursing,' an address to the Twenty-eighth Annual Convention of the National League of Nursing Education. *Annual Reports and Proceedings*, 1922. New York: National League of Nursing Education, 1922, 255–65
- 'Preparing for Nursing Service and Nursing Education in the New York Hospital–Cornell Medical College Association Project; An Experiment in Cooperative Planning,' *American Journal of Nursing*, XXXI (November 1931), 1295–1302
- 'The ICN Responsibility for International Education of Nurses,' *International Nursing Bulletin*, no. 7 (Winter 1951), 20–3
- 'Common Ground,' *The Canadian Home Economics Journal* (September 1955), 9–10

d In 'Just Plain Nursing'

Ethel Johns was both editor and writer for the 'Just Plain Nursing' series, which was published by the J.B. Lippincott Company. The first pamphlet appeared (undated) early in 1947; the final issue was published in October 1960. The number of issues yearly varied from one to four. A small bound volume which appeared early in 1953 contained the sixteen issues published up to and including January 1953, and featured a brief 'Foreword' by Ethel Johns, explaining how the series came to be inaugurated. Articles in the series to which reference was made in this biography are as follows:

Johns, Ethel. 'Something New,' vol. 1, no. 1 (1947), 2–3
- 'The Man Within,' vol. 10, no. 1 (1956), 1–5

e In the *Manitoba Free Press*

Johns, Ethel Incledon. 'War Bulletins Along Broadway: An exile from Winnipeg writes about her New York experiences,' *Manitoba Free Press*, 5 September 1914

Unpublished Writings by Ethel Johns

Johns, Ethel. Introductory chapters of her proposed autobiography, dealing

with her childhood, life on the Indian reserve, and training at the Winnipeg General Hospital Training School for Nurses
- Preliminary drafts for the following sections of Ethel Johns' proposed autobiography: 'The Fort William Unit'; 'The Teachers College Unit'; 'The Children's Hospital Unit': 'The Rockefeller Unit'
- Address to Staff and Pupils of the Training School and Members of the Training School Committee, Vancouver General Hospital (1919). Original in the Woodward Biomedical Library, the University of British Columbia
- 'The Influence of Latin Ideals and Traditions on Nursing Education,' a lecture given by Ethel Johns at Teachers College, Columbia University, as part of a series given under the auspices of the Department of Nursing Education, Teachers College. The ten-lecture series was provided through the Annie Goodrich Lectureship Fund between 12 February and 23 April 1931. Mimeographed paper is in the archives of the Department of Nursing Education, Teachers College.
- 'Blazing the Trail,' an address given by Ethel Johns at the 1952 Commencement Exercises of the Cornell University–New York Hospital School of Nursing. New York: Archives of the Cornell University–New York Hospital School of Nursing
- 'The Winnipeg General Strike,' memorandum written by Ethel Johns for Donald C. Masters, 17 October 1945

Letters written by Ethel Johns to: Mrs C.B. Brack, Miss Eileen Flanagan, Miss Amy Lee, Mr O.T. Leeman, Mrs Guthrie B. McVicar, Dr Muriel Uprichard, Miss Jean Wilson

B OTHER SOURCES

Books
Canadian Nurses' Association. *The Leaf and the Lamp*. Ottawa: The Association, 1968
Cavers, Anne S. *Our School of Nursing, 1899 to 1949*. Vancouver: The Vancouver General Hospital School of Nursing, n.d.
Christy, Teresa E. *Cornerstone for Nursing Education. A History of the Division of Nursing Education of Teachers College, Columbia University, 1899–1947*. New York: Teachers College Press, Teachers College, Columbia University
Crockford's Clerical Directory, 1969–1970
Dock, Lavinia L., and Isabel M. Stewart. *A Short History of Nursing from the Earliest Times to the Present Day*. New York and London: G.P. Putnam's Sons, 1920

Fosdick, Raymond B. *The Story of the Rockefeller Foundation.* New York: Harper and Brothers, 1952

Gibbon, John Murray. *The Victorian Order of Nurses for Canada, 50th Anniversary, 1897–1947.* Montreal: Southam Press [c. 1947]

Gibbon, John Murray, and Mary Mathewson. *Three Centuries of Canadian Nursing.* Toronto: Macmillan Company of Canada, 1947

Haig, Kennethe M. *Brave Harvest: The Life Story of E. Cora Hind, LL.D.* Toronto: Thomas Allen, 1945

Innis, Mary Q. (Ed.). *Nursing Education in a Changing Society.* Toronto: University of Toronto Press, 1970

Jordan, Helene Jamieson. *Cornell University–New York Hospital School of Nursing, 1877–1952.* New York: The Society of the New York Hospital, 1952

Masters, Donald C. *The Winnipeg General Strike.* Toronto: University of Toronto Press, 1950

Mitchell, Ross, M.D. *Medicine in Manitoba. The Story of Its Beginnings.* Winnipeg: Stovel-Advocate Press Limited, 1954

Morton, W.L. *Manitoba, a History.* Toronto: University of Toronto Press, 1957

Nursing and Nursing Education in the United States. Report of the Committee for the Study of Nursing Education and Report of a Survey by Josephine Goldmark. New York: Macmillan Company, 1923

Nursing Schools Today and Tomorrow: Final Report of the Committee on the Grading of Nursing Schools. New York: Committee on the Grading of Nursing Schools, 1934

Nutting, Mary Adelaide. *A Sound Economic Basis for Schools of Nursing and Other Addresses.* New York and London: G.P. Putnam's Sons, Knickerbocker Press, 1926

Roberts, Mary M. *American Nursing, History and Interpretation.* New York: Macmillan Company, 1954

Rudd, T.N., M.D. *The Nursing of the Elderly Sick, A Practical Handbook of Geriatric Nursing* (Modification and introduction by Ethel Johns). Philadelphia: J.B. Lippincott Company, 1954

Soward, Frederic H. *The Early History of the University of British Columbia.* Transcript in the Special Collections Division of the Library, University of British Columbia, 27 March 1930

– *Twenty-five Troubled Years, 1918–1943.* London, Toronto, New York: Oxford University Press, 1943

Stewart, Isabel Maitland. *Reminiscences of Isabel M. Stewart* (oral history). Research Office, Butler Library, Columbia University New York

– *The Education of Nurses: Historical Foundations and Modern Trends.* New York: Macmillan Company, 1953

Bibliography 313

Trevelyan, George Macaulay. *Illustrated English Social History, Vol. Four, The Nineteenth Century.* London, New York, Toronto: Longmans, Green and Company, 1949-1952
Weir, George M. *Survey of Nursing Education in Canada.* Toronto: University of Toronto Press, 1932
Williams, David. *A History of Modern Wales.* London: John Murray, reprinted (revised), 1965

Periodicals
'An Expression of Appreciation' (editorial), *The Canadian Nurse*, XL (July 1944), 468-9
'Annual Meeting of the Alumnae Association,' *Nurses' Alumnae Journal of the Winnipeg General Hospital* (June 1910), 14-15
Barrett, Caroline V. 'Impressions sur le Congrès Biennal,' *The Canadian Nurse*, XXX (September 1934), 413-14
'Campus Convention' (editorial), *The Canadian Nurse*, XLIV (August 1948), 615-22
Canadian Association of Nursing Education. Minutes of the Eleventh Meeting, 4-8 June 1918. *The Canadian Nurse*, XIV (July 1918), 1131-48
Canadian National Association of Trained Nurses. Proceedings of the Sixth Annual Convention, 14 and 15 June 1917. *The Canadian Nurse*, XIII (August 1917), 406-62
- Proceedings of the Seventh Annual Convention, 6-8 June 1918. *The Canadian Nurse*, XIV (August 1918), 1210-40
- Report of the General Meeting, June 1921. *The Canadian Nurse*, XVII (July 1921), 416-17
Canadian Society of Superintendents of Training Schools. Proceedings of Tenth Annual Convention, 12 and 13 June 1917. *The Canadian Nurse*, XIII (September 1917), 571-89
Christy, Teresa E. 'Portrait of a Leader: Isabel Maitland Stewart,' *Nursing Outlook*, XVII (October 1969), 44-8
Dickson, E. MacP. 'Report of the Thirteenth Annual Convention of the Canadian Association of Nursing Education,' *The Canadian Nurse*, XVI (August 1920), 454-7
Emory, Florence H.M. 'A Critical Period,' *The Canadian Nurse*, XXVIII (October 1932), 525
- 'The Appointment of an Editor,' *The Canadian Nurse*, XXVIII (October 1932), 527
- 'Report of Publications Committee,' *The Canadian Nurse*, XXVIII (September 1932), 481-2
- 'Yesterday and Tomorrow,' *The Canadian Nurse*, XXX (August 1934), 349-52

- 'Report of the Publications Committee,' in 'Notes from the National Office,' *The Canadian Nurse*, XXXI (February 1935), 77–8
Fairley, Grace M. 'Preparation and Peace,' *The Canadian Nurse*, XXXIV (November 1938), 637–8
- 'A National Emergency and a National Service,' *The Canadian Nurse*, XXXV (October 1939), 561
- 'A Letter to the Prime Minister of Canada,' *The Canadian Nurse*, XXXVI (January 1940), 10
- 'The Mary Agnes Snively Medal,' *The Canadian Nurse*, XXXVI (June 1940), 346
Hall, Gertrude. 'Administrative Aspects of Nursing Education in the Clinical Field,' *The Canadian Nurse*, XXXVI (September 1940), 555–61
Henderson, Virginia. 'Annie Warburton Goodrich,' *American Journal of Nursing*, LV (December 1955), 1488–92
'Higher Education for Nurses,' *Nurses' Alumnae Journal of the Winnipeg General Hospital* (September 1910), 9–11
Hind, E. Cora. 'Ethel Johns,' *The Canadian Nurse*, XXXVI (June 1940), 350
'Huge New York Hospital–Cornell Medical Centre Opened,' *Hospital Management* (September 1932), 26–9
Lindeburgh, Marion. 'Response from the Federal Government,' *The Canadian Nurse*, XXXVIII (August 1942), 543–4
- 'Report of the Committee on Post-war Planning,' *The Canadian Nurse*, XL (September 1944), 684–7
McLeod, Maude. 'The University and the Training School for Nurses, Vancouver General Hospital,' *The Canadian Nurse*, XV (November 1919), 2100–3
'Presentation to Miss Johns,' *Nurses' Alumnae Journal of the Winnipeg General Hospital* (July 1911), 7–8
'Resolutions Formulated and Passed at the General Session,' in 'Notes from the National Office,' contributed by Jean S. Wilson, *The Canadian Nurse*, XXX (November 1934), 533
'Resolutions from the General Meeting of the Canadian Nurses Association – 1936,' in 'Notes from the National Office,' *The Canadian Nurse*, XXXII (September 1936), 413–15
'Resolutions,' in 'Notes from the National Office,' *The Canadian Nurse*, XXXIV (September 1938), 520–1
'Resolutions from the Biennial Meeting, 1946,' in 'Notes from the National Office,' *The Canadian Nurse*, XLII (September 1946), 797–9
Simpson, Ruby M. 'A Call to Action,' *The Canadian Nurse*, XXXI (November 1935), 485–6
- 'Marching Orders,' *The Canadian Nurse*, XXXII (September 1936), 393–5
- 'Thirty Years of Growth,' *The Canadian Nurse*, XXXIV (August 1938), 411–16

Bibliography 315

Parker, Elizabeth. 'Report of the Honorary Secretary,' *The Canadian Alpine Journal*, vol. II, no. 2. Banff, Alberta: Alpine Club of Canada, 1910, 205-8
'Saskatchewan Registered Nurses' Association,' *The Canadian Nurse*, XV (May 1919), 1764
Snively, Mary A. A letter to the Editor, 18 March 1933. Published in *The Canadian Nurse*, XXIX (May 1933), 248
'Summer School for Nurses, University of Saskatchewan,' *The Canadian Nurse*, XVIII (September 1922), 541-3
'The Biennial Meeting,' *The Canadian Nurse*, XXVIII (August 1932), 397-8
'The Canadian Nurses' Association General Meeting, 1930,' *The Canadian Nurse*, XXVI (September 1930), 452-6
'The Canadian Nurses Association' (editorial), *American Journal of Nursing*, XXXII (November 1932), 1178
'Tribute for Splendid Service Rendered,' *The Canadian Nurse*, vol. VII (August 1911), 409-10
Walker, Florence H. 'Notes from the National Office,' *The Canadian Nurse*, XL (September 1944), 703
Wheeler, Arthur O. 'Report of the 1909 Camp,' *The Canadian Alpine Journal*, vol. II, no. 2 (1910), 211-22
Wilson, Jean S. 'Ourselves' (editorial), *The Canadian Nurse*, XXIX (January 1933), 6-7

Publications of Governments and Other Organizations
British Columbia Hospital Association. *Annual Reports*, 1918-25. Vancouver: The Association
Government of Canada, Department of Indian Affairs. *Annual Reports*, 1884-1903
Government of Manitoba. An Act respecting 'The Manitoba Association of Graduate Nurses,' III, CAP.114, 3 Geo. v., 15 February 1913
- *First Interim Report of the Public Welfare Commission of Manitoba*, 5 February 1918
- *Second Interim Report of the Public Welfare Commission of Manitoba*, February 1919
Goff, Hazel A. 'Nursing in Hungary, 1933,' Report for the Health Section of the League of Nations (mimeographed report)
Indian Work Investigation Commission, 1946. 'Report to the General Synod of the Church of England in Canada,' *Journal of Proceedings of the Sixteenth Session, Winnipeg, September 4-13, 1946.*, 1-2
National League of Nursing Education. *Proceedings of Twenty-eighth Annual Convention, June 26-July 1, 1922*. New York: The League, 1922
'Report of a Study Made by the National Organization for Public Health Nurs-

ing for the Committee on Nursing Organization of the New York Hospital,' in *Methods and Problems of Medical Education*, Twenty-first Series. New York: The Rockefeller Foundation, 1932

The Rockefeller Foundation. *Annual Reports* for the Years 1916–29. New York: The Foundation

Winslow, C.E.A., M.D. 'A Recent Study of the Education of the Nurse,' *Proceedings of the Twenty-eighth Annual Convention of the National League of Nursing Education*. New York: The League, pp. 175–7

Unpublished Materials

'History of the McKellar General Hospital,' a five-page, typed account of the institution's early years and growth. Archives of the McKellar General Hospital, Thunder Bay, Ontario

'Nursing Service in Canada – A Submission to the Department of National Health and Welfare by the Canadian Nurses' Association, September, 1946.' Ottawa: Archives of the Canadian Nurses' Association

Roberts, J.H.O., and S.L. Frost. 'An Account of the North Wales Hospital Written on the Occasion of the Hospital's Centenary in 1948' (Mimeographed paper)

Newspapers

'Commissioned to Missions of Mercy,' *Manitoba Free Press*, 20 May 1902

Lewis, Rowe. 'Fort William's Advantageous Commercial Position: A Prosperous Young City Destined by Nature to Occupy a Commanding Place in the Commerce and Industry of Canada,' *Manitoba Free Press*, 19 June 1909

'McKellar Auxiliary Story: Over 56 Years of Service,' *Daily Times Journal*, Fort William, 3 June 1958

'Much Routine in Nursing Might Be done Away With,' *Calgary Daily Herald*, 16 October 1923

'Nurses Are Opposed to Dixon Proposal,' *Manitoba Free Press*, 21 February 1919

'New Head Has Had Wide Experience,' *Manitoba Free Press*, 12 May 1915

Records and Reports (in files or archives)

a Alumnae Association of the Johns Hopkins Hospital School of Nursing: Files on the project to write a history of the School of Nursing

b Canadian Nurses' Association: Minutes, reports, and other reference materials related to: the Canadian Society of Superintendents of Training Schools; the Canadian Association of Nursing Education; the Canadian National Association of Trained Nurses; the Canadian Nurses' Association; *The Cana-*

dian Nurse, prior to 1933 and for the period of Ethel Johns' editorship, January 1933–June 1944
c The Children's Hospital of Winnipeg: Minutes of board of directors for the period, March 1909–January 1919; Annual reports of the superintendent, 1914–1920; Selected records in the files of the School of Nursing
d The Cornell University–New York Hospital School of Nursing: Records and reports of the Committee on Nursing Organization of the New York Hospital–Cornell Medical College Association Project; Reports of Ethel Johns, Director of Studies; Records of the commencement exercises, 1952
e Department of Nursing Education, Teachers College, Columbia University: Biography File – Ethel Johns; Calendar for the academic year 1914–1915; other material of historical interest
f Manitoba Association of Registered Nurses: Minutes of meetings (board and general), 1905–1911 and 1915–1919
g McKellar General Hospital and School of Nursing: Record book pertaining to student nurses enrolled in the School during the period 1911–1913
h National League for Nursing: Minutes of meeting of Board of Directors, National League of Nursing Education, January 25, 1945. Archives of the National League for Nursing, New York
i Registered Nurses' Association of British Columbia: Selected minutes of meetings of the Vancouver Graduate Nurses' Association, 4 June 1919 to 14 January 1925; Minutes of Council and general meetings, 1918–1925, of the Graduate Nurses' Association of British Columbia
j The University of British Columbia and School of Nursing: Minutes of meetings of the Senate, 1919–1925; Excerpts from minutes of meetings of the Board of Governors, 1919–1925; Reports and memoranda from the director of the Department of Nursing; Other reports and memoranda regarding the Department of Nursing for the period 1919–1925; Records in the files of the School of Nursing about students enrolled in the baccalaureate and diploma programmes during the period 1919–1928; Calendars of the University of British Columbia for the period 1918–1925
k The Vancouver General Hospital and School of Nursing: Annual reports of the superintendent and the director of nursing for the period 1918–1922; Excerpts from Board minutes; Student records in the files of the School of Nursing
l The Winnipeg General Hospital and School of Nursing: Minutes of meetings of the Board of Trustees and the Finance Committee, and Annual Reports, 1899–1911; File in the Department of Nursing on the project of the Alumnae Association to have a history of the School of Nursing written

Addendum

This book was in the final stage of production when certain papers were found which shed further light upon Ethel Johns' influence upon the early development of the nursing programme at the University of British Columbia. The author is greatly indebted to the University of Toronto Press for making last-minute adjustments to include in the book the following summary of significant data thus revealed.

1 Letter of 7 October 1919 from Ethel Johns to Dean R.W. Brock (one week after her arrival in Vancouver), recommending: (a) qualifications for entrance into the courses leading to the degree in nursing, with a summary of courses to be included in the preliminary two years of academic work in the University of British Columbia; (b) the appointment of a Committee on Standards for Training Schools for the Province, 'with representatives from the University, the British Columbia Hospitals Association, the Medical Council and the Graduate Nurses' Association of British Columbia, which shall provide a mechanism for the determination of the eligibility of graduates from various schools for the University degree'; and (c) 'that nurses now in training in or graduates of approved Training Schools for Nurses may be admitted to the degree on fulfilling the necessary academic qualifications.' [See supra, p. 127]

2 A statement, 'Basis for discussion of standards to be set for training schools desiring to affiliate with the University of British Columbia for the Combined Course in nursing leading to the University Degree,' on which is a hand-written note by Ethel Johns: 'Formulated in 1919 – Shortly after I took charge of the course.' This statement includes the University requirements for admission to the course, 'not subject to discussion,' and the proposed requirements as to the size and scope of the hospital to which the training school was attached, its faculty, curriculum, and teaching facilities. Concerning curriculum, Miss Johns recognized the responsibilities of both the Graduate Nurses' Association and the University: 'The course of study shall approximate as closely as possible that recommended by the British Columbia Association of Graduate Nurses, it being understood that necessary qualifications and changes may be made from time to time as desired by the University of British Columbia.' She further advocated that 'The University shall reserve the right to investigate and report upon all

Addendum 319

training schools asking affiliation privileges.' [NOTE: The above 'Basis for discussion of standards ...' was identical with the 'Standard for Nurses Training Schools' which the B.C.H.A. submitted to the Senate on 15 December 1920. This reinforces the assumption made above on page 129 that Ethel Johns influenced the statement of standards as finally approved by Senate.]

3 On 14 November 1919, Miss Johns wrote to Dean Brock enclosing 'an outline of the Combined Course now being given in the Department of Nursing and Health, Teachers College, Columbia University in conjunction with the Presbyterian Hospital, New York. It is interesting to note how closely our own plan, though arrived at independently, approximates theirs ...'

4 On 9 February 1920, Miss Johns sent to Dean Brock 'final suggestions re. Fifth Year.' [NOTE: This confirms the assumption made above on page 127.]

5 In a letter of 13 December 1919 to Ethel Johns, Mary Adelaide Nutting, as chairman of the Committee on Education of the N.L.N.E., requested information for a pamphlet on the subject of 'Nursing Courses in Colleges and Universities.' In her reply of 23 December 1919, Miss Johns commented: 'It seems logical that those who inspired this movement should be interested in its development and progress but I fear that I, among others, have drawn very heavily upon your resources of time and patience. As a matter of fact we have had no one else to whom to turn for help and advice in a very heavy undertaking ...' She then reported on the present status of the University nursing course, touched upon the 'somewhat anomalous' plan of organization of the department of nursing in the University, and her own status therein. She recognized the 'courage and vision' of Dr M.T. MacEachern 'to whom the movement here is really due.' Finally, Miss Johns commented that she foresaw many difficulties:

... The University itself is in its infancy, it is greatly hampered for funds and is housed in overcrowded temporary quarters. The nursing problem in this hospital and in others all over the province is acute. There is no chance at present of well ordered properly conducted efficient teaching work as you would judge of such things in Columbia. I myself do not come to my work adequately prepared. For many years we must submit to make shifts and to compromize. As I see it there is a fighting chance but not much more. The best that can be said for the experiment is that at least it is a courageous if somewhat rash piece of pioneer work ...

6 On 23 February 1923, Ethel Johns submitted to Dean Brock, for the information of the President, a memorandum on the progress of the Department of Nursing. Many of the Dean's remarks in his report of 23 May 1923 [see supra, page 147] were evidently based upon Miss Johns' memorandum. For example, Miss Johns had stated that active opposition to the course by the medical profession had practically ceased during the past year. 'This is probably due to two factors: first that the Director is no longer brought into conflict with Medical men in matters pertaining to Hospital administration and, second, that the aims and objects of the course are better understood. Here, again, the students are our best missionaries. The fact must be remembered that the majority of the Medical profession both in Canada and in the United States are bitterly opposed to higher education for nurses and that the situation is no worse here than in other parts of the continent.'

7 In a letter of 21 January 1924 to Dean Brock, Miss Johns reported upon a conference of 15 January which she had with Dr Mullin, at which she made suggestions as to the re-organization of the Departments of Nursing and Public Health. Included in these was a proposal that the two departments be amalgamated under one of the two following names: (a) Department of Nursing and Health, (b) Department of Nursing and Public Health. [NOTE: Based on this evidence, it is reasonable to assume that the idea for amalgamation which resulted in action by the Board of Governors three months later actually originated with Miss Johns. See supra, page 158.]

Index

Albert, Alice 228
Alberta Association of Graduate Nurses (name changed in 1921 to Alberta Association of Registered Nurses): E. Johns addresses meetings of 106–7, 158; R. Chittick president of 212; hostess to 1940 meeting of CNA 212
Allard, Mother Louise; receives Snively award 212
L'Alliance Française 258
Alpine Club of Canada: organized 1906 54; E. Johns attends 1909 Camp 54–7
American Journal of Nursing 43
American Nurses' Association Nursing Council on National Defence 223, 224, 226; Julia Stimson president of 229
Ashton, Dr H. 117
Association of Registered Nurses of the Province of Quebec: E.F. Upton secretary – registrar of 209; E. Johns gives address to 228
Auden, W.H. 270, 271

Barrett, Caroline 196, 220
Bayne-Jones, Dr S.: letters re E. Johns' address 265
Beard, Mary 175, 181, 201
Bell, Dr Fred C.: memories of E. Johns 39, 40, 54, 55, 56
Bellevue and Allied Hospitals 75, 254
Blanchard, Dr R.J. 29, 30, 66
Blayney, Lucille 258, 271, 275, 276, 278, 281, 282–3
Brack, Mrs C. Bernard: president, alumnae association 247, 248; chairman of history committee 255, 256; corresponds with E. Johns re history 259–63 *passim;* and meets with her 265; further correspondence with E. Johns 268, 269, 273, 274
British Association for the Advancement of Science 39, 54
British Columbia Hospitals Association 116, 119, 120: requests course in public health nursing 126; recommends standards for training schools 129; E. Johns addresses meeting of 131–3; and is appointed secretary of 141; annual meeting, 1923 156; tribute to E. Johns 161
Brock, Dr Reginald: dean, faculty of applied science, UBC 126, 127; reports on department of nursing 146, 147–8
Browne, Jean: elected president of CNATN, 1922 142; attends meeting of CANE, 1923 149; elected president of CNA 159; member of publications committee 188, 195; secretary of Joint Study Committee (CMA–CNA) 188; writes guest editorial 190, 191; receives Snively award 204
Brydone-Jack, Dr W.D. 117, 118
Buchanan, John M.: chancellor, UBC, presides over commemorative ceremony 284, 285

Calgary General Hospital: G.M. Hall, director of nursing 272
Cameron, Margaret 272
Canadian Alpine Journal: publishes article by E. Johns, 1910 57
Canadian Association of Nursing Education (CANE), new name of former Superintendents' Society 92; meeting in Toronto, 1918 95–7; meeting in Vancouver, 1919 119; meeting in Fort William and Port Arthur, 1920 134, 136; E. Johns gives speech 136; meeting in Toronto, 1923 149–55, 156; E. Johns chairs session, reports on degree programme 151–5, 156; decision to amalgamate with CNATN 150; becomes section of CNA 159. *See also* Canadian Society of Superintendents of Training Schools for Nurses
Canadian Home Economics Association: E. Johns addresses 272
Canadian Medical Association (CMA): co-sponsors survey of nursing education in Canada 177
Canadian National Association of Trained Nurses (CNATN) meeting in Winnipeg, 1916 87; E. Johns gives speech 88; meeting in Montreal, 1917 89, 92; J.I. Gunn elected president, E. Johns secretary of 92; meeting in Toronto, 1918 95; meeting in Vancouver, 1919, E. Johns re-elected secretary of 119; meeting in Fort William and Port Arthur, 1920, E. Johns gives speech and is elected second vice-president of 134–5; meeting in Quebec City, 1921, letter read from E. Johns 139, 140; meeting in Edmonton, 1922, E. Johns elected first vice-president of 142; meeting in Hamilton, 1924, name changed to Canadian Nurses' Association 159. *See also* Canadian Nurses' Association
Canadian Nurse: established, 1905 43; Dr H. MacMurchy editor of 43; aims of 43; E. Johns' support of 49; E. Johns' early writings for 50, 51, 52; H. Randal editor of 98, 138, 139, 140, 159; J. Wilson editor of 159; E. Johns editor of 187–233 *passim*; golden anniversary of, message from E. Johns 271. *See also* Johns, Ethel, 1933–1944; Randal, H.; and Wilson, J.
Canadian Nurses' Association (CNA): name of CNATN changed to CNA in 1924 159; E. Johns a councillor, and vice-chairman of new Nursing Education section 159; headquarters in Winnipeg, J. Wilson executive secretary 159; co-sponsors survey of nursing education 177; meeting in Regina, 1930, E. Johns gives speeches, F. Emory elected president 178–9; meeting in Saint John, 1932, decides to appoint full-time editor, discusses Weir Report, re-elects F. Emory as president 183–4; appoints E. Johns editor, moves national office to Montreal 187, 188; meeting in Toronto, 1934, 25th anniversary, establishes memorial to M.A. Snively, elects R. Simpson president 193–5; conducts circulation campaign for the Journal 198, 199; meeting in Vancouver, 1936, M. Lindeburgh presents *Proposed Curriculum,* and CNA gives first Snively awards and re-elects R. Simpson president 200–1, 202; meeting in

Halifax, 1938, discusses *Proposed Curriculum*, rejects Dominion registration, elects G.M. Fairley president, and E. Johns voices concern about the Journal 204-5; meeting in Calgary, 1940, M. Lindeburgh presents *Supplement*, CNA contributes to war effort, re-elects G.M. Fairley president, and E. Johns receives Snively award 212-15; CNA appoints E. Johns representative to Nursing Council on National Defence (ANA) 223; CNA executive confers with representatives of university departments of nursing 226, 227; and appoints national adviser and assistant 227; meeting in Montreal, 1942, elects M. Lindeburgh president 228, 229; receives grant from Federal government 229; submits brief on health insurance 231; J. Wilson retires and K.W. Ellis succeeds her 232; meeting in Winnipeg, 1944, pays tribute to E. Johns on retirement 232, 233; appoints E. Johns to committees 237, 238; meeting in Toronto, 1946, E. Johns gives speech, is named convener of Exchange of Nurses Committee 240-2; G.M. Hall general secretary of CNA 242; E. Johns prepares report for CNA 242, 243; meeting in Sackville, 1948, E. Johns honoured by Mount Allison University, gives address, and reports for the Exchange of Nurses Committee 251, 252, 254; E. Johns prepares brief for CNA 254; meeting in Ottawa, 1958, golden jubilee of CNA, confers honorary life membership on E. Johns 274

Canadian Red Cross Society 128, 136, 210
Canadian Society of Superintendents of Training Schools for Nurses: meeting in Winnipeg, 1916 87; appoints E. Johns convener of Committee on Standardization of Training Schools 89; meeting in Montreal, 1917, E. Johns reports, name changed to Canadian Association of Nursing Education, E. Johns elected second vice-president 89, 90-1, 92. *See also* Canadian Association of Nursing Education
Canadian Women's Press Club: E. Johns a member of 65
Carpenter, Herbert 57
Carrington, Archbishop Philip 3, 4, 221, 239
Carruthers, Elizabeth 85, 100
Cassidy, Dr and Mrs Harry 221
Catton, Mary 140
Chesney, Dr Alan 255
Children's Hospital of Winnipeg: appoints E. Johns 81; situation in 1915 84, 85; training school 85-6, 87; submission to Public Welfare Commission 93; impact of epidemic on 100; effects of Winnipeg General Strike on 108-11; resignation of E. Johns 111; H.E. Mallory a later appointee 225
Chittick, Rae: president of AARN 212; view of E. Johns' influence upon nursing 223, 233; commemorative address 284, 285 (*Note*: president of CNA, 1946-8)
Civic Hospitals of Lyon: president of Rockefeller Foundation comments on E. Johns' work in Lyon 170. *See also* Conseil Général d'Adminis-

tration des Hôpitaux Civils de Lyon
Clement, S.P. 117, 118
College of Physicians and Surgeons of British Columbia: Senate seeks advice of 118, 127; and receives reply 128, 129
Columbia University: Teachers College, department of nursing and health 46, 48, 62, 63, 72, 75–82, 97, 119, 166. *See also* Johns, E., 1914–15; Stewart, I.M.; and Teachers College
Conseil Général d'Administration des Hôpitaux Civils de Lyon: E. Johns' medallion from 170, 280. *See also* Civic Hospitals of Lyon
Coppinger, Dr H. 272
Cornell University: Medical College 174
Cornell University–New York Hospital School of Nursing 177, 182; graduation exercises, 1952, E. Johns gives address 263–5. *See also* New York Hospital School of Nursing
Cotter, Kate 65, 66
'The Creative Minority' 191, 220, 249
Crowell, F. Elizabeth 168, 170, 171

Darrach, Dr William 183
Dickens, Charles 5
Dickson, Edith MacPherson: convener, Committee on Standard Curriculum, CANE 95; president, CNATN, writes to E. Johns 139; re-elected president 140; convener of CNA committee on Dominion registration 201; receives Snively award 202
Dock, Lavinia 25, 77; E. Johns' memories of 79
Dominion registration for nurses 193, 201, 204

Duffield, Margaret 214, 275

Edith Cavell School of Nursing, Brussels: president of Rockefeller Foundation refers to E. Johns' association with 170. *See also* l'Institut Edith Cavell-Marie Depage
Ellis, Kathleen W.: director of nursing, VGH 141; relationships with department of nursing, UBC 155; professor of nursing, University of Saskatchewan, appointed national nursing adviser 227; general secretary, CNA 232
Embree, Dr Edwin R. 165, 166
Emory, Florence H.M. 142, 171; elected president of CNA, 1930 179; contacts with E. Johns re editorship 179, 182, 184; and announces appointment 187, 189; convenes publications committee 188, 194, 195; urges support of the Journal 190; presides over 1934 meeting of CNA 193, 194; memories of E. Johns 225; and view of her career 233

Fairley, Grace M. 149; elected president of CNA, 1938 206; messages to Canadian nurses 210, 211, 212; convenes publications committee 214; re-elected president 215; chairs conference 226; receives Snively award 229
Faris, Marion: memories of E. Johns 145, 146. *See also* Fisher, Marion
Feuz, Edouard 56
Fisher, Marion 121
Flanagan, Eileen C. 191, 220, 275, 281, 282; excerpts from E. Johns' letters to 249, 250, 256–7, 266, 269–76 *passim*, 277, 278, 280–1, 282

Flaws, Elizabeth 89; president, CANE 136
Florence Nightingale International Foundation: E. Johns convenes Canadian committee 242
Forbes, H. Stewart 284
Franklin, Helen (Johns) 46, 165, 166, 195, 230, 282. *See also* Johns family

Gilman, Alice Shepard 176, 263
Giroux, Suzanne 191, 220, 228; assistant to national nursing adviser 227
Goff, Hazel 171; memories of E. Johns 166, 168, 173
Good Samaritan Hospital, Los Angeles 71
Goodrich, Annie Warburton: E. Johns' memories of 77, 78, 79; attends NLNE convention 142, 143, 144; consultant to Committee on Nursing Organization 177; attends ICN congress 246
Grading of Nursing Schools, Committee on: E. Johns appointed to assist 182; membership, functions of 183; activity analysis of nursing (Johns and Pfefferkorn) 183
Graduate Nurses' Association of British Columbia 118, 133, 134, 146, 147; E. Johns convener of nursing education committee 148, 158; tributes to E. Johns 158, 161. *See also* Registered Nurses' Association of B.C.
Graduate Nurses' Association of Ontario 39, 136. *See also* Registered Nurses' Association of Ontario
Gray, Dr J.S.: addresses graduating class of 1902 28, 29
Gray, Mabel F. 53, 99, 100, 140; heads delegation 105; deputizes for E. Johns 119; attends meeting of CANE 149; and speaks 153; succeeds E. Johns at UBC 161, 165; retirement, and tribute by E. Johns 225; her memories of E. Johns 275; attends commemorative service 284
Greig, Janet 258, 275
Gunn, Jean I. 105, 149, 182, 214; member of committee on standardization of training schools, and secretary to CNATN 89; elected president of CNATN, 1917 92; ideas on nursing education 97, 152; presents report of Joint Study Committee (CMA-CNA) 179; leads campaign for subscriptions 198; receives Snively award 202; death, and tribute by E. Johns 225

Haig, Kennethe 71
Hall, Gertrude M.: gives speech [excerpt] 213, 214; general secretary of CNA 242; supports history project, spends day with E. Johns 272; E. Johns' comments on her death 274, 275
Hampton, Isabel (Mrs Hunter Robb) 25, 249, 250, 254
Healy, Margaret 121
Hersey, Mabel F. 149, 220; receives Snively award 202
Hespeler, William 28
Hind, E. Cora 20, 21, 53, 165, 166; meets E. Johns 16–17; her early influence upon E. Johns 17, 18; attends her graduation 28; friendship with Stewart family 38; is on staff of *Free Press* 38; interest in Johns family 71; political philosophy 108; tribute to E. Johns 212;

death, and bequest to E. Johns xii, 230
Holt, Mabel 199
Hospital for Sick Children, Toronto: E. Johns visits 99

Inglis, Dr M.S. 39, 66
International Council of Nurses (ICN): congress in London, 1937 204; E. Taylor, president, addresses CNA meeting 204; congress in Atlantic City, 1947, address by E. Johns [excerpts] 245, 246

Jean Moore Memorial Collection of Nightingale letters 282. *See also* UBC, Woodward Biomedical Library
Johns, Ethel
- 1879-1902
  childhood [excerpts, autobiog.]: ancestors 3-7; parents 5; birth 5; infant school 6; boarding-school 8-9; departs for Canada 9
  life on the reserve [excerpts, autobiog]: arrival at Wabigoon 10, 11: log house 11; attends school, influence of her father 11, 12; customs of Ojibway Indians 14, 15; death of father 15; helps with teaching 16; meets Cora Hind 16-17; applies to WGH training school 18, 19
  pupil nurse: enters training school 20; her experiences [excerpts, autobiog.] 22-7, 28; graduation 28-30
- 1902-1914
  early practice of nursing 33-40
  editor, *Nurses' Alumnae Journal* 44-51: writings [excerpts] 44-50 *passim*; tribute to I.M. Stewart 48; supports *The Canadian Nurse* 49; and nurse registration 43, 46, 47

alumnae association: early activity in 41, 42; president of 52, 58, 62
leisure activities 53-7: attends 1909 Camp, Alpine Club of Canada, and ascends Mount Huber 54-7; writes about [excerpts] 56, 57
other activities: third vice-president, MAGN 59; speech on registration [excerpts] 59-61; visits Chicago hospitals and describes [excerpts] 63, 64; member, Canadian Women's Press Club 65; president, MAGN 65; tributes on leaving Winnipeg 65, 67, 68; superintendent, McKellar General Hospital 65, 68-71 [excerpts, autobiog.]; resigns 71; head surgical nurse, Good Samaritan Hospital 71, 72; applies to Teachers College 72
- 1914-1919
  Teachers College: arrival in New York 75; I. Stewart helps her 75; courses 76, 77; writes for *Free Press* 76; her memories [autobiog.] of Clara D. Noyes, the outbreak of war, Mary A. Nutting, Annie W. Goodrich, Lavinia Dock, Edward L. Thorndike, her courses in biology, lecture on Freud, values of the programme [excerpts, autobiog.] 75-82 *passim*; applies to Children's Hospital of Winnipeg 81
Children's Hospital of Winnipeg: superintendent and principal of training school 82-111 *passim*: character of hospital in 1915 84, 85; training school 85-7; E. Johns corresponding secretary, convener of legislative committee, MAGN 87, 88, 89; gives speech 88; convener of standardization committee, CANE 89, 90-1; and second vice-president 92;

speaks on curriculum 95-6, 97; councillor, CANE 97; secretary of CNATN 92, 98, 105-6; appointed to Public Welfare Commission of Manitoba, member of committee on hospitals and nursing 92-3; surveys nursing in Manitoba 94, 95; and writes report 102-4; speaks to SRNA 106; and to AAGN [excerpts] 106, 107; influence of Winnipeg General Strike on her political philosophy and relationships 108-11; resigns from Children's Hospital 111
- 1919-1925
Vancouver General Hospital: is appointed director of nursing service and education 120-1; addresses mass meeting [excerpts] 122-5; surveys service and school 129, 130; appoints students council 130; confronts critical doctors 130; problems in 1920 130, 131; annual report, 1920 136-7; problems arising from dual appointments, VGH-UBC [excerpts from letter] 140, 141; resigns from Vancouver General Hospital 141
University of British Columbia: Board of Governors recognizes E. Johns' appointment by VGH, in connection with the department of nursing, UBC 121; and confers status of special lecturer, then assistant professor 128; E. Johns a full-time member of faculty 141; former students' memories of her 145, 146, 157, 158; E. Johns evaluates combined course 146, 147; directs summer course at University of Saskatchewan 144; and at UBC 156; re-appointed by Board of Governors 158; appreciates action of Board in combining departments of nursing and public health 158; attends summer session at Teachers College 159, 160; is approached by Rockefeller Foundation 160, 161; and resigns from department of nursing, UBC 161. *See also* Addendum 318-20
E. Johns' association activities, 1919-25: B.C. Hospitals Association: gives speech, 'The University in Relation to Nursing Education' [excerpts] 131-3; convener of nursing committee 133, 134; member of executive 134; and secretary 141, 156; tribute to her 161
Canadian Association of Nursing Education, attends meeting, June 1923: speaks on amalgamation of CANE and CNATN 150; gives views on records, reference books 150, 151; chairs session on Rockefeller report 151-5, 156; reports on combined course [excerpts] 153, 154-5, 156
Canadian National Association of Trained Nurses: is reelected secretary of 119; gives speech, is elected second vice-president 134-5; sends letter to be read at 1921 meeting 139; is elected first vice-president 142
Canadian Nurses' Association: is a councillor, and is elected vice-chairman, new nursing education section 159
Graduate Nurses' Association of British Columbia: is a member of the council of 129; convener of nursing education committee 141; tributes to her 158, 161

National League of Nursing Education (1922 convention): chairs session and gives speech on administration of nursing schools 143, 144
- 1925–1932
service under the Rockefeller Foundation [with excerpts, autobiog.] 165–73: appointed 165; makes study of status of Negro woman in nursing 166; arrives in Paris 166, 167; orientation 167–9, 170; assignments in field of nursing education 168; assigned to Roumania, visits Bulgaria and Turkey 170; responsible for nursing fellows in Europe 170; projects in Lyon and Brussels 170; assigned to Debrecen, Hungary 171; visits Cluj and Bucharest, Roumania, and has audience with Princess Helene 172; leaves service of Foundation 172–3
Director of Studies, Committee on Nursing Organization, New York Hospital–Cornell Medical College Association Project: appointed 174; nature of project 174; the Committee 175, 176; tasks as Director of Studies 175, 176, 177; completes assignment 181, 182
other activities: writes for *The Canadian Nurse* 177; speaks at 1930 meeting of CNA [excerpts] 178–9; at meeting of RNAO, Dist. Five [excerpts] 180, 181; and at convention of AHA 182
nurse associate to the director, study on grading of nursing schools: appointed 182; collaborates with B. Pfefferkorn in activity analysis of nursing 183; accepts editorship, *The Canadian Nurse* 184

- 1933–1944
Editor and business manager, *The Canadian Nurse* 187–233: organizational arrangements 187, 188; president of CNA announces appointment of 189; E. Johns' reports to biennial meetings of CNA 194, 201, 202, 204, 205, 214, 229; introduces 'Off Duty' page 191; development of the Journal 196; matter of French-language content 196, 197; campaigns for subscriptions 198, 199; move of office 207; Student Nurses' page 207, 208; receives Snively award 212; leisure activities [excerpts] 216–22; retires 231, 232; tributes to her 232, 233; views of her influence upon nursing, R. Chittick 223, 233, 284–5; and F. Emory 233
Excerpts from E. Johns' writings as editor: 'The Editor's Desk' 189; 'The Canadian Scene' 192, 193; 'Hail and Farewell' 194; 'The Editor's Desk' (New Year's message, 1935) 197, 198; 'The Editor's Desk' (innovation in staffing) 199–200; 'We Come of Age' 200; 'The Editor's Desk' (Stanley Park) 202; 'The Editor's Desk' (*Proposed Curriculum*) 203, 204; introduces Student Nurses' Page 207, 208; New Year's message (1939) 208, 209; 'A Gift and a Challenge' (Rockefeller endowment, University of Toronto School of Nursing) 209; Christmas message (1939) 211; 'The Time and Place of Meeting' 212, 213; 'Off Duty' essays 216–19, 222; 'The Shape of Things to Come' 223, 224; 'A Fine Record' (tribute to H. Randal) 224; tribute to Jean

Index 329

Gunn 225; editorial (shortage of nurses) 225, 226; 'Breaking a New Trail' 226, 227; 'A Christmas Candle' 227, 228; 'Meeting in Montreal' 228; 'Getting Down to Brass Tacks' 231; 'A Friendly Hearing' 231; 'A Turning Point' 232
- 1944-1968
post-retirement assignments: revision of faculty pamphlet, NLNE 238; surveys Indian schools 239, 240; committee activities, CNA 237, 238, 242; addresses biennial meeting of CNA, 1946 [excerpts] 240-1, 242; prepares brief for CNA 242, 243; begins writing *Just Plain Nursing* for Lippincott 243-4, 245; addresses Ninth Congress of ICN [excerpts] 245, 246; invited to write history of JHH School of Nursing 246, 247 the Johns Hopkins project: assists in organization of 248, 249; her impressions of Historical Library, residence [excerpt] 249, 250; initial research 250, 251; withdraws as editor 251; resumes work 254; gives progress report 255, 256; leaves Baltimore 256; B. Pfefferkorn, coauthor 259, 260, 261; correspondence with Mrs Brack 259-63 *passim*; sends manuscripts 260, 261, 262; receives honorarium 262 retirement in Vancouver: impressions of the West and her home [excerpts from letters] 256-7; memberships in clubs 258; friendships 258, 259; gives commencement address [excerpts] 263-4, 265; letters from Dr Bayne-Jones 265; relationships with Stewart family 267, 268, 269; adapts text on geriatric nursing 269; letters to friends [excerpts] 268-76 *passim*; writes golden jubilee message for *The Canadian Nurse* [excerpt] 271; Alumnae Association, WGH, seeks her advice about history project, appoints her author 271; gathers data, completes writing 272, 273; addresses Canadian Home Economics Association 272; is awarded honorary life' membership in CNA 274; her brother visits 274; death of brother 275; her illness 276; her religious beliefs, political convictions 277, 278; M. Uprichard visits, later receives letter from E. Johns 278, 279; UBC School of Nursing seeks her guidance 279, 280; and receives her medals 280; letters to E. Flanagan [excerpts] 277-82 *passim*; final illness and death xii, 282-3; commemorative ceremony 284-5
Johns family, members of
- Alexander Johns 9, 15, 53, 100, 274, 275
- Amy Robinson Johns 5, 7, 11, 15, 16, 19, 53, 71, 100, 195, 230
- Bennett George Johns 4, 5
- Charles Alexander Johns 3, 4
- Delphinea Sophia Hepburn Johns 4
- Delphinea (Dellie) Sophia Johns Adcock 4, 5
- Henry Incledon Johns 3, 5, 7, 12, 13, 15
- Owen Johns 5, 9, 53, 100, 165, 195, 230
- Helen Johns Franklin 46, 165, 166, 195, 230, 282
Johns Hopkins Hospital
- school of nursing: early influence on

E. Johns 25; Historical Library and residence [excerpt] 249, 250; and later reference to by E. Johns 279
— alumnae association: history project 246-57, 269; R. Chittick comments on *History* 285. *See also* Johns, E. 1944-1968; Brack, Mrs J. Bernard; and McVicar, Mrs Guthrie
Johns Hopkins Press 269
Johns Hopkins University: Welch Library 255
Johnson, Beatrice 121. *See also* Wood, Beatrice
Johnson, Thomas H. 93
Just Plain Nursing 243-4, 245, 252, 253, 269, 275; R. Chittick comments on E. Johns' writing of 285. *See also* Johns, E., 1944-1968; and Lippincott, J.B.

Kerr, Margaret 197, 213; succeeds E. Johns as editor 232
King George VI and Queen Elizabeth: visit to Canada 210
King, W.L. Mackenzie 211
Kingsley, Charles 3
Klinck, Dr L.S. 116, 119, 161

Lee, Amy 282; letters from E. Johns [excerpts] 238, 239
Leeman, O.T. 220, 221, 243, 244; memory of E. Johns 246; and correspondence with her 275
Leighton, Margaret 282
Lennox, Margaret 42, 58
Lindeburgh, Marion: convener of CNA curriculum committee 191; presents *Proposed Curriculum* 201; and *Supplement* 213; is elected president of CNA 229
Lippincott Company, J.B.: early contacts with E. Johns 220, 221; launches *Just Plain Nursing* 243-5; and binds collected issues of 269; E. Johns hostess in Lippincott Lounge 252; E. Johns adapts text for 269; last issue of JPN 275
Local Council of Women (Winnipeg): MAGN affiliates with 59; holds meeting on nurse registration, E. Johns speaker 59-61

McCann, Elizabeth: speaks at commemorative ceremony 284
MacEachern, Malcolm T.: proposes chair for nursing at UBC 115, 116; and writes letter to Senate 116, 117; as president of BCHA, speaks of UBC plan 119, 120; writes to President Klinck re E. Johns' appointment 121; applies for affiliation of training school 126; advocates placement of department of nursing in faculty of applied science 126; replies to Senate on behalf of BCHA 129; encourages E. Johns in extramural activities 131; supports combined course 131; is elected secretary of BCHA 134; leaves VGH 141; E. Johns speaks of him 154; he addresses BCHA meeting 156
McGill University 97, 99, 191, 256; School for Graduate Nurses, F.M. Shaw director of 144; alumnae association campaigns for funds 209; is locale of conference 226; E. Johns comments on history of school 279, 280, 281
McIntosh, Isabel: memories of E. Johns 243
McKechnie, Dr R.E.: chancellor, UBC, supports proposal for depart-

ment of nursing 115
McKellar General Hospital: appoints E. Johns superintendent 65; the hospital in 1911 67; early history of 69; ladies aid 69; problems in financing, 1911 69; appointment of dietitian [excerpt, autobiog.] 71; training school 69, 70; resignation of E. Johns 71
MacKenzie, Mary Ardcronie: chief lady superintendent, VON, opinions on maternity care 51; Red Cross instructor at UBC 128, 144; leaves UBC 161
MacKenzie, Norena 191, 254, 275
McLeod, Maude: writes about proposal for department of nursing at UBC [excerpt] 117
MacMurchy, Dr Helen: first editor, *The Canadian Nurse* 43; addresses MAGN 58; paper on 'University Training for the Nursing Profession' 98, 99
McPhedran, Eleanor: receives Snively award 229
McVicar, Mrs Guthrie B.: chairman, history committee, writes to E. Johns 246, 247; associate editor, history project 248, 249, 251, 254, 255; chairman of editorial committee 260, 261, 269
Maddin, Elizabeth (Betty) Stewart 268, 269
Mallory, Harriet Evelyn: president, MAGN 225; registrar and educational adviser, RNABC 225; succeeds Mabel Gray at UBC 225; E. McCann refers to her at commemorative ceremony 284
Manitoba, Province of
– Nurses' Act, 1913 62; and amendment, 1920 104–5
– proposed amendment to Minimum Wage Act 105
– Public Welfare Commission 83, 92; appointed, terms of reference of, E. Johns a commissioner, and member of committee on hospitals and nursing 93, 94; Second Interim Report 100; report of committee on hospitals and nursing 102–4; Board of Welfare Supervision 105; E. Johns refers to Commission 123
Manitoba Association of Graduate Nurses (name of MAGN changed in 1929 to Manitoba Association of Registered Nurses): organized 42; early steps towards nursing legislation 46, 58, 59; affiliation with Local Council of Women, 1906 59; incorporated 62; elects E. Johns president 65; E. Johns registers 87; is corresponding secretary of 87, 92; is convener of legislative committee 88; submission to Public Welfare Commission 93, 94; amendment to Act, 1920 104–5; resolution to Law Amendments Committee 105. *See also* Manitoba Association of Registered Nurses
Manitoba Association of Registered Nurses: G.M. Hall, secretary registrar of 213; H.E. Mallory, president of 225
Manitoba Free Press: account of 1902 graduation, WGH 28–9; E. Cora Hind on staff of 38; news item re E. Johns' work in X-ray department 39; reports E. Johns' speech on registration 59, 61, 62; article on Fort William 66, 67; reports E. Johns' resignation from McKellar General

Hospital 71; publishes her article 76; reports her appointment by Children's Hospital 83; reports on nursing delegation to Law Amendments Committee 105

Manitoba Medical College 22, 30

Mason, Mrs S. Ralph: president, alumnae association, thanks E. Johns 262

Maternity care: problems of, in Canadian west, 1908 49; E. Johns writes about 49–50; discussed at 1917 meeting of CNATN 92

Mathers, Dr A.T. 93

Mayall, Ann xii, 277, 282

Mayhew, Emily 258, 275, 276, 278, 282–3

Mayo, Adelaide A. 238

Mitchell, Dr Ross: memories of E. Johns 39, 40

Mount Allison University: honours E. Johns 251–3

Montreal General Hospital: M. Holt writes on staffing innovation, Western Division 199; and E. Johns comments on [excerpt] 199–200

Mount Royal Cemetery, Montreal: burial place of Amy, Owen, and Ethel Johns 230, 283

Mullin, Dr R.H.: President Wesbrook, UBC, refers to 99; dual positions, VGH-UBC 99, 116; advocates inclusion of department of nursing in faculty of applied science 126; appointed Red Cross Professor of Public Health, UBC 128; and head of department of nursing and health 158; death of 160

National League of Nursing Education (NLNE): 28th annual convention, 1922 142–3, 144; E. Johns chairs session and speaks 143, 144; E. Johns assists committee on revision of pamphlet 238

National Organization of Public Health Nursing (NOPHN) 176

New York Hospital 174, 176

– school of nursing 174–7 *passim*, 181, 263: alumnae association 175. *See also* New York Hospital–Cornell Medical College Association Project

New York Hospital–Cornell Medical College Association Project

– Nature of project 174

– Committee on Nursing Organization: E. Johns appointed director of studies 174; M. Beard chairman of 175; membership of 175; terms of reference of 175, 176; asks NOPHN to conduct study 176; A.S. Gilman consultant to 176; recommendations of 181; E. Johns' memories of 263, 264

Nightingale, Florence 21, 249

Noyes, Clara D.: E. Johns' memories of 75

Nutting, Mary Adelaide 25, 91, 95, 98, 99, 249: E. Johns' memories of [excerpts, autobiog.] 77, 78, 81–2; E. Johns gathers data about 254; and seeks to portray her 260; centenary of 274

Ojibway Indians 7, 12, 13; customs [excerpts, autobiog.] 14, 15. *See also* Johns, E., 1879–1902; and Wabigoon reserve

Olandt, Helen: memories of E. Johns 239

Parker, Elizabeth 54, 65

Patterson, Adah 24, 25
Paulson, Esther: memories of E. Johns 259
Pfefferkorn, Blanche: director of studies, NLNE 183, 238; collaborates with E. Johns in activity analysis 183; co-author with E. Johns 259–65 *passim*
Presbyterian Hospital School of Nursing, Chicago: E. Johns' observations of 63, 64
Princess Helene of Roumania: E. Johns' memories of [excerpt, autobiog.] 172
'Private Nurse' letter 138, 139, 140

Randal, Helen 145; president, Superintendents' Society 90; re-elected 92; first vice-president, CANE 97; editor, *The Canadian Nurse* 98, 159; matter of 'Private Nurse' letter 138, 139, 140; retirement, and tribute by E. Johns 224
Registered Nurses' Association of British Columbia subscription project, E. Johns' comments 214, 215; H.E. Mallory, registrar and educational adviser of 225. *See also* Graduate Nurses' Association of British Columbia
Registered Nurses' Association of Ontario: E. Johns addresses District Five 180, 181. *See also* Graduate Nurses' Association of Ontario
Registration of nurses: *The Canadian Nurse* supports 43; E. Johns supports 46–7; and gives speech on 59–61. *See also* Dominion registration for nurses
Roberts, Mary 246
Robinson, Dr G. Canby 174, 175, 176

Robinson, John 5, 6, 7
Rockefeller Foundation (RF) 142, 143, 144, 149, 151–3; approaches E. Johns 160, 161; and appoints her 165; study of status of Negro woman in nursing 166; philosophy, objectives of 167, 168; nursing programme in Europe 168, 171; nursing fellowships 169. *See also* Johns, E., 1925–1932
Russell, E. Kathleen: director, department of health nursing, University of Toronto 136; attends 1923 meeting of CANE 149, 156; E. Johns refers to her 209; receives Snively award 212

St James Church (Vancouver) 277, 282
St Luke's Hospital and School of Nursing 238, 239
Saskatchewan Registered Nurses' Association (SRNA): E. Johns addresses meeting, 1919 106; SRNA asks University of Saskatchewan to give short course for nurses 144
Shabaqua, Chief 13, 14
Shaw, Flora Madeline: director, McGill School for Graduate Nurses 144; chairs 1923 meeting of CANE 149; gives report and paper 151, 153; chairman, nursing education section, CNA 159
Simpson, Ruby: memories of E. Johns 107, 159, 160, 178; president of CNA, 1934 195; launches subscription campaign 198, 199; presides over 1936 meeting of CNA 200; and re-elected president 203; announces permanent appointment of E. Johns 203; presides over 1938 meeting of

CNA 205; member of publications committee 214
Smellie, Elizabeth 182, 204
Smith, Dr Harley [excerpt from paper] 39
Snively, Mary Agnes: appointed archivist of CNA 99; attends 1923 meeting of CANE 149; death 193, 194; CNA memorial to 194
Social Science Club of Winnipeg: E. Johns a member of 53
Stewart, Dr and Mrs David 89, 94
Stewart, Elizabeth (Mrs Charles Sharp) 166
Stewart, Elizabeth (Mrs W.S. Maddin) 268, 269
Stewart, Dr Helen 166, 267, 268, 275
Stewart, Isabel Maitland 183, 224, 254; classmate of E. Johns 25, 26, 29; has O.R. training under E. Johns [excerpt, oral history] 37; business editor, *Nurses' Alumnae Journal* 44; enrolment at Teachers College 46, 48; staff appointment at TC 48, 49, 63; tribute by E. Johns 48; visits Winnipeg 62, 63; befriends E. Johns 75; speaks in Toronto, Vancouver 95, 119; professor, department of nursing and health, TC 119; director, division of nursing education, TC 166; chairman, NLNE committee 238; sees E. Johns in Vancouver 267; eightieth birthday 274
Stewart, Jessie (Mrs M. Pierce) 267, 268
Stewart, Dr William 277
Stewart family: E. Johns' relationships with 37, 38, 267, 268, 281
Stimson, Julia 229
Survey of nursing education in Canada: co-sponsored by CNA and CMA, director, Dr G.M. Weir 177; interim report of 178; E. Johns quotes Dr Weir 180; final report of 183; steps to implement 187, 191–3 *passim*
Sutliffe, Irene: E. Johns' memories of 264, 265
Symington, H.Y. 93, 105

Taylor, Effie: president of ICN, addresses CNA meetings 204, 229; presents copy of *History* to JHH School of Nursing 269
Thorndike, Edward Lee: E. Johns' memories of 79, 80
Toronto General Hospital 42, 229
Trained attendants 98, 104–5, 135

United Nations Relief and Rehabilitation Administration (UNRRA) 237, 238
University of British Columbia 115, 116
– President Wesbrook writes to Dr H. MacMurchy 99, 116; Senate receives proposal for department of nursing 116–17; and appoints committee on nursing, receives reports 117, 118, 127; seeks advice of, receives reply from Medical Council 127, 128, 129; seeks advice of, receives reply from BCHA 129
– department of nursing: established 118; enrols first students 121; is included in faculty of applied science 126–7; makes recommendations 127; Board of Governors appoints E. Johns lecturer 128; and assistant professor 128; members of first class receive degrees 146; E. Johns evaluates combined course 146, 147; Dean Brock reports on course 147, 148; depart-

ments of nursing and public health combined, Dr R.H. Mullin, head 158; death of Dr Mullin 160; E. Johns resigns 161; M. Gray succeeds her 161, 165; M. Gray retires and is succeeded by H.E. Mallory 225
- school of nursing: library committee seeks E. Johns' advice 279, 280; golden jubilee ceremony honours memory of E. Johns 284-5
- Woodward Biomedical Library 122, 279; Jean Moore Memorial Collection of Nightingale letters 282; locale of commemorative ceremony 284-5
University of Manitoba 62, 93, 103
University of Saskatchewan: summer course for nurses, 1922, E. Johns director 144; K.W. Ellis, professor of nursing 227, 232
University of Toronto: host to 1918 meetings of CANE and CNATN 95; department of health nursing established 136; department of public health nursing 171; Rockefeller Foundation endows school of nursing, and E. Johns comments upon 209
University Women's Club (Vancouver): E. Johns a member of 258
Upham, Margory 254
Uprichard, Muriel: visits E. Johns 278, 279; and receives letter from her 279, 280; excerpts from letter 68, 120, 121, 126, 140, 141, 160, 161
Upton, E. Francis: secretary-registrar, ARNPQ, leads campaign for funds 209; receives Snively award 229

Vancouver General Hospital 99, 157
- Dr M.T. MacEachern suggests chair of nursing 115, 116; VGH submits proposal to Senate 117; appoints E. Johns director of nursing 120, 121; applies for affiliation with UBC department of nursing 126; situation of department of nursing, 1919-20 129, 130, 131; problem of dual appointments of director of nursing 140-1; E. Johns resigns 141; K.W. Ellis, director of nursing 141, 155; G.M. Fairley, director of nursing 206; fiftieth anniversary of school of nursing 274. See also Johns, E., 1919-25; MacEachern, Dr M.T.; and University of British Columbia
Victorian Order of Nurses 50, 51, 69, 97, 98, 141, 201

Wabigoon reserve: life on the reserve 10-19. See also Johns, E., 1879-1902; and Ojibway Indians
Walker, Mary 84
Ware, Dr Edith 250
Weir, Dr George M. 157; directs survey of nursing education 177; gives interim report 178; and final report 183; some proposals 192, 193; speaks at CNA meeting 201
Wesbrook, Dr F.F.: president, UBC, writes to Dr H. MacMurchy 99; problems of financing UBC 116
Wheeler, Arthur O.: president, Alpine Club of Canada quotation 54, 55, 56
White, Ada C. Newton 41, 42
Whiteford, Jean: president, WGH alumnae association, seeks E. Johns' advice re history, and assists her 271, 272
Wilson, Frederica 38; tribute to E. Johns 67, 68
Wilson, Jean S.: executive secretary, CNA, and editor, *The Canadian Nurse* 159; tribute to E. Johns 189; E. Johns thanks her 190; receives

Snively award 204; retires 230, 232
Winnipeg General Hospital 22, 28, 33
- training school for nurses: E. Johns applies 19; conditions in 1899 21, 22; E. Johns' experiences as pupil nurse [autobiog.] 22–8; graduation, 1902 28–30
- nurses' alumnae association: organized 41; aims 41; early work, and E. Johns participation in 41, 42; E. Johns president of 52, 62; tributes to E. Johns 67, 68; presents doctoral robes 252; history project, E. Johns author 271, 272, 273; R. Chittick refers to *History* 285
- *Nurses' Alumnae Journal*: established, 1907 44: E. Johns first editor 44–51; tributes to E. Johns 65, 68
Winnipeg General Strike 107–11
Winslow, Dr C.E.A. 142
Wolf, Anna 181, 247, 251
Wood, Beatrice (Johnson) 121, 145
Woodsworth, James 110
World War I 76
World War II 210, 211, 212
Wrinch, Dr H.C. 134

Young, Dr Henry Esson 115, 147

www.ingramcontent.com/pod-product-compliance
Lightning Source LLC
Chambersburg PA
CBHW020351080526
44584CB00014B/980